GO MATH

Grade 8

Differentiated Instruction

Contents

Description of Contents ix

Student Worksheets

Module 15   Two-Way Tables

Answers

Description of Contents

Using the Differentiated Instruction Worksheets	Integrating Language Arts
Practice and Problem Solving: A/B, C, D There are three worksheets for every lesson. All of these reinforce and practice the content of the lesson. Level A/B (slightly below/on level students) Level C (above level students) Level D (considerably below level students who require modified worksheets)	The *Differentiated Instruction* worksheets help students become successful learners by integrating the literacy grade-level expectations. The worksheets provide opportunities for students to:
Reteach (one worksheet per lesson) Provides an alternate way to teach or review the main concepts of the lesson, and for students to have further practice at a basic level.	• demonstrate independence as they become self-directed learners. • show their mastery of content through writing. • justify and defend their reasoning by using relevant evidence. • view critically and constructively the reasoning of others. • use technology appropriately.
Reading Strategies (one worksheet per lesson) Provides tools to help students master the math vocabulary or symbols, and comprehend word problems.	**LACC.68.RST.1.3** Follow precisely a multistep procedure… **LACC.68.RST.2.4** Determine the meaning of symbols, key terms…
Success for English Learners (one worksheet per lesson) Provides teaching strategies for differentiated instruction and alternate practice. The worksheets use a visual approach with fewer words, making them ideal for English language learners as well as other students who are having difficulties with the lesson concepts.	**LACC.68.RST.3.7** Integrate quantitative or technical information… **LACC.68.WHST.1.1** Write arguments focused on discipline-specific content…
Challenge (one worksheet per module) Provides extra non-routine problem solving opportunities, enhances critical thinking skills, and requires students to apply the math process skills.	**LACC.68.WHST.2.4** Produce clear and coherent writing…

**LESSON
1-1**

Rational and Irrational Numbers
Practice and Problem Solving: A/B

Write each fraction as a decimal.

1. $\dfrac{1}{8}$

2. $\dfrac{9}{16}$

3. $\dfrac{11}{20}$

4. $5\dfrac{8}{25}$

_____

5. $\dfrac{14}{15}$

6. $2\dfrac{7}{12}$

7. $\dfrac{3}{100}$

8. $\dfrac{16}{5}$

_____

Find the two square roots of each number.

9. 25

10. 1

11. $\dfrac{25}{4}$

12. $\dfrac{121}{49}$

_____

Find the cube root of each number.

13. 8

14. 216

15. 1

16. 2197

_____

Approximate each irrational number to the nearest hundredth without using a calculator.

17. $\sqrt{32}$

18. $\sqrt{118}$

19. $\sqrt{18}$

20. $\sqrt{319}$

_____

Approximate each irrational number to the nearest hundredth without using a calculator. Then plot each number on a number line.

21. $\sqrt{8}$ _____

22. $\sqrt{75}$ _____

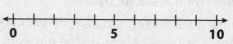

23. A tablet weighs 1.23 pounds. What is its weight written as a mixed number?

_____

24. The area of a square mirror is 256 in^2. A rectangular mirror has a width the same as the square mirror's width. Its length is two inches longer than its width. What is the area of the rectangular mirror?

_____

_____

LESSON
1-1

Rational and Irrational Numbers

Practice and Problem Solving: C

Solve.

1. One nickel is $\frac{39}{500}$ inch thick. Fifteen nickels are stacked vertically.
   How many inches tall is the stack? Give your answer as a decimal.

   _____

2. One quarter is $\frac{191}{200}$ inch in diameter. Eight quarters are placed
   side-by-side along a line. How many inches long is the line of
   quarters? Give your answer as a decimal.

   _____

3. Is $\frac{41}{50}$ closer to $\frac{9}{11}$ or $\frac{10}{11}$? Verify your answer.

   _____

   _____

**Find the two square roots of each number. (Hint: First write the
decimal as a fraction.)**

4. 0.25 _____   5. 0.0625 _____   6. $0.\overline{4}$ _____

**Approximate each irrational number to the nearest hundredth without
using a calculator. Then plot each lettered point on the number line.**

7. *A:* $\sqrt{3}$ _____   8. *B:* $\sqrt{18}$ _____

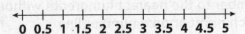

0   0.5   1   1.5   2   2.5   3   3.5   4   4.5   5

Answer the questions below.

9. How does finding a cube root differ from finding a square root of a
   positive integer? How do the answers differ?

   _____

   _____

10. Each page of a photo album holds 3 rows of 4 square photos. The
    area of each photo is 25 cm². There is 2 cm space between photos
    and a 3 cm border around the group of pictures. What are the
    dimensions of one page of the photo album?

    _____

LESSON 1-1

Rational and Irrational Numbers
Practice and Problem Solving: D

Write each fraction as a decimal. The first one is done for you.

1. $\frac{1}{9}$

    $0.\overline{1}$

2. $\frac{11}{20}$

3. $\frac{9}{16}$

Write each decimal as a fraction in simplest form. The first one is done for you.

4. 0.258

    $\frac{258}{1000} = \frac{129}{500}$

5. 4.8

6. 0.333

Find the two square roots of each number. The first one is done for you.

7. 16

    4, −4

8. 49

9. $\frac{25}{4}$

Find the cube root of each number. The first one is done for you.

10. 343

    $7 \times 7 \times 7 = 343, 7$

11. 1

12. $\frac{8}{27}$

Approximate each irrational number to the nearest hundredth without using a calculator. The first one is done for you.

13. $\sqrt{32}$

    5.66

14. $\sqrt{59}$

15. $\sqrt{118}$

Solve.

16. The world's smallest country is Vatican City. It covers $\frac{17}{100}$ square mile. What is Vatican City's area written as a decimal?

    _____

17. A square sandbox has an area of 25 ft². What is the length of each of its sides? (Hint: side = $\sqrt{25}$)

    _____

LESSON 1-1

Rational and Irrational Numbers
Reteach

To write a fraction as a decimal, divide the numerator by the denominator.

A decimal may terminate.

$$\frac{3}{4} = 4\overline{)3.00}$$
$$\begin{array}{r} 0.75 \\ \underline{-28}\downarrow \\ 20 \\ \underline{-20} \\ 0 \end{array}$$

A decimal may repeat.

$$\frac{1}{3} = 3\overline{)1.00}$$
$$\begin{array}{r} 0.\overline{3} \\ \underline{-9}\downarrow \\ 10 \\ \underline{-9} \\ 1 \end{array}$$

Complete to write each fraction as a decimal.

1. $\frac{15}{4} = 4\overline{)15.00}$

2. $\frac{5}{6} = 6\overline{)5.00}$

3. $\frac{11}{3} = 3\overline{)11.00}$

Every positive number has two square roots, one positive and one negative.

Since $5 \times 5 = 25$ and also $-5 \times -5 = 25$, both 5 and -5 are square roots of 25.

$\sqrt{25} = 5$ and $-\sqrt{25} = -5$

Every positive number has one cube root.
Since $4 \times 4 \times 4 = 64$, 4 is the cube root of 64.

Find the two square roots for each number.

4. 81

5. 49

6. $\frac{25}{36}$

_____ _____ _____

Find the cube root for each number.

7. 27

8. 125

9. 729

_____ _____ _____

LESSON 1-1

Rational and Irrational Numbers
Reading Strategies: Compare and Contrast

Are Real Numbers

Can be written as a fraction.

Cannot be written as a fraction.

Rational Numbers

Irrational Numbers

Examples:

$8 = \dfrac{8}{1}, -2.5 = -2\dfrac{1}{2}, \sqrt{\dfrac{49}{81}} = \dfrac{7}{9},$

$-\sqrt{\dfrac{49}{81}} = -\dfrac{7}{9}; \ 0.\overline{6} = \dfrac{2}{3}, \ 0.375 = \dfrac{3}{8}$

Examples:

$\sqrt{2} = 1.414213..., \ \pi = 3.141592...$

$\sqrt{24} = 4.8989794...$

Decimals terminate or repeat.

Can be written as a decimal.

Decimals are infinite and nonrepeating.

Use the chart to answer the following questions.

1. Is 0.62 a rational number? Why or why not?

   _____

2. Is $\sqrt{7}$ a rational number? Why or why not?

   _____

3. Can an irrational number be a decimal? If so, give an example.

   _____

4. Can a rational number be a repeating decimal? If so, give an example.

   _____

5. What kind of decimal is an irrational number? Give an example.

   _____

   _____

6. What do rational and irrational numbers have in common?

   _____

LESSON 1-1 Rational and Irrational Numbers

Success for English Learners

Problem 1

Think about decimal equivalents of common fractions to rewrite $\frac{2}{3}$ as a decimal.

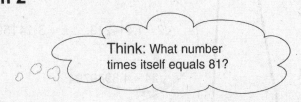

$\frac{1}{2} = 0.5$ $\qquad$ $\frac{1}{4} = 0.25$ $\qquad$ $\frac{1}{3} = 0.\overline{3}$ $\qquad$ $\frac{3}{4} = 0.75$ $\qquad$ $\frac{2}{3} = 0.\overline{6}$

So, $\frac{2}{3} = 0.\overline{6}$.

Problem 2

Think: What number times itself equals 81?

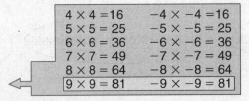

$\sqrt{81}$

$\sqrt{81}$ $\quad = \quad$ 9

$-\sqrt{81}$ $\quad = \quad$ -9

$4 \times 4 = 16$	$-4 \times -4 = 16$
$5 \times 5 = 25$	$-5 \times -5 = 25$
$6 \times 6 = 36$	$-6 \times -6 = 36$
$7 \times 7 = 49$	$-7 \times -7 = 49$
$8 \times 8 = 64$	$-8 \times -8 = 64$
$9 \times 9 = 81$	$-9 \times -9 = 81$

Problem 3

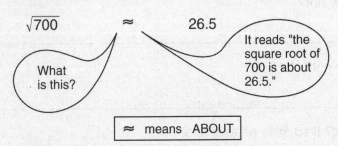

$\sqrt{700}$ $\qquad \approx \qquad$ 26.5

What is this?

It reads "the square root of 700 is about 26.5."

$\approx$ means ABOUT

1. Which decimal equivalent of a common fraction would you use to rewrite $1\frac{1}{4}$ as a decimal?

   _____

2. Why is 5^2 read as "five squared"?

   _____

   _____

3. Why do you use the term "about" when reading the answer to Problem 3 above?

   _____

LESSON 1-2

Sets of Real Numbers
Practice and Problem Solving: A/B

List all number sets that apply to each number.

1. $-\dfrac{4}{5}$ _____

2. $\sqrt{15}$ _____

3. -2 _____

4. -25 _____

5. $0.\overline{3}$ _____

6. $\dfrac{20}{4}$ _____

Tell whether the given statement is true or false. Explain your choice.

7. All real numbers are rational.

_____

8. All whole numbers are integers.

_____

Identify the set of numbers that best describes each situation. Explain your choice.

9. the amount of money in a bank account

_____

10. the exact temperature of a glass of water in degrees Celsius

_____

Place each number in the correct location on the Venn diagram.

11. $-\dfrac{5}{9}$

12. $-\sqrt{100}$

13. π

14. $\sqrt{25}$

Real Numbers	
Rational Numbers	Irrational Numbers
Integers	
Whole Numbers	

LESSON 1-2 Sets of Real Numbers
Practice and Problem Solving: C

List all number sets that apply to each number.

1. $-\sqrt{18}$

   _____

2. $-\dfrac{16}{2}$

   _____

3. 0.125

   _____

4. $\dfrac{\sqrt{25}}{5}$

   _____

5. $\dfrac{18}{19}$

   _____

6. $\dfrac{4}{5} \cdot \dfrac{10}{4}$

   _____

Identify the set of numbers that best describes each situation. Explain your choice.

7. the possible scores in a card game in which points are added or deducted after each hand

   _____

8. elevation of land compared to sea level

   _____

Answer each question.

9. Is it possible to count the number of rational numbers there are between any two integers?

   _____

10. If you take the square root of every whole number from 1 through 100, how many of them will be whole numbers? How many will be irrational numbers?

    _____

11. What numbers are integers but not whole numbers?

    _____

12. What negative numbers are not integers?

    _____

LESSON 1-2 Sets of Real Numbers
Practice and Problem Solving: D

List all number sets that apply to each number. The first one is done for you.

1. $-\dfrac{1}{2}$

　　real, rational

2. $\sqrt{3}$

3. 0.9

4. −3

5. $0.\overline{6}$

6. 18

Tell whether the given statement is true or false. Explain your choice.

7. All fractions are real numbers.

_____

8. All negative numbers are integers.

_____

Identify the set of numbers that best describes each situation. Explain your choice.

9. the number of people in a movie theater

_____

10. roll a pair of number cubes and take the square root of the sum

_____

Place each of the given numbers in the correct location on the Venn diagram. The first one is done for you.

11. $\dfrac{2}{3}$

12. −99

13. $\dfrac{10}{11}$

14. 1,000

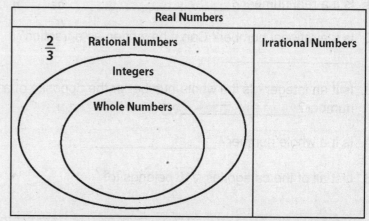

LESSON 1-2   **Sets of Real Numbers**

Reteach

Numbers can be organized into groups. Each number can be placed into one or more of the groups.

Real numbers include all rational and irrational numbers. All of the numbers that we use in everyday life are real numbers.

- If a real number can be written as a fraction, it is a **rational number**. If it cannot be written as a fraction, it is an **irrational number**.

- If a rational number is a whole number, or the opposite of a whole number, then it is an **integer**.

- If an integer is positive or 0, then it is a **whole number**.

You can use these facts to categorize any number.

A. What kind of number is 10?

Is it a real number? *Yes.*

Is it a rational number? Can it be written as a fraction? *Yes:* $\dfrac{10}{1}$

Is it an integer? Is it a whole number or the opposite of a whole number? *Yes.*

Is it a whole number? *Yes.*

So 10 is a real number, a rational number, an integer, and a whole number.

B. What kind of number is $\sqrt{\dfrac{9}{3}}$?

Is it a real number? *Yes.*

Is it a rational number? Can it be written as a fraction? *No.* $\dfrac{9}{3}$ *simplifies to 3. If you try to find the square root of 3, you will get a decimal answer that goes on forever but does not repeat: 1.7320508… This cannot be written as a fraction.*

So $\sqrt{\dfrac{9}{3}}$ is a real and an irrational number.

Answer each question to identify the categories the given number belongs to.

$\sqrt{16}$

1. Is it a real number? _____

2. Is it a rational number? Can it be written as a fraction?

   _____

3. Is it an integer? Is it a whole number or the opposite of a whole number? _____

4. Is it a whole number? _____

5. List all of the categories $\sqrt{16}$ belongs to.

_____

LESSON 1-2

Sets of Real Numbers

Reading Strategies: Use a Venn Diagram

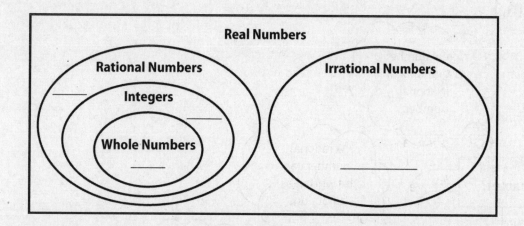

1. A real number is a _____ or an _____ number.

2. A rational number can be written as a _____ or a

   _____ .

3. Both _____ and _____ decimals are rational
   numbers.

4. A set of integers is the set of whole numbers, their _____ ,
   and zero.

5. The whole numbers are the set of _____ numbers and
   zero.

6. Place each number on the proper line on the Venn diagram.

   a. −5   b. 0.34   c. 11   d. π

LESSON 1-2 Sets of Real Numbers
Success for English Learners

Problem 1

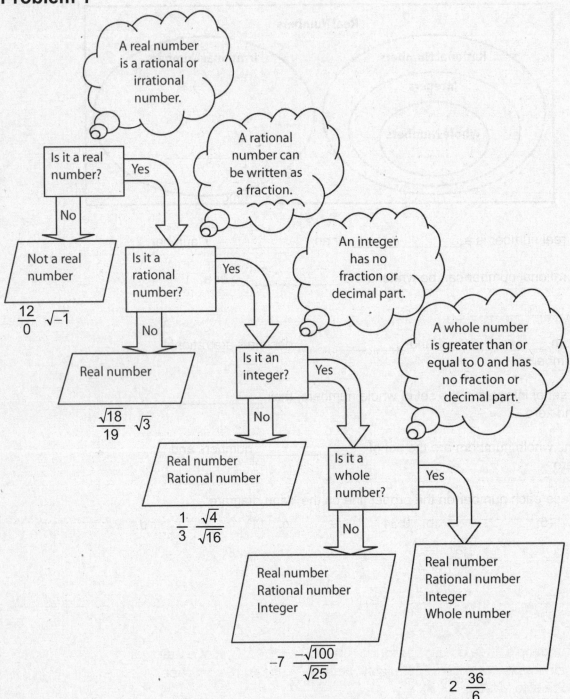

Classify each number. Use the flowchart to help you.

1. $\sqrt{15}$ _____

2. $\dfrac{3}{0}$ _____

3. $\sqrt{\dfrac{1}{9}}$ _____

4. -13 _____

_____ _____ _____ _____

LESSON 1-3	**Ordering Real Numbers**

Practice and Problem Solving: A/B

Compare. Write <, >, or = .

1. $\sqrt{5} + 3 \bigcirc \sqrt{5} + 4$

2. $\sqrt{6} + 13 \bigcirc \sqrt{10} + 13$

3. $\sqrt{7} + 4 \bigcirc 5 + \sqrt{6}$

4. $8 + \sqrt{2} \bigcirc \sqrt{8} + 2$

5. $3 + \sqrt{3} \bigcirc \sqrt{13} - 7$

6. $11 - \sqrt{3} \bigcirc 5 - \sqrt{3}$

Use the table to answer the questions.

7. List the butterflies in order from greatest to least wingspan.

_____

_____

_____

_____

Butterfly	Wingspan (in.)
Great white	3.75
Large orange sulphur	$3\frac{3}{8}$
Apricot sulphur	2.625
White-angled sulphur	3.5

8. The pink-spotted swallowtail's wingspan can measure $3\frac{5}{16}$ inches.

Between which two butterflies should the pink-spotted swallowtail be in your list from question 7?

_____

Order each group of numbers from least to greatest.

9. $\sqrt{8}, 2, \frac{\sqrt{7}}{2}$

10. $\sqrt{12}, \pi, 3.5$

_____

_____

11. $\sqrt{26}, -20, 13.5, \sqrt{35}$

12. $\sqrt{6}, -5.25, \frac{3}{2}, 5$

_____

_____

Solve.

13. Four people have used different methods to find the height of a wall. Their results are shown in the table. Order their measurements from greatest to least. $\pi \approx 3.14$

Wall Height (m)			
Allie	**Byron**	**Justin**	**Rosa**
$\sqrt{12} - 1$	$\frac{5}{2}$	2.25	$1 + \frac{\pi}{2}$

_____

LESSON
1-3

Ordering Real Numbers

Practice and Problem Solving: C

1. Order $4.\overline{6}$, $\sqrt{13} + 1$, and $2\pi - 1.68$ from least to greatest. Use $\pi \approx 3.14$.

   a. From least to greatest, the numbers are:

   _____

   b. Would the order change if you used $\pi \approx \dfrac{22}{7}$? Explain.

   _____

2. Four people are using different methods to measure the width of shelves to be installed in a closet using 3.5-centimeter brackets. Their results are shown in the table.

Shelf Width (m)			
Allie	**Byron**	**Justin**	**Rosa**
$\sqrt{12} - 2.2$	$\dfrac{\sqrt{23}}{2} - 1$	1.18	$1 + \dfrac{\pi}{9}$

   a. Order their measurements from greatest to least.

   _____

   b. The width of the closet, 1.2 meters, is shown on the number line. Graph the four measurements shown in the table.

   _____

   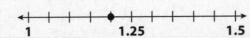

   c. Whose shelf or shelves would be suitable to use in the closet? Explain.

   _____

   _____

   _____

Name _____ Date _____ Class_____

Ordering Real Numbers
Practice and Problem Solving: D

Compare. Write <, >, or = . The first one is done for you.

1. $\sqrt{2}+1$ $\bigcirc\!\!<$ $\sqrt{2}+8$ 2. $\sqrt{2}+5$ $\bigcirc$ $\sqrt{2}+3$

3. $\sqrt{3}+5$ $\bigcirc$ $5+\sqrt{6}$ 4. $8+\sqrt{2}$ $\bigcirc$ $\sqrt{8}+2$

5. $3+\sqrt{3}$ $\bigcirc$ $\sqrt{7}-3$ 6. $5-\sqrt{3}$ $\bigcirc$ $-\sqrt{3}+5$

Graph the numbers on the number line. Then order them from least to greatest.

7. $\sqrt{2}$, π, 4.5

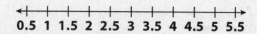

0.5   1   1.5   2   2.5   3   3.5   4   4.5   5   5.5

From least to greatest, the numbers are _____, _____, and _____.

Order the numbers from least to greatest. The first one is done for you.

8. 2, $\dfrac{\sqrt{2}}{2}$, -10 9. 7, π, $\sqrt{3}$

$$-10, \frac{\sqrt{2}}{2}, 2$$

_____   _____

10. $\sqrt{8}$, -4, 1.5 11. $\sqrt{6}$, -5.5, $\dfrac{3}{2}$

_____   _____

Solve.

12. Four people have measured the height of a wall using different methods. Their results are shown in the table. Order their measurements from least to greatest.

Wall Height (m)			
Allie	**Byron**	**Justin**	**Rosa**
$\sqrt{8}$	$\dfrac{5}{2}$	2.6	$1+\sqrt{3}$

_____

LESSON 1-3

Ordering Real Numbers

Reteach

Compare and order real numbers from least to greatest.

Order $\sqrt{22}$, $\pi + 1$, and $4\frac{1}{2}$ from least to greatest.

You can use a calculator to approximate irrational numbers.

$\sqrt{22} \approx 4.69$

You know that $\pi \approx 3.14$, so you can find the approximate value of $\pi + 1$.

$\pi + 1 \approx 3.14 + 1 \approx 4.14$

Plot $\sqrt{22}$, $\pi + 1$, and $4\frac{1}{2}$ on a number line.

On a number line, the values of numbers increase as you move from left to right. So, to order these numbers from least to greatest, list them from left to right.

$\pi + 1$, $4\frac{1}{2}$, and $\sqrt{22}$

Order each group of numbers from least to greatest.

1. 4, π, $\sqrt{8}$

_____

2. 5, $\dfrac{17}{3}$, $\pi + 2$

_____

3. $\sqrt{2}$, 1.7, -2

_____

4. 2.5, $\sqrt{5}$, $\dfrac{3}{2}$

_____

5. 3.7, $\sqrt{13}$, $\pi + 1$

_____

6. $\dfrac{5}{4}$, $\pi - 2$, $\dfrac{\sqrt{5}}{2}$

_____

Name _____ Date _____ Class_____

Ordering Real Numbers

Reading Strategies: Connect Words with Symbols

To compare real numbers, you can use the symbols <, >, and =.

To approximate irrational numbers, you can use the symbol ≈.

The symbol < means "less than."

$$\frac{1}{2} < 2$$ ←——— Read as "$\frac{1}{2}$ is less than 2."

The symbol > means "greater than":

$$\sqrt{6} > \sqrt{5}$$ ←——— Read as "The square root of 6 is greater than the square root of 5."

The symbol = means "equal to":

$$\sqrt{16} = 4$$ ←——— Read as
"The square root of 16 is equal to 4" OR
"The square root of 16 equals 4."

The sign ≈ means "approximately equal to":

$$\pi \approx 3.14$$ ←——— Read as
"π is approximately equal to 3.14." OR
"π is approximately 3.14."

Write in words.

1. $\sqrt{13} < 4$

_____

2. $0.501 \approx \frac{1}{2}$

_____

3. $\sqrt{25} = 5$

_____

4. $\pi + 1 > \frac{2}{3}$

_____

Write using symbols.

5. Eighteen-halves is equal to nine. _____

6. 5.17 is greater than the square root of twenty-three.

    _____

7. Two-thirds is less than pi. _____

Ordering Real Numbers
Success for English Learners

Problem 1

Compare. Write <, >, or =.

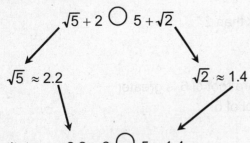

$\sqrt{5} + 2 \bigcirc 5 + \sqrt{2}$

> Find approximate values for $\sqrt{5}$ and $\sqrt{2}$. Use a calculator.

$\sqrt{5} \approx 2.2$ $\qquad$ $\sqrt{2} \approx 1.4$

Substitute. $\quad 2.2 + 2 \bigcirc 5 + 1.4$

Add. $\qquad 4.2 \bigcirc 6.4$

$\qquad 4.2 \lessdot 6.4$, so $\sqrt{5} + 2 \lessdot 5 + \sqrt{2}$.

Problem 2

Order $\sqrt{7}$, $\pi - 1$, and 2.5 from least to greatest.

Find approximate values for $\sqrt{7}$ and $\pi - 1$.

$\sqrt{7} \approx 2.65 \qquad\qquad \pi - 1 \approx 3.14 - 1$

$\qquad\qquad\qquad\qquad\qquad \approx 2.14$

Plot the three values on a number line.

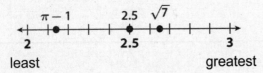

From least to greatest, the numbers are $\pi - 1$, 2.5, and $\sqrt{7}$.

1. Compare. Write <, >, or =.

$\sqrt{13} + 8 \bigcirc \sqrt{8} + 13$

2. Order $\sqrt{19}$, $\pi + 1$, and 4.4 from least to greatest. _____

3. Name a situation in which it would be very important to know the order of a series of numbers.

_____

MODULE 1

Real Numbers
Challenge

Venn Diagrams

Diagrams using circles can show relationships between classes or sets. These diagrams are named after the English mathematician John Venn who introduced them.

Here are some examples using integers, even numbers, odd numbers, and primes. Remember that just one prime number, 2, is even. A shaded region is empty. A region marked *x* has at least one member.

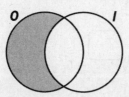
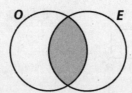
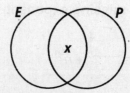

All odd numbers are integers.	No odd numbers are even.	Some even numbers are prime.
All *O* is *I*.	No *O* is *E*.	Some *E* is *P*.

Describe each diagram using both words and letters. Set *S* is the square numbers.

1.
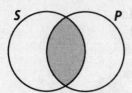

_____

2.
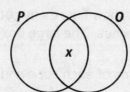

_____

3.
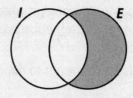

_____

Draw a Venn diagram for each statement.

4. Some square numbers are odd.

5. No prime numbers are squares.

6. All square numbers are integers.

7. Some odd numbers are not prime.

Integer Exponents
Practice and Problem Solving: A/B

Find the value of each power.

1. $5^3 =$ _____

2. $7^{-2} =$ _____

3. $51^1 =$ _____

4. $3^{-4} =$ _____

5. $1^{12} =$ _____

6. $64^0 =$ _____

7. $4^{-3} =$ _____

8. $4^3 =$ _____

9. $10^5 =$ _____

Find the missing exponent.

10. $n^3 = n^{\boxed{}} \cdot n^{-3}$

11. $\dfrac{a^{\boxed{}}}{a^2} = a^4$

12. $(r^4)^{\boxed{}} = r^{12}$

Simplify each expression.

13. $(9 - 3)^2 - (5 \cdot 4)^0 =$ _____

14. $(2 + 3)^5 \div (5^2)^2 =$ _____

15. $4^2 \div (6 - 2)^4 =$ _____

16. $[(1 + 7)^2]^2 \cdot (12^2)^0 =$ _____

Use the description below to complete Exercises 17–20.

A shipping company makes a display to show how many cubes can fit into
a large box. Each cube has sides of 2 inches. The large box has sides of
10 inches.

17. Use exponents to express the volume of each cube and the large box.

   Volume of cube = _____   Volume of large box = _____

18. Find how many cubes will fit in the box. _____

19. Suppose the shipping company were packing balls with a diameter of
    2 inches instead of cubes. Would the large box hold more balls or
    fewer balls than boxes? Explain your answer.

    _____

    _____

    _____

20. Suppose the size of each cube is doubled and the size of the large box
    is doubled. How many of these new cubes will fit in that new large box?
    Explain how you found your answer.

    _____

LESSON 2-1 Integer Exponents

Practice and Problem Solving: C

Simplify each expression.

1. $(7-3)^2 \cdot (6-2)^3 =$ _____

2. $(7-3)^2 \div (6-2)^3 =$ _____

3. $(2 \cdot 5^3) \div (9-4)^4 =$ _____

4. $[(3+7)^2]^2 \cdot (10^2)^0 =$ _____

5. $(3 \cdot 4)^2 \div (6 \cdot 2)^4 =$ _____

6. $[(2^2)^2]^2 \cdot 2^3 =$ _____

Answer each question.

7. Andrea quickly gave the answer to the problem below. Can you do the same? Explain how you found your answer.

   Find the value of $a^n \cdot a^{n-1} \cdot a^{n-2} \cdot a^{n-3} \cdot a^{n-4} \cdot a^{n-5} \cdot a^{n-6}$
   when $a = 2$ and $n = 3$.

   _____

   _____

For each experiment, make a prediction first. Then complete the given table. Finally, try the experiment and see if your prediction is correct.

   Experiment 1: Fold a piece of paper in half over and over again to make smaller and smaller rectangles.

8. Predict the maximum number of small rectangles you can make before

   you cannot fold the paper any further. _____

9.

Number of Folds	0	1	2	3	4	5	6	7	8	9	10
Number of Rectangles	2^0, 1	2^1, 2									

10. Do the experiment. How many rectangles could you make? _____

   Experiment 2: Cut a piece of paper in half. Make a single pile of the pieces. Cut the pile in half. Continue making a single pile of the pieces and cutting the pile in half.

11. Predict the maximum number of pieces you can make before you cannot cut the paper any further. _____

12. Do the experiment. How many pieces could you make? _____

LESSON 2-1

Integer Exponents

Practice and Problem Solving: D

Write each expression without exponents. Then find the value. The first one is done for you.

1. $4^{-4} = \dfrac{1}{4 \times 4 \times 4 \times 4} = \dfrac{1}{256}$

2. $6^2 = $ _____

3. $3^5 = $ _____

4. $24^0 = $ _____

5. $7^{-2} = $ _____

6. $10^5 = $ _____

Simplify each expression. Show your work. The first is done for you.

7. $\dfrac{(3 \cdot 2)^6}{(7 - 1)^4} = \dfrac{6^6}{6^4} = \dfrac{6^6}{6^4}$

$= 6^{6-4} = 6^2$

$= 36$

8. $(3)^2 \bullet (3^1)$

9. $4^2 \bullet 4^3$

10. $(4^2)^3$

11. $(4 - 3)^2 \bullet (5 \bullet 4)^0$

12. $(2 + 3)^5 \div (5^2)^2$

Answer the question.

13. Find the value of $(2^2)^3$. Then find the value of $(2^3)^2$. What is true about the results? Explain why.

_____

_____

_____

Integer Exponents
Reteach

A positive exponent tells you how many times to multiply the base as a factor. A negative exponent tells you how many times to divide by the base. Any number to the 0 power is equal to 1.

$$4^2 = 4 \bullet 4 = 16 \qquad 4^5 = 4 \bullet 4 \bullet 4 \bullet 4 \bullet 4 = 1{,}024 \qquad a^3 = a \bullet a \bullet a$$

$$4^{-2} = \frac{1}{4^2} = \frac{1}{4 \bullet 4} = \frac{1}{16} \qquad 4^{-5} = \frac{1}{4^5} = \frac{1}{4 \bullet 4 \bullet 4 \bullet 4 \bullet 4} = \frac{1}{1{,}024} \qquad a^{-3} = \frac{1}{a^3} = \frac{1}{a \bullet a \bullet a}$$

When you work with integers, certain properties are always true. With integer exponents, there are also certain properties that are always true.

When the bases are the same and you multiply, you add exponents.

$$2^2 \bullet 2^4 = 2^{2+4}$$

$$2 \bullet 2 \bullet 2 \bullet 2 \bullet 2 \bullet 2 = 2^6 \qquad\qquad a^m \bullet a^n = a^{m+n}$$

When the bases are the same and you divide, you subtract exponents.

$$\frac{2^5}{2^3} = 2^{5-3}$$

$$\frac{2 \bullet 2 \bullet \cancel{2} \bullet \cancel{2} \bullet \cancel{2}}{\cancel{2} \bullet \cancel{2} \bullet \cancel{2}} = 2^2 \qquad\qquad \frac{a^m}{a^n} = a^{m-n}$$

When you raise a power to a power, you multiply.

$$(2^3)^2 = 2^{3 \bullet 2}$$

$$(2 \bullet 2 \bullet 2)^2$$

$$(2 \bullet 2 \bullet 2) \bullet (2 \bullet 2 \bullet 2) = 2^6 \qquad\qquad (a^m)^n = a^{m \bullet n}$$

Tell whether you will add, subtract, or multiply the exponents. Then simplify by finding the value of the expression.

1. $\dfrac{3^6}{3^3} \rightarrow$ _____

2. $8^2 \bullet 8^{-3} \rightarrow$ _____

3. $(3^2)^3 \rightarrow$ _____

4. $5^3 \bullet 5^1 \rightarrow$ _____

5. $\dfrac{4^2}{4^4} \rightarrow$ _____

6. $(6^2)^2 \rightarrow$ _____

Name _____ Date _____ Class _____

Integer Exponents

Reading Strategies: Using Patterns

You can use patterns to help evaluate powers.

Look at the patterns in each column. As you move down the column, you will note that the products are getting smaller. That is because there is one less factor when the powers are positive and one more factor when the powers are negative.

Column 1	Column 2	Column 3
$2^3 = 8$	$3^3 = 27$	$4^3 = 64$
$2^2 = 4$	$3^2 = 9$	$4^2 = 16$
$2^1 = 2$	$3^1 = 3$	$4^1 = 4$
$2^0 = 1$	$3^0 = 1$	$4^0 = 1$
$2^{-1} = \dfrac{1}{2}$	$3^{-1} = \dfrac{1}{3}$	$4^{-1} = \dfrac{1}{4}$
$2^{-2} = \dfrac{1}{4}$	$3^{-2} = \dfrac{1}{9}$	$4^{-2} = \dfrac{1}{16}$

Use the table to answer each question.

1. Describe the pattern of the exponents in each column.

   _____

2. What is the base of column 2?   _____

3. In column 2, what is the product divided by
   each time to get the product in the cell below?   _____

4. What is the base of column 3?   _____

5. In column 3, what is the product divided by
   each time to get the product in the cell below?   _____

Complete the table, using the table above as a guide.

6.

Column 1	Column 2	Column 3
$5^3 = 125$	$6^3 = 216$	$10^3 = 1,000$
$5^2 = 25$	$6^2 = 36$	$10^2 = 100$

LESSON
2-1

Integer Exponents
Success for English Learners

The set of integers is the set of whole numbers and their opposites, such as 3, 2, 1, 0, −1, −2, and −3. Integer exponents are powers of a number where the power is a whole number or its opposite.

Problem 1

$$4^2 = 4 \cdot 4 = 16 \qquad 4^5 = 4 \cdot 4 \cdot 4 \cdot 4 \cdot 4 = 1{,}024 \qquad a^3 = a \cdot a \cdot a$$

$$4^{-2} = \frac{1}{4^2} = \frac{1}{4 \cdot 4} = \frac{1}{16} \qquad 4^{-5} = \frac{1}{4^5} = \frac{1}{4 \cdot 4 \cdot 4 \cdot 4 \cdot 4} = \frac{1}{1{,}024} \qquad a^{-3} = \frac{1}{a^3} = \frac{1}{a \cdot a \cdot a}$$

Problem 2

When you work with integers, certain properties are always true. With integer exponents, there are also certain properties that are always true.

Use properties of exponents to simplify each expression.

$$\overbrace{2^2} \cdot \overbrace{2^4} = 2^{2+4}$$

$$\underbrace{2 \cdot 2} \cdot \underbrace{2 \cdot 2 \cdot 2 \cdot 2} = 2^6 \qquad\qquad a^m \cdot a^n = a^{m+n}$$

$$\frac{2^5}{2^3} = 2^{5-3}$$

$$\frac{2 \cdot 2 \cdot \cancel{2} \cdot \cancel{2} \cdot \cancel{2}}{\cancel{2} \cdot \cancel{2} \cdot \cancel{2}} = 2^2 \qquad\qquad \frac{a^m}{a^n} = a^{m-n}$$

$$(2^3)^2 = 2^{3 \cdot 2}$$

$$(2 \cdot 2 \cdot 2)^2$$

$$(2 \cdot 2 \cdot 2) \cdot (2 \cdot 2 \cdot 2) = 2^6 \qquad\qquad (a^m)^n = a^{m \cdot n}$$

Complete.

1. Explain in your own words what a negative exponent means.

_____

_____

Use properties of exponents to simplify each expression.

2. $\dfrac{3^6}{3^4} =$ _____

3. $4^2 \cdot 4^1 =$ _____

4. $(x^5)^4 =$ _____

5. $(4^2)^3 =$ _____

6. $12^3 \cdot 12^{-2} =$ _____

7. $z^6 \cdot z^6 =$ _____

LESSON 2-2

Scientific Notation with Positive Powers of 10
Practice and Problem Solving: A/B

Write each number as a power of 10.

1. 100   2. 10,000   3. 100,000   4. 10,000,000

_____ _____ _____ _____

5. 1,000,000   6. 1,000   7. 1,000,000,000   8. 1

_____ _____ _____ _____

Write each power of ten in standard notation.

9. 10^3 10. 10^5 11. 10   12. 10^6

_____ _____ _____ _____

13. 10^2 14. 10^0 15. 10^4 16. 10^7

_____ _____ _____ _____

Write each number in scientific notation.

17. 2,500   18. 300   19. 47,300   20. 24

_____ _____ _____ _____

21. 14,565   22. 7,001   23. 19,050,000   24. 33

_____ _____ _____ _____

Write each number in standard notation.

25. 6×10^3 26. 4.5×10^2 27. 7×10^7 28. 1.05×10^4

_____ _____ _____ _____

29. 3.052×10^3 30. 5×10^0 31. 9.87×10^1 32. 5.43×10^1

_____ _____ _____ _____

Solve.

33. The average distance of the Moon from Earth is about 384,400 kilometers. Write this number in scientific notation.

_____

34. The radius of Earth is about 6.38×10^3 kilometers. Write this distance in standard notation.

_____

LESSON 2-2 Scientific Notation with Positive Powers of 10

Practice and Problem Solving: C

Write each pair of numbers in standard notation. Use the symbols >, <, or = to compare them. Show your work.

1. 2.5×10^3 ____ 2.5×10^6

   _____

2. 5×10^6 ____ 2.5×10^6

   _____

3. 3×10^0 ____ 1×10^1

   _____

4. 4.025×10^3 ____ 1.025×10^4

   _____

Write each pair of numbers in scientific notation. Write the numbers in scientific notation on the correct side of the comparison symbol.

5. 1,200; 450

   _____ < _____

6. 230,000; 32,000

   _____ > _____

Write the numbers from least to greatest.

7. 3.25×10^6, 5.32×10^5, 2.35×10^6, 5.32×10^6, 3.25×10^5, 2.35×10^5

   _____

8. 5×10^0, 1×10^1, 0×10^0, 1×10^0, 5×10^1

   _____

Use the fact that 1 meter equals 10^3 millimeters and 1 centimeter equals 10^1 millimeters to label each of these statements as true or false. Show your work.

9. 1×10^3 m $> 1 \times 10^5$ cm

   True or false?

   _____

10. 9×10^1 m $= 9 \times 10^1$ mm

    True or false?

    _____

Solve.

11. An athletic stadium has a capacity of 1.5×10^4 fans. If 9×10^3 fans buy advance tickets to an event at the stadium, how many tickets will be available at the box office on the day of the event? Show your work. Use standard notation.

    _____

12. A town's most popular drive-in restaurant has 2,500 followers on a social networking website. The town's high school athletic program has 1.5×10^4 followers on the same website. Which is more popular according to this data, the drive-in or the athletic program? Show your work. Use standard notation.

    _____

**LESSON
2-2**

Scientific Notation with Positive Powers of 10

Practice and Problem Solving: D

Write each product in standard form. The first one is done for you.

1. $10 \times 10 =$

   _____**100**_____

2. $10 \times 10 \times 10 \times 10 \times 10 =$

   _____

3. $10 \times 10 \times 10 \times 10 =$

   _____

4. $10 \times 10 \times 10 =$

   _____

Write each number as a product of tens. The first one is done for you.

5. $100,000 =$

   ___**$10 \times 10 \times 10 \times 10 \times 10$**___

6. $10,000,000 =$

   _____

7. $10,000 =$

   _____

8. $100,000,000,000 =$

   _____

Write each number as a power of ten and an exponent. The first one is done for you.

9. $1,000 =$ ___**10^3**___

10. $10 =$ _____

11. $100,000 =$ _____

Write each power of ten in standard form. The first one is done for you.

12. 10^1

   _____**10**_____

13. 10^3

   _____

14. 10^4

   _____

15. 10^9

   _____

16. 10^5

   _____

17. 10^0

   _____

Write the exponent for the question mark. The first one is done for you.

18. $3,600 = 3.6 \times 10^? $ __**3**__

19. $450 = 4.5 \times 10^? $ ____

20. $5,000,000 = 5 \times 10^? $ ____

21. $6 = 6 \times 10^? $ ____

Write each number in standard form. The first one is done for you.

22. $3.56 \times 10^3 =$

   _____**3,560**_____

23. $9 \times 10^3 =$

   _____

24. $6.875 \times 10^4 =$

   _____

25. $4.005 \times 10^6 =$

   _____

Solve.

26. The volume of a cube is 10 feet times 10 feet times 10 feet. Write this product as one number in standard form.

   _____

LESSON 2-2 Scientific Notation with Positive Powers of 10
Reteach

You can change a number from standard notation to scientific notation in 3 steps.

1. Place the decimal point between the first and second digits on the left to make a number between 1 and 10.
2. Count from the decimal point to the right of the last digit on the right.
3. Use the number of places counted in Step 2 as the power of ten.

Example

Write 125,000 in scientific notation.

1.25

1) The first and second digits to the left are 1 and 2, so place the decimal point between the two digits to make the number 1.25.

125,000

‿‿‿‿

1.25×10^5 2) The last digit in 125,000 is 5 places to the right.
3) The power of 10 is 5.

You can change a number from scientific notation to standard notation in 3 steps.

1. Find the power of 10.
2. Count that number of places to the right.
3. Add zeros as needed.

Example

Write 5.96×10^4 in standard notation.

10^4 1) The power of 10 is 4.

5.9600

‿‿‿

59,600   2) Move the decimal point 4 places to the right.
3) Add two zeros.

Complete to write each number in scientific notation.

1. 34,600

   The number between 1 and 10: _____

   The power of 10: _____

   The number in scientific notation:

   _____

2. 1,050,200

   The number between 1 and 10: _____

   The power of 10: _____

   The number in scientific notation:

   _____

Write each number in standard notation.

3. 1.057×10^3 4. 3×10^8 5. 5.24×10^5

_____   _____   _____

Name _____ Date _____ Class _____

Scientific Notation with Positive Powers of 10

Reading Strategies: Follow a List of Steps

Lists can help you understand the steps of changing from standard notation to scientific notation.

Change a number from standard notation to scientific notation

A   Locate the digit that is on the left end of the number. For example, if the number is 2,350, the digit on the far left is "2."

B   Place the decimal point *after* or *to the right* of that digit. For example, in the example 2,350, moving the decimal makes the number "2.350". This gives a number between 1 and 10.

C   Count places to the right from the new decimal point to the end of the number. How many is that? In the example, it is *three places* from the new decimal point to the right end of the number.

D   Use the number of places as the *exponent* or *power* of ten after you write the number between 1 and 10, a times sign, and a "10." In this example, the "3" goes with the "10." This gives 2.350×10^3. After moving the decimal, zeros at the end of the number can be dropped, so 10^3 can be written as 2.35×10^3.

Fill in the steps in the list below each number as you write it in scientific notation.

1. 295

A: _____

B: _____

C: _____

D: _____

2. 10,500

A: _____

B: _____

C: _____

D: _____

3. 4,505,000

A: _____

B: _____

C: _____

D: _____

Change a number from scientific notation to standard notation

A   Find the decimal point in the number between 1 and 10 in a number written in scientific notation. For example, in 4.56×10^7 the decimal is between the digits "4" and "5".

B   Locate the exponent or power of 10. In the example 4.56×10^7 the power of 10 is "7."

C   Starting at the decimal, count seven places to the right. If there are no numbers to be counted, write zeros. In the example 4.56×10^7, you would count the "5" and the "6" as two places, and add five zeros. This would give 45600000, or 45,600,000.

Fill in the steps below each number as you write it in standard notation.

4. 2.5×10^4

A: _____

B: _____

C: _____

5. 7×10^5

A: _____

B: _____

C: _____

6. 1.234×10^3

A: _____

B: _____

C: _____

LESSON 2-2

Scientific Notation with Positive Powers of 10

Success for English Learners

Problem 1

Write 3.12×10^9 in standard notation.

Which way should you move the decimal point?

Think about the number line.

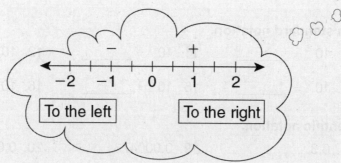

The exponent 9 is positive, so the decimal point moves to the *right*.

So, 3.12×10^9 in standard notation is 3,120,000,000.

Problem 2

Write 7,505,000 in scientific notation.

7,505,000 ⟵——— Move decimal point *six* places to the *left*.

When you move the decimal to the left, the exponent of 10 is positive.

So, 7,505,000 in scientific notation is 7.505×10^6.

1. Which number is greater, 3.28×10^5 or 3.28×10^3? Prove your answer by writing each number in standard notation.

   _____

2. Is 3×10^6 grams more likely to be the mass of a car or the mass of an eyelash? Explain.

   _____

   _____

3. Write 186,000 in scientific notation.

   _____

4. Write 4.56789×10^3 in standard form.

   _____

Scientific Notation with Negative Powers of 10
Practice and Problem Solving: A/B

Write each number as a negative power of ten.

1. $\dfrac{1}{10^2}$ = _____

2. $\dfrac{1}{10^4}$ = _____

3. $\dfrac{1}{10^5}$ = _____

4. $\dfrac{1}{10^7}$ = _____

5. $\dfrac{1}{10^6}$ = _____

6. $\dfrac{1}{10^3}$ = _____

7. $\dfrac{1}{10^9}$ = _____

8. $\dfrac{1}{10^1}$ = _____

Write each power of ten in standard notation.

9. 10^{-3} = _____

10. 10^{-5} = _____

11. 10^{-1} = _____

12. 10^{-6} = _____

13. 10^{-2} = _____

14. 10^{-9} = _____

15. 10^{-4} = _____

16. 10^{-7} = _____

Write each number in scientific notation.

17. 0.025

18. 0.3

19. 0.000473

20. 0.0024

_____

_____

_____

_____

21. 0.000014565

22. 0.70010

23. 0.0190500

24. 0.00330000

_____

_____

_____

_____

Write each number in standard notation.

25. 6×10^{-3}

26. 4.5×10^{-2}

27. 7×10^{-7}

28. 1.05×10^{-6}

_____

_____

_____

_____

29. 3.052×10^{-8}

30. 5×10^{-1}

31. 9.87×10^{-4}

32. 5.43×10^{-5}

_____

_____

_____

_____

Solve.

33. An *E. coli* bacterium has a diameter of about 5×10^{-7} meter. Write
this measurement as a decimal in standard notation.

_____

34. A human hair has an average diameter of about 0.000017 meter.
Write this measurement in scientific notation.

_____

LESSON 2-3 Scientific Notation with Negative Powers of 10

Practice and Problem Solving: C

Write each pair of numbers in standard notation. Use the symbols >, <, or = to compare them.

1. $5.2 \times 10^{-3} \bigcirc 5.2 \times 10^{-6}$

2. $5 \times 10^{-6} \bigcirc 2.5 \times 10^{-5}$

_____

_____

3. $3 \times 10^{0} \bigcirc 1 \times 10^{-1}$

4. $5.02 \times 10^{-3} \bigcirc 2.05 \times 10^{-4}$

_____

_____

Write each pair of numbers in scientific notation. Write the numbers in scientific notation on the correct side of the comparison symbol.

5. 0.0012; 0.45

6. 0.0000023; 0.00032

_____ < _____

_____ > _____

List the numbers in order from least to greatest.

7. $3.25 \times 10^{-6}, 5.32 \times 10^{-5}, 2.35 \times 10^{-6}, 5.32 \times 10^{-6}, 3.25 \times 10^{-5}, 2.35 \times 10^{-5}$

_____

8. $5 \times 10^{0}, 1 \times 10^{-1}, 0 \times 10^{0}, 1 \times 10^{0}, 5 \times 10^{-1}$

_____

Identify whether each statement is true or false. Circle the correct answer. Show your work. (1 m = 10^{3} mm; 1 cm = 10^{1} mm)

9. 1×10^{-3} m > 1×10^{-1} cm

   True or false?

10. 7×10^{-1} cm < 7×10^{-3} m

    True or false?

11. 3.5×10^{-1} cm = 3.5×10^{-3} m

    True or false?

12. 9×10^{-1} mm = 9×10^{-4} m

    True or false?

Solve.

13. A test tube used in science class has a volume capacity of 9×10^{-3} liter. How many drops of a solution will it take to fill the test tube if each drop's volume is 3×10^{-5} liter? Write these numbers in standard notation and then calculate the answer.

_____

14. A logic array on a semiconductor chip has a rectangular shape. Its length is 0.00025 meter and its width is 0.000125 meter. What is the logic array's area? Write these numbers in scientific notation.

_____

LESSON 2-3

Scientific Notation with Negative Powers of 10

Practice and Problem Solving: D

Write each product in standard form. The first one is done for you.

1. $\dfrac{1}{10 \times 10} = \dfrac{1}{100}$

2. $\dfrac{1}{10 \times 10 \times 10 \times 10 \times 10} = $ _____

3. $\dfrac{1}{10 \times 10 \times 10 \times 10} = $ _____

4. $\dfrac{1}{10 \times 10 \times 10} = $ _____

Write each number as a product of tens. The first one is done for you.

5. $\dfrac{1}{100,000} = \dfrac{1}{10 \times 10 \times 10 \times 10 \times 10}$

6. $\dfrac{1}{10,000,000} = $ _____

7. $\dfrac{1}{10,000} = $ _____

8. $\dfrac{1}{100,000,000,000} = $ _____

Write each number as both a power of ten and a negative exponent. The first one is done for you.

9. $\dfrac{1}{1,000} = \dfrac{1}{10^3} = 10^{-3}$

10. $\dfrac{1}{10} = $ _____

11. $\dfrac{1}{100} = $ _____

12. $\dfrac{1}{10,000} = $ _____

Write in standard form. The first one is done for you.

13. $\dfrac{1}{10^1} = \dfrac{1}{10}$

14. $\dfrac{1}{10^3} = $ _____

15. $\dfrac{1}{10^4} = $ _____

16. $\dfrac{1}{10^9} = $ _____

17. $\dfrac{1}{10^5} = $ _____

18. $\dfrac{1}{10^{12}} = $ _____

Identify the unknown exponent. The first one is done for you.

19. $0.00036 = 3.6 \times 10^?$ ___−4___

20. $0.450 = 4.5 \times 10^?$ _____

21. $0.00000005 = 5 \times 10^?$ _____

22. $0.00600 = 6 \times 10^?$ _____

Write each number in standard form. The first one is done for you.

23. $3.56 \times 10^{-3} = $ ___0.00356___

24. $9 \times 10^{-5} = $ _____

25. $6.875 \times 10^{-4} = $ _____

26. $4.005 \times 10^{-6} = $ _____

Solve.

27. The volume of a box is found by multiplying its length, width, and height. The three sides are 0.5 foot, 0.75 foot, and 0.4 foot. Find the product. Write it in scientific notation.

_____

LESSON 2-3

Scientific Notation with Negative Powers of 10
Reteach

You can convert a number from standard form to scientific notation in 3 steps.
1. Starting from the left, find the first non-zero digit. To the right of this digit is the new location of your decimal point.
2. Count the number of places you moved the decimal point. This number will be used in the exponent in the power of ten.
3. Since the original decimal value was less than 1, your power of ten must be negative. Place a negative sign in front of the exponent.

Example
Write 0.00496 in standard notation.

4.96	1) The first non-zero digit is 4, so move the decimal point to the right of the 4.
4.96×10^3	2) The decimal point moved 3 places, so the whole number in the power of ten is 3.
4.96×10^{-3}	3) Since 0.00496 is less than 1, the power of ten must be negative.

You can convert a number from scientific notation to standard form in 3 steps.
1. Find the power of ten.
2. If the exponent is negative, you must move the decimal point to the left. Move it the number of places indicated by the whole number in the exponent.
3. Insert a leading zero before the decimal point.

Example
Write 1.23×10^{-5} in standard notation.

10^{-5}	1) Find the power of ten.
.0000123	2) The exponent is −5, so move the decimal point 5 places to the left.
0.0000123	3) Insert a leading zero before the decimal point.

Write each number in scientific notation.

1. 0.0279

2. 0.00007100

3. 0.0000005060

_____ _____ _____

Write each number in standard notation.

4. 2.350×10^{-4}

5. 6.5×10^{-3}

6. 7.07×10^{-5}

_____ _____ _____

LESSON 2-3 Scientific Notation with Negative Powers of 10

Reading Strategies: Use Graphic Aids

Change a number from standard notation to scientific notation

Change 0.0000003 to scientific notation.

  A. What is the first non-zero digit? It is 3.

  B. Move the decimal point until it is directly to the right of the 3.
     0.0000003 ◄─── The decimal point moves 7 places *to the right*.

  C. The decimal point moved 7 places to the *right*. So, the power of ten is 7,
     and it must be must be *negative*. The power of ten is –7.

  D. So, the number in scientific notation is 3.0×10^{-7}.

Fill in the steps below each number to write it in scientific notation.

1. 0.00123

   First non-zero digit: _____

   Number of places from decimal: _____

   Direction decimal point moves: _____

   Power of 10: _____

   Scientific notation: _____

2. 0.00000567

   First non-zero digit: _____

   Number of places from decimal: _____

   Direction decimal point moves: _____

   Power of 10: _____

   Scientific notation: _____

Change a number from scientific notation to standard notation

Change 2.5×10^{-4} to standard notation.

  A. What is the power of 10? It is –4.

  B. Since the power of 10 is negative, the decimal must move *left*.
     0002.5 ◄─── Move the decimal point 4 places *to the left*.

  C. So, the number in standard notation is 0.00025.

Fill in the steps below each number to write it in standard notation.

3. 6.7×10^{-8}

   Power of 10: _____

   Direction decimal point moves: _____

   Number of places: _____

   Standard notation: _____

4. 3.21×10^{-4}

   Power of 10: _____

   Direction decimal point moves: _____

   Number of places: _____

   Standard notation: _____

**LESSON
2-3**
Scientific Notation with Negative Powers of 10
Success for English Learners

Problem 1

Write 5.43×10^{-6} in standard notation.

Which way should you move the decimal point?

Think about the number line.

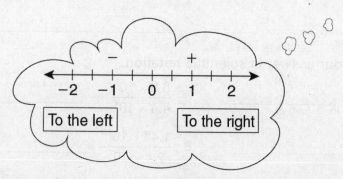

The exponent (–6) is negative, so the decimal point moves to the *left*.

So, 5.43×10^{-6} in standard notation is 0.00000543.

Problem 2

Write 0.00000456 in scientific notation.

0.00000456 ⟵—— Move decimal point *six* places to the *right*.

When you move the decimal to the right, the exponent is negative.

So, 0.00000456 in scientific notation is 4.56×10^{-6}.

1. Which number is greater, 5.75×10^{-3} or 5.75×10^{-4}? Prove your answer by writing each number in standard notation.

   _____

2. Is 3×10^{-7} grams more likely to be the mass of a bicycle or the mass of a hair? Explain.

   _____

   _____

3. Write 0.000493 in scientific notation.

   _____

4. Write 3.21×10^{-5} in standard form.

   _____

LESSON 2-4

Operations with Scientific Notation

Practice and Problem Solving: A/B

Add or subtract. Write your answer in scientific notation.

1. $6.4 \times 10^3 + 1.4 \times 10^4 + 7.5 \times 10^3$

   _____

2. $4.2 \times 10^6 - 1.2 \times 10^5 - 2.5 \times 10^5$

   _____

3. $3.3 \times 10^9 + 2.6 \times 10^9 + 7.7 \times 10^8$

   _____

4. $8.0 \times 10^4 - 3.4 \times 10^4 - 1.2 \times 10^3$

   _____

Multiply or divide. Write your answer in scientific notation.

5. $(3.2 \times 10^8)(1.3 \times 10^9) =$ _____

6. $\dfrac{8.8 \times 10^7}{4.4 \times 10^4} =$ _____

7. $(1.5 \times 10^6)(5.9 \times 10^4) =$ _____

8. $\dfrac{1.44 \times 10^{10}}{2.4 \times 10^2} =$ _____

Write each number using calculator notation.

9. $4.1 \times 10^4 =$ _____

10. $9.4 \times 10^{-6} =$ _____

Write each number using scientific notation.

11. $5.2E–6 =$ _____

12. $8.3E+2 =$ _____

Use the situation below to complete Exercises 13–16. Express each answer in scientific notation.

A runner tries to keep a consistent stride length in a marathon. But, the length will change during the race. A runner has a stride length of 5 feet for the first half of the race and a stride length of 4.5 feet for the second half.

13. A marathon is 26 miles 385 yards long. That is about 1.4×10^5 feet. How many feet long is half a marathon?

    _____

14. How many strides would it take to finish the first half of the marathon?

    _____

15. How many strides would it take to finish the second half of the marathon?

    _____

Hint: Write 5 ft as 5.0×10^0 and 4.5 feet as 4.5×10^0.

16. How many strides would it take the runner to complete marathon? Express your answer in both scientific notation and standard notation.

    _____

LESSON 2-4

Operations with Scientific Notation

Practice and Problem Solving: C

Add or subtract. Write your answer in scientific notation.

1. $2.4 \times 10^2 + 3.4 \times 10^4 + 1.5 \times 10^3$

   _____

2. $6.2 \times 10^4 - 3.4 \times 10^2 - 7.5 \times 10^3$

   _____

3. $8.3 \times 10^5 + 1.6 \times 10^7 + 6.7 \times 10^4$

   _____

4. $8.0 \times 10^3 - 0.8 \times 10^3 - 1.2 \times 10^2$

   _____

Multiply or divide. Write your answer in scientific notation.

5. $(5.2 \times 10^8)(4.8 \times 10^4) = $ _____

6. $\dfrac{9.8 \times 10^7}{1.4 \times 10^{-5}} = $ _____

7. $(8.5 \times 10^2)(3.4 \times 10^{-5}) = $ _____

8. $\dfrac{1.702 \times 10^5}{7.4 \times 10^8} = $ _____

Use the information below to complete Exercises 9–13.

A 60-watt light bulb uses 60 watt hours of electricity in 1 hour. Suppose everyone in the United States left one unneeded 60 watt light bulb on for one hour every day for a year.

9. Electricity is billed in kilowatt hours. So 60 watt hours is equal to sixty divided by one thousand. Express the electricity used by a 60-watt light bulb in one hour in kilowatt hours in scientific notation.

   _____

10. Express the number of days in a year in scientific notation.

   _____

11. There are about 315,000,000 people in the United States. Write that number in scientific notation.

   _____

12. Now find how many kilowatt hours of electricity would be wasted if every person in the United States left on one unneeded 60-watt light bulb one hour a day for a whole year. Express your answer in both scientific notation and standard notation.

   _____

13. The average household uses about 15,000 kilowatt hours per year. How many households could use that wasted electricity from item 12 and have light for a year? Express your answer in standard notation.

   _____

LESSON 2-4

Operations with Scientific Notation

Practice and Problem Solving: D

Add or subtract. Write your answer in scientific notation. The first one is done for you.

1. $2.4 \times 10^2 + 3.3 \times 10^4 + 7.2 \times 10^3$

   $240 + 33,000 + 7,200 = 40,440$
   $= 4.044 \times 10^4$

2. $1.2 \times 10^4 - 1.5 \times 10^3 - 2.2 \times 10^2$

   _____

   _____

3. $7.3 \times 10^5 + 1.6 \times 10^6 + 4.7 \times 10^5$

   _____

   _____

4. $8.2 \times 10^4 - 2.4 \times 10^4 - 1.5 \times 10^3$

   _____

   _____

Multiply or divide. Write your answer in scientific notation. The first one is done for you.

5. $(3.2 \times 10^3)(6.4 \times 10^9) = \underline{(3.2 \times 6.4) \times (10^3 \times 10^9)}$

   $= \underline{20.48 \times 10^{3+9}}$

   $= \underline{20.48 \times 10^{12}}$

   $= \underline{2.048 \times 10^{13}}$

6. $\dfrac{9.6 \times 10^5}{5 \times 10^4} =$

   _____

7. $(2.5 \times 10^4)(4.1 \times 10^4) = \underline{\hspace{2cm}}$

   _____

   _____

8. $\dfrac{6.4 \times 10^{10}}{3.2 \times 10^2} = \underline{\hspace{2cm}}$

   _____

   _____

Write each number using calculator notation. The first one is done for you.

9.	Scientific notation	7.1×10^5		4.4×10^{-3}	
10.	Calculator notation	**7.1E+5**	3.3E–3		6.9E+5

Answer the questions.

11. How do you write one million in scientific notation? _____

12. A day is 8.64×10^4 seconds long. Write and solve an expression to find how many days are in one million seconds. Give your answer in standard form.

_____

LESSON 2-4

Operations with Scientific Notation
Reteach

To add or subtract numbers written in scientific notation:

> Check that the exponents of powers of 10 are the same.
> If not, adjust the decimal numbers and the exponents.
> Add or subtract the decimal numbers.
> Write the sum or difference and the common power of 10 in
>   scientific notation format.
> Check whether the answer is in scientific notation.
> If it is not, adjust the decimal and the exponent.

$(a \times 10^n) + (b \times 10^n) = (a + b) \times 10^n$ $(1.2 \times 10^5) - (9.5 \times 10^4)$

$(a \times 10^n) - (b \times 10^n) = (a - b) \times 10^n$ $(1.2 \times 10^5) - (0.95 \times 10^5)$ ← Adjust to get same

                                                      $(1.2 - 0.95) \times 10^5$ exponent.

                                                           0.25×10^5 ← Not in scientific notation.

                                                           2.5×10^4 ← Answer

To multiply numbers written in scientific notation:

> Multiply the decimal numbers.
> Add the exponents in the powers of 10.
> Check whether the answer is in scientific notation.
> If it is not, adjust the decimal numbers and the exponent.

$(a \times 10^n) \times (b \times 10^m) = ab \times 10^{n+m}$ $(2.7 \times 10^8) \times (8.9 \times 10^4)$

                                                           $(2.7 \times 8.9) \times 10^{8+4}$

                                                           24.03×10^{12} ← Not in scientific notation.

                                                           2.403×10^{13} ← Answer

To divide numbers written in scientific notation:

> Divide the decimal numbers.
> Subtract the exponents in the powers of 10.
> Check whether the answer is in scientific notation.
> If it is not, adjust the decimal numbers and the exponent.

$(a \times 10^n) \div (b \times 10^m) = a \div b \times 10^{n-m}$ $(6.3 \times 10^7) \div (9.0 \times 10^3)$

                                                           $(6.3 \div 9.0) \times 10^{7-3}$

                                                           0.7×10^4 ← Not in scientific notation.

                                                           7.0×10^3 ← Answer

Compute. Write each answer in scientific notation.

1. $(2.21 \times 10^7) \div (3.4 \times 10^4)$ 2. $(5.8 \times 10^6) - (4.3 \times 10^6)$ 3. $(2.8 \times 10^3)(7.5 \times 10^4)$

_____   _____   _____

Operations with Scientific Notation
Reading Strategies: Follow a Flowchart

A flowchart gives you a plan. You can use a flowchart to compute with numbers given in scientific notation.

To multiply numbers in scientific notation:

| **1** Multiply the decimal numbers. | 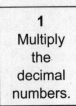 | **2** Add the exponents of 10. | 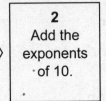 | **3** Write the product from Step 1 and the power from Step 2 in the format of scientific notation. | | **4** Check that the decimal is between 1 and 10. If not, adjust the decimal and the exponent so the answer is in scientific notation. |

To divide numbers in scientific notation:

| **1** Divide the decimal numbers. | | **2** Subtract the exponents of 10. | | **3** Write the quotient from Step 1 and the power from Step 2 in the format of scientific notation. | | **4** Check that the decimal is between 1 and 10. If not, adjust the decimal and the exponent so the answer is in scientific notation. |

To add or subtract numbers in scientific notation:

| **1** Check that the exponents on powers of 10 are the same. If not, adjust the decimal and the exponent. | | **2** As long as the exponents match, add or subtract the decimal numbers. | | **3** Write the sum or difference from Step 2 and the power from Step 1 in the format of scientific notation. | | **4** Check that the decimal is between 1 and 10. If not, adjust the decimal and the exponent so the answer is in scientific notation. |

Identify which flowchart to follow. Perform the indicated operation.

1. $4.2 \times 10^3 + 2.4 \times 10^4$

2. $(1.2 \times 10^4)(1.6 \times 10^6)$

3. $\dfrac{8.8 \times 10^7}{4.4 \times 10^4}$

_____   _____   _____

4. $(6.4 \times 10^3) \div (3.2 \times 10^4)$

5. $(3.2 \times 10^8) - (1.3 \times 10^7)$

6. $(7.0 \times 10^6)(4.7 \times 10^3)$

_____   _____   _____

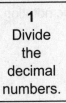
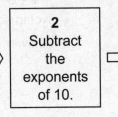

LESSON 2-4 Operations with Scientific Notation
Success for English Learners

When completing mathematical operations with integers, there are procedures that simplify the process.

Problem 1

You can add or subtract numbers in scientific notation.

$(5.9 \times 10^5) - (5.4 \times 10^4)$ ← Check to see if each power of 10 has the same exponent.

$(5.9 \times 10^5) - (0.54 \times 10^5)$ ← Adjust to get the same exponent.

$(5.9 - 0.54) \times 10^5$ ← Add or subtract the decimal parts. Use 10 to the common power.

5.36×10^5 ← Check that the answer is in scientific notation. ✓

Problem 2

You can multiply or divide numbers in scientific notation.

$(3.5 \times 10^8) \times (9.1 \times 10^4)$
$(3.5 \times 9.1) \times (10^8 \times 10^4)$ ← Regroup so decimals and powers of 10 are grouped.

$(3.5 \times 9.1) \times 10^{8+4}$ ← Multiply or divide the decimal parts. If multiplying, add exponents. If dividing, subtract exponents.

31.85×10^{12} ← Check that the answer is in scientific notation.

3.185×10^{13} ← Answer in scientific notation.

Complete.

1. When is scientific notation most useful?

_____

_____

Compute. Write each answer in scientific notation.

2. $(1.43 \times 10^5) \div (2.6 \times 10^2)$ 3. $(2.8 \times 10^6) - (1.3 \times 10^6)$ 4. $(5.8 \times 10^6)(2.5 \times 10^3)$

_____   _____   _____

_____   _____   _____

5. $(2.9 \times 10^5) + (8.4 \times 10^4)$ 6. $(1.8 \times 10^3)(3.4 \times 10^8)$ 7. $(3.024 \times 10^9) \div (5.4 \times 10^4)$

_____   _____   _____

_____   _____   _____

MODULE
2
Exponents and Scientific Notation
Challenge

Astronomical Distances

1. A light year is the distance light travels in a vacuum in one year. It is about 9.4605284×10^{15} meters. Write this in standard form.

_____

2. Change a light year to kilometers. Write it in both standard form and scientific notation. About how many trillions is this number?

_____

3. Distances to stars are often measured in parsecs rather than in light years. One parsec is about 3.26 light years. Use scientific notation to write the number of kilometers in one parsec to three significant digits.

_____

Subatomic Distances

4. Dimensions of subatomic particles are often described in nanometers. A nanometer is one-billionth of a meter. Write a nanometer in both standard form and scientific notation.

_____

5. Sometimes atomic scale dimensions are written in angstroms. An angstrom equals 0.1 nanometer. Use scientific notation to show the value of an angstrom in meters.

_____

6. A nanometer equals $\dfrac{1}{1,000}$ of a micron. Use scientific notation to show the value of a micron in meters.

_____

7. How many times larger than a nanometer is a parsec?

_____

Representing Proportional Relationships
Practice and Problem Solving: A/B

Use the table to complete Exercises 1–3.

Feet	1		3	4		6
Inches		24			60	

1. The table shows the relationship between lengths in feet and lengths in inches. Complete the table.

2. Write each pair as a ratio. $\dfrac{\text{inches}}{\text{feet}} \rightarrow \dfrac{}{1} = \dfrac{24}{} = \dfrac{}{3} = \dfrac{}{4} = \dfrac{60}{} = \dfrac{}{6}$

   Each ratio is equal to _____.

3. Let *x* represent feet. Let *y* represent inches.

   An equation that describes the relationship is _____.

Use the table to complete Exercises 4 and 5. Tell whether each relationship is proportional. If it is proportional, write an equation that describes the relationship. First define your variables.

Lemonade Recipe

Lemons	1	2	3	4	5	6
Sugar (c)	1.5	3	4.5	6	7.5	9
Water (c)	7	14	21	28	35	42

4. the ratio of lemons to cups of sugar

   _____

5. the ratio of cups of sugar to cups of water

   _____

Use the table to complete Exercise 6.

Distance Traveled Daily on a Family Road Trip

Hours	6	4.5	9	2	3.25	5.75
Distance (mi)	270	229.5	495	60	188.5	281.75

6. Is the relationship shown in the table below proportional? If so, what is the ratio of the hours driven to miles traveled?

   _____

LESSON 3-1 Representing Proportional Relationships
Practice and Problem Solving: C

Use the table for Exercises 1 and 2.

Length (ft)	2.85	5.7	7.6	9.88	11.4
Width (ft)	1.5	3	4	5.2	6

1. The table shows the length and width of various United States flags.

   a. Is the relationship proportional? _____

   b. If so, write the equation that describes the relationship.
   Let *x* represent the width of the flags. Let *y* represent the length of the flags.

   _____

2. Another flag in the same collection has a length of 12.6 feet.

   How wide would you expect the flag to be? _____

Use the table for Exercise 3.

Map Distance, *x* (in.)	$1\frac{1}{2}$	$3\frac{1}{2}$	4	5	$7\frac{1}{4}$
Actual Distance, *y* (mi)	75	175	200	250	$362\frac{1}{2}$

3. The table shows the distance between various cities on a map in inches, *x*, and the actual distance between the cities in miles, *y*.

   a. Is the relationship proportional? _____

   b. If so, write the equation that describes the relationship.

   _____

   c. The distance between Jacksonville and Daly City on the map is $9\frac{1}{8}$ inches.

   How far apart are the cities in miles?_____

   d. San Diego, CA, and San Francisco, CA, are about 550 miles apart.
   If you were putting these two cities on a map, how many inches apart would they be?

   _____

LESSON 3-1 Representing Proportional Relationships
Practice and Problem Solving: D

Use the table to answer Exercises 1–3:

Yards	1	2		4		6
Feet	3		9		15	

1. The table shows the relationship between lengths in feet and lengths in yards. Complete the table. The first column has been done for you.

2. Write each pair as a ratio. $\dfrac{feet}{yards} \rightarrow \dfrac{3}{1} = \dfrac{6}{\rule{1cm}{0.15mm}} = \dfrac{\rule{1cm}{0.15mm}}{3} = \dfrac{12}{\rule{1cm}{0.15mm}} = \dfrac{\rule{1cm}{0.15mm}}{\rule{1cm}{0.15mm}} = \dfrac{18}{6}$

   Each ratio is equal to _____.

3. Let x represent the number of yards. Let y represent the number of

   feet. The equation that describes the relationship is _____.

Write the equation that describes the relationship.

4. There are 50 stars on each United States flag. Two flags have 100 stars. Three flags have 150 stars.

   Let x be the number of flags. Let y be the number of stars.

   The equation that describes the relationship is _____.

Use the table to answer problems 5–7. Tell whether each relationship is proportional. The first one is done for you.

Lemonade Recipe

Lemons	1	2	3	4	5	6
Sugar (cups)	1.5	3	4.5	6	7.5	9
Water (cups)	7	14	21	28	35	42

5. the ratio of lemons to cups of sugar _____**yes**_____

6. the ratio of cups of sugar to cups of water _____

7. the ratio of lemons to cups of water _____

Representing Proportional Relationships
Reteach

A **proportional relationship** is a relationship between two sets of quantities in which the ratio of one quantity to the other quantity is constant. If you divide any number in one group by the corresponding number in the other group, you will always get the same quotient.

    Example: Martin mixes a cleaning spray that is 1 part vinegar to 5 parts water.

Proportional relationships can be shown in tables, graphs, or equations.

Table

The table below shows the number of cups of vinegar Martin needs to add to certain amounts of water to mix his cleaning spray.

Martin's Cleaning Spray

Water (c)	5	10	15	20	25
Vinegar (c)	1	2	3	4	5

Notice that if you divide the amount of water by the amount of vinegar, the quotient is always 5.

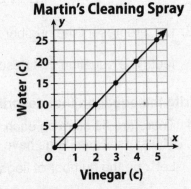

Martin's Cleaning Spray

Graph

On the graph, you can see that for every 1 unit you move to the right on the *x*-axis, you move up 5 units on the *y*-axis.

Equation

Let *y* represent the number of cups of water.
Let *x* represent the cups of vinegar.

    $y = 5x$

Use the table below for Exercises 1–3.

Distance Driven (mi)	100	200		400		600
Gas Used (gal)	5		15			30

1. There is a proportional relationship between the distance a car drives and the amount of gas used. Complete the table.

2. Find each ratio. $\dfrac{\text{miles}}{\text{gallons}} \rightarrow \dfrac{100}{5} = \dfrac{200}{\underline{\quad}} = \dfrac{\underline{\quad}}{15} = \dfrac{400}{\underline{\quad}} = \dfrac{\underline{\quad}}{\underline{\quad}} = \dfrac{600}{30}$

    Each ratio is equal to _____.

3. a. Let *x* represent gallons of gas used. Let *y* represent _____.

    b. The equation that describes the relationship is _____.

Representing Proportional Relationships

Reading Strategies: Identify Relationships

A **proportional relationship** is a relationship between two sets of numbers in which the ratio of one set to the other set is constant.

When you divide any member of the first set by the corresponding member of the second set, the quotient is the same.

The quotient is called the **constant of proportionality**.

Number of Quarters	5	15	30	50	100
Value	$1.25	$3.75	$7.50	$12.50	$25
Ratio	5 ÷ 1.25 = 4	15 ÷ 3.75 = 4	30 ÷ 7.5 = 4	50 ÷ 12.5 = 4	100 ÷ 25 = 4

The value of a quarter is $0.25.
To find the value of any quantity of quarters, you multiply the quantity by 0.25.

0.25 is the **constant of proportionality.**

Use the table above for Exercises 1 and 2.

1. Let x represent the number of quarters in a jar. Let y represent the value of the quarters. Write an equation that shows the relationship.

_____

2. What is the value of 350 quarters? _____

Use the table below for Exercises 3 and 4.

Planet	Mercury	Venus	Earth	Mars	Jupiter
Diameter (mi)	3,032	7,521	7,926	4,222	88,846
Distance from Sun (millions of mi)	36.0	67.2	93.0	141.6	483.6
Ratio					

3. Complete the table. Round the ratios to the nearest tenth.

4. Is there a proportional relationship between a planet's diameter and its distance from the sun? Explain.

_____

LESSON 3-1 Representing Proportional Relationships

Success for English Learners

Problem 1

Look at the map of Sand County.

> Look at the key at the bottom.

> 1 inch = 10 miles

The key sets up a ratio.

$$\frac{\text{real-world distance}}{\text{distance on map}} = \frac{10}{1} = 10$$

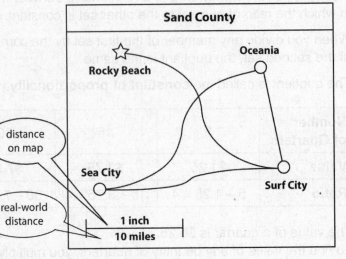

Sand County

Oceania

Rocky Beach

Sea City

Surf City

distance on map

real-world distance

1 inch
10 miles

The table shows distances between cities on the map.

	Rocky Beach to Surf City	Rocky Beach to Oceania	Oceania to Surf City
Real-World Distance (mi)	22	20	11
Distance on Map (in.)	$2\frac{1}{5}$	2	$1\frac{1}{10}$
Ratio	$22 \div 2\frac{1}{5} = 10$	$20 \div 2 = 10$	$11 \div 1\frac{1}{10} = 10$

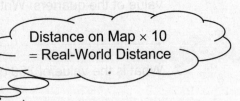

Distance on Map × 10
= Real-World Distance

Problem 2

Write an equation to show the **proportional relationship** in the table.

> Let y = Real-World Distance.

> Let x = Distance on Map.

The equation is $y = 10x$. ◄——— 10 is the **constant of proportionality.**

1. Two places on the map are $3\frac{1}{10}$ inches apart. What is the distance

   between them in the real world? _____

2. Is real-world distance greater or less than the distance on the map?
   Explain.

_____

_____

**LESSON
3-2**

Rate of Change and Slope
Practice and Problem Solving: A/B

Find the slope of each line.

1. slope = _____

2. slope = _____

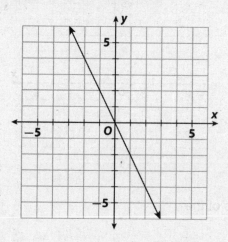

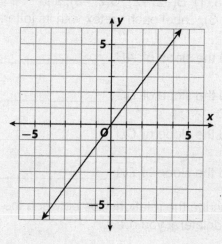

Solve.

3. Jasmine bought 7 yards of fabric. The total cost was $45.43. What was the average cost per yard of the fabric she bought?

_____

4. A train traveled 325 miles in 5 hours. What was the train's average rate of speed in miles per hour?

_____

5. The graph at the right shows the amount of water in a tank that is being filled. What is the average rate of change in gallons per minute?

_____

Water in a Tank

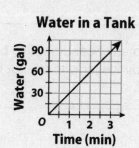

6. Suppose the size of the tank in question 5 is doubled. Will the average rate of change in gallons per minute change? Explain your answer.

_____

_____

7. A line passes through (1, 1), (−2, 4), and (6, n). Find the value of n.

_____

Name _____ Date _____ Class_____

Rate of Change and Slope

Practice and Problem Solving: C

Use the grid at the right for 1–7.

1. Draw a quadrilateral with vertices at
   A(–3, 1), B(–2, –2), C(2, –3), and
   D(0, 3). Label each vertex with its letter.

2. Find the slope of $\overline{AB}$. _____

3. Find the slope of $\overline{BC}$. _____

4. Find the slope of $\overline{CD}$. _____

5. Find the slope of $\overline{DA}$. _____

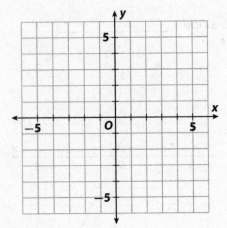

6. Describe the relationships between the opposite sides of the
   quadrilateral you drew.

   _____

   _____

7. What kind of quadrilateral did you draw? _____

**The table at the right shows how many peanuts one company uses
to make peanut butter.**

8. Suppose you graph the information in the table.
   Find the slope of a line drawn through the points.

   _____

9. How many peanuts would be needed to fill
   a 40-ounce jar with peanut butter?

   _____

**Number of Peanuts
Needed to Make Peanut Butter**

Peanuts, x	368	552	828
Amount Made (oz), y	8	12	18

Solve.

10. You graph a triangle on grid paper. The slopes of the sides are 0, –3,
    and undefined. What kind of triangle did you draw? Explain how you
    know.

    _____

    _____

LESSON 3-2

Rate of Change and Slope

Practice and Problem Solving: D

Tell whether the rates of change are constant or variable. The first one is done for you.

1. calories per serving _____constant_____

Servings	1	2	5	7
Calories	150	300	750	1,050

2. distance jumped _____

Jumps	2	4	7	10
Distance (ft)	12	24	35	55

Find the slope of each line. The first one is done for you.

3. slope = _____−3_____

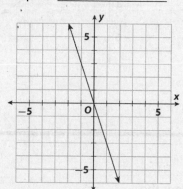

4. slope = _____

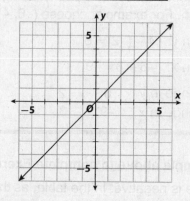

5. slope = _____

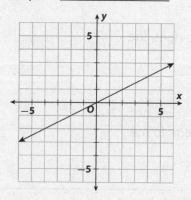

6. slope = _____

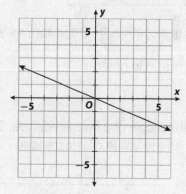

Solve. The first one is done for you.

7. In 3 hours, 654 gallons of water passed through a pipe. What was the average rate in gallons per hour at which the water passed through the pipe?

   218 gallons per hour

8. A car traveled 200 miles in 4 hours. What was the car's average rate of speed in miles per hour?

   _____

LESSON 3-2
Rate of Change and Slope
Reteach

Look at the relationships between the table, the graph, and the slope.

First value (x)	Second value (y)
–6	4
–3	2
0	0
3	–2

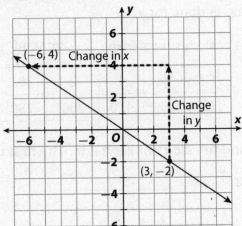

To find the slope, choose two points, using the
table or graph. For example, choose (–6, 4) and (3, –2).

Change in y: $4 - (-2) = 6$

Change in x: $-6 - 3 = -9$

$$\text{Slope} = \frac{\text{change in } y}{\text{change in } x} = \frac{6}{-9} = -\frac{2}{3}$$

Use the example above to complete Exercises 1 and 2.

1. The slope is negative. In the table, as the values of x decrease, the

   values of y _____.

2. The slope is negative. In the graph, as you move from left to right, the

   line of the graph is going _____ (up or down).

Solve.

3. Suppose the slope of a line is positive. Describe what happens to the
   value of x as the value of y increases.

   _____

   _____

4. Suppose the slope of a line is positive. Describe what happens to the
   graph of the line as you move from left to right.

   _____

   _____

5. Two points on a line are (3, 8) and (–3, 2). What is the slope of the line?

   _____

Name _____ Date _____ Class_____

Rate of Change and Slope

Reading Strategies: Read a Table

Data that show a relationship between two quantities can be displayed in a table. Each pair of numbers in the table can be written as an ordered pair. The ordered pairs can be plotted as points on a grid.

Homemade Orange Juice

Oranges	Juice (oz)
4	12
6	18
9	27

Ordered Pair (x, y)	Distance from Origin
(4, 12)	Right 4, Up 12
(6, 18)	Right 6, Up 18
(9, 27)	Right 9, Up 27

Homemade Orange Juice

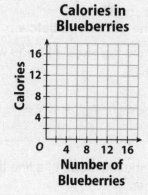

A line drawn through the points represents the relationship between the number of oranges and the amount of juice made.

The slope of the line represents the rate of change.

To identify the slope of the line, choose 2 points on it.

Examples:

Slope = $\dfrac{\text{change in } y}{\text{change in } x}$

A. Use (6, 18) and (4, 12).

$\dfrac{18 - 12}{6 - 4}$

$\dfrac{6}{2} = \dfrac{3}{1}$ or 3

B. Use (4, 12) and (9, 27).

$\dfrac{12 - 27}{4 - 9}$

$\dfrac{-15}{-5} = \dfrac{3}{1}$ or 3

Use the information in the table for 1–4.

Calories in Blueberries

Number of Blueberries	5	10	15
Number of Calories	4	8	12

1. List the ordered pairs.

   _____

2. Plot the ordered pairs on the grid at right, and draw a line connecting them.

3. Find the slope of the line you graphed. Show your work.

   _____

4. When finding the slope, does it matter which two points you use? Explain why or why not.

   _____

   _____

Calories in Blueberries

LESSON 3-2
Rate of Change and Slope
Success for English Learners

Problem 1

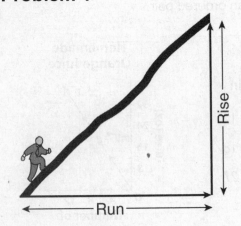

$$\text{Slope} = \frac{\text{rise}}{\text{run}} = \frac{\text{Change in } y}{\text{Change in } x}$$

Problem 2

Main School Theater	
Tickets Sold	Amount Collected
50	$225
100	$450
150	$675
200	$900

$$\text{Slope} = \frac{\text{rise}}{\text{run}} = \frac{y_2 - y_1}{x_2 - x_1}$$

Choose any two points.

For (50, 225) and (100, 450):

$$\frac{225 - 450}{50 - 100} = \frac{-225}{-50} = 4.5$$

For (200, 900) and (100, 450):

$$\frac{900 - 450}{200 - 100} = \frac{450}{100} = 4.5$$

The slope is the same!

Answer the questions below.

1. Describe the slope of a line when both the rise and the run are positive numbers.

_____

_____

2. Describe the slope of a line if either the rise or the run is a negative number.

_____

_____

3. In Exercise 2, explain why it does not matter which 2 points you use to find the slope of a line.

_____

_____

LESSON 3-3 Interpreting the Unit Rate as Slope

Practice and Problem Solving: A/B

Find the slope. Name the unit rate.

1. **Benjamin Hiking**

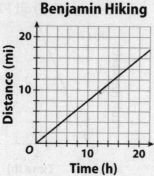

2. **Marcy Hiking**

Time (h)	5	10	15	20
Distance (mi)	6	12	18	24

Slope = _____

Unit rate: _____

Slope = _____

Unit rate: _____

3. The equation $y = 3.5x$ represents the rate, in miles per hour, at which Laura walks.

Piyush Walking

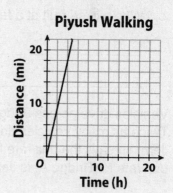

The graph at right represents the rate at which Piyush walks. Determine who walks faster. Explain.

_____

_____

4. Rain fell at a steady rate of 2 inches every 3 hours.

a. Complete the table to describe the relationship.

Rainfall

Time (h)	3			12
Rainfall (in.)		4	6	

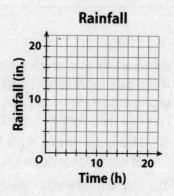

b. Graph the data in the table on the coordinate grid at right. Draw the line.

c. Find the slope.

_____

d. Identify the unit rate.

_____

Name _____ Date _____ Class_____

Interpreting the Unit Rate as Slope

Practice and Problem Solving: C

Solve.

1. Shawn picked 4 bushels of apples and 5 bushels of pears in 2 hours. Carla picked 4 bushels of apples and 6 bushels of pears in 3 hours.

   a. The graph at right shows the rate at which Shawn picked fruit. Find the slope and name the unit rate.

   _____

   b. The table below shows the rate at which Carla picked fruit. Complete the table.

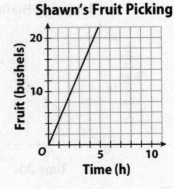

Shawn's Fruit Picking

Carla's Fruit Picking

Time (h)		6	9	
Fruit (bushels)	10			40

   c. Who picked fruit at a faster pace? Explain.

   _____

   _____

2. Vehicles drive across Bridge A at a steady rate of 20 cars per hour. Twice as many vehicles drive across Bridge B in twice as much time. Jermain says the unit rate for Bridge B would be twice as great as the unit rate for Bridge A. Is Jermain correct? Explain.

   _____

   _____

3. Alicia works at a pretzel factory. In the graph at right, the x-axis represents time in minutes and the y-axis represents the number of pretzels twisted. Line A represents the rate at which Alicia can twist pretzels.

   a. Using the graph, draw line B representing the rate of someone who twists pretzels more slowly than Alicia.

   b. Explain how you determined where to draw line B.

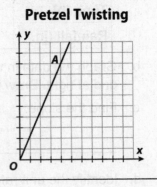

Pretzel Twisting

   _____

   _____

   _____

   _____

LESSON 3-3

Interpreting the Unit Rate as Slope

Practice and Problem Solving: D

Find the slope. Name the unit rate. The first one is done for you.

1. **Miguel Hiking**

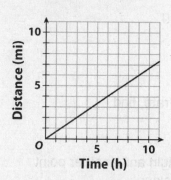

2. **Brianna Hiking**

Time (h)	2	4	6	8
Distance (mi)	1	2	3	4

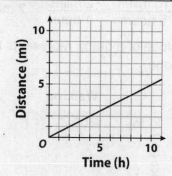

Slope = $\dfrac{2}{3}$

Unit rate: $\dfrac{2}{3}$ **mile/hour**

Slope = _____

Unit rate: _____

3. The graph at right represents the rate at which Poonam walks.

   Poonam Walking

   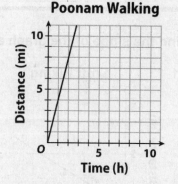

   a. What is the slope of the line?

   _____

   b. What is the speed (unit rate) at which Poonam walks?

   _____

   The equation $y = 3x$ represents the rate, in miles per hour, at which Latrice walks.

   c. The graph of the equation is a line. What is the slope of the line?

   _____

   d. What is the unit rate at which Latrice walks?

   _____

   e. Who walks faster, Poonam or Latrice? Explain

   _____

   _____

LESSON
3-3

Interpreting the Unit Rate as Slope
Reteach

A rate is a comparison of two quantities that have different units.

A **unit rate** is a rate in which the second quantity is 1 unit.

For example, walking 10 miles every *5 hours* is a rate. Walking
2 miles every *1 hour* is the equivalent unit rate.

$$\frac{10 \text{ miles}}{5 \text{ hours}} = \frac{2 \text{ miles}}{1 \text{ hour}} = 2 \text{ mi/h}$$

The slope of a graph represents the unit rate. To find the unit rate, find
the slope.

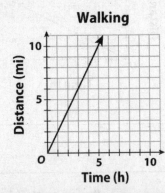

Walking

Step 1: Use the origin and another point
to find the slope.

$$\text{slope} = \frac{\text{rise}}{\text{run}} = \frac{10 - 0}{5 - 0} = \frac{10}{5} = 2$$

Step 2: Write the slope as the unit rate.

slope = unit rate = 2 mi/h

Find the slope of the graph and the unit rate.

1.   **Scott Hiking**

2.   **Rebecca Hiking**

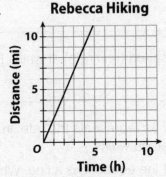

slope = $\frac{\text{rise}}{\text{run}}$ = _____

unit rate = _____ mi/h

slope = $\frac{\text{rise}}{\text{run}}$ = _____

unit rate = _____ mi/h

LESSON 3-3

Interpreting the Unit Rate as Slope
Reading Strategies: Analyze Information

Information about rates can be presented in different ways. For example, a graph and a table can present the same type of information in different formats.

Use the graph to complete Exercises 1–3.

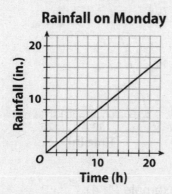

Rainfall on Monday

1. How many inches of rain fell in 10 hours? _____

2. How many inches of rain fell in 1 hour? _____

3. What is the slope of the graph and the unit rate?

   _____

Use the table to complete Exercises 4–7.

Rainfall on Tuesday

Time (h)	1	2	3	4
Rainfall (in.)	3	6	9	12

4. How many inches of rain fell in 4 hours? _____

5. How many inches of rain fell in 1 hour? _____

6. What is the unit rate? _____

7. What would be the slope of the graph of the data in the table? Explain how you know.

   _____

**LESSON
3-3**

Interpreting the Unit Rate as Slope

Success for English Learners

Problem 1

Who walks faster, Carlos or Lucy?

Carlos Walking

Time (h)	1	2	3	4
Distance (mi)	4	8	12	16

Lucy Walking

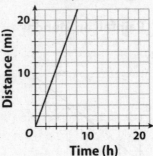

STEP 1: Find each slope. The slope is the unit rate.

For Carlos: Choose any pair from the table, for example (1, 4).

$$\text{slope} = \frac{4}{1} = 4$$

So, Carlos's unit rate is 4 mi/h.

For Lucy: Choose any point on the line, for example (3, 8).

$$\text{slope} = \frac{8}{3}$$

So, Lucy's unit rate is $\frac{8}{3}$ mi/h, or $2\frac{2}{3}$ mi/h.

STEP 2: Compare the two unit rates.

$4 > 2\frac{2}{3}$ Carlos's unit rate is **greater than** Lucy's unit rate.

So, Carlos walks faster than Lucy.

Answer.

1. How many miles can Carlos walk in 1 hour?

_____

2. How many miles can Lucy walk in 1 hour?
   Round your answer to the nearest tenth.

_____

MODULE 3 — Proportional Relationships
Challenge

Are Giants Possible?

An equation of the general form $y = kx^n$ represents a proportional relationship called **nth power variation**. Two specific examples of *nth* power variation are:

    quadratic variation: $y = kx^2$ **cubic variation:** $y = kx^3$

These variation equations can be used to show why giants with normal human proportions, although often found in folklore, are anatomically impossible.

Solve to explore the possibility of giants. Show your work. Round to the nearest 0.01.

1. The weight of a person of average build varies directly with the cube of that person's height. Use a person 6 feet tall who weighs 200 pounds to find the equation of variation.

    _____

2. The weight that a person's legs will support is proportional to the square of that person's height. Find this equation of variation using the 6-foot, 200-pound person.

    _____

3. Use the equation you found in Exercise 1. How much would an imaginary giant 20 feet tall weigh?

    _____

4. Use the equation you found in Exercise 2. How much weight could a 20-foot tall giant's legs support?

    _____

5. Explain why a 20-foot tall giant with normal human proportions isn't possible.

    _____

    _____

6. Use a graphing calculator. Graph the two variation equations and show them on the coordinate plane below. Then graph the lines $x = 6$ and $x = 20$ on the same coordinate plane. Label all graphs with their equations and what the equations represent.

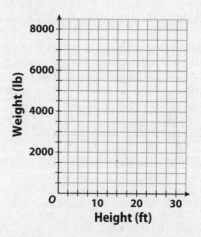

7. Explain how the graph shows that a 20-foot giant is not possible.

    _____

    _____

Name _____ Date _____ Class _____

Representing Linear Nonproportional Relationships

Practice and Problem Solving: A/B

Make a table of values for each equation.

1. $y = 4x + 3$

x	−2	−1	0	1	2
y					

2. $y = \frac{1}{4}x - 2$

x	−8	−4	0	4	8
y					

3. $y = -0.5x + 1$

x	−4	−2	0	2	4
y					

4. $y = 3x + 5$

x	−2	−1	0	1	2
y					

Make a table of values and graph the solutions of each equation.

5. $y = 2x + 1$

x	−2	−1	0	1	2
y					

6. $y = -\frac{1}{2}x - 3$

x	−4	−2	0	2	4
y					

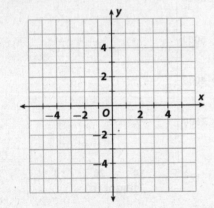

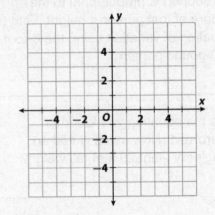

State whether the graph of each linear relationship is a solid line or a set of unconnected points. Explain your reasoning.

7. The relationship between the height of a tree and the time since the tree was planted.

_____

_____

8. The relationship between the number of $12 DVDs you buy and the total cost.

_____

LESSON 4-1 Representing Linear Nonproportional Relationships

Practice and Problem Solving: C

Make a table of values for each equation.

1. $y = \frac{1}{3}x + 1$

2. $y = 0.2x - 4$

x	−6	−3	0	3	6
y					

x					
y					

Make a table of values and graph the solutions of the equation.

3. $y = \frac{1}{4}x + 2$

x				
y				

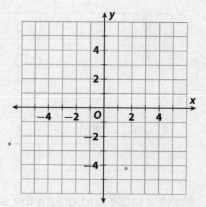

4. A medical delivery service charges $10 for a house call plus $0.50 per mile. The situation is represented by the equation $y = 0.5x + 10$, where x represents the number of miles the delivery is from the office and y represents the cost of the delivery.

a. Make a table of values for this situation.

x (Number of Miles)					
y (Cost of Delivery)					

b. Draw a graph to represent the situation.

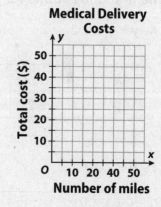

Medical Delivery Costs

c. Explain why this relationship is not proportional.

_____

_____

d. Do all points on the graph represent valid charges? Explain.

_____

_____

LESSON 4-1

Representing Linear Nonproportional Relationships

Practice and Problem Solving: D

Make a table of values for each equation. The first one is done for you.

1. $y = 3x + 2$

x	−2	−1	0	1	2
y	−4	−1	2	5	8

2. $y = -x - 1$

x	−2	−1	0	1	2
y					

3. $y = 5x + 3$

x	−2	−1	0	1	2
y					

Make a table and graph the solutions of each equation. The first one is done for you.

4. $y = \frac{1}{2}x + 3$

x	−4	−2	0	2	4
y	1	2	3	4	5

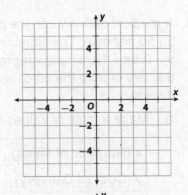

5. $y = x - 2$

x	−2	−1	0	1	2
y					

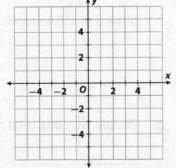

6. $y = -2x + 1$

x	−2	−1	0	1	2
y					

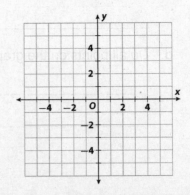

LESSON 4-1 Representing Linear Nonproportional Relationships
Reteach

A relationship will be proportional if the ratios in a table of values of the relationship are constant. The graph of a proportional relationship will be a straight line through the origin. If either of these is not true, the relationship is nonproportional.

To graph the solutions of an equation, make a table of values. Choose values that will give integer solutions.

A. Graph the solutions of $y = x + 2$.

x	−2	−1	0	1	2
y	0	1	2	3	4

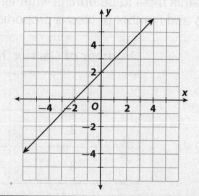

B. Tell whether the relationship is proportional. Explain.

The graph is a straight line, but it does **not** go through the origin, so the relationship is not proportional.

Make a table and graph the solutions of each equation.

1. $y = 3x + 1$

x	−2	−1	0	1	2
y					

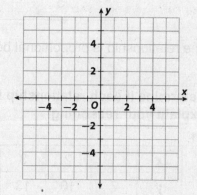

2. $y = -x - 2$

x	−2	−1	0	1	2
y					

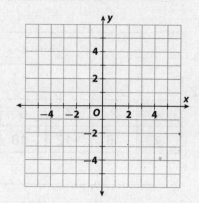

LESSON 4-1

Representing Linear Nonproportional Relationships

Reading Strategies: Identify Relationships

You can tell if a relationship is proportional or nonproportional when you analyze data in a table.

First, you need to understand the terms *proportional* and *nonproportional*.

- A **proportional** relationship has a constant ratio of *y*-values to *x*-values.

- A **nonproportional** relationship does not have a constant ratio of *y*-values to *x*-values.

Use this table to determine whether the relationship between number of cars and number of tires is proportional:

Number of Cars, x	Number of Tires, y	$\dfrac{y}{x}$
1	4	$\dfrac{4}{1} = 4$
2	8	$\dfrac{8}{2} = 4$
3	12	$\dfrac{12}{3} = 4$
4	16	$\dfrac{16}{4} = 4$
5	20	$\dfrac{20}{5} = 4$

The relationship is proportional because each $\dfrac{y}{x}$ ratio has the same value, 4.

Determine if each relationship is proportional or nonproportional. Explain your reasoning.

1.

x	1	2	3	4
y	7	10	13	16

_____

_____

2.

x	2	4	6	8
y	−6	−12	−18	−24

_____

_____

LESSON 4-1
Representing Linear Nonproportional Relationships
Success for English Learners

Problem 1

When given a table, calculate $\frac{y}{x}$ values to see if the relationship is proportional. If the ratio is constant, the relationship is proportional.

x	3	4	5	6	7
y	9	12	15	18	21

> In this table, every ratio $\frac{y}{x} = 3$, so the relationship is proportional.

x	3	4	5	6	7
y	9	10	11	12	13

> In this table, every ratio $\frac{y}{x}$ is **not** the same value, so the relationship is not proportional, or **nonproportional**.

Problem 2

When given a graph, if the graph is a line through the origin, the relationship is proportional. If the graph does not pass through the origin, the relationship is not proportional.

> This graph passes through the origin, so the relationship is proportional.

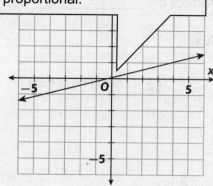

> This graph does not pass through the origin, so the relationship is not proportional.

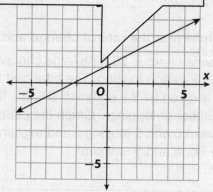

1. How can you tell from a table of values if a relationship is proportional?

   _____

   _____

2. How can you tell from a graph if a relationship is proportional?

   _____

   _____

LESSON 4-2

Determining Slope and y-Intercept

Practice and Problem Solving: A/B

Find the slope and y-intercept of the line in each graph.

1.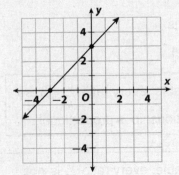

2.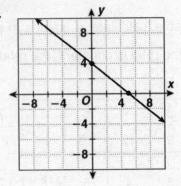

slope m = _____

slope m = _____

y-intercept b = _____

y-intercept b = _____

Find the slope and y-intercept of the line represented by each table.

3.

x	0	3	6	9	12
y		10	19	28	37

4.

x	0	2	4	6	8
y		2	3	4	5

slope m = _____

slope m = _____

y-intercept b = _____

y-intercept b = _____

Find and interpret the rate of change and the initial value.

5. A pizzeria charges $8 for a large cheese pizza, plus $2 for each topping. The total cost for a large pizza is given by the equation $C = 2t + 8$, where t is the number of toppings. Graph the equation for t between 0 and 5 toppings, and explain the meaning of the slope and y-intercept.

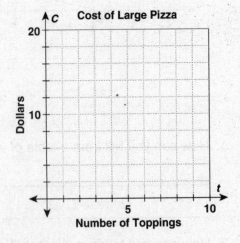

_____

_____

_____

LESSON 4-2

Determining Slope and *y*-Intercept
Practice and Problem Solving: C

1. The total daily cost for a rental truck based on mileage is shown.

   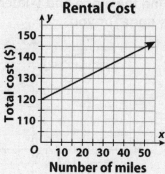

   Rental Cost

   a. Find the cost to rent a truck for the day and the rate to use the truck for each mile.

   _____

   b. What will Amanda pay if she rents a truck and drives 45 miles and splits the total cost with two friends? Explain.

   _____

2. Some amusement park costs are shown in the table. The relationship is linear. Find and interpret the rate of change and the initial value for this situation.

Number of Rides	1	2	3	4	5
Cost ($)	14.50	17.00	19.50	22.00	24.50

_____

3. The amount a tutor is compensated for one-hour individual or group tutoring sessions is shown in the table. The relationship between compensation and number of sessions is linear.

Sessions	1	2	3	4	5
Group ($)	39.50	69.00	98.50	128.00	157.50
Individual ($)	29.50	49.00	68.50	88.00	107.50

   a. Find the rate of change and the initial value for the group sessions.

   _____

   b. Find the rate of change and the initial value for individual sessions.

   _____

   c. Compare and contrast the rates of change and initial value.

   _____

4. Miguel works for a landscaping company. He earns a fixed weekly salary of $150 plus a fee of $30 for each lawn he mows. At what point does Miguel begin to earn more from fees than his fixed salary? Explain.

_____

_____

**LESSON
4-2**

Determining Slope and y-Intercept
Practice and Problem Solving: D

**Find the slope and y-intercept of the line in each graph. The first one
is done for you.**

1.
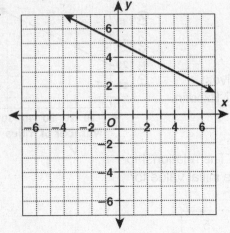

slope $m =$ _____$-\dfrac{1}{2}$_____

y-intercept $b =$ _____**5**_____

2.
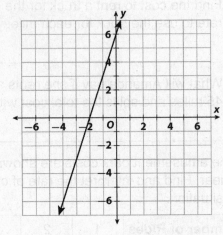

slope $m =$ _____

y-intercept $b =$ _____

3.
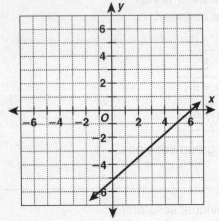

slope $m =$ _____

y-intercept $b =$ _____

4.
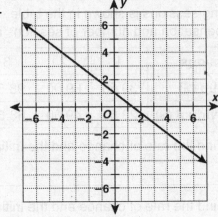

slope $m =$ _____

y-intercept $b =$ _____

Find the slope and y-intercept of the line represented by each table.

5.

x	0	5	10	15	20
y	3	13	23	33	43

slope $m =$ _____

y-intercept $b =$ _____

6.

x	0	2	4	6	8
y	5	6	7	8	9

slope $m =$ _____

y-intercept $b =$ _____

LESSON 4-2

Determining Slope and y-Intercept
Reteach

The **slope** of a line is a measure of its tilt, or slant.

The slope of a straight line is a constant ratio, the "rise over run," or the **vertical change** over the **horizontal change.**

You can find the slope of a line by comparing any two of its points.

The vertical change is the difference between the two y-values, and the horizontal change is the difference between the two x-values.

The **y-intercept** is the point where the line crosses the y-axis.

A. Find the slope of the line shown.

    point A: (3, 2)   point B: (4, 4)

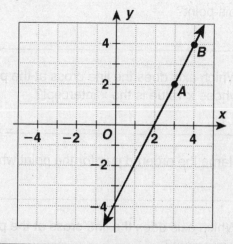

$$\text{slope} = \frac{4-2}{4-3}$$

$$= \frac{2}{1}, \text{ or } 2$$

So, the slope of the line is 2.

B. Find the y-intercept of the line shown.
The line crosses the y-axis at (0, −4).
So, the y-intercept is −4.

Find the slope and y-intercept of the line in each graph.

1.

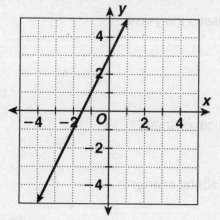

slope m = _____

y-intercept b = _____

2.

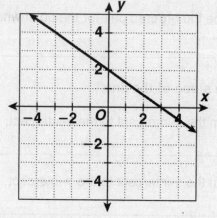

slope m = _____

y-intercept b = _____

Name _____ Date _____ Class _____

Determining Slope and *y*-Intercept

Reading Strategies: Use a Visual Model

Refer to the coordinate plane at the right. Find the point where the line crosses the *x*-axis. The *x*-value of this point is called the **x-intercept**.

1. What is the *y*-value of the ordered pair for this point?

   _____

Find the point where the line crosses the *y*-axis. The *y*-value of this point is called the **y-intercept**.

2. What is the *x*-value of the ordered pair for this point?

   _____

3. Which axis does the line cross at the point whose *x*-value is the *x*-intercept?

   _____

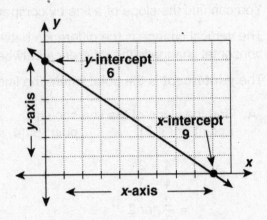

4. Name the ordered pair for the point where the line crosses the *x*-axis.

   _____

5. Which axis does the line cross at the point whose *y*-value is the *y*-intercept?

   _____

6. Name the ordered pair for the point where the line crosses the *y*-axis.

   _____

Find the slope of the line.

7. From the *x*-intercept to the *y*-intercept, what is the vertical change?

   _____

8. From the *x*-intercept to the *y*-intercept, what is the horizontal change?

   _____

9. The slope is the ratio of the vertical change to the horizontal change. What is the slope of the line?

   _____

LESSON 4-2
Determining Slope and *y*-Intercept
Success for English Learners

Problem 1

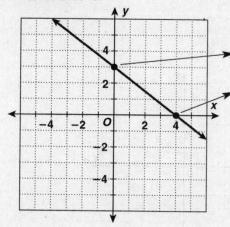

$3x + 4y = 12$

The *y*-intercept is 3.

The *x*-intercept is 4.

LOOK!

Problem 2

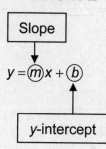

Slope

$y = \textcircled{m}x + \textcircled{b}$

y-intercept

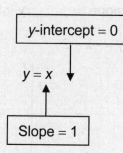

y-intercept = 0

$y = x$

Slope = 1

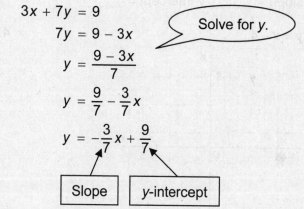

$3x + 7y = 9$

$7y = 9 - 3x$

$y = \dfrac{9 - 3x}{7}$

$y = \dfrac{9}{7} - \dfrac{3}{7}x$

$y = -\dfrac{3}{7}x + \dfrac{9}{7}$

Slope   *y*-intercept

Solve for *y*.

1. What do the *x*-intercept and the *y*-intercept have in common?
   How are they different?

   _____

   _____

2. What is the slope of the line in Problem 1?

   _____

   _____

3. Describe the graph of the line in Problem 2.

   _____

   _____

LESSON 4-3

Graphing Linear Nonproportional Relationships Using Slope and y-Intercept

Practice and Problem Solving: A/B

Graph each equation using the slope and the y-intercept.

1. $y = 2x - 1$

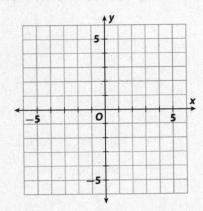

slope = _____ y-intercept = _____

2. $y = \frac{1}{2}x + 3$

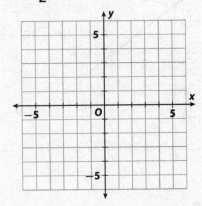

slope = _____ y-intercept = _____

3. $y = x - 4$

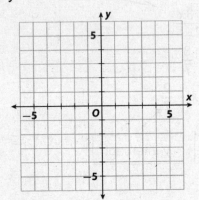

slope = _____ y-intercept = _____

4. $y = -x - 2$

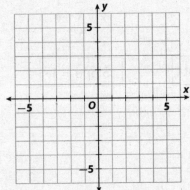

slope = _____ y-intercept = _____

5. The equation $y = 15x + 10$ gives your score on a math quiz, where x is the number of questions you answered correctly.

   a. Graph the equation.

   b. Interpret the slope and y-intercept of the line.

   _____

   _____

   c. What is your score if you answered 5 questions correctly?

   _____

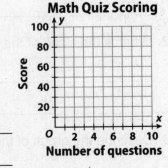

Math Quiz Scoring

LESSON 4-3

Graphing Linear Nonproportional Relationships Using Slope and *y*-Intercept

Practice and Problem Solving: C

Graph each equation using the slope and the *y*-intercept. Then interpret the slope and *y*-intercept of each line.

1. The equation $y = -0.04x + 12$ gives the number of gallons of gas in your car, where x is the number of miles driven.

   a. Graph the equation.

   b. Interpret the slope and *y*-intercept of the line.

   _____

   _____

   c. How many gallons of gas are left after driving 200 miles?

   _____

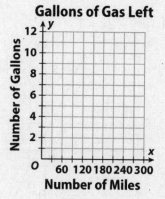

Gallons of Gas Left

2. The equation $y = 100x + 250$ gives the amount in your savings account, where x is the amount you deposit each month.

   a. Graph the equation.

   b. Interpret the slope and *y*-intercept of the line.

   _____

   _____

   c. What is the amount in your account after 7 months?

   _____

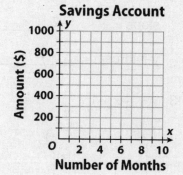

Savings Account

3. The equation $y = 0.1x + 50$ gives the monthly cost of a cell phone plan, where x is the number of text messages you sent and received.

   a. Graph the equation.

   b. Interpret the slope and *y*-intercept of the line.

   _____

   _____

   c. What is the cost of your cell phone plan if you sent and received 315 text messages?

   _____

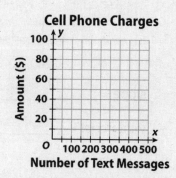

Cell Phone Charges

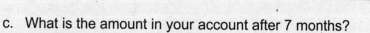

LESSON 4-3

Graphing Linear Nonproportional Relationships Using Slope and *y*-Intercept

Practice and Problem Solving: D

**Graph each equation using the slope and the *y*-intercept.
The first one is done for you.**

1. $y = -2x + 1$

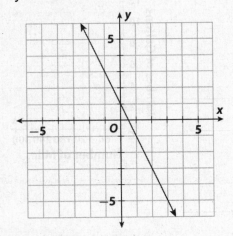

slope = _____-2_____

y-intercept = _____1_____

2. $y = 3x - 2$

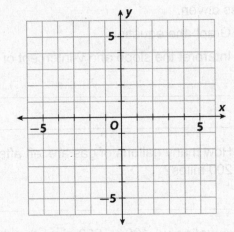

slope = _____

y-intercept = _____

3. $y = \frac{1}{3}x + 1$

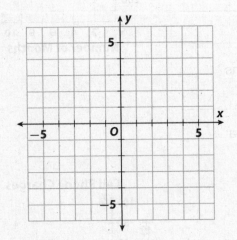

slope = _____

y-intercept = _____

4. $y = -x + 3$

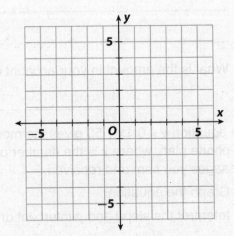

slope = _____

y-intercept = _____

LESSON 4-3

Graphing Linear Nonproportional Relationships Using Slope and *y*-Intercept

Reteach

You can graph a linear function by graphing the *y*-intercept of the line and then using the slope to find other points on the line.

The graph shows $y = x + 2$.

To graph the line, first graph the *y*-intercept which is located at (0, 2).

Because the slope is 1 or $\frac{1}{1}$, from the *y*-intercept,

rise 1 and run 1 to graph the next point.

Connect the points with a straight line.

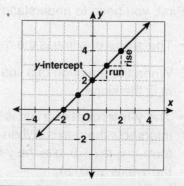

Graph each equation using the slope and the *y*-intercept.

1. $y = 4x - 1$

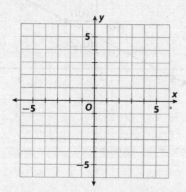

slope = _____ *y*-intercept = _____

2. $y = -\frac{1}{2}x + 2$

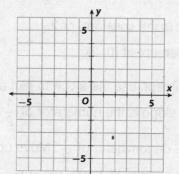

slope = _____ *y*-intercept = _____

3. $y = -x + 1$

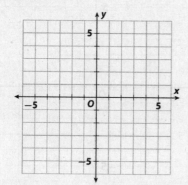

slope = _____ *y*-intercept = _____

4. $y = 2x - 3$

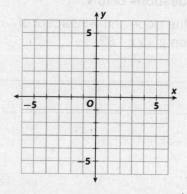

slope = _____ *y*-intercept = _____

LESSON 4-3

Graphing Linear Nonproportional Relationships Using Slope and y-Intercept

Reading Strategies: Build Vocabulary

You can graph a line of an equation in slope-intercept form,

$y = mx + b$.

First, you need to understand the terms *slope* and *y-intercept*.

- The **slope** of a line is the ratio of change in *y* to change in *x*, or $\dfrac{\text{rise}}{\text{run}}$.

  When the equation of a line is in slope-intercept form, $y = mx + b$, *m* is the slope.

- The **y-intercept** of a line is the *y*-coordinate of the point where the graph intersects the *y*-axis. When the equation of a line is in slope-intercept form, $y = mx + b$, *b* is the *y*-intercept. The point where the line intersects the *y*-axis is (0, *b*).

Example: Graph $y = \dfrac{1}{2}x + 2$:

The slope is the value before *x*, or $\dfrac{1}{2}$.

The *y*-intercept is the constant, or 2.

Graph the *y*-intercept at (0, 2).

From the *y*-intercept, use the slope to plot another point.

The rise of the slope is the numerator of $\dfrac{1}{2}$. The run of

the slope is the denominator of $\dfrac{1}{2}$. Move up 1 unit and

to the right 2 units from (0, 2). Connect the points with a line.

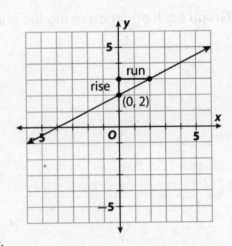

You try it. Show your work.

Answer the questions below.

1. What are the slope and *y*-intercept of the equation $y = 2x - 8$?

   _____

   _____

2. Graph $y = -3x + 4$.

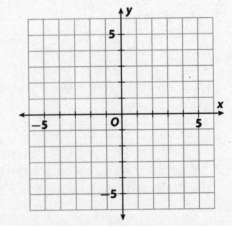

LESSON 4-3

Graphing Linear Nonproportional Relationships Using Slope and *y*-Intercept

Success for English Learners

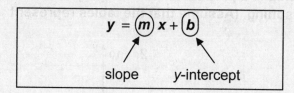

Problem 1

Graph $y = x - 3$

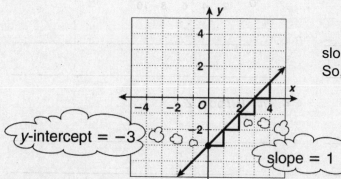

The function is:

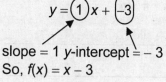

slope = 1 *y*-intercept = −3

So, $f(x) = x - 3$

Problem 2

The plane starts at an altitude of 700 feet.

The rate of change is −15 feet per second.

After 3 seconds, it is at 655 feet.

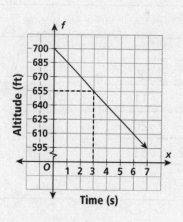

1. How do you graph a line if you know the *y*-intercept and the slope of the line?

   _____

2. What does the slope of a graph tell you about the situation represented by the graph? What does the *y*-intercept tell you?

   _____

LESSON 4-4

Proportional and Nonproportional Situations

Practice and Problem Solving: A/B

Determine if each relationship is a proportional or nonproportional situation. Explain your reasoning. (Assume that the tables represent linear relationships.)

1.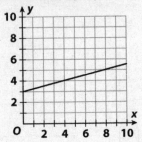

_____
_____

2.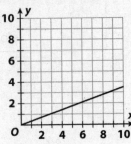

_____
_____

3. $t = 15d$

_____
_____

4. $m = 0.75d - 2$

_____
_____

5. $y = \sqrt{x}$

_____
_____

6. $r = b^2 + 1$

_____
_____

7.

x	y
2	11
5	26
12	61

_____
_____

8.

x	y
4	36
10	90
13	117

_____
_____

Name _____ Date _____ Class_____

Proportional and Nonproportional Situations

Practice and Problem Solving: C

Answer the questions below.

1. The values in the table represent the numbers of dogs and cats at animal shelters. The relationship is linear. Describe the relationship in other ways.

Number of Dogs	Number of Cats
40	50
60	48
24	30

_____

_____

_____

2. The graph shows the amount of time it takes Brittany to jog different numbers of miles.

   a. Is the relationship proportional or nonproportional? Explain.

   _____

   _____

   _____

   b. Identify and interpret the slope and *y*-intercept.

   _____

   _____

3. The variables *F*, *I*, and *C* represent feet, inches, and centimeters respectively.

   Equation A
   $I = 12F$

   Equation B
   $I = 0.39C$

Table C	
Centimeters	**Inches**
5	1.95
8	3.12
22	8.58

   a. Is the relationship between centimeters and inches proportional? Justify your answer in two different ways.

   _____

   _____

   b. Is the relationship between inches and feet proportional? Why or why not?

   _____

   _____

LESSON
4-4

Proportional and Nonproportional Situations

Practice and Problem Solving: D

Determine if each relationship is a proportional or nonproportional situation. Explain your reasoning. (Assume that the tables represent linear relationships.) The first one is done for you.

1. $y = 6x + 3$

   nonproportional; when the

   equation is written in the form

   $y = mx + b$, the value of b is not 0.

2. $c = 5t$

   _____

   _____

   _____

3.

x	y
5	40
8	64
11	88

_____

_____

4.

x	y
6	17
10	25
12	29

_____

_____

5.

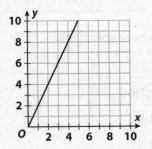

_____

_____

6.

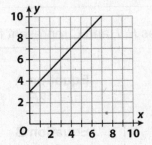

_____

_____

LESSON 4-4

Proportional and Nonproportional Situations
Reteach

To decide whether a relationship is proportional or nonproportional, consider how the relationship is presented.

If the relationship is a **graph**: Ask: Is the graph a straight line? Does the straight line go through the origin?
The graph at the right shows a proportional relationship.

If the relationship is a **table**:
Ask: For every number pair, is the quotient of y and x constant? Will $(0, 0)$ fit the pattern?
The table at the right shows a proportional relationship. The quotient for every number pair is 5. Since each y-value is 5 times each x-value, $(0, 0)$ will fit the pattern.

x	y
4	20
6	30
7	35

If the relationship is an **equation**:
Ask: Is the equation linear? When the equation is written in the form $y = mx + b$ is the value of b equal to 0?
The equation at the right shows a proportional relationship.

$$y = 0.8x$$

Determine if each relationship is a proportional or nonproportional situation. Explain your reasoning.

1.

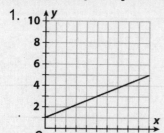

2.

x	y
3	36
5	60
8	96

_____

_____

_____

_____

3. $y = x^3$

4. $q = 4b$

_____

_____

_____

_____

LESSON
4-4

Proportional and Nonproportional Situations

Reading Strategies: Use a Graphic Organizer

You can tell if a relationship is proportional or nonproportional when you analyze graphs, equations, and tables.

Use this graphic organizer to determine if graphs, equations, or tables have a proportional or nonproportional relationship:

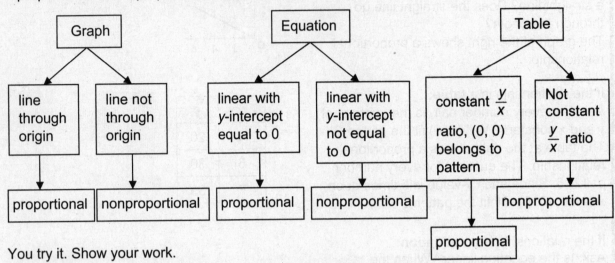

You try it. Show your work.

Determine if each relationship is proportional or nonproportional.
Explain your reasoning.

1.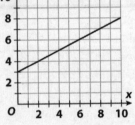

2.

x	y
2	6
3	9
5	15

_____   _____

_____   _____

3. $y = 5x$

4. $y = 9x + 3$

_____   _____

_____   _____

LESSON 4-4 Proportional and Nonproportional Situations
Success for English Learners

Problem 1

If a graph is a straight line through the origin, the relationship is **proportional.**

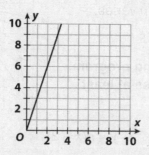

Problem 2

When an equation is not linear, it is not proportional, or **nonproportional.**
When an equation is linear in the form $y = mx + b$, it is a proportional relationship when $b = 0$.

$y = 10x$ is proportional

$y = 5x + 2$ is **not** proportional (or nonproportional)

1. What does the graph of a proportional relationship look like?

_____

_____

2. When does an equation describe a proportional relationship?

_____

_____

MODULE
4

Nonproportional Relationships

Challenge

Exploring Systems

The figure shows a **pencil of lines**, a system of lines that all pass through the same point. A set of lines that are all parallel is also called a pencil of lines.

The figure shows $y - 3 = n(x + 2)$. The parameter n varies. For each value of n, you get a different line.

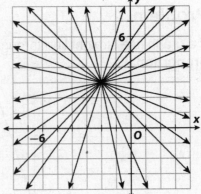

Use a graphing calculator or computer graphing program. Graph each system and describe the result. Use at least five values of n.

1. $y = nx + 6$

2. $y = n(x - 2)$

_____   _____

3. $y = 3x + n$

4. $y = -0.5x + n$

_____   _____

5. $y - 6 = n(x - 4)$

6. $y + 6 = n(x + 4)$

_____   _____

7. $y + 6 = n(x - 4)$

8. $y + 6 = 2(x + n)$

_____   _____

9. Use your graphs to write a conclusion about the system represented by $y - k = n(x - h)$, where (h, k) is a fixed point and n varies.

_____

For these problems, use equations of the form $A_1x + B_1y = C_1$ and $A_2x + B_2y = C_2$.

10. Create two equations such that $\dfrac{A_1}{B_1} = \dfrac{A_2}{B_2}$. Graph your equations.

11. Create two equations such that $\dfrac{A_1}{B_1} = -\dfrac{B_2}{A_2}$. Graph your equations.

12. Repeat problems 10 and 11 a few times. Then write a conclusion.

_____

_____

LESSON 5-1

Writing Linear Equations from Situations and Graphs

Practice and Problem Solving: A/B

For each situation described in Exercises 1–4, first write an equation in the form $y = mx + b$. Then, solve each problem.

1. A sales associate is given a $500 hiring bonus with a new job. She earns an average commission of $250 per week for the next 12 weeks. How much does she earn?

_____

_____

2. A farm has 75 acres of wheat. The farmer can harvest the wheat from 12 acres per day. In how many days will all of the fields be harvested?

_____

_____

3. A contractor's crew can frame 3 houses in a week. How long will it take them to frame 54 houses if they frame the same number each week?

_____

_____

4. A water tank holds 18,000 gallons. How long will it take for the water level to reach 6,000 gallons if the water is used at an average rate of 450 gallons per day?

_____

_____

Write an equation in the form $y = mx + b$ for each situation.

5.

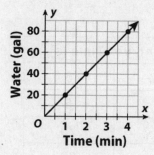

6.

Height (m)y	Time (s)x
360	0
300	10
240	20
180	30
120	40

_____   _____

Name _____ Date _____ Class_____

Writing Linear Equations from Situations and Graphs

Practice and Problem Solving: C

For each situation described in Exercises 1–4, first write an equation
in the form $y = mx + b$. Then, solve each problem. Show your work.

1. Mrs. Sanchez is given a $550 hiring bonus with a new job. She earns
   an average commission of $275 per week. If $68 is subtracted each
   week for taxes and benefits, how much does she earn in a year?

   _____

   _____

2. A large farm has 75 acres of wheat and 62.5 acres of corn. The farm
   crew can harvest the wheat from 12 acres and the corn from 10 acres
   per day. In how many days will all of the fields be harvested?

   _____

   _____

3. An electrician can wire on average 4.5 houses in a week. How many
   months will it take her to wire 55 houses if she wires the same number
   each week and figures on 4.5 weeks per month?

   _____

   _____

4. A water tank holds 24,000 gallons. How many hours will it take for $\frac{2}{3}$

   of the water to be used if the water is used at an average rate of 650
   gallons per day?

   _____

   _____

Write an equation in the form $y = mx + b$ for each situation.

5.

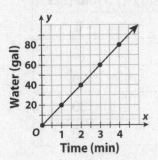

6.

Height (m), y	Time (s), x
360	0
330	5
240	20
162	33
120	40

_____   _____

Name _____ Date _____ Class _____

Writing Linear Equations from Situations and Graphs
Practice and Problem Solving: D

Use the graph to complete Exercises 1–6. A fish tank is being drained. The graph shows the number of quarts of water, *y*, in the tank after *x* minutes. Write the correct answer. The first one is done for you.

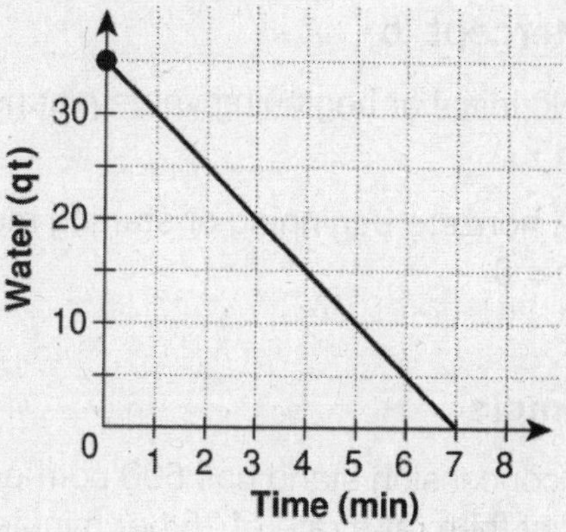

1. In the slope-intercept form for a linear equation, $y = mx + b$, *b* is the *y*-intercept, or the *y* value where the line crosses the *y*-axis. What is *b*?

   _____ **35** _____

2. Select any two points on the line. What is the "rise," going vertically from one point to the other on the line?

   _____

3. What is the "run," going from left to right between the same two points?

   _____

4. What is the "rise" divided by the "run"?

   _____

5. The slope, *m*, is the "rise" of the *y* values of any two points divided by the "run" of the *x* values of the points, taken in the same order. What is the slope?

   _____

6. What is the equation of the line? $y =$ _____ $x +$ _____

Use the graph to answer the questions.

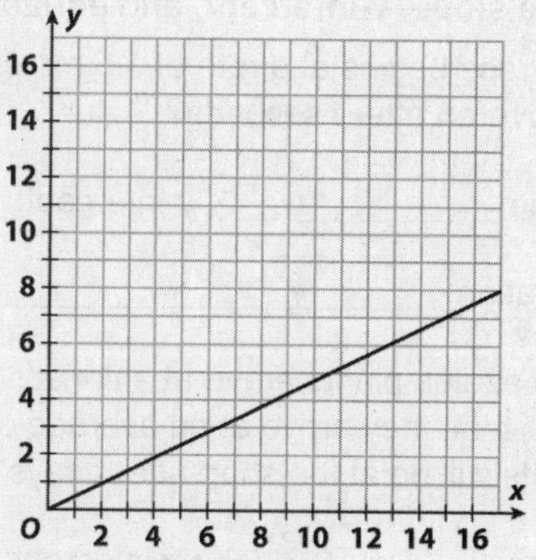

7. What is the *y*-intercept, *b*?

   _____

8. What is the slope, *m*?

   _____

9. What is the equation of the line?

   _____

10. In order to have a *y*-intercept of 4, and the same slope, how would you need to change the line?

    _____

    _____

LESSON 5-1 Writing Linear Equations from Situations and Graphs
Reteach

You will be asked to find the slope (m) and the y-intercept (b) of graphs of linear equations in the form $y = mx + b$. Both slope and y-intercept can be identified from the wording of a problem.

y-intercept, b

- No initial or beginning value means $b = 0$.

- A nonzero beginning or starting means $b \neq 0$.

slope, m

- A rate indicates slope, m.

- A change "per" some variable;

  o   increasing ($m > 0$)

  o   decreasing ($m < 0$)

Example

The concession stand has 500 pom-poms before the game. The fans bought them at a rate of 25 per minute. How long will it take for the supply to be gone?

What is b? ⟶ $b = 500$

What is m and why is it negative? ⟶ $m = -25$, because 25 are being sold each minute.

What else do you know? ⟶ In the equation, $y = 0$ when all of the pom-poms are sold.

Replace the variables in the equation: $\qquad y = mx + b$ ⟶ $0 = -25t + 500$

$\qquad\qquad\qquad\qquad\qquad\qquad\qquad\qquad 25t = 500$

Solve for t $\qquad\qquad\qquad\qquad\qquad\qquad t = 20$ minutes

Write the slope, y-intercept, and equation for each situation.

1. The race begins at a rate of 1.5 meters per second. What distance, d, is covered after t seconds?

   Slope _____; y-intercept: _____

   Equation: _____

2. Fifty azalea plants arrive at a florist's shop on the first day of the week. After that, they arrive at an average of 75 plants per day. How many plants will be at the shop after t days?

   Slope: _____; y-intercept: _____

   Equation: _____

LESSON 5-1 Writing Linear Equations from Situations and Graphs

Reading Strategies: Interpreting a Graph

The table lists the time and speed of Mrs. Smith's walk and run through the neighborhood.

- Mrs. Smith walks at a rate of 4 miles per hour.
- She runs at a rate of 8 miles per hour.
- Sometimes she stops to talk to neighbors.

Time	Speed (mph)
2:00 P.M.	0
2:05 P.M.	4
2:10 P.M.	4
2:15 P.M.	0
2:18 P.M.	8
2:20 P.M.	8
2:25 P.M.	8
2:30 P.M.	0

The graph below pictures the same data. Answer the questions.

1. Where is time shown on the graph?

   _____

2. Where is speed shown on the graph?

   _____

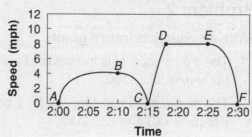

3. Which letters on the graph identify segments or parts of the walk-and-run that can be described by linear equations?

   _____

4. What is the slope of the line segment *CD*? Use the table if you need help.

   _____

5. Describe Mrs. Smith's walking or jogging from points *C* to *D* and from *D* to *E*.

   _____

   _____

6. Why can't the parts *ABC* and *EF* of Mrs. Smith's graph be described by linear equations?

   _____

   _____

Writing Linear Equations from Situations and Graphs

LESSON 5-1

Success for English Learners

Problem 1

Write an equation from a table.

Step 1: What happens to the depth with each minute that passes?

"The submarine goes 50 feet deeper."

Step 2: The *y*-intercept, *b*, is the depth at a time of 0.

"The depth starts at 0 feet."

Step 3: The slope, *m*, is the change in depth divided by the change in time.

"–50 feet divided by 1 minute is –50 feet per minute."

Step 4: Write the equation for the line using the slope and *y*-intercept.

$$d = -50t + 0, \text{ or } d = -50t$$

Submarine Depth	
Minutes (*m*)	**Depth (*d*) In Feet**
0	0
1	–50
2	–100

Problem 2

Write an equation from a graph.

1. The *y*-intercept, *b*, is the value of *y* where the line meets the *y*-axis. $b = -100$

2. The slope, *m*, is rise over run for 2 points on the line. For (0, –100) and (2, –200),

$$m = \frac{-100 - (-200)}{0 - 2} = \frac{100}{-2} = -50$$

3. Put the slope and *y*-intercept in the equation for the line:

$$d = -50t - 100$$

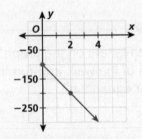

Find the slope, *y*-intercept, and equation for the data in the table and in the graph.

1.

x	0	1	2	3	4
y	0	3	6	9	12

Slope: ____; *y*-intercept: ____

Equation: _____

2.

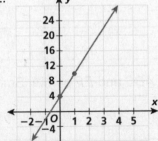

Slope: ____

y-intercept: ____

Equation:

_____

LESSON 5-2

Writing Linear Equations from a Table
Practice and Problem Solving: A/B

Graph the data, and find the slope and *y*-intercept from the graph. Then write an equation for the graph in slope-intercept form.

1.

Weight (oz), x	2	4	8	10
Cost ($), y	12	16	24	28

2.

Time (min), x	5	20	30	35
Elevation (ft), y	4	10	14	16

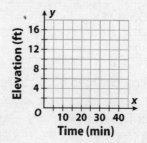

slope: _____

y-intercept: _____

equation: _____

slope: _____

y-intercept: _____

equation: _____

Write an equation in slope-intercept form that represents the data.

3.

Sales Per Day, x	0	1	2	3
Daily Pay ($), y	100	105	110	115

equation: _____

4.

Time Since Turning Oven Off (min), x	0	5	10	15
Temperature of Oven (°F), y	375	325	275	225

equation: _____

The table shows the linear relationship of the height *y* (in inches) of a tomato plant *x* weeks after it was planted.

5. Write an equation that shows the height of the tomato plant.

_____

6. Use the equation to find the height of the tomato plant 6 weeks after it was planted.

_____

Weeks After Planting, x	Height (in.), y
0	8
1	11
2	14
3	17

Writing Linear Equations from a Table

LESSON 5-2

Practice and Problem Solving: C

Complete each table to model the linear relationship. Then write an equation in slope-intercept form for each relationship.

1. A single-serve coffee maker costs $70 plus $0.20 for the coffee for each serving.

Servings, *x*	0	1	2	3
Total Cost ($), *y*				

Equation: _____

2. A bowling alley charges $3.00 to rent shoes and $1.50 per game bowled.

Games Bowled, *x*	1	2	3	4
Total Cost ($), *y*				

Equation: _____

3. The table shows the height *y* (in feet) of a rock climber *x* minutes after she starts rappelling down a rock-climbing wall. Will the slope that represents this linear relationship be positive or negative? Explain.

Time (m), *x*	1	2	3	4
Height (ft), *y*	24	18	12	6

_____

4. The table shows the linear relationship of how the number of months of membership at two gyms relates to the total cost of the membership, including the membership fee.

   a. Write an equation for the total cost *y* for *x* months of membership at each gym. Explain the meaning of the slope and *y*-intercept in this situation.

Month	Total Cost for Gym A ($)	Total Cost for Gym B ($)
1	70.00	55.00
2	90.00	80.00
3	110.00	105.00

_____

_____

   b. Suppose you plan to be a member for 10 months. Which gym will cost less? Explain.

_____

_____

LESSON 5-2

Writing Linear Equations from a Table
Practice and Problem Solving: D

The table and the graph show the total cost for party invitations, which includes a design fee. Choose the correct answer. The first one is done for you.

Invitations Printed, x	10	20	30	40
Total Cost ($), y	20.00	25.00	30.00	35.00

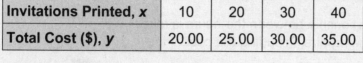

1. The slope of the line is __**B**__.

   A −0.5　　　　　　　B 0.5　　　　　　　C 5

2. The *y*-intercept of the line is ____.

   A 0　　　　　　　　B 5　　　　　　　　C 15

3. An equation for the line is ____.

   A $y = -0.5x + 15$　　　B $y = 0.5x$　　　C $y = 0.5x + 15$

The tables show linear relationships between *x* and *y*. Find the slope *m* or the *y*-intercept *b*. The first one is done for you.

4.

x	0	1	2	3
y	5	13	21	29

$$m = \frac{y_2 - y_1}{x_2 - x_1} = \frac{\boxed{21} - \boxed{13}}{\boxed{2} - \boxed{1}} = \underline{8}$$

5.

x	4	8	12	16
y	3	4	5	6

$$m = \frac{y_2 - y_1}{x_2 - x_1} = \frac{\boxed{} - \boxed{}}{\boxed{} - \boxed{}} = \underline{}$$

6.

x	2	3	4	5
y	15	22	29	36

$y = 7x + b$

$b = $ _____

7.

x	1	2	3	4
y	1	−2	−5	−8

$y = -3x + b$

$b = $ _____

The table shows the linear relationship of the cost *y* (in dollars) of *x* swimming lessons, including the membership fee for the swim club.

Number of Swimming Lessons, x	1	3	4	7
Total Cost ($), y	21.00	33.00	39.00	57.00

8. Find the slope for this relationship.

_____

9. Find the *y*-intercept for this relationship.

_____

10. Write an equation in slope-intercept form that represents this relationship.

_____

11. Use your equation to find the total cost (in dollars) for 12 swimming lessons.

_____

Name _____ Date _____ Class_____

Writing Linear Equations from a Table
Reteach

A linear relationship can be described using an equation in slope-intercept form, $y = mx + b$, where m is the slope and b is the y-intercept. Recall that the y-intercept b is where the graph of the equation crosses the y-axis, which is at point $(0, b)$.

The table below shows the linear relationship between the hours is takes to repair a car and the total cost of the repairs, including the cost of the parts.

Look for an x-value of 0.
The corresponding y-value, 325, is the y-intercept.

Hours Worked, x	Total Cost ($), y
0	325
2	425
4	525
6	625

+2   +100

Find changes in x-values and y-values.
Then use the values to find the slope:

$$m = \frac{\text{change in } y\text{-values}}{\text{change in } x\text{-values}} = \frac{100}{2} = 50$$

Using x-values that differ by 1 will require the least calculation.

Use the y-intercept, $b = 325$, and the slope, $m = 50$ to write an equation for the relationship.
$$y = mx + b$$
$$y = 50x + 325$$

Write an equation in slope-intercept form for each linear relationship.

1. The total monthly cost, y, for smartphone service depends on the number of text messages, x.

Text Messages, x	0	10	20	30
Cost ($), y	40.00	42.00	44.00	46.00

slope: _____

y-intercept: _____

equation: _____

2. The total cost, y, for a taxi ride depends on the number of miles traveled, x.

Distance (mi), x	0	1	5	10
Total Cost ($), y	2.50	5.00	15.00	27.50

slope: _____

y-intercept: _____

equation: _____

Writing Linear Equations from a Table

LESSON 5-2

Reading Strategies: Analyze Information

An equation can be used to describe a linear relationship shown in a table. The slope-intercept form of a **linear equation** is shown below.

$$y = mx + b$$

m is the slope.

b is the *y*-intercept.

The *y*-intercept *b* is where the line crosses the *y*-axis, which is at the point (0, *b*).

The slope *m* of a line is the ratio of the change in the *y*-values to the change in *x*-values. Two points (x_1, y_1) and (x_2, y_2) can be used to calculate the slope as shown.

$$m = \frac{\text{change in } y\text{-values}}{\text{change in } x\text{-values}} = \frac{y_2 - y_1}{x_2 - x_1}$$

The table shows a linear relationship between the height of a fast-growing bamboo plant and the number of days since it was planted.

Days Planted, *x*	0	2	4	6
Height (in.), *y*	15	20	25	30

1. What do the variables *x* and *y* represent in this relationship?

   _____

2. Read the description of the relationship above the table. How do you know that the relationship can be represented by a linear equation?

   _____

3. Can you tell whether the relationship has a positive or negative slope just by looking at the data in the table? Explain.

   _____

4. What rate does the slope represent in this situation?

   _____

5. Choose two points from the table and calculate the slope.

   _____

6. Suppose you graph the points given in the table. Where does the point (0, 15) lie? Use this information to find the *y*-intercept.

   _____

7. Write an equation in slope-intercept form that represents this relationship.

   _____

LESSON 5-2

Writing Linear Equations from a Table
Success for English Learners

Problem 1

Identify the important information given.

x-values

Matthew receives an installment loan to pay for a used car. He has to give a down payment and then make monthly payments. The table shows the linear relationship between the number of monthly payments made and the total amount of money paid toward the loan, including the down payment. Write an equation in slope-intercept form for this relationship.

A linear equation can be used.

y-values

The answer should be in slope-intercept form.

Monthly Payments Made, x	1	2	3	4
Amount of Loan Paid ($), y	1,050	1,300	1,550	1,800

Problem 2

Make a plan to write an equation in slope-intercept form.

1

Find the slope using two points.

2

Find the *y*-intercept using the slope and one point.

3

Write an equation using the slope and *y*-intercept.

1. Find the slope.

   Choose two points:

   (,) and (,)

   Use formula for slope:

   $$m = \frac{y_2 - y_1}{x_2 - x_1} =$$

   slope:_____

2. Find the *y*-intercept.

   Use $m =$ and (,).

   y-intercept: _____

3. Write an equation.

   equation: _____

4. How can a graph be used to find the *y*-intercept for a linear relationship given as a table? Explain any problems with using this method.

   _____

   _____

LESSON 5-3

Linear Relationships and Bivariate Data

Practice and Problem Solving: A/B

Does each of the tables represent a linear relationship? Explain why or why not.

1.

Months	0	1	2
Account balance ($)	220	240	260

_____

_____

2.

Time (sec)	2	3	4
Distance (ft)	8	12	15

_____

_____

Write an equation for each linear relationship.

3.

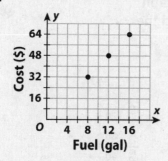

_____

4.

Weight (lb), x	Total cost ($), y
1	10
2	12
4	16
6	20

_____

The graph shows the relationship between the number of rows in a friendship bracelet and the time it takes Mia to make the bracelet, including the time it takes to prepare the threads.

5. Determine whether the relationship is linear.
   If so, write an equation for the relationship.

   _____

6. How long will it take for Mia to complete
   14 rows?

   _____

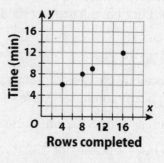

7. Mia teaches Brynn how to make a bracelet. Graph these points to
   show Brynn's progress: (2, 6), (4, 8), (8, 10), (12, 12). Is the time y it
   takes Brynn to make a bracelet with x rows a linear relationship?
   Explain.

   _____

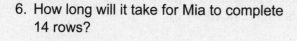

Linear Relationships and Bivariate Data

LESSON 5-3

Practice and Problem Solving: C

Does each of the tables represent a linear relationship? Explain why or why not. If the relationship is linear, then write an equation for the relationship.

1.

Time Filling Tank (min)	5	8	12
Water in Tank (gal)	37	55	79

2.

Time (h)	2	6	9
Distance Traveled (mi)	124	372	552

_____

_____

_____

_____

Adrian regularly deposits money in his saving account. The graph shows the relationship between the balance in his account and the number of weeks he has been making deposits.

3. Find the balance of Adrian's account after he makes deposits for 5 weeks.

_____

4. How many weeks does it take for the balance of Adrian's account to be $140?

_____

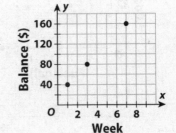

5. Adrian's sister, Lara, makes deposits to her savings account when Adrian makes his deposits. The balance *y* in dollars of Lara's account after *x* weeks is $y = 10x + 80$. Does Adrian or Lara have a greater balance after 4 weeks? Explain.

_____

6. A ticket agency charges a processing fee for ticket purchases. The following ticket purchases were made for tickets to a concert.

- William spends $132 on 4 tickets.

- Theo buys 2 tickets for $72.

- The ticket agency charges Ellis $252 for 8 tickets.

Use the information to complete the table. Then determine whether the relationship between tickets purchased and total cost is linear. If so, find the cost of 7 tickets.

Tickets	Total Cost ($)

_____

_____

LESSON
5-3
Linear Relationships and Bivariate Data
Practice and Problem Solving: D

Does each graph represent a linear relationship? Explain why or why not. The first one is done for you.

1.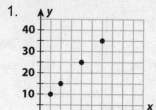

Yes, because the rate of

change is constant.

2.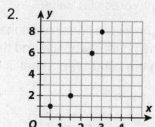

_____

_____

The graph shows the linear relationship between the number of days renting a car and the total cost, including the initial fees. Choose the correct answer.

3. The slope of the line is ____.

   A 30   B 60   C 90

4. The *y*-intercept of the line is ____.

   A 30   B 60   C 90

5. An equation for the line is ____.

   A $y = 30x + 30$ B $y = 90x$ C $y = 30x + 60$

6. The cost for renting a car for 3 days is ____.

   A $120   B $150   C $160

Explain whether or not you think each relationship is linear. The first one is done for you.

7. The total pay and hours worked for babysitter who gets paid per hour

   linear; The rate of change is the babysitter's pay per hour, which is constant.

8. The height of a kicked football and the horizontal distance traveled by the ball.

_____

9. The perimeter of a square and its side length

_____

Name _____ Date _____ Class _____

LESSON 5-3

Linear Relationships and Bivariate Data
Reteach

You have used an equation of a linear relationship to predict a value between two data points that you know. You can also use a table of a linear relationship to predict a value.

The table below shows the linear relationship between the number of months a company hosts a website and the total cost of hosting the website, including the set-up fee. What is the cost for 4 months of web hosting?

Months	Total Cost ($)
2	125
6	265
8	335

+2   +70

Months	Total Cost ($)
2	125
3	160
4	195
5	230
6	265
8	335

+35
+35
+35

Find rate of change.
An increase of 2 months increases the cost by $70. So, the monthly cost increase is:

$$\frac{\text{change in cost}}{\text{change in months}} = \frac{70}{2} = 35$$

Fill in missing values.
Use the rate of change, 35, to fill in the numbers between the given numbers. Start at month 2.

Looking at the second table, the cost for 4 months of web hosting is $195.

Use the table of each linear relationship to find each value.

1. Determine the amount of snow on the ground after 3 hours.

2. Determine the total cost of 6 prints of a digital photo.

Time (h)	Snow Accumulation (in.)
1	5
4	11
5	13

Prints	Total Cost ($)
2	3.00
4	6.00
7	10.50

LESSON 5-3

Linear Relationships and Bivariate Data

Reading Strategies: Use Graphic Aids

Linear Relationship	Nonlinear Relationship
Rate of change, 45, is constant.	Rate of change is not constant.

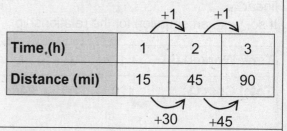

Time (h)	1	2	3
Distance (mi)	45	90	135

+1 +1
+45 +45

Time (h)	1	2	3
Distance (mi)	15	45	90

+1 +1
+30 +45

Points lie on a straight line. Two points on the line can be used to write an equation for the line.	Points do not lie on a straight line.

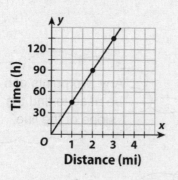

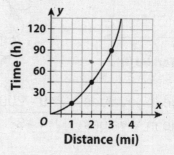

1. How do you determine whether a relationship represented as a graph is linear or nonlinear?

   _____

2. Describe the difference between the rate of change of a linear relationship and the rate of change of a nonlinear relationship.

   _____

3. How do you determine whether a relationship represented as a table is linear or nonlinear?

   _____

4. Can you use the graph of a linear relationship to write an equation for the line in slope-intercept form? Explain.

   _____

LESSON 5-3 Linear Relationships and Bivariate Data

Success for English Learners

Problem 1

The table shows the total cost for a plumber to fix a broken pipe, including his hourly rate and the cost for the materials. Is the relationship linear?
If so, write an equation for the relationship.

Time Worked (h)	1	3	4
Total Cost ($)	120	200	240

Linear means the points lie on a line.

Do these points lie on a line?

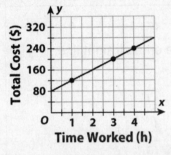

Yes. The relationship is linear.

$$m = \frac{\text{change in } y\text{-values}}{\text{change in } x\text{-values}} = \frac{240-200}{4-3} = \frac{40}{1} = 40$$

Any two points can be used to find the slope of the line.

$$y = mx + b$$
$$240 = 40(4) + b$$
$$240 = 160 + b$$
$$80 = b$$

The slope and any point can be used to find the y-intercept.

An equation for the relationship is $y = 40x + 80$.

1. What do the slope and y-intercept represent in the situation above?

_____

_____

2. A linear relationship is shown in the table. Describe a real-world situation that can be represented by the table.

x	2	3	6
y	100	150	300

_____

_____

MODULE 5

Writing Linear Equations
Challenge

The **standard form** of a line is $Ax + By = C$ where A, B, and C are real numbers.

To write an equation of a line, you need to know two pieces of information.

When the slope and the y-intercept are known, use $y = mx + b$.

When the slope and a point on the line are known, use $y - y_1 = m(x - x_1)$.

You can use either the slope-intercept form or the point-slope form to write an equation in standard form.

Write an equation in standard form for the line that contains side AB of triangle ABC.

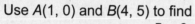

Use $A(1, 0)$ and $B(4, 5)$ to find

the slope of $\overrightarrow{AB}$. $m = \dfrac{5 - 0}{4 - 1} = \dfrac{5}{3}$.

Substitute $m = \dfrac{5}{3}$ and $(x_1, y_1) = (1, 0)$

into point-slope form. $y - 0 = \dfrac{5}{3}(x - 1)$

Write the equation in standard form.

clear fractions	$3y = 5(x - 1)$
distribute	$3y = 5x - 5$
add and subtract	$5x - 3y = 5$

Write the standard form of the equation for the line that contains each indicated side or diagonal.

1.

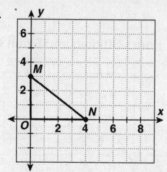

$\overline{MN}$ of right triangle MNO

_____

_____

2.

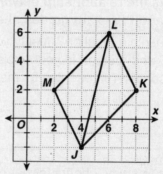

$\overline{JL}$ of parallelogram $JKLM$

_____

_____

Name _____ Date _____ Class_____

Identifying and Representing Functions
Practice and Problem Solving: A/B

Tell whether each relationship is a function.

1.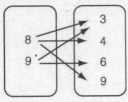

2.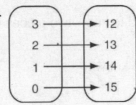

3.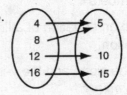

_____

4.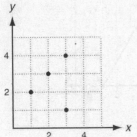

5.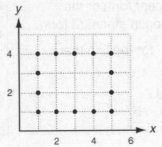

6.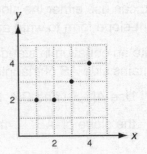

_____

7.

Input	0	1	2	3
Output	4	1	0	4

8.

Input	1	2	0	1	2
Output	4	5	6	7	8

_____

9. {(0, 0), (2, 4), (3, 6), (5, 5), (7, 6)}

10. {(0, 8), (1, 2), (3, 7), (5, 9), (3, 6)}

**The graph shows the relationship between the hours
Rachel studied and the exam grades she earned.**

11. Is the relationship a function? Justify your answer. Use the
words "input" and "output" in your explanation, and connect
them to the context represented by the graph.

Hours Studied and Exam Grade

_____

_____

12. Rachel plans to study 2 hours for her next exam. How might
plotting her grade on the same graph change your answer
to Exercise 11? Explain your reasoning.

_____

_____

LESSON 6-1 Identifying and Representing Functions
Practice and Problem Solving: C

Determine whether each relationship is a function. Explain.

1. {(2, 9), (3, 12), (4, 12), (2, 8), (1, 6)}

_____

_____

2. {(0, 0), (1, 2), (2, 3), (3, 4), (4, 5)}

_____

_____

Solve.

3. Connor is a gardener. He made a graph showing the relationship between the day of the week he worked, Monday through Saturday, and the number of square feet of mulch he used. His graph covered one month. Is the relationship represented by Connor's graph a function? Explain.

_____

_____

_____

4. Chana pays $7.35 per pound for up to19 pounds of beads. For more than 19 pounds, she pays $5.35 per pound. Is the amount Chana pays a function of the weight of the beads she buys? Explain your reasoning.

_____

_____

_____

An animal adoption agency tracked the number of animals remaining to be adopted, as shown in the graph.

5. Explain why the relationship represented by the graph is a function.

_____

_____

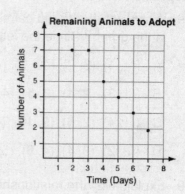

6. If another animal adoption agency tracked the number of animals they have remaining to be adopted on this same graph, would the graph still represent a function? Explain.

_____

_____

Name _____ Date _____ Class _____

Identifying and Representing Functions

Practice and Problem Solving: D

Tell whether each relationship is a function. The first one is done for you.

1.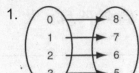

2.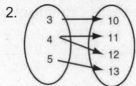

3.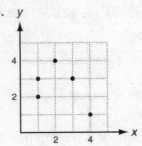

_____ **function** _____

_____

_____

4.

Input	Output
0	8
1	7
2	6
3	5

5.

Input	Output
2	3
2	6
5	9
8	12

6.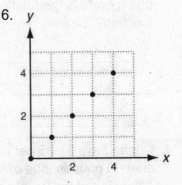

_____

_____

_____

7. {(1, 8), (1, 2), (1, 7), (2, 9)}

8. {(0, 0), (1, 4), (2, 6), (3, 5)}

_____

_____

The graph shows the relationship between the number of years and the number of elephants in one herd of Asian elephants.

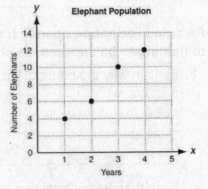

9. Which set of ordered pairs represents the information in the graph? Circle the letter.

A {(4, 1), (6, 2), (10, 3), (4, 12)}

B {(1, 3), (2, 4), (3, 5), (4, 6)}

C {(1, 4), (2, 6), (3, 10), (4, 12)}

D {(2, 2), (3, 4), (4, 6), (5, 8)}

10. Explain why the relationship shown in the graph is a function.

_____

_____

_____

LESSON 6-1 Identifying and Representing Functions
Reteach

A **relation** is a set of ordered pairs.	{(1, 2), (3, 4), (5, 6)}
The **input** values are the first numbers in each pair.	{(**1**, 2), (**3**, 4), (**5**, 6)}
The **output** values are the second numbers in each pair.	{(1, **2**), (3, **4**), (5, **6**)}

Circle each input value. Underline each output value.

1. {(1, 1), (2, 3), (3, 5)}

2. {(6, 2), (5, 3), (4, 8)}

A relation is a **function** when each input value is paired with *only one* output value.

The relation below is a function.

Input   Output

2 ——→ 5

1 ——→ 1

3 ——→

Input value 2 is paired with *only one* output, 5.

Input value 1 is paired with *only one* output, 1.

Input value 3 is paired with *only one* output, 1.

The relation below is **not** a function.

Input   Output

3 ——→ 5

2 ——→ 4

1 ——→ 1

      3

Input value 1 is paired with *two* outputs, 1 and 3.

Tell whether each relation is a function. Explain how you know.

3. {(1, 5), (3, 7), (6, 5), (9, 8)}

_____

_____

4. {(1, 2), (1, 8), (3, 6), (4, 8)}

_____

_____

5.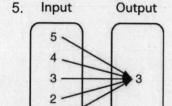

_____

_____

6.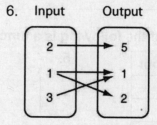

_____

_____

Identifying and Representing Functions

Reading Strategies: Use Examples and Non-Examples

LESSON 6-1

In a **function** no input value can have more than one output value.

Examples	Non-Examples
{(1, 3), (2, 4), (3, 5), (6, 8)}	{(1, 3), (2, 4), (3, 5), (3, 8)}

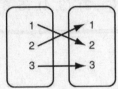
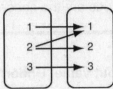

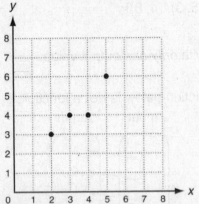
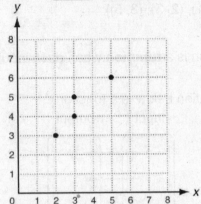

Input	1	2	3	4	5
Output	4	5	6	6	8

Input	2	2	2	2	2
Output	4	5	6	6	8

Answer the following.

1. Give your own example of a function in table form.

Input				
Output				

2. Draw a mapping that is **not** a function.

3. Explain why the relation in Exercise 2 is not a function.

_____

Tell whether each of the following is a function. Write *yes* or *no*.

4.

Input	Output
3	8
2	5
1	4
1	6

5.

6.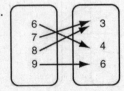

_____   _____   _____

LESSON 6-1
Identifying and Representing Functions
Success for English Learners

In a **function**, each *x*-value is paired with only one *y*-value.

Problem 1

4 ways to represent a function:

List: {(4, 3), (3, 6), (2, 2), (1, 0)}

Table:

Input	2	3	4	5
Output	3	6	9	2

Mapping Diagram:

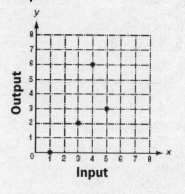

Graph:

Problem 2

How to tell a relationship is **NOT** a function:

List: {(5, **3**), (5, **6**), (2, 2), (1, 0)}

5 is paired with *both* 3 and 6.

Table:

Input	1	2	0	1
Output	**4**	5	6	**7**

1 is paired with *both* 4 and 7.

Mapping Diagram:

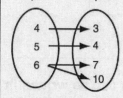

6 is paired with *both* 7 and 10.

Graph:

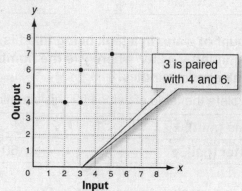

3 is paired with 4 and 6.

Solve.

1. How you can tell from the graph of a relation whether it is a function?

_____

2. Julie listed the relationship {(1, 3), (3, 2), (4, 6), (5, 2)}. Both 3 and 5 are paired with 2. Is this relationship a function?

_____

_____

LESSON 6-2

Describing Functions

Practice and Problem Solving: A/B

Graph each equation. Tell whether the equation is linear or nonlinear.

1. $y = 3x$

Input, x	–1	0	1	2	4
Output, y					

2. $y = x^2 + 1$

Input, x	–2	–1	0	1	2
Output, y					

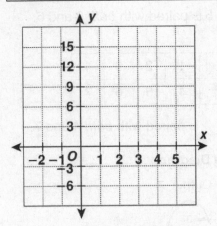

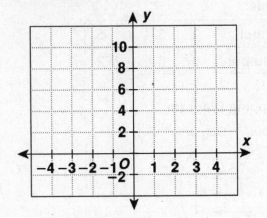

_____

_____

Tell whether each equation can be written in the form $y = mx + b$.
Write *yes* or *no*. If *yes*, write the equation in the form $y = mx + b$.

3. $y = 8 - x^2$

4. $y = 4 + x$

5. $y = 3 - 2x$

_____   _____   _____

The amount of water in a tank being filled is represented by the equation $y = 20x$, where y is the number of gallons in the tank after x minutes.

6. Complete the table of values for this situation.

Time (min), x	0	1	2		4
Water (gal), y				60	

7. Sketch a graph of the equation.

8. Use your graph to predict the amount of water in the tank after 6 minutes.

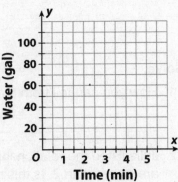

_____

9. Explain how you know whether relationship between x and y is linear or nonlinear.

_____

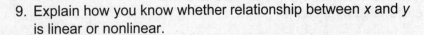

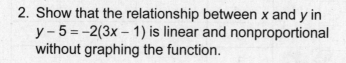

LESSON 6-2 Describing Functions

Practice and Problem Solving: C

Solve.

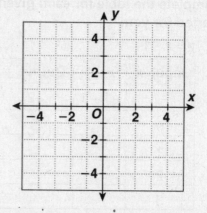

1. State whether the relationship between *x* and *y* in
   $3y = -2x + 6$ is proportional or nonproportional.
   Then graph the function.

   _____

2. Show that the relationship between *x* and *y* in
   $y - 5 = -2(3x - 1)$ is linear and nonproportional
   without graphing the function.

   _____

   _____

   _____

3. Juanita usually spends $3 more than twice her transportation costs on
   groceries. If *x* is the amount she spends on transportation, and *y* is the
   amount she spends on groceries, the amount she spends on groceries
   can be represented by the equation $y = 2x + 3$. Is the relationship
   between *x* and *y* linear? Is it proportional? How much would Juanita
   spend on groceries if she spent $30 on transportation? Explain.

   _____

   _____

   _____

4. The number of hours, *x*, Ryan rides his bike and the total number of
   miles, *y*, he rides is a linear relationship. Ryan has already ridden
   5 miles, and he can ride at a constant rate of 12 miles per hour. Write
   an equation relating *x* hours and *y* miles. Then predict how many
   minutes will pass for Ryan to have traveled a total of 60 miles.

   _____

   _____

   _____

5. When $x = 2$, $|x| = 2$. When $x = -2$, $|x| = 2$. Is the relationship between
   x and *y* in the equation $y = |x|$ linear? Is it proportional? Explain.

   _____

   _____

Describing Functions

Practice and Problem Solving: D

Complete the table for each given equation. The first row has been started for you.

1. $y = x - 1$

Input, x	x – 1	Output, y	(x, y)
–1	–1 – 1	–2	(–1, –2)
0			
1			
2			
3			

2. $y = 2x + 6$

Input, x	2x + 6	Output, y	(x, y)
–2	2(–2) + 6		
–1			
0			
1			

Complete the table and graph the equation.

3. $y = -2x + 2$

Input, x	–2x + 2	Output, y	(x, y)
–2	–2(–2) + 2	6	(–2, 6)
–1			
0			
1			
2			

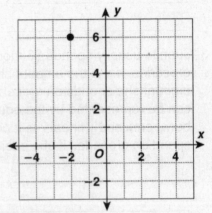

A cyclist rides at an average speed of 20 miles per hour. The equation $y = 20x$ shows the distance y, the cyclist travels in x hours.

4. Complete the table of values for this situation.

Input, x	20x	Output, y	(x, y)
0	20(0) = 0	0	(0, 0)
1	20(1) = 20	20	(1, 20)
2			
3			

5. Complete the graph of the equation at the right.

6. Is the relationship between x and y linear or nonlinear?

_____

7. How do you know the relationship between x and y is proportional?

_____

LESSON 6-2

Describing Functions
Reteach

Graph $y = x + 2$.

Step 1: Make a table of values.

Input, x	$x + 2$	Output, y	(x, y)
−2	−2 + 2 = 0	0	(−2, 0)
0	0 + 2 = 2	2	(0, 2)
2	2 + 2 = 4	4	(2, 4)
3	3 + 2 = 5	5	(3, 5)

Step 2: Graph the ordered pairs, (x, y).

Step 3: Draw a line through the points.

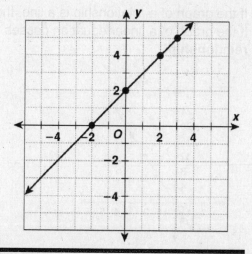

Complete the table. Graph the function.

1. $y = x + 4$

Input, x	$x + 4$	Output, y	(x, y)
−2	−2 + 4 = ___		(−2, ___)
0	___ + 4 = ___		
2			
6			
8			

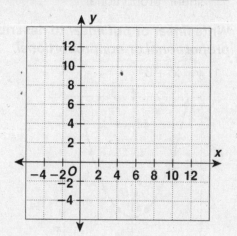

A function is **linear** if:
- the graph is a line, and
- the equation can be written in the form $y = mx + b$.

A linear function is **proportional** if its graph passes through the origin, (0, 0).

If the graph is not a line, then the function is **nonlinear**.

Linear: $\quad y = mx + b$
$y = 4 - 3x \longrightarrow y = -3x + 4$
$y = 5x \longrightarrow y = 5x + 0$

Proportional: $\quad y = 5x$
$\qquad\qquad\quad 0 = 5(0)$

Not proportional: $y = 4 - 3x$
$\qquad\qquad\qquad 0 \neq 4 - 3(0)$

Describe each function. Write *linear*, *proportional*, or *nonlinear*.

2.

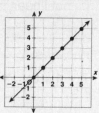

_____

3. $y = -2x + 5$

_____

4.

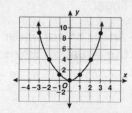

_____

Name _____ Date _____ Class _____

Describing Functions

Reading Strategies: Build Vocabulary

If the graph of a relationship is a line, the equation is a **linear equation**.
If the graph of a linear equation passes through (0, 0), it is a **proportional relationship**.

$y = 6x$

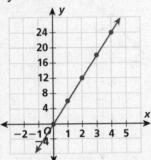

$y = 2x - 1$

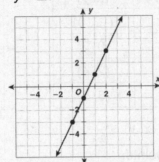

$y = x^2 + 3$

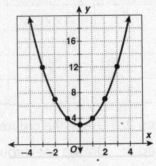

linear, proportional   linear, nonproportional   not linear

Write *linear* or *not linear* to describe each graph. If it is linear, write *proportional* or *nonproportional*.

1. $y = x^2 + 3$

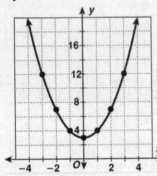

2. $y = x$

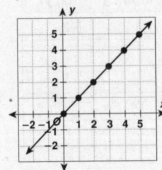

3. $y = -2x + 5$

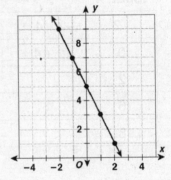

_____   _____   _____

_____   _____   _____

An equation of the form $y = mx + b$ is a **linear equation**.
Equations that cannot be written in this form are not linear equations.

$y = 4 + 3x$	$y = 5x$	$x = 7$	$y = 3x^2 + 1$
↓	↓	↓	↓
$y = 3x + 4$	$y = 5x + 0$	$0y = x - 7$	x is squared
↓	↓	↓	↓
linear	linear	linear	not linear

Write *linear* or *not linear* to describe each equation. If it is linear, write the equation in $y = mx + b$ form.

4. $y = 1 - 2x$ 5. $4x = 3$ 6. $y = 6x^2 - 2$ 7. $-1 + 8x = y$

_____   _____   _____   _____

_____   _____   _____   _____

LESSON 6-2

Describing Functions
Success for English Learners

Problem 1

To graph point *M* at (4, 2), start at (0, 0).

    Move 4 units right. $\longrightarrow$

    Move 2 units up. $\uparrow$

Draw the point. Label it *M*.

To graph point *N* at (−3, −3), start at (0, 0).

    Move 3 units left. $\longleftarrow$

    Move 3 units down. $\downarrow$

Draw the point. Label it *N*.

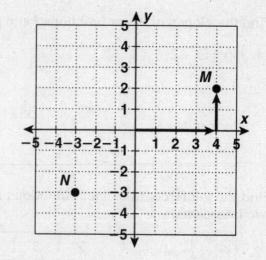

Problem 2

Graph the equation $y = 3x - 5$.

    • Make a table of ordered pairs.

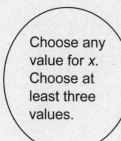
Choose any value for *x*. Choose at least three values.

x	3x − 5	y	(x, y)
2	3(2) − 5 = 1	1	(2, 1)
3	3(3) − 5 = 4	4	(3, 4)
4	3(4) − 5 = 7	7	(4, 7)

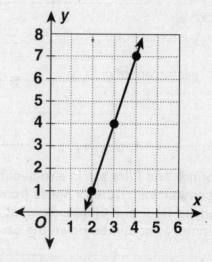

    • Graph the ordered pairs on a coordinate grid.

    • Connect the points.

Is the graph of an equation a line? Then it is called a **linear equation**.

Solve.

1. To graph Point *R* at (5, 6), Arlen started at (0, 0), moved 5 units right and then 6 units left. What mistake did he make?

_____

2. Nancy's table of ordered pairs for the equation $y = 3x - 5$ included letting $x = 1$. What ordered pair should she graph for this value of *x*?

_____

3. How could you tell if the equation $y = 2x + 3$ is a linear equation?

_____

LESSON 6-3 Comparing Functions

Practice and Problem Solving: A/B

Find the slopes of linear functions *f* and *g*. Then compare the slopes.

1. $f(x) = 5x - 2$

x	0	1	2	3	4
g(x)	−3	−1	1	3	5

slope of *f* = _____   slope of *g* = _____

_____

Find the *y*-intercepts of linear functions *f* and *g*. Then compare the two intercepts.

2.

x	0	1	2	3	4
f(x)	−3	−1	1	3	5

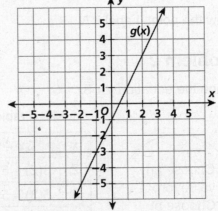

y-intercept of *f*: _____

y-intercept of *g*: _____

_____

_____

Connor and Pilar are in a rock-climbing club. They are climbing down a canyon wall. Connor starts from a cliff that is 200 feet above the canyon floor and climbs down at an average speed of 10 feet per minute. Pilar climbs down the canyon wall as shown in the table.

Time (min)	0	1	2	3
Pilar's height (ft)	242	234	226	218

3. Interpret the rates of change and initial values of the linear functions in terms of the situations that they model. Compare the results and what they mean.

Connor   Pilar

Initial value: _____   Initial value: _____

Rate of change: _____   Rate of change: _____

_____

_____

LESSON 6-3

Comparing Functions

Practice and Problem Solving: C

Find the slopes and *y*-intercepts of the linear functions *f* and *g*. Then compare the graphs. Tell whether the lines are parallel, perpendicular, or neither. If they intersect, name the point of intersection.

1. $f(x) = -3x + 5$

x	−1	0	1	2	3
g(x)	4	1	−2	−5	−8

slope of *f* = _____   slope of *g* = _____

y-intercept of *f:* _____   *y*-intercept of *g:* _____

_____

_____

The function *f*(*x*) has a slope of $\frac{1}{3}$ and a *y*-intercept of −2. The function *g*(*x*) is shown at right.

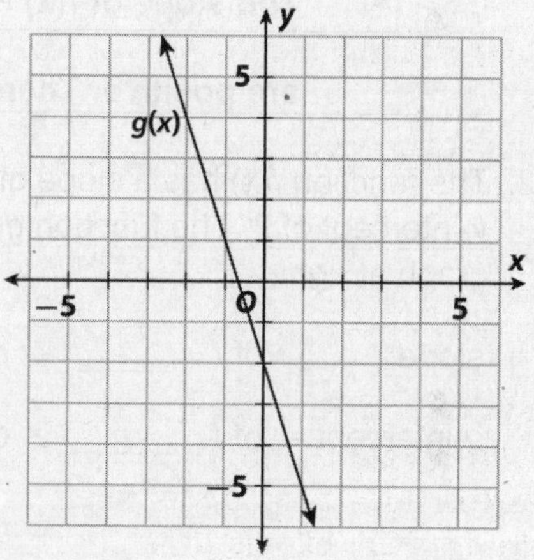

2. Compare the rates of change and the initial values of the functions. Tell whether the lines are parallel, perpendicular, or neither. If the lines intersect, name the point of intersection.

_____

_____

_____

Jing just got a new job. She started at a pay rate of $12.50 per hour and will get a $0.50 raise each year. Max started a job where his salary is found by the equation: *f*(*x*) = *x* + 10, where *x* is the number of years.

3. Interpret the rates of change and initial values of the linear functions in terms of the situations they model. Compare the results and what they mean. How many years must they both work for Max to earn more per hour than Jing?

<u>Jing</u>

Initial value: _____

Rate of change: _____

<u>Max</u>

Initial value: _____

Rate of change: _____

_____

_____

**LESSON
6-3**

Comparing Functions

Practice and Problem Solving: D

Find the slopes and *y*-intercepts of the linear functions *f* and *g*.
Then compare the graphs of the two functions. The first one is
done for you.

1.

x	−1	0	1	2	3
f(x)	−2	−1	0	1	2

↑ *y*-intercept

Think:

$$\text{slope} = \frac{-2-(-1)}{-1-0} = \frac{-1}{-1} = 1$$

$g(x) = 2x + 4$

↑ slope   ↑ *y*-intercept

slope of *f* = __**1**__   slope of *g* = __**2**__

y-intercept of *f*: __**−1**__   *y*-intercept of *g*: __**4**__

__The slope of *f(x)* is less steep than the slope of *g(x)*. Both slopes__

__are positive. There are 5 units between the *y*-intercepts.__

2. The function *f(x)* has a slope of −2 and a
y-intercept of 2. The function *g(x)* is shown in the
graph at right.

slope: of *f* = _____   of *g* = _____

y-intercept: of *f* = _____ of *g* = _____

_____

_____

_____

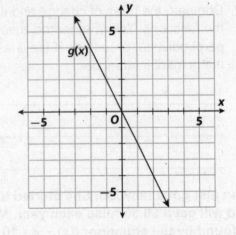

3.

x	−1	0	1	2	3
f(x)	5	4	3	2	1

slope: of *f* = _____   of *g* = _____

y-intercept: of *f* = _____ of *g* = _____

_____

_____

_____

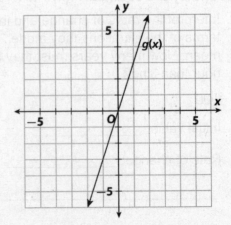

LESSON
6-3

Comparing Functions
Reteach

Functions can be represented in many forms. You can identify the slope and *y*-intercept from any format.

Representation	Slope	*y*-intercept
Equation written in slope-intercept form: $y = mx + b$	Value of *m*	Value of *b*
Table of values	Substitute any two ordered pairs into the slope formula. $m = \dfrac{y_2 - y_1}{x_2 - x_1}$	Substitute the slope and one ordered pair (*x*, *y*) into the slope-intercept formula. $y = mx + b$ Solve for *b*.
Graph	Choose two points on the line. Find the ratio of vertical change to horizontal change.	Find the point where the line crosses the *y*-axis. You may need to extend the graph.

**Find the slopes and *y*-intercepts of the linear functions *f* and *g*.
Then compare the graphs of the two functions.**

1. $f(x) = -\dfrac{1}{2}x - 2$

x	–2	0	2	4	6
g(x)	4	1	–2	–5	–8

slope of *f* = _____   slope of *g* = _____

y-intercept of *f*: _____   *y*-intercept of *g*: _____

_____

_____

2. $f(x) = 6x - 1$

slope: of *f* = _____   of *g* = _____

y-intercept: of *f* = _____   of *g* = _____

_____

_____

_____

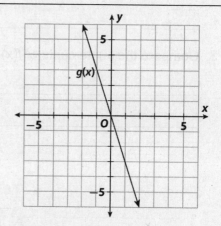

LESSON
6-3

Comparing Functions

Reading Strategies: Use Graphic Aids

When comparing functions, graphing is one way to
see similarities and differences.

Example: Compare the two functions.

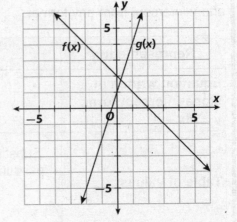

x	f(x)
2	0
0	2
−2	4

$g(x) = 3x + 1$

Look at the graphs and compare the functions.

- The slope of $g(x)$ is steeper than the slope of $f(x)$.

- The slope of $g(x)$ is positive, while the slope of
  $f(x)$ is negative.

- There is 1 unit difference in the y-intercepts.

Use the functions below for 1–3.

x	−4	−2	0
f(x)	−4	0	4

$g(x) = 2x$

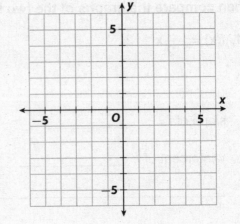

1. Graph $f(x)$ and $g(x)$ on the coordinate grid at right.

2. Compare the slopes of $f(x)$ and $g(x)$.

    _____

    _____

    _____

3. Compare the y-intercepts of $f(x)$ and $g(x)$.

    _____

    _____

Name ______________________ Date ______________ Class ______________

LESSON 6-3

Comparing Functions

Success for English Learners

Problem 1

<table>
<tr><th></th><th>Example</th><th>Rate of Change</th><th>Initial Value</th></tr>
<tr><td>Words</td><td>A bird in the sky flies down.
It starts 700 feet above the ground.
Each second it gets 15 feet lower.</td><td>Flies down 15 ft/s:
$m = -15$</td><td>Starts at 700 ft:
$b = 700$</td></tr>
<tr><td>Graph</td><td>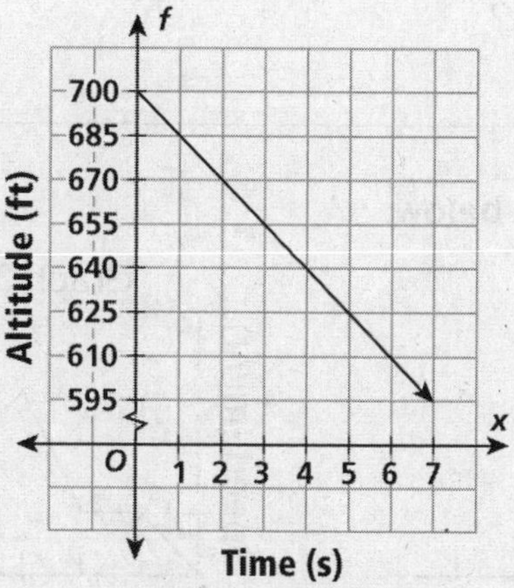
f
x
O
700
685
670
655
640
625
610
595
1 2 3 4 5 6 7
Altitude (ft)
Time (s)</td><td>For every 1-second increase on the x-axis (Time), there is a 15-foot decrease on the f-axis.
$m = \frac{-15}{1}$
$= -15$</td><td>The line crosses the f-axis at 700.
$b = 700$</td></tr>
<tr><td>Table</td><td><table><tr><th>Time (s)</th><th>Height (ft)</th></tr><tr><td>0</td><td>700</td></tr><tr><td>1</td><td>685</td></tr><tr><td>2</td><td>670</td></tr><tr><td>3</td><td>655</td></tr><tr><td>4</td><td>640</td></tr></table></td><td>Using points (0, 700) and (1, 685):
$m = \frac{700 - 685}{0 - 1}$
$= \frac{15}{-1}$
$= -15$</td><td>When Time is 0 s, Height is 700 ft.
$b = 700$</td></tr>
<tr><td>Equation</td><td>$f(x) = -15x + 700$</td><td>THINK:
$f(x) = mx + b$
$m = -15$</td><td>THINK:
$f(x) = mx + b$
$b = 700$</td></tr>
</table>

1. How can you find the rate of change from a table?

____

2. Which function representation is easiest for you to use? Explain.

____

____

Analyzing Graphs

Practice and Problem Solving: A/B

Use the situation for 1–2.

Dan is going to fix dinner. He turns on the oven. The graph
shows the temperature over time.

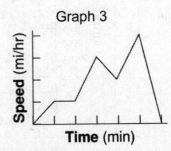

1. Why does the graph not start at zero?

   _____

   _____

2. What does it mean when the graph flattens out?

   _____

Tell which graph corresponds to each situation below.

Graph 1   Graph 2   Graph 3

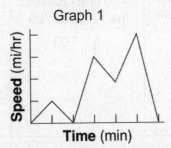   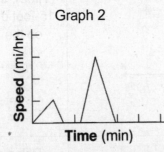

3. A car eases into traffic and then slows down and stops
   at an intersection. Next it enters the highway and adjusts
   speed to traffic until it exits and stops at home.   _____

4. A car eases into traffic, maintains speed for a short time.
   Next it enters the highway and adjusts speed to traffic
   until it exits and stops at home.   _____

5. Which graph did you not choose for Exercise 3 or Exercise 4?
   Write a description that describes what happened in that graph.

   _____

   _____

Use the graph at the right for 6–7.

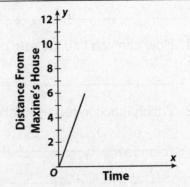

6. Maxine bikes 6 miles from home. She then rests for a
   short time before biking 4 more miles. After a short rest,
   she bikes home. Complete the graph so it shows the
   distance Maxine is from home compared to the time.

7. Find the total number of miles Maxine biked.

   _____

LESSON 6-4

Analyzing Graphs

Practice and Problem Solving: C

Tell which graph corresponds to each situation below.

Graph A   Graph B   Graph C

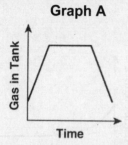   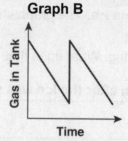   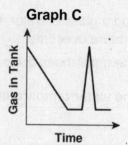

1. Mr. Alison drives in city traffic to the gas station. He also shops for bread and milk at the gas station. After filling

   up his car, he drives home on the highway. _____

2. Mr. Alison fills up his car at the gas station. He also gets a car wash at the station and visits with the manager.

   Then he drives to the next town on business._____

3. Which graph did you not choose for Exercise 1 or Exercise 2? Write a description that describes what happened in that graph.

   _____

   _____

Use the graph at the right for 4.

4. Jenny starts her walk at home. The graph shows her distance from home in relation to time. Write a story that could be represented by the graph.

   _____

   _____

   _____

Jenny's Distance from Home

[Graph: Jenny's Distance from Home. Y-axis: Distance From Home (mi), values 0 to 12. Points rise to 6, stay at 6, rise to 10, stay at 10, drop to 8, stay at 8, drop to 0.]

Use the graph at the right for 5.

5. Yolanda took 16 weeks to save money for a trip. For the first 8 weeks, she saved $50 each week. For the next 4 weeks Yolanda did not save any money. Then Yolanda saved $50 a week for 4 weeks. When Yolanda took the trip, she spent $500 of her savings. Complete the graph so that it shows Yolanda's savings compared to time.

6. Use your graph to find the amount of money Yolanda had left after the trip. _____

[Graph: Y-axis: Yolanda's Savings ($), values 0 to 800 in increments of 100. X-axis: Time.]

LESSON 6-4

Analyzing Graphs
Practice and Problem Solving: D

Use the situation for 1–2. The first one is done for you.

Dan had a glass of water. He added some ice. The graph shows the temperature over time.

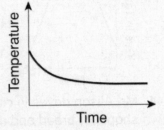

1. The graph goes down at the beginning. What does that mean?

   The water temperature went down after the ice was put in.

   _____

2. What does it mean when the graph flattens out?

   _____

   _____

Tell which graph corresponds to each situation below. The first one is done for you.

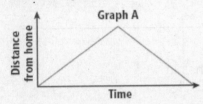
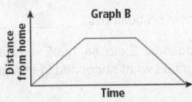
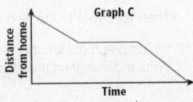

3. Alexia starts from home and jogs to the store. She shops for a while and then jogs home.   **Graph B**

4. Alexia jogs to the store from school. She shops for a while and then jogs home.   _____

5. Which graph did you not choose for Exercise 3 or Exercise 4? Write a description that describes what happened in that graph.

   _____

   _____

Use the graph at the right for 6–7.

6. Talia hiked 4 miles from her house, and stopped to eat lunch. Then she hiked back to where she started. Complete the graph. Show the distance from Talia's house compared to the time that she took.

7. Use your graph to find the total number of miles Talia hiked.

   _____

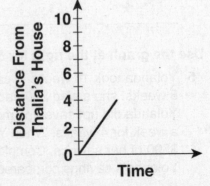

Original content Copyright © by Houghton Mifflin Harcourt. Additions and changes to the original content are the responsibility of the instructor.

LESSON 6-4

Analyzing Graphs
Reteach

Graphs are often used to model situations. This graph shows Shavawn's daily jogging routine. She jogs uphill at a steady speed. When she starts to run downhill, her speed increases.

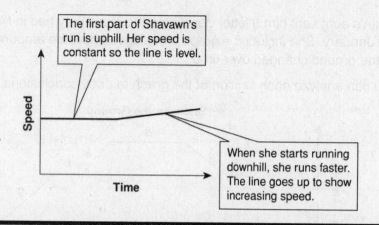

The first part of Shavawn's run is uphill. Her speed is constant so the line is level.

When she starts running downhill, she runs faster. The line goes up to show increasing speed.

You have a savings account in a bank. The graphs below show how the amount in your account changes. Describe what each graph shows.

1.

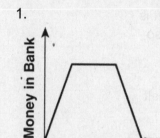

_____

_____

_____

2.

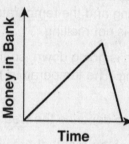

_____

_____

_____

Complete the graph for each situation.

3. Mr. Wyatt drives for a while at a steady speed. A traffic jam slows him down. Then he resumes his normal speed.

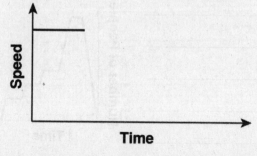

4. You are watching television. You turn down the volume during a commercial. You turn the volume back up after the commercial.

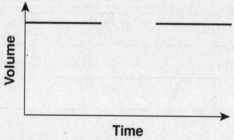

Analyzing Graphs

Reading Strategies: Draw Conclusions

Aiden's aunt sent him a letter describing the snow they had in Minnesota last January. She included a graph that showed how the amount of snow on the ground changed over time.

You can analyze each section of the graph to draw conclusions.

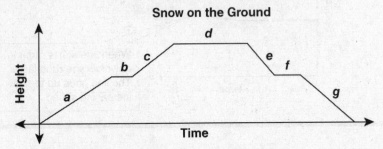

Snow on the Ground

Parts a and c: The graph is going up, so the height of snow is increasing. It must be snowing.

Parts b, d, and f: The graph is horizontal, so the height is not changing. It is not snowing and the temperature is staying cold enough so the snow is not melting.

Parts e and g: The graph is going down, so the height of the snow is decreasing. The temperature must be warm enough to melt the snow.

You use what you know to describe the weather in Minnesota last January.

> At the beginning of the month there was no snow on the ground. There were two snowstorms in the first half of the month. The temperature stayed cold for two-thirds of the month. Toward the end of January the weather warmed up and the snow was gone by the end of the month.

Analyze the graph below. Explain what each part of the graph shows. Then describe how the number of people at the amusement park on Monday changed over time.

_____

_____

_____

_____

_____

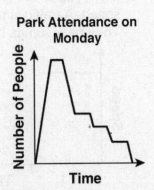

LESSON 6-4

Analyzing Graphs
Success for English Learners

Graphs can model what happens in real-life situations.

Problem 1

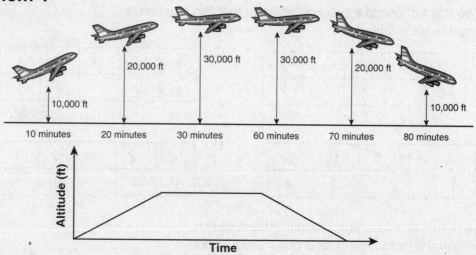

Problem 2

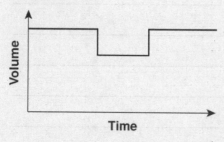

The graph at the left could model the situation of watching a television program, turning down the volume for a commercial, and then turning the volume back up for the rest of the program.

Use the graph at the right to answer each question.

1. What does the graph represent?

_____

_____

2. How long did it take the plane to reach its maximum altitude?

_____

3. What does the part of the line with a negative slope represent?

_____

_____

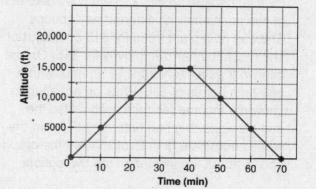

Name _____ Date _____ Class_____

Functions
Challenge

Solve.

1. Each table represents some values of a function. If the slope
   between two pairs of points are equal, assume that the function is
   linear. Complete each table.

A

x	−2	−1	0	1	2
y	−5		1		7

C

x	−2	−1	0	1	2
y	2		0	1	

B

x	−2	−1	0	1	2
y	4			−2	−4

D

x	−2	−1	0	1	2
y	4		0	1	

Describe each function as a proportional linear function,
a nonproportional linear function, or a nonlinear function.
Explain how you decided.

_____

_____

_____

_____

_____

2. Sasha just accepted a short-term job working
   for a landscape architect. Sasha can take either
   of two positions with different pay options.
   She can help plant trees for $15 an hour, but
   she must buy her own gloves for $18. Or she
   can work as a cashier for $9 an hour with a
   one-time bonus of $30. Write an equation to
   show the income for each option. Use the
   grid provided to graph both equations on the
   same coordinate grid. Explain what the graph
   shows about the income of the two options.

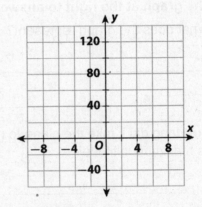

_____

_____

_____

_____

LESSON 7-1

Equations with the Variable on Both Sides
Practice and Problem Solving: A/B

Use algebra tiles to model and solve each equation.

1. $x + 3 = -x - 5$

2. $1 - 2x = -x - 3$

3. $x - 2 = -3x + 2$

_____   _____   _____

Fill in the boxes to solve each equation.

4. $4a - 3 = 2a + 7$
   $\underline{-2a \qquad -[\ ]}$
   $2a - 3 = 7$
   $\underline{+[\ ] \quad +3}$
   $2a = [\ ]$
   $\dfrac{2a}{[\ ]} = \dfrac{10}{[\ ]}$
   $a = [\ ]$

5. $7x - 1 = 2x + 5$
   $\underline{-[\ ] \qquad -2x}$
   $5x - 1 = [\ ]$
   $\underline{+[\ ] \quad +1}$
   $5x = [\ ]$
   $\dfrac{5x}{[\ ]} = \dfrac{6}{[\ ]}$
   $x = [\ ]$

6. $-3r + 9 = -4r + 5$
   $\underline{+[\ ] \qquad +4r}$
   $r + 9 = 5$
   $\underline{-[\ ] \quad -9}$
   $r = [\ ]$

Solve.

7. $3y + 1 = 4y - 6$

8. $2 + 6x = 1 - x$

9. $5y + 4 = 4y + 5$

_____   _____   _____

Write an equation to represent each relationship. Then solve the equation.

10. Ten less than 3 times a number is the same as the number plus 4.

_____

11. Six times a number plus 4 is the same as the number minus 11.

_____

12. Fifteen more than twice the hours Carla worked last week is the same as three times the hours she worked this week decreased by 15. She worked the same number of hours each week. How many hours did she work each week?

_____

LESSON 7-1

Equations with the Variable on Both Sides
Practice and Problem Solving: C

Solve.

1. $-v + 5 + 4v = 1 + 5v + 3$

2. $15 - x = 2(x + 3)$

3. $5(r - 1) = 2(r - 4) - 6$

_____ _____ _____

4. $6m - 11 = 2 + 9m - 1$

5. $4(3x - 1) = 3 + 8x - 11$

6. $-2(t + 2) + 5t = 6t + 11$

_____ _____ _____

Write an equation to represent each relationship. Then solve.

7. Twelve decreased by twice a number is the same as 8 times the sum of the number plus 4. What is the number?

8. Three added to 8 times a number is the same as 3 times the value of 2 times the number minus 1. What is the number?

_____ _____

9. Company A offers a starting salary of $28,000 with a raise of $3,000 each year. Company B offers a starting salary of $36,000 with a raise of $2,000 per year. Company C offers a starting salary of $18,000. After how many years would the salaries for Companies A and B be the same? How much of a raise per year would Company C have to offer to equal the salaries of Companies A and B in the year in which the salaries of those two companies are the same?

_____

_____

Write a real-world situation that could be modeled by the equation. Then solve for the unknown in the situation.

10. $60 + 25x = 35x + 20$

_____

_____

_____

_____

LESSON 7-1

Equations with the Variable on Both Sides

Practice and Problem Solving: D

Use algebra tiles to model and solve each equation. The first one is done for you.

1. $x + 2 = 2x - 1$

$$x = 3$$

2. $2x - 1 = x - 3$

Fill in the boxes to solve each equation. The first one is done for you.

3.
$$7y + 1 = 3y + 13$$
$$-[3y] \quad -3y$$
$$\overline{\quad 4y + 1 = 13 \quad}$$
$$-1 \quad -[1]$$
$$\overline{\quad 4y = [12] \quad}$$
$$\frac{4y}{4} = \frac{12}{[4]}$$
$$y = [3]$$

4.
$$4w + 3 = 2w + 7$$
$$-[\quad] \quad -2w$$
$$\overline{\quad 2w + 3 = 7 \quad}$$
$$-3 \quad -[\quad]$$
$$\overline{\quad 2w = [\quad] \quad}$$
$$\frac{2w}{2} = \frac{4}{[\quad]}$$
$$w = [\quad]$$

5.
$$-2r + 4 = -3r + 9$$
$$+[\quad] \quad +3r$$
$$\overline{\quad r + 4 = 9 \quad}$$
$$-[\quad] \quad -4$$
$$\overline{\quad r = [\quad] \quad}$$

Solve. The first one is done for you.

6.
$$2y + 1 = 3y - 5$$
$$-2y \quad -2y$$
$$\overline{\quad 1 = y - 5 \quad}$$
$$+5 \quad +5$$
$$\overline{\quad 6 = y \quad}$$

$$y = 6$$

7. $4x + 6 = -x + 1$

8. $-2y + 3 = 8y - 7$

Write an equation to represent each relationship. Then solve the equation. The first one is done for you.

9. Four times a number minus 5 is the same as twice the number plus 3.

$$4n - 5 = 2n + 3; \; n = 4$$

10. Seven minus 2 times a number is the same as the number minus 2.

LESSON 7-1

Equations with the Variable on Both Sides
Reteach

If there are variable terms on both sides of an equation, first collect them on one side. Do this by adding or subtracting. When possible, collect the variables on the side of the equation where the coefficient will be positive.

Solve the equation $5x = 2x + 12$. $\begin{aligned} 5x &= 2x + 12 \\ \underline{-2x \quad -2x} \\ 3x &= \quad\quad 12 \\ \dfrac{3x}{3} &= \dfrac{12}{3} \\ x &= 4 \end{aligned}$	To collect on left side, subtract $2x$ from both sides of the equation. Divide by 3.	**Check:** Substitute into the original equation. $5x = 2x + 12$ $5(4) \stackrel{?}{=} 2(4) + 12$ $20 \stackrel{?}{=} 8 + 12$ $20 = 20$
Solve the equation $-6z + 28 = 9z - 2$ $\begin{aligned} -6z + 28 &= 9z - 2 \\ \underline{+6z \quad\quad +6z} \\ 28 &= 15z - 2 \\ \underline{+2 \quad\quad +2} \\ 30 &= 15z \\ \dfrac{30}{15} &= \dfrac{15z}{15} \\ 2 &= z \end{aligned}$	To collect on right side, add $6z$ to both sides of the equation. Add 2 to both sides of the equation. Divide by 15.	**Check:** Substitute into the original equation. $-6z + 28 = 9z - 2$ $-6(2) + 28 \stackrel{?}{=} 9(2) - 2$ $-12 + 28 \stackrel{?}{=} 18 - 2$ $16 = 16$

Complete to solve and check each equation.

1. $9m + 2 = 3m - 10$

$\begin{aligned} 9m + 2 &= 3m - 10 \\ \underline{-[\ ] \quad\quad -[\ ]} \\ 6m + 2 &= \quad\quad -10 \\ \underline{-[\ ] \quad\quad -[\ ]} \\ 6m &= \quad [\ \ ] \\ \dfrac{6m}{[\ ]} &= \dfrac{-12}{[\ ]} \\ m &= [\ ] \end{aligned}$

To collect on left side, subtract ____ from both sides.

Subtract ____ from both sides.

Divide by ____.

Check: Substitute into the original equation.

$9m + 2 = 3m - 10$
$9(\underline{\ \ \ }) + 2 \stackrel{?}{=} 3(\underline{\ \ \ }) - 10$
$\underline{\ \ \ } + 2 \stackrel{?}{=} \underline{\ \ \ } - 10$
$\underline{\ \ \ } = \underline{\ \ \ }$

2. $-7d - 22 = 4d$

$\begin{aligned} -7d - 22 &= 4d \\ \underline{+[\ ] \quad\quad +[\ ]} \\ -22 &= 11d \\ \dfrac{-22}{[\ ]} &= \dfrac{11d}{[\ ]} \\ [\ \ ] &= d \end{aligned}$

To collect on right side, add ____ to both sides.

Divide by ____.

Check: Substitute into the original equation.
$-7d - 22 = 4d$
$-7(\underline{\ \ \ }) - 22 \stackrel{?}{=} 4(\underline{\ \ \ })$
$\underline{\ \ \ } - 22 \stackrel{?}{=} \underline{\ \ \ }$
$\underline{\ \ \ } = \underline{\ \ \ }$

LESSON 7-1 Equations with the Variable on Both Sides
Reading Strategies: Follow a Procedure

Equations may have variables on both sides. Follow these steps to get the variables on one side of the equation.

> Solve $6x - 7 = 2x + 5$.

Step 1: Get all variables on one side of the equation.

$$6x - 7 = 2x + 5$$
$$\underline{-2x \qquad\qquad -2x}$$
Subtract 2x from both sides.
$$4x - 7 = \qquad 5$$

Step 2: Get all constants on the other side of the equation.

$$\underline{+7 \qquad\qquad +7}$$
Add 7 to both sides.
$$4x \qquad = \qquad 12$$

Step 3: Solve.

$$\frac{4x}{4} = \frac{12}{4}$$
Divide both sides by 4.
$$x = 3$$

Use the above procedure to answer each question.

1. What is the first step to solve equations with variables on both sides?

   _____

2. What was done to get the variables on one side?

   _____

3. Write the equation with the variables on one side only.

   _____

4. What is the second step in solving the equation?

   _____

5. What was done to get the constants on one side?

   _____

6. What was the last step to solve the equation?

   _____

LESSON 7-1

Equations with the Variable on Both Sides

Success for English Learners

Problem 1

On <u>Monday</u> Elaine ran <u>5 miles and 3 laps</u> around a trail. On <u>Tuesday</u> she ran <u>6 miles and 2 laps</u> around a trail. She ran the <u>same distance both days</u>. How many miles long is one lap around the trail?

What information is given?

Monday's distance: **5 miles + 3 laps** Tuesday's distance: **6 miles + 2 laps**

Monday's **distance** = Tuesday's **distance**

x is the length in miles of one lap around the trail.

Write an equation: $5 + 3x = 6 + 2x$

Solve the equation:

$5 + 3x = 6 + 2x$	Get all variables on one side.
$\underline{\quad -2x \quad\quad -2x}$	Subtract 2x.
$5 + x = 6$	Get all constants on one side.
$\underline{-5 \quad\quad -5}$	Subtract 5.
$x = 1$	One lap is 1 mile long.

Solve.

1. Why should the length of the trail be the variable?

   _____

2. What do 2x and 3x represent?

   _____

3. To solve for the variable, what must all be together on one side of the equation?

   _____

4. Write a real-world situation that could be modeled by the equation $8 + 2x = 6x$. Then solve the problem.

   _____

   _____

   _____

LESSON 7-2

Equations with Rational Numbers

Practice and Problem Solving: A/B

Write the least common multiple of the denominators in the equation.

1. $9 + \dfrac{3}{4}x = \dfrac{7}{8}x - 10$ _____

2. $\dfrac{2}{3}x + \dfrac{1}{6} = -\dfrac{3}{4}x + 1$ _____

Describe the operations used to solve the equation.

3. $\dfrac{5}{6}x - 2 = -\dfrac{2}{3}x + 1$

$$6\left(\dfrac{5}{6}x - 2\right) = 6\left(-\dfrac{2}{3}x + 1\right)$$ _____

$$5x - 12 = -4x + 6$$ _____

$$\begin{array}{c} +4x \qquad\qquad +4x \\ \hline 9x - 12 = \qquad\quad 6 \end{array}$$ _____

$$\begin{array}{c} +12 \qquad +12 \\ \hline 9x = 18 \end{array}$$ _____

$$\dfrac{9x}{9} = \dfrac{18}{9}$$

$$x = 2$$

Solve.

4. $\dfrac{2}{3}x + \dfrac{1}{3} = \dfrac{1}{3}x + \dfrac{2}{3}$

_____

5. $\dfrac{3}{5}n + \dfrac{9}{10} = -\dfrac{1}{5}n - \dfrac{23}{10}$

_____

6. $\dfrac{5}{6}h - \dfrac{7}{12} = -\dfrac{3}{4}h - \dfrac{13}{6}$

_____

7. $4.5w = 5.1w - 30$

_____

8. $\dfrac{4}{7}y - 2 = \dfrac{3}{7}y + \dfrac{3}{14}$

_____

9. $-0.8a - 8 = 0.2a$

_____

10. Write and solve a real-world problem that can be modeled by the equation $0.75x - 18.50 = 0.65x$.

_____

_____

_____

LESSON
7-2
Equations with Rational Numbers
Practice and Problem Solving: C

Solve.

1. $-\dfrac{2}{3}(x+2)=\dfrac{1}{6}(x+6)$

2. $0.15-0.2x=0.3(x+3)$

3. $\dfrac{2}{5}(r-2)=\dfrac{3}{20}(r-4)$

_____

_____

_____

4. $\dfrac{1}{3}\left(x+\dfrac{2}{3}\right)=\dfrac{1}{6}(x-4)$

5. $0.4(0.3x-1)=2+0.75x$

6. $-\dfrac{1}{2}(t+9)+5\dfrac{3}{4}t=\dfrac{3}{8}t$

_____

_____

_____

Answer each of the following.

7. If $4\left(x-\dfrac{2}{3}\right)=-18$, what is the value of $2x$?

8. If $0.9x-1.3=-3.1$, what is the value of $x-0.8$?

_____

_____

9. Nikos sold muffins at his club's bake sale. He spent $28.50 on supplies. He sold his muffins for $0.75 each, and made a profit of $36.75. Write and solve an equation to find out how many muffins Nikos sold.

_____

_____

Write a real-world situation that could be modeled by the equation. Then solve for the unknown in the situation.

10. $3+\dfrac{2}{3}x=\dfrac{5}{6}x-\dfrac{7}{8}$

_____

_____

_____

LESSON 7-2

Equations with Rational Numbers

Practice and Problem Solving: D

Write the least common multiple of the denominators in the equation. The first one is done for you.

1. $6 + \dfrac{3}{4}x = \dfrac{1}{2}x - 4$ _____**4**_____

2. $\dfrac{2}{3}x + \dfrac{1}{6} = -3x + 4$ _____

Describe the operations used to solve the equation. The first one is done for you.

3. $\dfrac{7}{10}x - 2 = \dfrac{2}{5}x + 1$

$10\left(\dfrac{7}{10}x - 2\right) = 10\left(\dfrac{2}{5}x + 1\right)$ **Multiply both sides by the LCM of 10 and 5,**

$7x - 20 = 4x + 10$ **which is 10. Simplify.**

$\begin{array}{ll} \underline{-4x \qquad\quad -4x} & \text{_____} \\ 3x - 20 = \qquad 10 & \text{_____} \\ \underline{+20 \qquad\qquad +20} & \text{_____} \\ 3x \quad = \qquad 30 & \text{_____} \\ \dfrac{3x}{3} = \dfrac{30}{3} & \text{_____} \\ x = 10 \end{array}$

Solve. The first one is done for you.

4. $\dfrac{7}{9} + n = 3n + \dfrac{1}{9}$

$7 + 9n = 27n + 1$
$7 = 18n + 1$
$6 = 18n$
$n = \dfrac{1}{3}$

5. $\dfrac{1}{4} - \dfrac{1}{2}r = -\dfrac{3}{4}r$

6. $12.5 - 4g = -2g - 3.5$

_____   _____   _____

LESSON 7-2

Equations with Rational Numbers

Reteach

To solve an equation with a variable on both sides that involves fractions, first get rid of the fractions.

Solve $\dfrac{3}{4}m + 2 = \dfrac{2}{3}m + 5$.

$$12\left(\dfrac{3}{4}m + 2\right) = 12\left(\dfrac{2}{3}m + 5\right)$$

$$12\left(\dfrac{3}{4}m\right) + 12(2) = 12\left(\dfrac{2}{3}m\right) + 12(5)$$

$$\begin{array}{rcl} 9m + 24 &=& 8m + 60 \\ -8m \quad\quad & & -8m \\ \hline m + 24 &=& 60 \\ -24 & & -24 \\ \hline m &=& 36 \end{array}$$

Multiply both sides of the equation by 12, the LCM of 4 and 3.

Multiply each term by 12.

Simplify.
Subtract 8*m* from both sides.
Simplify.
Subtract 24 from both sides.
Simplify.

Check: Substitute into the original equation.

$$\dfrac{3}{4}m + 2 = \dfrac{2}{3}m + 5$$

$$\dfrac{3}{4}(36) + 2 \overset{?}{=} \dfrac{2}{3}(36) + 5$$

$$27 + 2 \overset{?}{=} 24 + 5$$

$$29 = 29$$

Complete to solve and check your answer.

1. $\dfrac{1}{4}x + 2 = \dfrac{2}{5}x - 1$

$$[\;\;]\left(\dfrac{1}{4}x + 2\right) = [\;\;]\left(\dfrac{2}{5}x - 1\right)$$

$$[\;\;]\left(\dfrac{1}{4}x\right) + [\;\;](2) = [\;\;]\left(\dfrac{2}{5}x\right) - [\;\;](1)$$

$$\begin{array}{rcl} [\;\;]x + [\;\;] &=& [\;\;]x - [\;\;] \\ -5x & & -5x \\ \hline 40 &=& 3x - 20 \\ +20 & & +20 \\ \hline [\;\;] &=& 3x \end{array}$$

$$\dfrac{60}{[\;\;]} = \dfrac{3x}{[\;\;]}$$

$$[\;\;] = x$$

Multiply both sides of the equation by ____ the LCM of 4 and 5.

Multiply each term by____.

Simplify.

Subtract ____.

Simplify.

Add____.

Simplify.

Divide both sides by

_____

Simplify.

Check: Substitute into the original equation.

$$\dfrac{1}{4}x + 2 = \dfrac{2}{5}x - 1$$

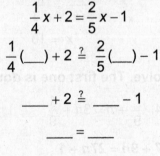

$$\dfrac{1}{4}(\_\_\_) + 2 \overset{?}{=} \dfrac{2}{5}(\_\_\_) - 1$$

$$\_\_\_ + 2 \overset{?}{=} \_\_\_ - 1$$

$$\_\_\_ = \_\_\_$$

LESSON 7-2

Equations with Rational Numbers
Reading Strategies: Use a Sequence Chain

Use the sequence chain below to guide you in solving equations with
rational numbers.

Are there fractions or decimals in the equation?

If fractions, multiply every term by the LCM.

If decimals, multiply every term by the same power of 10 to clear the decimals.

Are there variables on both sides of the = sign?

If yes, add or subtract to get them on one side.

Is a number being added or subtracted from the variable?

If yes, do the opposite to both sides.

Is the variable multiplied or divided by a number?

If yes, do the opposite to both sides.

Does your answer check using substitution?

If yes, you are done! If no, try again.

Answer each question.

1. When an equation contains fractions, what should you do before getting the variables together on one side?

   _____

2. When an equation contains decimals, what should you do before getting the variables together on one side?

   _____

Solve each equation using the sequence chain.

3. $\dfrac{3}{8}x - 4 = \dfrac{1}{8}x - 5$

4. $0.8 + 0.8k = 0.6k + 0.9$

5. $\dfrac{1}{3}y + 1 = \dfrac{1}{2}y - 3$

   _____

LESSON 7-2

Equations with Rational Numbers

Success for English Learners

Problem 1

Solve $2 + \dfrac{2}{5}x = \dfrac{3}{8}x - 1$.

How can I make this equation simpler?

Eliminate the fractions.

LCM (5, 8) = 40

$$40\left(2 + \frac{2}{5}x\right) = 40\left(\frac{3}{8}x - 1\right)$$

$$40(2) + \overset{8}{4\,0}\left(\frac{2}{5}x\right) = \overset{5}{4\,0}\left(\frac{3}{8}x\right) - 40(1)$$

$$80 + 16x = 15x - 40$$

The fractions are gone!

Problem 2

Solve $0.4x = 0.375x + 1$.

How can I make this equation simpler?

Multiplying by 1,000 clears the decimals.

Clear the decimals.

$$1000(0.4x) = 1{,}000(0.375x + 1)$$

$$1000(0.4x) = 1{,}000(0.375x) + 1{,}000(1)$$

$$400x = 375x + 1{,}000$$

The decimals are gone!

Solve.

1. Explain how you would solve the equation, $80 + 16x = 15x - 40$, in Problem 1. Then solve for x.

   _____

2. Write a real-world situation that could be modeled by the equation, $0.4x = 0.375x + 1$, in Problem 2. Then solve for x.

   _____

   _____

   _____

3. When an equation has fractions with denominators of 2, 3, and 4, what can you multiply the equation by to eliminate the fractions?

   _____

4. When an equation has decimals that are in tenths and hundredths, what can you multiply the equation by to clear the decimals?

   _____

LESSON 7-3

Equations with the Distributive Property
Practice and Problem Solving: A/B

Solve each equation.

1. $4(x - 2) = x + 10$

2. $\frac{2}{3}(n - 6) = 5n - 43$

_____

_____

3. $-2(y + 12) = y - 9$

4. $8(12 - k) = 3(k + 21)$

_____

_____

5. $8(-1 + m) + 3 = 2\left(m - 5\frac{1}{2}\right)$

6. $2y - 3(2y - 3) + 2 = 31$

_____

_____

Use the situation below to complete Exercises 7–8.

A taxi company charges $2.25 for the first mile and then $0.20 per mile for each additional mile, or $F = \$2.25 + \$0.20(m - 1)$ where F is the fare and m is the number of miles.

7. If Juan's taxi fare was $6.05, how many miles did he travel in the taxi?

_____

8. If Juan's taxi fare was $7.65, how many miles did he travel in the taxi?

_____

Use the situation below to complete Exercises 9–11.

The equation used to estimate typing speed is $S = \frac{1}{5}(w - 10e)$, where S is the accurate typing speed, w is the number of words typed in 5 minutes and e is the number of errors.

9. Ignacio can type 55 words per minute (wpm). In 5 minutes, she types 285 words. How many errors would you expect her to make?

_____

10. If Alexis types 300 words in 5 minutes with 5 errors, what is his typing speed?

_____

11. Johanna receives a report that says her typing speed is 65 words per minute. She knows that she made 4 errors in the 5-minute test. How many words did she type in 5 minutes?

_____

LESSON 7-3

Equations with the Distributive Property

Practice and Problem Solving: C

Solve each equation.

1. $2(x - 1) = x + 4$

2. $3(n - 6) = -5n - 2$

_____

3. $-2(y - 5) = y + 1$

4. $8(8 - k) = -2(k - 5)$

_____

5. $2\left(-4\dfrac{1}{2} + m\right) + 3 = 4(m - 3) + 5\dfrac{1}{2}$

6. $0.5(x - 12) + 2 = 1.25(x + 8) - 9.5$

_____

Write and solve an equation to find each solution.

7. One bag of trail mix has 5 ounces of raisins and some almonds. Lon buys 3 bags of trail mix and has 48 ounces of trail mix altogether. How many ounces of almonds are in each bag of trail mix?

_____

8. A moving van charges a flat rate of $25 per day plus $0.12 per mile for every mile over 100 driven. If Millie's bill was $29.46 how many miles to the nearest mile did she drive in all?

_____

9. Benjamin is 4 years younger than Kevan. William is 4 years less than twice Benjamin's age. If William is 22, how old are Kevan and Benjamin?

_____

10. A taxi company charges $2 for the first mile and then $0.25 per mile for each additional mile. If Lupita's fare was $4.50, how many miles did she travel in the taxi?

_____

11. Parker has quarters and dimes in his piggy bank. He has 4 more dimes than quarters, and he has a total of $7.05 in his bank. How many dimes and quarters does Parker have?

_____

Equations with the Distributive Property

LESSON 7-3

Practice and Problem Solving: D

Solve each equation. The first one has been done for you.

1. $2(x - 5) = 10$

   $x = 10$ _____

2. $3(n - 6) = 27$

   _____

3. $9(4 - s) = 10 + 4s$

   _____

4. $8(2 - p) = 24p$

   _____

5. $-2(y - 3) = y + 24$

   _____

6. $8(8 - k) = -72k$

   _____

7. $-3(12 - m) = -1(m - 8)$

   _____

8. $10(2 + x) = 15(x - 1) + 5$

   _____

Answer each question to solve the problem. The first one is done for you.

9. Kevan is 6 years younger than his sister Katie. Melanie is twice as old as Kevan. How old are all three siblings?

   a. If you let *k* represent Katie's current age, what expression can you use to represent Kevan's current age?

   k – 6 _____

   b. Based on your answer to part a, what expression represents Melanie's age?

   _____

   c. If Melanie is 18 years old, what equation can you write to solve the problem?

   _____

   d. Solve the equation. How old are Kevan and Katie?

   _____

Name _____ Date _____ Class _____

Equations with the Distributive Property

Reteach

When solving an equation, it is important to simplify on both sides of the equal sign before you try to isolate the variable.

$3(x + 4) + 2 = x + 10$	Since you cannot combine x and 4, multiply both by 3 using the Distributive Property.
$3x + 12 + 2 = x + 10$	Then combine like terms.
$3x + 14 = x + 10$	Subtract 14 to begin to isolate the variable term.
$\underline{-14 \qquad -14}$	
$3x = x - 4$	Subtract x to get the variables to one side of the equation.
$\underline{-x \quad -x}$	
$\dfrac{2x}{2} = \dfrac{-4}{2}$	Divide by 2 to isolate the variable.
$x = -2$	The solution is -2.

Solve.

1. $5(i + 2) - 9 = -17 - i$

2. $-3(n + 2) = n - 22$

_____

You may need to distribute on both sides of the equal sign before simplifying.

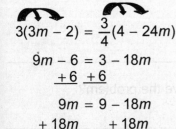

$3(3m - 2) = \dfrac{3}{4}(4 - 24m)$	Use the Distributive Property on both sides of the equation to remove the parentheses.
$9m - 6 = 3 - 18m$	
$\underline{+6 \quad +6}$	Add 6 to begin to isolate the variable term.
$9m = 9 - 18m$	Add $18m$ to get the variables to one side of the equation.
$\underline{+18m \qquad +18m}$	
$\dfrac{27m}{27} = \dfrac{9}{27}$	Divide by 27 to isolate the variable.
$m = \dfrac{1}{3}$	The solution is $\dfrac{1}{3}$.

Solve.

3. $9(y - 4) = -10\left(y + 2\dfrac{1}{3}\right)$

4. $-7\left(-6 - \dfrac{6}{7}x\right) = 12\left(x - 3\dfrac{1}{2}\right)$

_____

LESSON 7-3

Equations with the Distributive Property

Reading Strategies: Follow a Procedure

Use the steps below to understand the procedure for solving equations using the distributive property.

Solve $2(x + 5) + 3 = 4(x + 2) - 11$.

$$2(x + 5) + 3 = 4(x + 2) - 11$$
$$2x + 10 + 3 = 4x + 8 - 11$$
$$2x + 10 + 3 = 4x + 8 - 11$$
$$2x + 13 = 4x - 3$$
$$\underline{-13 \qquad -13}$$
$$2x = 4x - 16$$
$$\underline{-4x \quad -4x}$$
$$\frac{-2x}{-2} = \frac{-16}{-2}$$
$$x = 8$$

1. Use the Distributive Property.

2. Identify and combine like terms.

3. "Undo" addition to isolate the variable term.

4. "Undo" multiplication to isolate the variable.

Solve each equation using the procedure shown. Show all your steps.

1. $-4(j + 2) - 3j = 6$

2. $4n + 6 - 2n = 3(n + 3) - 11$

3. $5(r - 1) = 2(r - 4) - 6$

4. $2\left(n + \dfrac{1}{3}\right) = \dfrac{3}{2}n + 1$

LESSON 7-3

Equations with the Distributive Property
Success for English Learners

Problem 1

| Distribute on both sides. | $3\left(q + \dfrac{1}{2}\right) = 4(q + 2) - 2\dfrac{1}{2}$ |

THINK: 8 and $-2\dfrac{1}{2}$ are like terms.

| Combine like terms. | $3q + 1\dfrac{1}{2} = 4q \boxed{+ 8} \boxed{- 2\dfrac{1}{2}}$ |

$3q + 1\dfrac{1}{2} = 4q + 5\dfrac{1}{2}$

$\quad\quad -1\dfrac{1}{2} \quad\quad\quad -1\dfrac{1}{2}$

THINK: I need the q terms on one side of the equation.

$3q = 4q + 4$
$-4q \quad -4q$

$\dfrac{-q}{-1} = \dfrac{4}{-1}$

$q = -4$

Problem 2

Geri has exactly $3 in dimes and nickels. She has 9 more dimes than nickels. How many of each coin does Geri have?

*Let **n*** = the number of nickels.   × n = value of the nickels

There are 9 more dimes than nickels.

The number of dimes = n + 9   × (n + 9) = value of the dimes

Equation: value of the nickels + value of the dimes = $3

$\quad .05n \quad\quad + \quad\quad 0.10(n + 9) \quad = 3$

$0.05n + 0.10(n + 9) = 3$

$0.05n + 0.10n + 0.9 = 3$

$0.15n + 0.9 = 3$

$0.15n = 2.1$

$n = 14$

Geri has 14 nickels and 14 + 9 or 23 dimes.

Solve.

1. $-1(x + 8) + 3 = x - 15$

2. Portia has 9 more pennies than quarters. Altogether she has $2.95 in pennies and quarters. How many of each coin does Portia have?

_____   _____

Equations with Many Solutions or No Solution

LESSON 7-4

Practice and Problem Solving: A/B

Tell whether each equation has one, zero, or infinitely many solutions. If the equation has one solution, solve the equation.

1. $4(x-2) = 4x + 10$

2. $\frac{1}{2}n + 7 = \frac{n+14}{2}$

3. $6(x-1) = 6x-1$

4. $6n + 7 - 2n - 14 = 5n + 1$

5. $4x + 5 = 9 + 4x$

6. $\frac{1}{2}(8-x) = \frac{8-x}{2}$

7. $8(y + 4) = 7y + 38$

8. $4(-8x + 12) = -26 - 32x$

9. $2(x + 12) = 3x + 24 - x$

10. $3x - 14 + 2(x - 9) = 2x - 2$

Solve.

11. Cell phone company A charges $20 per month plus $0.05 per text message. Cell phone company B charges $10 per month plus $0.07 per text message. Is there any number of text messages that will result in the exact same charge from both companies?

12. Lisa's pet shop has 2 fish tanks. Tank A contains smaller fish who are fed 1 gram of food each per day. Tank B contains larger fish who are fed 2 grams of food each per day. If Tank B contains $\frac{2}{3}$ the number of fish that Tank A contains, will Lisa ever feed both tanks the same amount of food?

Equations with Many Solutions or No Solution

LESSON 7-4

Practice and Problem Solving: C

Tell whether each equation has one, zero, or infinitely many solutions. If the equation has one solution, solve the equation.

1. $-(2x-1)-2x=4(1-x)$

2. $1=-\dfrac{m-3}{4}+\dfrac{m+3}{5}$

_____

_____

3. $-3(2p+1)+4(2p-3)=2p-15$

4. $6n+7-2n-14=5n+1$

_____

_____

5. $\dfrac{4r+2}{2}+1=r+16$

6. $5(3-m)+10=5(5-m)$

_____

_____

7. $16+\dfrac{1}{4}(x+8)=9(x+2)$

8. $-(q-5)=\dfrac{8q-4}{-4}$

_____

_____

Solve.

9. Latrice and Meagan are collecting coins. Latrice doubled her coin collection the first month, and then added 200 coins to her collection the second month. Meagan added 85 coins to her collection the first week, and then doubled her total the second week. Now Latrice and Meagan have the same number of coins. Did they begin with the same number of coins? Explain.

_____

10. Domingo picks up 5 coins from his collection of quarters and nickels. Is it possible for him to pick up exactly $0.50?

a. Write an equation.

_____

b. Solve the equation.

_____

c. Does the equation have a solution?

_____

d. Does the word problem have a solution?

_____

LESSON 7-4

Equations with Many Solutions or No Solution

Practice and Problem Solving: D

Tell whether each equation has one, zero, or infinitely many solutions. The first one has been done for you. If the equation has one solution, solve the equation.

1. $2x - 1 = 2x + 3$

   zero solutions _____

2. $3(y - 2) = 3y - 6$

   _____

3. $\dfrac{m - 3}{4} = \dfrac{m - 3}{5}$

   _____

4. $6n + 7 - 2n - 14 = 4n + 8$

   _____

5. $4r + 2 = r + 8$

   _____

6. $3m + 8 = 3(4 + m) - 4$

   _____

7. $\dfrac{1}{4}(x + 3) = 4(x + 3)$

   _____

8. $t - 2 = \dfrac{3t}{10} + 5$

   _____

9. $6(d - 4) = 18d$

   _____

10. $2(d + 7) - 1 = \dfrac{8d}{4} + 13$

   _____

Answer each question. Begin with the equation $x = x$. The first one has been done for you.

11. Add the same number to both sides of the equation $x = x$.

   $x + 5 = x + 5$ _____

12. Does your new equation have 0, 1 or many solutions?

   _____

13. Multiply both sides of your new equation by the same number. Be sure to use parentheses to group the sums before multiplying.

   _____

14. Does your new equation have 0, 1 or many solutions?

   _____

15. Use the Distributive Property on one side of your equation so that the two sides look different.

   _____

16. Does your new equation have 0, 1 or many solutions?

   _____

Name _____ Date _____ Class_____

LESSON 7-4

Equations with Many Solutions or No Solution
Reteach

When you solve a linear equation, you are trying to find a value for the variable that makes the equation true. Often there is only one value that makes an equation true – one solution. But sometimes there is no value that will make the equation true. Other times there are many values that make the equation true.

$x + 3 = 8$ $x = 5$	**Use properties of equality to solve.** If you get a statement that tells you what the variable equals, the equation has **one solution**.
$x + 3 = x + 4$ $3 = 4$	If you get a false statement with no variables, the equation has **no solution**.
$x + 3 = x + 3$ $3 = 3$	If you get a true statement with no variables, the equation has **infinitely many solutions**.

Tell whether each equation has one, zero, or infinitely many solutions.

1. $5(i + 2) = 8(i - 1)$

_____

2. $-3(n + 2) = -3n - 6$

_____

You can write an equation with one solution, no solution, or infinitely many solutions.

One solution: Start with a variable on one side and a constant on the other. This is your solution. Add, subtract, multiply or divide both sides of the equation by the same constant(s). Your equation has one solution. **Example:** $3(r + 2) = 30$

No solution: Start with a false statement of equality about two constants, such as $3 = 4$. Now add, subtract, multiply or divide the same variable from both sides. You may then add, subtract, multiply or divide additional constants to both sides. Your equation has no solution. **Example:** $k + 3 = k + 4$

Infinitely many solutions: Start with a true statement of equality about two constants, such as $5 = 5$. Now add, subtract, multiply or divide the same variable from both sides. You may then add, subtract, multiply or divide additional constants to both sides. Your equation has many solutions. **Example:** $5(n - 3) = 5n - 15$

Solve.

3. Write an equation with one solution. _____

4. Write an equation with no solution. _____

5. Write an equation with infinitely many solutions. _____

LESSON 7-4 Equations with Many Solutions or No Solution
Reading Strategies: Compare and Contrast

Compare equations with zero, one, or many solutions.

	One Solution	Zero Solutions	Infinitely Many Solutions
Equation	$3(y + 2) = 30$	$5(2 + c) = 45 + 5c$	$2(v - 2) = 2v - 4$
Use properties of equality	$3y + 6 = 30$ $3y = 24$ $y = 8$	$10 + 5c = 45 + 5c$ $10 = 45$	$2v - 4 = 2v - 4$ $-4 = -4$
End result	one solution	no solution	Infinitely many solutions

Tell whether each equation has 0, 1, or infinitely many solutions.

1. $2p + 8 = 2(p + 4)$

2. $4(t + 8) = 8t + 8 - 4t$

_____   _____

Compare how to write an equation with zero, one, or infinitely many solutions.

	One Solution	Zero Solutions	Infinitely Many Solutions
Begin with	Solution: variable = constant $y = 8$	False statement: constant = constant $2 = 9$	True statement: constant = constant $-2 = -2$
Make a change	$+, -, \times, \div$ by the same number on both sides $y + 2 = 8 + 2$ $y + 2 = 10$	$+, -, \times, \div$ by the same variable on both sides $2 + c = 9 + c$	$+, -, \times, \div$ by the same variable on both sides $v - 2 = v - 2$
Make another change (optional)	$+, -, \times, \div$ by another number on both sides $3(y + 2) = 30$	$+, -, \times, \div$ by the same number on both sides $5(2 + c) = 45 + 5c$	$+, -, \times, \div$ by the same number on both sides $2(v - 2) = 2v - 4$

Solve.

3. Write an equation with one solution. _____

4. Write an equation with no solution. _____

5. Write an equation with many solutions. _____

LESSON 7-4

Equations with Many Solutions or No Solution

Success for English Learners

Problem 1

Write an equation with no solution.

$4 = -2$ | Start with a false statement.

$4y = -2y$ | Add, subtract, multiply, or divide by the same variable on both sides.

$4y + 9 = -2y + 9$ | Add, subtract, multiply, or divide by the same constant on both sides.

1. Write your own equation with no solution. Use at least two operations.

_____

_____

Problem 2

Write an equation with infinitely many solutions.

$9 = 9$ | Start with a true statement.

$9 - r = 9 - r$ | $+, -, \times, \div$ by the same variable on both sides

$2(9 - r) = 18 - 2r$ | $+, -, \times, \div$ by the same constant on both sides

2. Write your own equation with infinitely many solutions. Use at least two operations.

_____

_____

_____

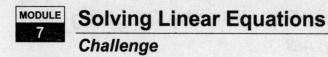

MODULE 7

Solving Linear Equations
Challenge

Use the information to complete Exercises 1–7.

Happy Trails Ranch charges $25.00 for equipment rental plus $8.50 an hour to ride a horse. Rough Riders Ranch charges $20.75 for equipment rental plus $9.75 an hour to ride.

1. Which is the better deal if a customer plans on riding for 2.5 hours? Show your work.

   _____

   _____

2. When would the two ranches charge the same amount? Show your work.

   _____

   _____

3. Rewrite your equation from Exercise 2 using the Distributive Property and 5 as a factor. Solve.

   _____

   _____

4. How many solutions are there to $25.00 + 8.50x = 5(5 + 1.7x)$? Explain your answer.

   _____

   _____

5. Tina started riding at noon at Happy Trails and rode for 3.4 hours. At what time did she finish her ride? What did her ride cost?

   _____

6. Pierre rode for 3.4 hours at Rough Riders. Without doing any computation can you tell how much his ride cost? Explain your reasoning.

   _____

7. If a customer planned on riding for 5 hours, at which ranch would he or she get the better deal? Explain.

   _____

   _____

LESSON 8-1

Solving Systems of Linear Equations by Graphing

Practice and Problem Solving: A/B

Solve each linear system by graphing. Check your answer.

1. $y = -1$
   $y = 2x - 7$

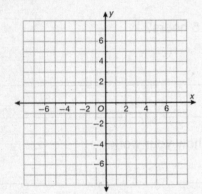

2. $x - y = 6$
   $2x = 12 + 2y$

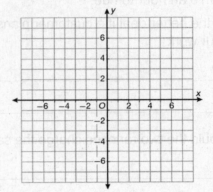

3. $\frac{1}{2} x - y = 4$
   $2y = x + 6$

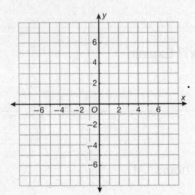

4. $y = 4x - 3$
   $2y - 3x = 4$

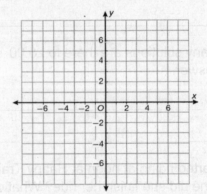

5. Two skaters are racing toward the finish line of a race. The first skater has a 40 meter lead and is traveling at a rate of 12 meters per second. The second skater is traveling at a rate of 14 meters per second. How long will it take for the second skater to pass the first skater?

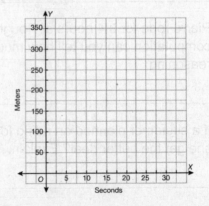

LESSON 8-1

Solving Systems of Linear Equations by Graphing

Practice and Problem Solving: C

Use the information below to complete Exercises 1–4.

Kelly needs to order lunch for orders 6 people at a business meeting. Her menu choices are chicken salad for a cost of $5 per person and egg salad for a cost of $4 per person. She only has $28 to spend. More people want chicken salad.

1. Write and graph one equation in a system for this situation. _____

2. Write a second equation in the system. Graph it on the same grid.

   _____

3. What do *x* and *y* represent?

   _____

   _____

4. How many of each type of lunch can she order?

   _____

   _____

Graph the lines for the two sets of linear data. Find the intersection of the lines.

5.

x	y
−2	0
0	1
2	2
4	3

x	y
−2	−1.5
0	−3.5
2	−5.5
4	−7.5

_____

6. A softball team bought a box of sweatshirts for $240. Each sweatshirt cost $12 to print and will sell for $18. Graph a system of equations to find the number of sweatshirts the softball team needs to sell in order to break even.

_____

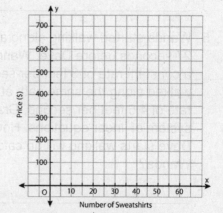

Price ($)

Number of Sweatshirts

LESSON 8-1
Solving Systems of Linear Equations by Graphing

Practice and Problem Solving: D

Solve each linear system by graphing. Check your answer. The first one is done for you.

1. $y = x + 3$
   $y = -2x + 6$

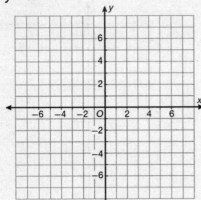

_____ **(1, 4)**

2. $3x = y$
   $y = 2x + 2$

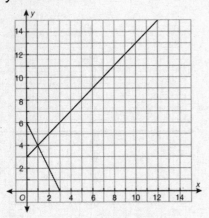

_____

3. $x = 3y$
   $y = x - 4$

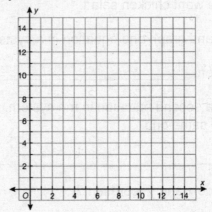

_____

4. $y = 5x - 4$
   $y - 5x = 1$

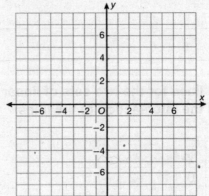

_____

5. Wanda started walking along a path 27 seconds before Dave. Wanda walked at a constant rate of 3 feet per second. Dave walked along the same path at a constant rate of 4.5 feet per second. Graph the system of linear equations. How long after Dave starts walking will he catch up with Wanda?

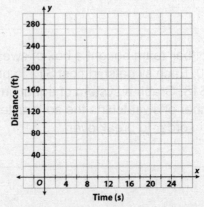

_____

LESSON 8-1
Solving Systems of Linear Equations by Graphing
Reteach

When solving a system of linear equations by graphing, first write each equation in slope-intercept form. Do this by solving each equation for y.

Solve the following system of equations by graphing.

$y = -2x + 3$
$y + 4x = -1$

The first equation is already solved for y.

Write the second equation in slope-intercept form. Solve for y.

$y + 4x - 4x = -1 - 4x$

$y = -4x - 1$

Graph both equations on the coordinate plane.

The lines intersect at $(-2, 7)$. This is the solution to the system of linear equations.

To check the answer, substitute -2 for x and 7 for y in the original equations.

$y = -2x + 3$; $7 = -2(-2) + 3$; $7 = 4 + 3$; $7 = 7$

$y + 4x = -1$; $7 + 4(-2) = -1$; $7 - 8 = -1$; $-1 = -1$

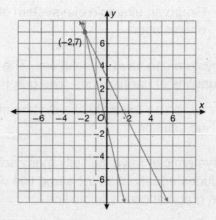

Solve each linear system by graphing. Check your answer.

1. $y = x + 1$
   $y = -x + 5$

2. $y + 3x = 1$
   $y - 6 = 2x$

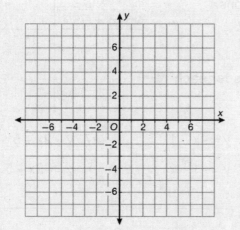

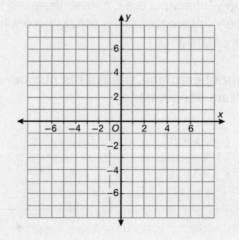

_____

_____

LESSON 8-1

Solving Systems of Linear Equations by Graphing

Reading Strategies: Identify Relationships

A **system of linear equations** has two or more equations that are graphed on the same **coordinate grid**. The solution for the system is the ordered pair of the point where all of the equations intersect.

The solution to a system can come in three forms.

A system can have one solution. The system includes equations of different lines. The graph shows lines that intersect in one point.

1. Graph an example of a system of two equations that has one solution.

A system can have no solutions. The system includes equations of parallel lines. The graph shows parallel lines.

2. Graph an example of a system of two equations that has no solution.

A system can have infinitely many solutions. The system includes equations of the same line written in different forms. The graph shows a single line.

3. Graph an example of a system of two equations that has infinitely many solutions.

1.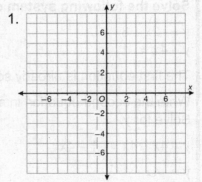

2.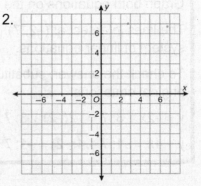

3.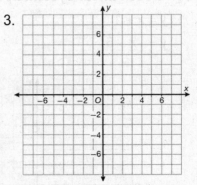

If you write all of the equations in a system in slope-intercept form, you can often tell how many solutions there are before you graph it. Look at the slopes.

If the slopes are different, there will be one solution.
If the slopes are the same, look at the *y*-intercept.
If the *y*-intercepts are different, there will be no solutions.
If the *y*-intercepts are the same, there will be infinitely many solutions.

Without graphing, predict the number of solutions for each system of equations.

4. $y = 2x + 5$
   $y = 2x - 1$

5. $y = \dfrac{3}{2}x$
   $y = 4x + 7$

6. $y = -x - 1$
   $y = -1 - x$

7. $y = 2x + 5$
   $y = -2x + 5$

_____   _____   _____   _____

Solving Systems of Linear Equations by Graphing

LESSON 8-1

Success for English Learners

Problem 1

Two Questions ➡ **Two Equations** ➡ **One or Two Lines**

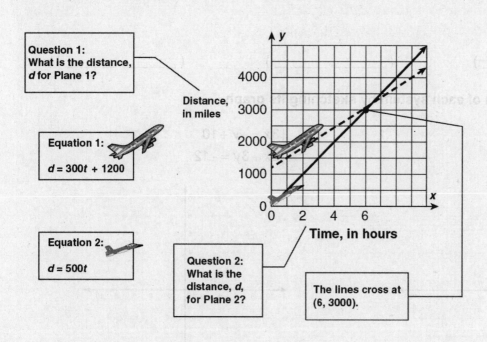

Question 1:
What is the distance, *d* for Plane 1?

Distance, in miles

Equation 1:

$d = 300t + 1200$

Time, in hours

Equation 2:

$d = 500t$

Question 2:
What is the distance, *d*, for Plane 2?

The lines cross at (6, 3000).

1. How do you know that the system of equations shown in Problem 1 has only one solution?

   _____

2. Explain how to check that the ordered pair in Problem 1 is the correct solution to the system of equations.

   _____

   _____

3. Explain how to graph the two linear equations in Problem 1.

   _____

   _____

LESSON 8-2

Solving Systems by Substitution
Practice and Problem Solving: A/B

Solve each system by substitution. Check your answer.

1. $\begin{cases} y = x - 2 \\ y = 4x + 1 \end{cases}$

2. $\begin{cases} 2x - y = 6 \\ x + y = -3 \end{cases}$

3. $\begin{cases} 3x - 2y = 7 \\ x + 3y = -5 \end{cases}$

(_____ , _____)   (_____ , _____)   (_____ , _____)

Estimate the solution of each system by sketching its graph.

4. $\begin{cases} y = -4x + 5 \\ 3x + 2y = 0 \end{cases}$

5. $\begin{cases} 3x = -y + 10 \\ 2x + 3y = -12 \end{cases}$

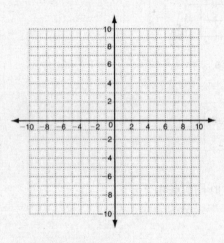

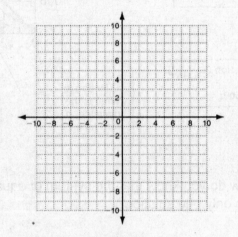

Estimated solution:

(about _____ , about _____)

Estimated solution:

(about _____ , about _____)

6. A sales associate in a department store earns a commission on each suit and each pair of shoes sold. One week, she earned $47 in commission for selling 3 suits and a pair of shoes. The next week, she earned $107 in commission for selling 7 suits and 2 pairs of shoes. How much commission does she earn for selling each suit and each pair of shoes? Solve by substitution.

_____

LESSON 8-2

Solving Systems by Substitution

Practice and Problem Solving: C

Use the information below to complete Exercises 1–3.

The following three equations are shown on the graph:

A: $x + y = 2$
B: $-3x + y = -2$
C: $y = 1$

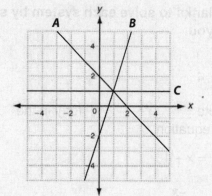

1. What is the solution of this system?

   (_____ , _____)

2. How can you re-write Equation *C* so that it is satisfied by the system solution?

   _____

3. Two weavers are selling their products at a crafts fair. One weaver sells 4 blankets and 6 sweaters for $150. The other weaver sells 8 blankets and 12 sweaters for $400. Do the weavers charge the same amount for blankets and sweaters? Write and solve a system of equations to support your answer.

   _____

Re-write these systems to make it easier to estimate a solution.

4. $\begin{cases} 4.13x - \dfrac{23}{34}y = 5.754 \\ -1.804x = 10.04 + \dfrac{56}{11}y \end{cases}$

5. $\begin{cases} y = 0.005 \\ 0.006x + 0.00812y = 0.00087 \end{cases}$

The linear equation $195x - 221y = 65$ has an infinite number of solutions for x and y. These are given by the linear equations $x = 40 - 17n$ and $y = 35 - 15n$, where n is any integer.

6. What is the smallest integer that will make $x < 0$ and $y < 0$?

   _____

7. Is there any integer that will give the values $x = 20$ and $y = 30$? Prove that your answer is correct.

   _____

LESSON 8-2

Solving Systems by Substitution

Practice and Problem Solving: D

Fill in the blanks to solve each system by substitution. The first one is started for you.

1. $\begin{cases} y = 3x \\ y = x + 4 \end{cases}$

Substitute ____**3x**____ for y in the second equation.

____**3x**____ $= x + 4$

$\underline{\quad -\textbf{x} \quad} \quad \underline{-\textbf{x}}$

_____ $= 4$

$\div$ _____ $\div$ _____

_____ $=$ _____

Since $x =$ ____, substitute ____ for x in one of the equations to find the value of y:

$y = 3x$

$y = 3(\underline{\quad\cdot\quad})$

$y = $ _____

Solution: (____ , ____)

2. $\begin{cases} 3x + y = 25 \\ y = x - 3 \end{cases}$

Substitute _____ for y in the first equation.

$3x + ($ _____ $) = 25$

_____ -3 $= 25$

$\underline{\quad +3 \quad} \quad \underline{+3}$

_____ $= 28$

$\div$ _____ $\div$ _____

_____ $=$ _____

Since $x =$ _____, substitute _____ for x in one of the equations to find the value of y.

$y = x - 3$

$y =$ _____ -3

$y = $ _____

Solution: (____ , ____)

Solve each system by substitution. Check your answer.

3. $\begin{cases} y = 4x \\ y = 2x + 6 \end{cases}$

_____

4. $\begin{cases} y = x - 2 \\ 2x + y = 4 \end{cases}$

_____

5. A decorator charges a $75 consultation fee, plus $50 per hour. Another decorator charges a $50 consultation fee, plus $60 per hour. When do the decorators change the same amount? How much is it? Solve.

1st decorator: $y =$ _____ $x +$ _____   2nd decorator: $y =$ _____ $x +$ _____
Write a system of equations for this problem.

1st equation: _____   2nd equation: _____

Solve the system of equations by substitution. $x =$ _____ hours; $y = \$$ _____

LESSON 8-2 Solving Systems by Substitution

Reteach

You can use substitution to solve a system of equations if one of the
equations is already solved for a variable.

Solve $\begin{cases} y = x + 2 \\ 3x + y = 10 \end{cases}$

Step 1: Choose the equation to use as the
substitute.
Use the first equation $y = x + 2$
because it is already solved for a variable.

Step 2: Solve by substitution.

$$\boxed{x + 2}$$

$$3x + y = 10$$
$$3x + (x + 2) = 10 \qquad \text{\textit{Substitute } x + 2 \text{ \textit{for} } y.}$$
$$4x + 2 = 10 \qquad \text{\textit{Combine like terms.}}$$
$$\underline{-2 \quad -2}$$
$$4x = 8$$
$$\frac{4x}{4} = \frac{8}{4}$$
$$x = 2$$

Step 3: Now substitute $x = 2$ back into
one of the original equations to
find the value of y.

$$y = x + 2$$
$$y = 2 + 2$$
$$y = 4$$

The solution is $(2, 4)$.

Check:

Substitute $(2, 4)$ into both equations.

$$y = x + 2 \qquad\qquad 3x + y = 10$$
$$4 \overset{?}{=} 2 + 2 \qquad\qquad 3(2) + 4 \overset{?}{=} 10$$
$$4 \overset{?}{=} 4 \checkmark \qquad\qquad 6 + 4 \overset{?}{=} 10$$
$$10 \overset{?}{=} 10 \checkmark$$

Solve each system by substitution. Check your answer.

1. $\begin{cases} x = y - 1 \\ x + 2y = 8 \end{cases}$

2. $\begin{cases} y = x + 2 \\ y = 2x - 5 \end{cases}$

3. $\begin{cases} y = x + 5 \\ 3x + y = -11 \end{cases}$

4. $\begin{cases} x = y + 10 \\ x = 2y + 3 \end{cases}$

Solving Systems by Substitution
Reading Strategies: Build Vocabulary

When you solve and check a system of equations by **substitution**,
you may see words such as "in the place of," or "replace."

Example

Solve the system by substitution.

$$4x - y = 8$$
$$-2x + 3y = -6$$

Solution

The term **substitution** means to *replace* one of the variables, x or y, in one
of the equations with its value from the *other* equation. Look at the
equations and decide which variable would be the easiest to find.

Here, it's the y in $4x - y = 8$. Add a "$+y$" to both sides of the equation, and
subtract 8 from both sides of the equation to give $4x - 8 = y$.

Then, **substitute** this value for y in the other equation and simplify:

$$-2x + 3y = -6 \qquad \longrightarrow \qquad -2x + 3(4x - 8) = -6$$
$$\longrightarrow \qquad -2x + 12x - 24 = -6, \text{ or } 10x = 18$$

This gives $x = \dfrac{9}{5}$. Next, **replace** x with $\dfrac{9}{5}$ in *either* of the equations in the

system. For the first equation, this gives $4\left(\dfrac{9}{5}\right) - y = 8$, which simplifies to

$36 - 5y = 40$, or $y = -\dfrac{4}{5}$. So, the solution of the system is $\left(\dfrac{9}{5}, -\dfrac{4}{5}\right)$.

Check

You might graph the equations on a coordinate plane to check your
answer. If you **round** the numbers in the solutions, **about** where will you
find the point of intersection?

The x value of $\dfrac{9}{5}$ is **about** 2. The y value of $-\dfrac{4}{5}$ is **about** -1. So, the point
of intersection would be at **about** $(2, -1)$.

Solve each system by *substitution*.

1. $\begin{cases} 2x = 3y \\ y = x - 2 \end{cases}$

2. $\begin{cases} x + y = 2 \\ -x = 2y - 7 \end{cases}$

Solution: (_____, _____)

Solution: (_____, _____)

Name _____ Date _____ Class _____

LESSON 8-2

Solving Systems by Substitution
Success for English Learners

Problem 1

Step 1: Substitute

Equation 1

$2x + y = 5$

$2x + (x - 4) = 5$

Step 2: Solve

$2x + x - 4 = 5$

$3x - 4 = 5$

Wait! You're not done yet!

$3x = 9$

$x = 3$

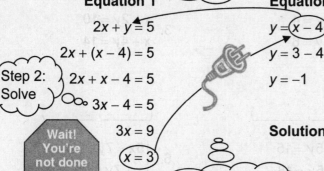

Equation 2

$y = (x - 4)$

$y = 3 - 4$

$y = -1$

Graph to Check:

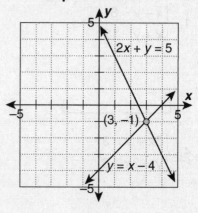

$2x + y = 5$

$(3, -1)$

$y = x - 4$

Solution: (3, −1)

Step 3: Re-substitute

Problem 2

Option #1

This will cost $50.

Let m = number of months.

$m = 1$	$m = 2$	$m = 3$	$m = 4$	$m = 5$	$m = 6$	$m = 7$
$80	$110	$140	$170	$200	$230	$260

Total	= Set-Up Fee	+	(Monthly fee)	(number of months)
T	= $50	+	$30	• m

Option #2

This is FREE!

Let m = number of months.

$m = 1$	$m = 2$	$m = 3$	$m = 4$	$m = 5$	$m = 6$	$m = 7$
$40	$80	$120	$160	$200	$240	$280

Total	= Set-Up Fee	+	(Monthly fee)	(number of months)
T	= $0	+	$40	• m

1. Once you find the value of x in Problem 1, what do you need to do?

_____

2. Describe the two differences between Options 1 and 2 in Problem 2.

_____

LESSON 8-3

Solving Systems by Elimination
Practice and Problem Solving: A/B

Solve each system by eliminating one of the variables by addition or subtraction. Check your answer.

1. $\begin{cases} x - y = 8 \\ x + y = 12 \end{cases}$

2. $\begin{cases} 2x - y = 4 \\ 3x + y = 6 \end{cases}$

3. $\begin{aligned} x + 2y = 10 \\ x + 4y = 14 \end{aligned}$

(_____, _____)   (_____, _____)   (_____, _____)

4. $\begin{cases} 3x + y = 9 \\ y = 3x + 6 \end{cases}$

5. $\begin{cases} 4x + 5y = 15 \\ 6x - 5y = 18 \end{cases}$

6. $\begin{cases} 5x = 7y \\ x + 7y = 21 \end{cases}$

(_____, _____)   (_____, _____)   (_____, _____)

Write a system of equations for each problem. Solve the system using elimination. Show your work and check your answers.

7. Aaron bought a bagel and 3 muffins for $7.25. Bea bought a bagel and 2 muffins for $6. How much is a bagel and how much is a muffin?

_____

8. Two movie tickets and 3 snacks are $24. Three movie tickets and 4 snacks are $35. How much is a movie ticket and how much is a snack?

_____

Explain why the system has the answer given. Solve each system by elimination to prove your answer.

9. $\begin{cases} x + 2y = 8 \\ x + 2y = 20 \end{cases}$

No solution

10. $\begin{cases} 3x + y = 9 \\ 3x = 9 - y \end{cases}$

Infinitely many solutions

_____   _____

_____   _____

LESSON 8-3 Solving Systems by Elimination
Practice and Problem Solving: C

Answer the questions below.

1. Solve the system by elimination: $x - y = 4$ Equation A

                                         $x + z = 6$ Equation B

                                         $y - z = 8$ Equation C

    a. $x + y =$ _____   Equation D

    b.   Add the new Equation D to Equation A to eliminate the variable y.

        _____

    c. $x =$ ____

        Substitute $x = 9$ into Equation A to find y and into Equation B to find z.

        $x - y = 4$ ⟶ $9 - y = 4$, or $y = 5$

    d. $x + z = 6$ ⟶ $9 + z = 6$, or $z =$ _____

    e.   The solution is $x =$ ____, $y =$ ____, and $z =$ ____, which can be

        written as an **ordered triple** (_____).

Solve by elimination.

2. $2x = y + 4$
    $y = 2z + 5$
    $2z = x + 3$
    (_____, _____, _____)

3. $2a + 3b = 5$
    $a + 3c = 6$
    $3b + c = 7$
    (_____, _____, _____)

4. $2b - c = 5$
    $a + c = 10$
    $2b - a = 1$
    (_____, _____, _____)

5. $2x + y = 1$
    $y + z = -2$
    $3x - 2z = 4.5$
    (_____, _____, _____)

LESSON
8-3
Solving Systems by Elimination
Practice and Problem Solving: D

Solve the systems by elimination. The first one is started for you.

1. $\begin{cases} x + 3y = 14 \\ 2x - 3y = -8 \end{cases}$

2. $\begin{cases} 2x + 2y = 4 \\ 3x + 2y = 7 \end{cases}$

3. $\begin{cases} 3x + 4y = 26 \\ x - 2y = -8 \end{cases}$

Add the equations:
$$x + 3y = 14$$
$$\underline{+2x - 3y = -8}$$
$$3x + \underline{\ 0\ } = 6$$

$$\frac{3x}{} = 6$$
$$\div \underline{\ 3\ } \div \underline{\ 3\ }$$
$$x = \underline{\ 2\ }$$

Substitute ___ for x in
one of the equations:
$$x + 3y = 14$$
$$\underline{\ \ \ } + 3y = 14$$
$$-\underline{\ \ \ } \quad -\underline{\ \ \ }$$
$$3y = \underline{\ \ \ \ }$$
$$\div 3 \ \div 3$$
$$y = \underline{\ \ \ }$$
Solution: (___ , ___)

Subtract the equations:
$$2x + 2y = 4$$
$$-(3x + 2y = 7)$$

or

$$2x + 2y = 4$$
$$\underline{-3x - \underline{\ \ \ } = \underline{\ \ \ }}$$
$$-x + \underline{\ \ \ } = \underline{\ \ \ }$$
$$-x = \underline{\ \ \ }$$
$$\div \underline{\ \ \ } \div \underline{\ \ \ }$$
$$x = \underline{\ \ \ \ }$$

Substitute ___ for x in
one of the equations:
$$3x + 2y = 7$$
$$3(\underline{\ \ }) + 2y = 7$$
$$\underline{\ \ \ } + 2y = 7$$
$$-\underline{\ \ \ } \quad -\underline{\ \ \ }$$
$$2y = \underline{\ \ \ }$$
$$\div \underline{\ \ \ } \div \underline{\ \ \ }$$
$$y = \underline{\ \ \ \ }$$
Solution: (___ , ___)

Multiply the second
equation by 2. Then,
add the equations:
$$\begin{cases} 3x + 4y = 26 \\ 2(x - 2y = -8) \end{cases}$$

$$3x + 4y = 26$$
$$\underline{+\underline{\ \ }x - \underline{\ \ }y = \underline{\ \ \ }}$$
$$\underline{\ \ \ }x + 0 = \underline{\ \ \ }$$
$$\underline{\ \ \ }x = \underline{\ \ \ }$$
$$\div \underline{\ \ \ } \div \underline{\ \ \ }$$
$$x = \underline{\ \ \ }$$

Substitute ____ for x in
one of the equations:
$$x - 2y = -8$$
$$\underline{\ \ \ } - 2y = -8$$
$$-\underline{\ \ \ } \quad -\underline{\ \ \ }$$
$$-2y = \underline{\ \ \ }$$
$$\div \underline{\ \ \ } \div \underline{\ \ \ }$$
$$y = \underline{\ \ \ }$$
Solution: (___ , ___)

Solve each system by elimination.

4. $\begin{cases} 3x - 2y = 1 \\ 2x + 2y = 14 \end{cases}$

5. $\begin{cases} x + y = 4 \\ 3x + y = 16 \end{cases}$

6. $\begin{cases} 3x + 2y = -26 \\ 2x - 6y = -10 \end{cases}$

_____   _____   _____

LESSON 8-3

Solving Systems by Elimination
Reteach

Solving a system of two equations in two unknowns by **elimination** can be done by adding or subtracting one equation from the other.

Elimination by Adding

Solve the system: $x + 4y = 8$
$$3x - 4y = 8$$

Solution

Notice that the terms "+4y" and "–4y" are opposites. This means that the two equations can be added without changing the signs.

$$x + 4y = 8$$
$$\underline{3x - 4y = 8}$$
$$4x + 0 = 16$$
$$4x = 16, \text{ or } x = 4$$

Substitute $x = 4$ in either of the equations to find y: $x + 4y = 8 \longrightarrow 4 + 4y = 8$
$$4y = 4, \text{ or}$$
$$y = 1$$

The solution of this system is (4, 1).

Elimination by Subtracting

Solve the system: $2x - 5y = 15$
$$2x + 3y = -9$$

Solution

Notice that the terms "2x" are common to both equations. However, to eliminate them, it is necessary to *subtract* one equation from the other. This means that the *signs* of one equation will change. Here, the top equation stays the same. The signs of the bottom equation change.

$$2x - 5y = 15$$
$$\underline{(-)2x\,(-)3y = (+)9}$$
$$0 - 8y = 24, \text{ or } y = -3$$

Substitute $y = -3$ in either of the original equations to find x:
$$2x - 5y = 15 \longrightarrow 2x - 5(-3) = 15$$
$$2x + 15 = 15, \text{ or}$$
$$x = 0$$

The solution of this system is (0, –3).

Solve the following systems by elimination. State whether addition or subtraction is used to eliminate one of the variables.

1. $3x + 2y = 10$
    $3x - 2y = 14$

    Operation: _____

    Solution: (_____, _____)

2. $\begin{cases} x + y = 12 \\ 2x + y = 6 \end{cases}$

    Operation: _____

    Solution: (_____, _____)

Solving Systems by Elimination

Reading Strategies: Analyze Information

When solving word problems using systems, identify the two variables. This is especially important if you are trying to find a variable with the same coefficient that can be eliminated by addition or subtraction.

Example

A welcome kit contains 3 grocery store coupons and 7 drug store coupons. The coupons are worth $45. Another welcome kit contains 3 grocery store coupons and 6 drug store coupons, worth $42. What is the value of each grocery coupon and each drug store coupon?

Solution

To use the elimination method, it is important to notice that *both* welcome kits contain 3 grocery store coupons. This means that the grocery-store coupon variable can be eliminated by subtracting one equation from the other.

The equation for the first welcome kit is $3g + 7d = 45$.

The equation for the second welcome kit is $3g + 6d = 42$. Write one equation over the other and subtract the like terms:

$$
\begin{array}{r}
3g + 7d = 45 \\
(-)3g\ (-)6d = (-)42 \\
\hline
1d = \quad 3
\end{array}
$$

The drug store coupons have a value of $3.

Substitute to find the average value of the grocery coupon:

$3g + 7(3) = 45$, $3g = 24$, and $g = 8$

The grocery store coupons have a value of $8.

Identify the variable that is the same in each equation in the system that is used to solve the problem. Then, add or subtract to eliminate that variable. Finally, solve the system.

1. Joy bought 2 bath towels from a linen store, but returned 3 hand towels. Kay bought 3 bath towels and 3 hand towels. Joy's bill was $5. Kay's bill was $45. What are the prices of the bath and hand towels?

   _____

2. One family spent $45 on movie tickets for 2 adults and 3 children. Another family spent $40 for 2 adults and 2 children. What are the prices of the adult movie tickets and the child movie tickets?

   _____

Solving Systems by Elimination

LESSON 8-3

Success for English Learners

Problem 1

STEP 1:

$$\begin{cases} x - 2y = -19 \\ 5x + 2y = 1 \end{cases}$$

STEP 2:

$$\begin{array}{r} x - 2y = -19 \\ 5x + 2y = 1 \\ \hline 6x + 0 = -18 \\ 6x = -18 \\ x = -3 \end{array}$$

Wait! You're not done yet!

Graph to Check:

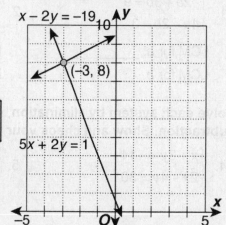

STEP 3:

$$\begin{array}{r} x - 2y = -19 \\ -3 - 2y = -19 \\ +3 \qquad +3 \\ \hline -2y = -16 \\ y = 8 \end{array}$$

STEP 4:

Write the solution: $(-3, 8)$

Problem 2

A family buys 3 lunch combos and 2 desserts for $24. Another family buys 5 lunch combos and 2 desserts for $40. Write a system of equations for the dinners and desserts bought by the families.

Let **L** stand for the number of lunch combos. Let **D** stand for the number of desserts.

1st family: **3L + 2D = $24**
2nd family: **5L + 2D = $40**
Do you *add* or *subtract*?

1. In Problem 1, what happens to the *y*-variable in Step 2 when the equations are added?

_____

2. In Problem 2, what do you get if you subtract the top equation from the bottom equation? How much is a lunch combo?

_____

Solving Systems by Elimination with Multiplication

Practice and Problem Solving: A/B

Name the *least common multiple* (LCM) of the coefficients of each pair of variables. Ignore the signs.

1. $\begin{cases} -2a + 3b = 9 \\ 4a - 2b = 3 \end{cases}$

2. $\begin{cases} 7x + 5y = 20 \\ 6x - 18y = 11 \end{cases}$

3. $\begin{array}{l} -8m - 5n = 3 \\ 3m - 12n = -1 \end{array}$

LCM for *a*: _____   LCM for *x*: _____   LCM for *m*: _____

LCM for *b*: _____   LCM for *y*: _____   LCM for *n*: _____

Solve each system by elimination, multiplication, and addition or subtraction. Show and check your work.

4. $\begin{cases} x + 3y = -14 \\ 2x - 4y = 30 \end{cases}$

5. $\begin{cases} 4x - y = -5 \\ -2x + 3y = 10 \end{cases}$

6. $\begin{cases} y - 3x = 11 \\ 2y - x = 2 \end{cases}$

(_____ , _____)   (_____ , _____)   (_____ , _____)

Write and solve a system of linear equations for each problem. Show and check your work.

7. One family spends $134 on 2 adult tickets and 3 youth tickets at an amusement park. Another family spends $146 on 3 adult tickets and 2 youth tickets at the same park. What is the price of a youth ticket?

_____

_____

8. A baker buys 19 apples of two different varieties to make pies. The total cost of the apples is $5.10. Granny Smith apples cost $0.25 each and Gala apples cost $0.30. How many of each type of apple did the baker buy?

_____

_____

LESSON 8-4

Solving Systems by Elimination with Multiplication

Practice and Problem Solving: C

Find the solution to each system.

1. $\begin{cases} 2x - 3y = 4 \\ 3x - 4y = 5 \end{cases}$

2. $\begin{cases} 3x - 4y = 5 \\ 4x - 5y = 6 \end{cases}$

3. $\begin{cases} 4x - 5y = 6 \\ 5x - 6y = 7 \end{cases}$

(_____, _____)   (_____, _____)   (_____, _____)

4. What do you notice about the coefficients of the variables and the constants on each system?

_____

5. What do you predict the solution for the system $5x - 6y = 7$ and $6x - 7y = 8$ will be? Explain your answer.

_____

6. Write the equations in Exercise 1 in slope-intercept form. How do the slopes compare?

_____

7. What is happening to the slopes of the lines in Exercises 1–3? Toward what number are the slopes approaching?

_____

8. What would the graph of the six equations in Exercises 1–3 look like?

_____

Find the solution to the system in Exercise 9. Then, write two systems for Exercise 10 and 11 that have the same solution. Verify your equations by solving those systems.

9. $\begin{cases} 2x + 3y = 4 \\ 3x + 4y = 5 \end{cases}$

10. _____

11. _____

_____   _____

(_____, _____)   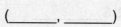   (_____, _____)

Solving Systems by Elimination with Multiplication

LESSON 8-4

Practice and Problem Solving: D

Fill in the blanks to solve each system by elimination with multiplication. The first one has been started for you.

1. $\begin{cases} 3x + 4y = 26 \\ x - 2y = -8 \end{cases}$

   Multiply the second equation by 2. Then, add the equations:

   $\begin{cases} 3x + 4y = 26 \\ 2(x - 2y = -8) \end{cases}$

   $3x + 4y = 26$

   $+ \underline{\mathbf{2}} x - \underline{\mathbf{4}} y = \underline{\mathbf{-16}}$

   $\underline{} x + 0 = \underline{}$

   $ x = \underline{}$

   $\div \underline{} \quad \div \underline{}$

   $x = \underline{}$

   Substitute _____ for x in one of the equations:

   $x - 2y = -8$

   $\underline{} - 2y = -8$

   $- \underline{} \quad - \underline{}$

   $-2y = \underline{}$

   $\div \underline{} \quad \div \underline{}$

   $y = \underline{}$

   Solution: (_____, _____)

2. Last month, Stephanie spent $57 on 4 allergy shots and 1 office visit. This month, she spent $9 after 1 office visit and a refund for 2 allergy shots from her insurance company. How much do an allergy shot and an office visit cost?

   Complete the equations:

   $4a + 1v = \underline{}$

   $-2a + 1v = \underline{}$

   Allergy shot: $_____; office visit: $_____

LESSON 8-4

Solving Systems by Elimination with Multiplication
Reteach

Elimination is used to solve a system of equations by adding like terms. Sometimes, it is necessary to multiply one or both equations by a number to use this method. You should examine the equations carefully and choose the coefficients that are easiest to eliminate.

Multiplying *one* equation by a number	Multiplying *both* equations by a number
$\begin{cases} 2x + 5y = 9 \\ x - 3y = 10 \end{cases}$	$\begin{cases} 5x + 3y = 2 \\ 4x + 2y = 10 \end{cases}$

The easiest variable to work with is x.
Multiply the second equation by -2.

$$2x + 5y = 9$$
$$-2(x - 3y) = -2(10)$$

$$2x + 5y = 9$$
$$\underline{-2x + 6y = -20}$$
$$0 + 11y = -11$$

So, $y = -1$, and $2x + 5(-1) = 9$, or $x = 7$.
The solution is $(7, -1)$.

The *least common multiple* (LCM) of 4 and 5 is 20, and the LCM of 2 and 3 is 6. So, multiply the first equation by -2 and the second equation by 3.

$$-2(5x + 3y = 2)$$
$$\underline{3(4x + 2y = 10)}$$

$$-10x - 6y = -4$$
$$\underline{12x + 6y = 30}$$
$$2x + 0 = 26$$

So, $x = 13$, and $5(13) + 3y = 2$, so $y = -21$.
The solution is $(13, -21)$.

Solve each system by elimination.

1. $\begin{cases} 2x - y = 20 \\ 3x + 2y = 19 \end{cases}$

2. $\begin{cases} -3a + 4b = 15 \\ 5a - 6b = 12 \end{cases}$

(_____, _____)

(_____, _____)

3. $\begin{cases} 3m + 5n = 20 \\ 4m - 6n = 30 \end{cases}$

4. $\begin{cases} 3u - v = 20 \\ -4u - 2v = 13 \end{cases}$

(_____, _____)

(_____, _____)

LESSON 8-4

Solving Systems by Elimination with Multiplication

Reading Strategies: Connect Concepts

When solving systems of linear equations using elimination, you will sometimes need to multiply one or both equations by a factor in order to get the same coefficients for a variable. This process is very similar to getting a common denominator for fractions. Look at the example below.

$$\begin{cases} 6x - 5y = 16 \\ 4x - 3y = 12 \end{cases}$$

To eliminate the x-terms, you need to get the same or opposite coefficients for x in both equations.

Add: $\dfrac{5}{6} + \dfrac{1}{4} = ?$

Think about finding a common denominator for 4 and 6.

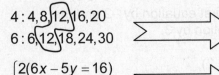

Find the least common multiple (LCM) of 4 and 6 by listing their multiples in order. The LCM is 12.

$$\begin{cases} 2(6x - 5y = 16) \\ 3(4x - 3y = 12) \end{cases}$$

Determine what you have to multiply 4 and 6 by to get 12. Multiply each equation by the appropriate number.

$$\begin{cases} 12x - 10y = 32 \\ 12x - 9y = 36 \end{cases}$$

Now either add or subtract the equations. In this case, you will subtract the equations.

1. Describe how you would get common y-coefficients (instead of x-) in the example above.

_____

_____

2. Show how to get a set of common y-coefficients for the system $\begin{cases} 9x - 10y = 7 \\ 5x + 8y = 31 \end{cases}$

_____

Solve each system of equations by elimination.

3. $\begin{cases} 9x - 2y = 15 \\ 4x + 3y = -5 \end{cases}$

4. $\begin{cases} 2x - 3y = 50 \\ 7x + 8y = -10 \end{cases}$

(_____,_____)

(_____,_____)

LESSON 8-4

Solving Systems by Elimination with Multiplication

Success for English Learners

Problem 1

Solve the system by elimination and use multiplication.

$$\begin{cases} 2x + y = 3 \\ -x + 3y = -12 \end{cases}$$
$$x + 4y = -9$$

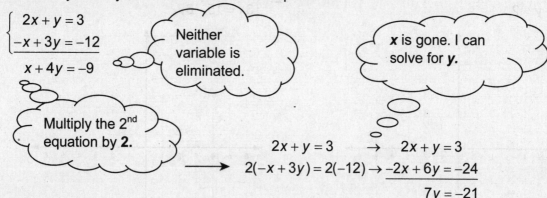

Neither variable is eliminated.

x is gone. I can solve for y.

Multiply the 2nd equation by 2.

$$2x + y = 3 \quad \rightarrow \quad 2x + y = 3$$
$$2(-x + 3y) = 2(-12) \rightarrow \underline{-2x + 6y = -24}$$
$$7y = -21$$

Solution: (3, −3)

Problem 2

How do you eliminate a variable in a system like this?

$$\begin{cases} 2a + 3b = 4 \\ 3a - 4b = 8 \end{cases}$$

$$4(2a + 3b) = 4(4) \rightarrow 8a + 12b = 16$$
$$3(3a - 4b) = 8(3) \rightarrow \underline{9a - 12b = 24}$$
$$17a = 40 \quad a = \frac{40}{17} = 2\frac{6}{17}$$

Notice that 3b and −4b have opposite signs. What is the smallest number that 3 and 4 divide evenly? 12

Multiply the 1st equation by 4. Multiply the 2nd equation by 3. The b is eliminated.

Solution: $\left(2\frac{6}{17}, \frac{-4}{17} \right)$

1. In Problem 1, what would you multiply the first equation by to eliminate the *y* variable?

_____

2. In Problem 2, what would you multiply the equations by to eliminate the variable *a*? (*Hint*: There are two different numbers, one for each equation.)

_____

Solving Special Systems

Practice and Problem Solving: A/B

Graph each system. Describe the solution.

1. $\begin{cases} y = x + 2 \\ x - y = 2 \end{cases}$

2. $\begin{cases} x + 2y = 5 \\ 3x = 15 - 6y \end{cases}$

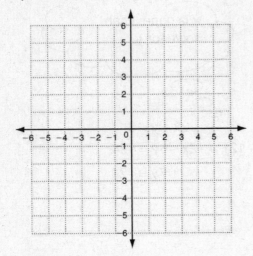

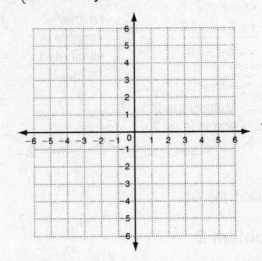

Solution:

_____

_____

Solution:

_____

_____

Re-write each system in the form $y = mx + b$. Then, state whether the system has one solution, no solution, or many solutions without actually solving the system.

3. $\begin{cases} 2x + y = 1 \\ 2x + y = -3 \end{cases}$

4. $\begin{cases} y - 2 = -5x \\ y - 5x = 2 \end{cases}$

5. $\begin{cases} y - 3x + 2 = 0 \\ 2 = -y + 3x \end{cases}$

_____

_____

_____

Solve.

6. Two sisters open savings accounts with $60 each that their grandmother gave them. The first sister adds $20 each month to her account. The second sister adds $40 every two months to her $60. If the sisters continue to make deposits at the same rate, when will they have the same amount of money?

_____

LESSON 8-5

Solving Special Systems

Practice and Problem Solving: C

Answer the questions about the graph.

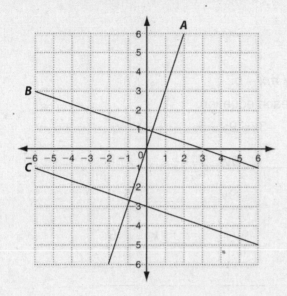

1. Give the slope of the lines.

   Slope of *A*: _____

   Slope of *B*: _____

   Slope of *C*: _____

2. Write the equation of each line.

   Line *A*:

   _____

   Line *B*:

   _____

   Line *C*:

   _____

3. What is the relationship of the slopes of lines *A* and *B*?

   _____

4. What is the relationship of the slopes of lines *B* and *C*?

   _____

5. Solve the system of equations represented by lines *A* and *B*.

   _____

6. Describe how you would use the distance formula,

   $d = \sqrt{(x_2 - x_1)^2 + (y_2 - y_1)^2}$, and the Pythagorean Theorem to show

   that lines *A* and *B* are perpendicular.

   _____

Which lines are perpendicular? Write "yes" or "no." Explain.

7. $\begin{cases} x + 3y = 6 \\ 3x - y = 9 \end{cases}$ 8: $\begin{cases} -2x + y = 10 \\ 2x - 4y = 15 \end{cases}$ 9. $\begin{cases} 3x - 5y = 21 \\ 5x + 3y = 25 \end{cases}$

_____   _____   _____

_____   _____   _____

LESSON 8-5

Solving Special Systems
Practice and Problem Solving: D

Answer the questions about the system. The first one is done for you.

$$\begin{cases} 2x + 6y = 15 \\ -3x - 9y = 5 \end{cases}$$

Write each equation in slope-intercept form, $y = mx + b$.

1. **Step 1** Subtract the x term from both sides of each equation.

   $2x + 6y = 15$ $-3x - 9y = 5$

   $2x \underline{- \mathbf{2x}} + 6y = 15 \underline{- \mathbf{2x}}$ $-3x + \underline{} - 9y = 5 + \underline{} x$

   $6y = \underline{-\mathbf{2x}} + 15$ $-9y = \underline{} x + 5$

   $\dfrac{6y}{\underline{6}} = \dfrac{-2x}{\underline{6}} + \dfrac{15}{\underline{6}}$ $\dfrac{-9y}{\underline{}} = \dfrac{\underline{}x}{\underline{}} + \dfrac{5}{\underline{}}$

   $y = \dfrac{-1x}{\underline{3}} + \dfrac{5}{\underline{2}}$ $y = \dfrac{\underline{}x}{\underline{}} - \dfrac{5}{\underline{}}$

2. **Step 2** Write the slope, m, of each equation.

   Slope of 1st equation: $-\dfrac{1}{\underline{3}}$ Slope of 2nd equation: _____

3. **Step 3** Compare the y-intercept, b, of each equation.

   y-intercept, 1st equation: $\dfrac{5}{\underline{2}}$ y-intercept, 2nd equation: _____

4. Based on your answers to Exercises 2 and 3, how many solutions does this system have? Explain.

   _____

How many solutions do these systems have: none, many, or one? The first one is done for you.

5. $\begin{aligned} 2y + 5x &= 8 \\ 5x + 2y &= 17 \end{aligned}$ 6. $\begin{aligned} 3x - 5y &= 40 \\ 3x - 5y &= 80 \end{aligned}$ 7. $\begin{aligned} x - y &= 100 \\ 10x - 10y &= 1{,}000 \end{aligned}$

    __**none**__   _____   _____

LESSON 8-5

Solving Special Systems
Reteach

When solving equations in one variable, it is possible to have one solution, no solutions, or infinitely many solutions. The same results can occur when graphing systems of equations.

Solve $\begin{cases} 4x + 2y = 2 \\ 2x + y = 4 \end{cases}$ Solve $\begin{cases} y = 4 - 3x \\ 3x + y = 4 \end{cases}$

Multiplying the second equation by −2 will eliminate the *x*-terms.

$$4x + 2y = 2$$
$$-2(2x + y = 4)$$

$\longrightarrow$

$$4x + 2y = 2$$
$$\underline{-4x - 2y = -8}$$
$$0 + 0 = -6$$
$$0 = -6 \; \text{✗}$$

Because the first equation is solved for a variable, use substitution.

$$3x + y = 4$$
$$3x + (4 - 3x) = 4 \quad \textit{Substitute } 4 - 3x \textit{ for } y$$
$$0 + 4 = 4$$
$$4 = 4 \; ✓$$

The equation is false. **There is no solution.**

The equation is true for all values of *x* and *y*. **There are infinitely many solutions.**

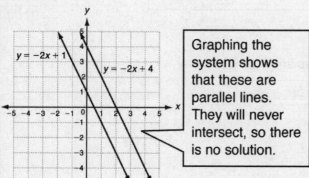

Graphing the system shows that these are parallel lines. They will never intersect, so there is no solution.

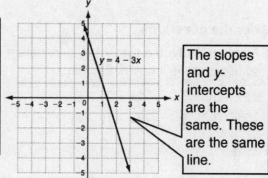

The slopes and *y*-intercepts are the same. These are the same line.

Solve each system of linear equations algebraically.

1. $\begin{cases} y = 3x \\ 2y = 6x \end{cases}$

2. $\begin{cases} y = 2x + 5 \\ y - 2x = 1 \end{cases}$

3. $\begin{cases} 3x - 2y = 9 \\ -6x + 4y = 1 \end{cases}$

_____   _____   _____

**LESSON
8-5**

Solving Special Systems

Reading Strategies: Use a Table

A table can help you answer questions about special systems of equations.

Number of Solutions	Similarities and Differences in $y = mx + b$	Description of Graphed Lines
1	different slopes (m)	intersecting
infinitely many	same slope (m) same y-int. (b)	same lines
0	same slope (m) different y-int. (b)	parallel

Answer the questions.

1. A student solved a system by elimination as shown. How many solutions does it have? Explain.

$$\begin{cases} 2x + 3y = 5 \\ 2x + 3y = 7 \end{cases} \qquad \begin{aligned} 2x + 3y &= 5 \\ \underline{-(2x + 3y = 7)} \\ 0 &= -2 \end{aligned}$$

_____

2. The graph of a system consists of two intersecting lines. How many solutions does the system have?

_____

Name _____ Date _____ Class_____

LESSON 8-5
Solving Special Systems
Success for English Learners

Problem 1

$\begin{cases} y = x - 1 \\ -x + y = 2 \end{cases}$ → $\begin{aligned} -x + y &= -1 \\ x - y &= -2 \end{aligned}$ → $\begin{aligned} \cancel{-x} + \cancel{y} &= -1 \\ + \cancel{x} - \cancel{y} &= -2 \\ \hline 0 &= -3 \end{aligned}$	$\begin{cases} y = 2x + 1 \\ 2x - y + 1 = 0 \end{cases}$ → $\begin{aligned} -2x + y &= 1 \\ 2x - y &= -1 \end{aligned}$ → $\begin{aligned} \cancel{-2x} + \cancel{y} &= 1 \\ + \cancel{2x} - \cancel{y} &= -1 \\ \hline 0 &= 0 \end{aligned}$
⇩	⇩
FALSE. There is **no solution**.	TRUE. There are **infinitely many solutions**.

Problem 2

Number of Solutions	1	∞ = Infinitely many	∅ = No Solution
Description of Equation	**Different** slopes: $m = -1$ and $m = 3$	**Same** slopes: $m = -1$ and $m = -1$ **Same** y-intercepts: $b = 2$ and $b = 2$	**Same** slopes: $m = -1$ and $m = -1$ **Different** y-intercepts: $b = 2$ and $b = -2$
Description of Graph	Intersecting lines	Same line	Parallel lines
Examples of Graphs	$y = -x + 2$ $m = -1$ $b = 2$ (1, 1) $y = 3x - 2$ $m = 3$ $b = -2$	$y = -x + 2$ or $2x + 2y = 4$	$y = -x + 2$ $m = -1$ $b = 2$ $y = -x - 2$ $m = -1$ $b = -2$

1. In Problem 1, two different outcomes occur when the equations are added together. What are those outcomes?

_____

2. How do the outcomes in Exercise 1 relate to the number of solutions of the system?

_____

_____

Solving Systems of Linear Equations

Challenge

In a village, 200 bushels of corn are distributed among 100 persons. Each child under the age of 6 gets one bushel of corn, each person age 60 or older gets two bushels of corn, and every other person gets three bushels of corn.

1. Let the variables c, e, and p stand for each child, older person, and other person, respectively. Write a linear equation that relates the variables to the total number of persons in the village.

   _____

2. Write a linear equation for the way the 200 bushels of corn is distributed among the 100 persons using the variables c, e, and p.

   _____

3. Write a system of equations using your answers to Exercises 1 and 2.

   _____

4. Subtract the equation from Exercise 1 from the equation for Exercise 2. What do you get?

   _____

A third equation is needed to completely solve this problem, because there are three variables.

5. Use your answer to Exercise 4 to give three values for the variables in the new equation.

   _____

6. Check the values in Exercise 5 against the equations in Exercises 1 and 2 to make sure that a reasonable value for the third variable results. Then, write three possible values for all three of the variables.

   c: _____ bushels e: _____ bushels p: _____ bushels

   c: _____ bushels e: _____ bushels p: _____ bushels

   c: _____ bushels e: _____ bushels p: _____ bushels

LESSON 9-1

Properties of Translations

Practice and Problem Solving: A/B

Describe the translation that maps point *A* to point *A'*.

1.

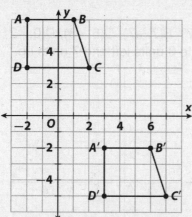

2.

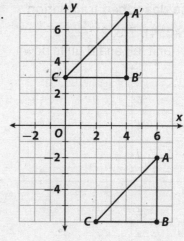

_____

Draw the image of the figure after each translation.

3. 3 units left and 9 units down

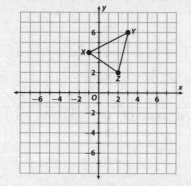

4. 3 units right and 6 units up

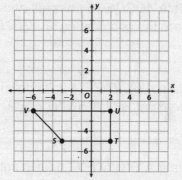

5. a. Graph rectangle *J'K'L'M'*, the image of rectangle *JKLM,* after a translation of 1 unit right and 9 units up.

   b. Find the area of each rectangle.

   _____

   c. Is it possible for the area of a figure to change after it is translated? Explain.

   _____

   _____

**LESSON
9-1**

Properties of Translations

Practice and Problem Solving: C

The vertices of a figure are given. Draw the figure. Then draw its image after the described translation.

1. $R(-4, 4)$, $S(3, 4)$, $T(3, 2)$
   Translate 1 unit left and 6 units down.

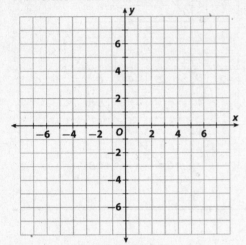

2. $A(-3, -7)$, $B(7, -7)$, $C(6, -3)$, $D(0, -2)$
   Translate 3 units left and 7 units up.

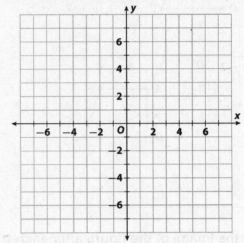

3. Figure *ABCDEF* is given.

   a. Translate *ABCDEF* 6 units left and 2 units down. What are the coordinates of *A'B'C'D'E'F'*?

   _____

   b. Translate *A'B'C'D'E'F'* 4 units down. What are the coordinates of *A"B"C"D"E"F"*?

   _____

   c. Translate *A"B"C"D"E"F"* 6 units right and 2 units up. What are the coordinates of *A'''B'''C'''D'''E'''F'''*?

   _____

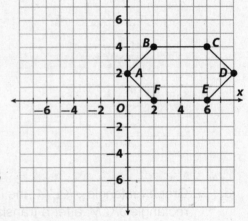

   d. A pattern of a figure that repeats and covers a plane without overlapping and without gaps is called a *tessellation*. Can figure *ABCDEF* be translated to create a tessellation? Explain.

   _____

4. A translation of each point (x, y) of a figure can be described using the coordinate notation $(x, y) \rightarrow (x + a, y + b)$, where *a* represents the horizontal distance moved and *b* represents the vertical distance moved. For triangle *PQR* with vertices $P(-3, -1)$, $Q(0, -1)$, and $R(-1, -3)$, find the coordinates of the vertices of the image after the translation $(x, y) \rightarrow (x - 5, y + 7)$.

_____

**LESSON
9-1**

Properties of Translations

Practice and Problem Solving: D

**Answer the questions about the given translation of triangle *ABC*
onto triangle *A'B'C'*. The first one is done for you.**

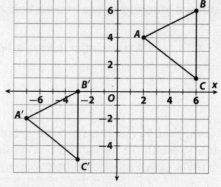

1. What is the image of *A*(2, 4)?___*A'*(−7, −2)___

2. What is the preimage of *B'*(−3, 0)?_____

3. What is the image of *C*(6, 1)?_____

4. Which side is congruent to side *AB*?_____

5. Which angle is congruent to angle *C*?_____

6. How would you describe the translation?

_____

7. Quadrilateral *PQRS* is given.

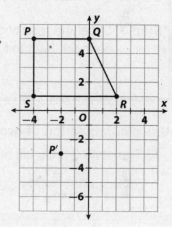

a. Vertex *P* is translated to point *P'* as shown.
   Describe the translation.

_____

b. Use the same translation to translate the remaining
   vertices. Draw quadrilateral *P'Q'R'S'*.

c. How do quadrilateral *PQRS* and quadrilateral *P'Q'R'S'*
   compare?

_____

Draw the image of the figure after each translation.

8. 3 units right and 4 units down

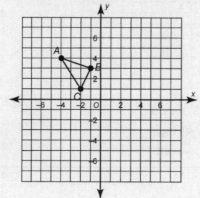

9. 5 units left and 2 units up

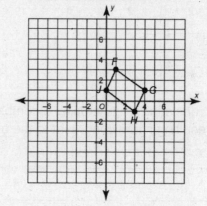

**LESSON
9-1**

Properties of Translations
Reteach

The description of a translation in a coordinate plane uses a combination of two translations – one translation slides the figure in a horizontal direction, and the other slides the figure in a vertical direction. An example is shown below.

A translation slides a figure 8 units right and 5 units down.

horizontal distance   vertical distance

Triangle *LMN* is shown in the graph. The triangle can be translated 8 units right and 5 units down as shown below.

Step 1 Translate each vertex 8 units right.

Step 2 Translate each vertex 5 units down.

Step 3 Label the resulting vertices and connect them to form triangle *L'M'N'*.

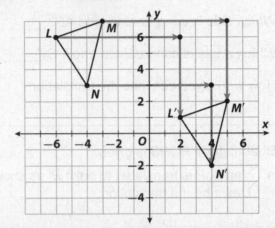

Use a combination of two translations to draw the image of the figure.

1. Translate 6 units left and 7 units down.

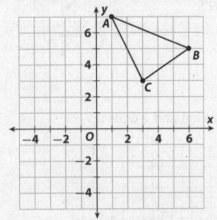

2. Translate 7 units right and 9 units up.

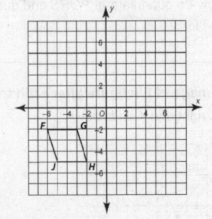

3. When translating a figure using a combination of two translations, is the resulting figure congruent to the original figure? Explain.

_____

_____

LESSON 9-1 Properties of Translations

Reading Strategies: Build Vocabulary

A **transformation** is an operation that describes a change in the position, size, or shape of a figure. A **translation** is one kind of transformation.

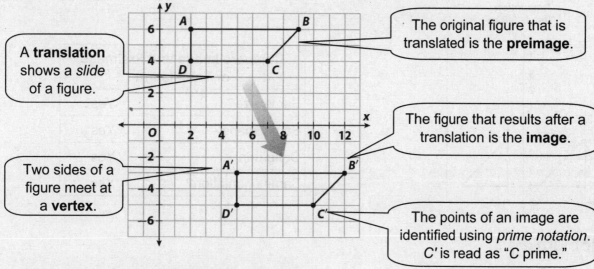

A **translation** shows a *slide* of a figure.

The original figure that is translated is the **preimage**.

The figure that results after a translation is the **image**.

Two sides of a figure meet at a **vertex**.

The points of an image are identified using *prime notation*. *C'* is read as "*C* prime."

In Exercises 1–5, use the translation shown.

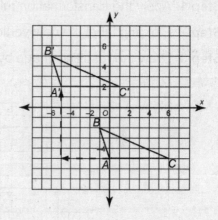

1. What is the image of the translation?

   _____

2. What is the preimage of the translation?

   _____

3. How many vertices does the preimage have?

   _____

4. Is the image congruent to the preimage? Explain.

   _____

   _____

5. Describe the translation.

   _____

6. Describe the difference between a transformation and a translation.

   _____

   _____

LESSON
9-1

Properties of Translations

Success for English Learners

Problem 1

Translation
Think: *Slide*

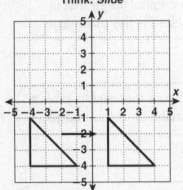

Compare Image and Preimage of Translation		
Same size?		Yes
Same shape?		Yes
Congruent?		Yes
Same orientation?		Yes

Problem 2

Steps for Translating a Figure

Step 1 Apply the transformation rule to each vertex.

Step 2 Plot and label the new vertices on the same coordinate grid.

Step 3 Draw the resulting image by connecting the vertices.

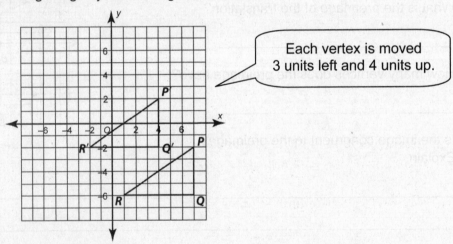

Each vertex is moved
3 units left and 4 units up.

1. Describe the translation in Problem 1.

_____

_____

2. In Problem 2, suppose triangle *PQR* is translated using the translation "4 units up and 3 units left." Is the resulting image the same as in Problem 2? Explain why or why not.

_____

_____

LESSON 9-2

Properties of Reflections

Practice and Problem Solving: A/B

Use the graph for Exercises 1–3.

1. Quadrilateral *J* is reflected across the *x*-axis. What is the image of the reflection?

   _____

2. Which two quadrilaterals are reflections of each other across the *y*-axis?

   _____

3. How are quadrilaterals *H* and *J* related?

   _____

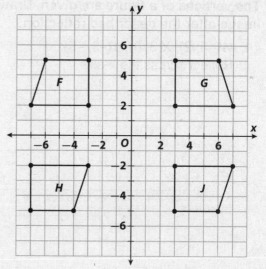

Draw the image of the figure after each reflection.

4. across the *x*-axis

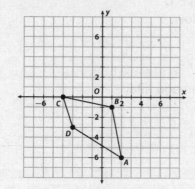

5. across the *y*-axis

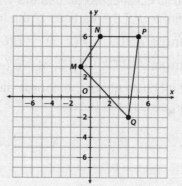

6. a. Graph rectangle *K'L'M'N'*, the image of rectangle *KLMN* after a reflection across the *y*-axis.

   b. What is the perimeter of each rectangle?

   _____

   c. Is it possible for the perimeter of a figure to change after it is reflected? Explain.

   _____

   _____

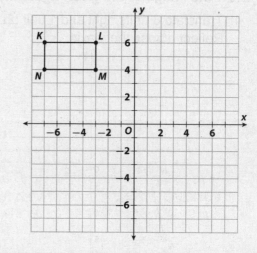

LESSON
9-2

Properties of Reflections

Practice and Problem Solving: C

The vertices of a figure are given. Draw the figure. Then draw its image after the described reflection.

1. $W(-5, 2)$, $X(3, 0)$, $Y(-2, -5)$
   Reflect across the x-axis.

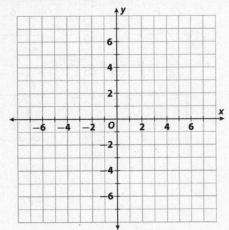

2. $G(3, -3)$, $H(-5, -1)$, $J(-4, 3)$, $K(2, 2)$
   Reflect across the y-axis.

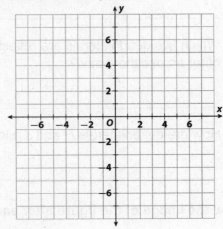

3. Triangle ABC is reflected across the y-axis to form triangle $A'B'C'$.
   The coordinates of the vertices of the triangles are given below.

   Triangle ABC: $A(2, 3)$ $B(6, 7)$ $C(4, 1)$

   Triangle $A'B'C'$: $A'(-2, 3)$ $B'(-6, 7)$ $C'(-4, 1)$

   Make a conjecture about the coordinates of a figure and its image after
   a reflection across the y-axis.

   _____

   _____

Draw the image of the given figure after the two transformations.

4. Translate 8 units right and 1 unit up.
   Reflect across the x-axis.

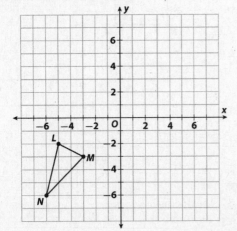

5. Reflect across the y-axis.
   Translate 2 units left and 5 units up.

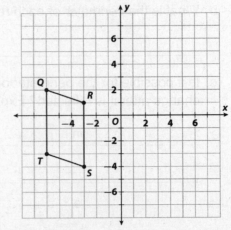

LESSON 9-2

Properties of Reflections
Practice and Problem Solving: D

**Answer the questions about the given reflection of quadrilateral
ABCD onto quadrilateral *A'B'C'D'*. The first one is done for you.**

1. What is the image of *A*(−6, 2)? ___*A'*(6, 2)___

2. What is the preimage of *B'*(5, 6)? _____

3. What is the image of *C*(−3, 7)? _____

4. Which side is congruent to side *CD*? _____

5. Which angle is congruent to angle *D*? _____

6. How would you describe the reflection?

   _____

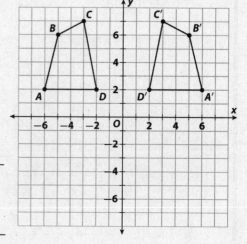

Draw the image of the figure after each reflection.

7. across the *x*-axis

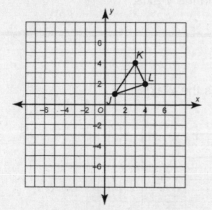

8. across the *y*-axis

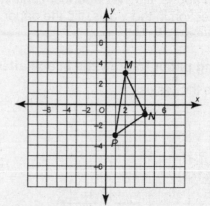

**Choose the word in parentheses that makes the statement true.
The first one is done for you.**

9. A reflection is a transformation that (*slides, flips, turns*) a figure across

   a line. ___*flips*___

10. The image of a reflection is (*sometimes, always, never*) congruent to

    the original figure. _____

11. In a reflection across the *x*-axis, the (*x*-coordinate, *y*-coordinate)

    changes. _____

LESSON
9-2

Properties of Reflections
Reteach

You can use tracing paper to reflect a figure in the coordinate plane. The graphs below show how to reflect a triangle across the *y*-axis.

Start by tracing the figure and the axes on tracing paper.

Flip the tracing paper over, making sure to align the axes. Transfer the flipped image onto the coordinate plane.

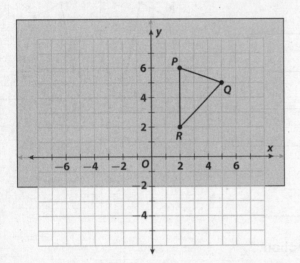
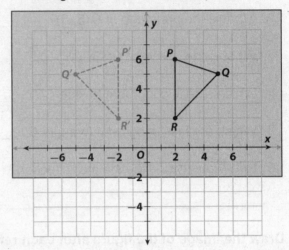

As shown above, flip the paper horizontally for a reflection in the *y*-axis.
For a reflection in the *x*-axis, flip the paper vertically.

Use tracing paper to draw the image after the reflection.

1. across the *y*-axis

2. across the *x*-axis

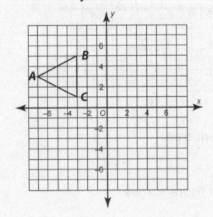
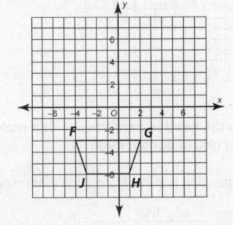

Name _____ Date _____ Class _____

Properties of Reflections
Reading Strategies: Analyze Graphs

A **transformation** is an operation that describes a change in the position, size, or shape of a figure. A **reflection** is one kind of transformation.

In a **reflection**, a figure is flipped across a line.

Corresponding vertices can be easily identified when *prime notation* is used.

The original figure is quadrilateral *ABCD*.

The figure is reflected across the *x*-axis.

The image of the reflection is quadrilateral *A'B'C'D'*, which is read as "*A* prime, *B* prime, *C* prime, *D* prime."

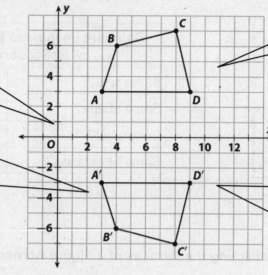

In Exercises 1–4, use the reflection shown.

1. What is the image of the reflection?

_____

2. What is the original figure of the reflection?

_____

3. Name a pair of corresponding vertices.

_____

4. Describe the reflection.

_____

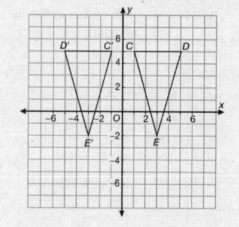

5. Quadrilateral *P'Q'R'S'* is the image of a figure that is flipped across the *x*-axis. Complete each statement about the transformation.

   a. The name of the original figure is _____.

   b. The transformation is called a _____.

6. Suppose a figure is reflected across a line. Describe the relationship between a point on the original figure and its corresponding point on the image.

_____

Properties of Reflections

Success for English Learners

Problem 1

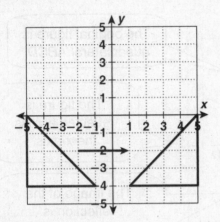

Compare Image and Preimage of Reflection	
Same size?	Yes
Same shape?	Yes
Congruent?	Yes
Same orientation?	No

Problem 2

Steps for Reflecting the Vertices of a Figure Across a Line

Step 1
Find distance from the line of reflection to each vertex in the original figure.

Step 2
Move the same distance in the opposite direction to plot the vertices of the image.

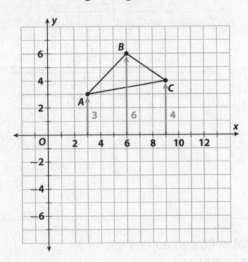

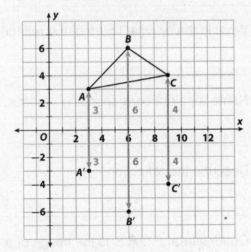

1. Describe the reflection in Problem 1.

_____

2. In Problem 2, what other step is needed to complete the reflection of the original figure?

_____

LESSON 9-3

Properties of Rotations
Practice and Problem Solving: A/B

Use the figures at the right for Exercises 1–5. Triangle *A* has been rotated about the origin.

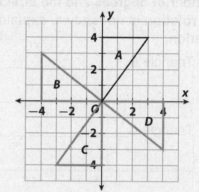

1. Which triangle shows a 90° counterclockwise rotation? ____

2. Which triangle shows a 180° counterclockwise rotation? ____

3. Which triangle shows a 270° clockwise rotation? ____

4. Which triangle shows a 270° counterclockwise rotation? ____

5. If the sides of triangle *A* have lengths of 30 cm, 40 cm, and 50 cm, what are the lengths of the sides of triangle *D*?

_____

Use the figures at the right for Exercises 6–10. Figure *A* is to be rotated about the origin.

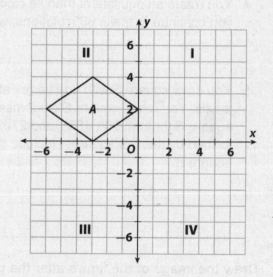

6. If you rotate figure *A* 90° counterclockwise, what quadrant will the image be in? ____

7. If you rotate figure *A* 270° counterclockwise, what quadrant will the image be in? ____

8. If you rotate figure *A* 180° clockwise, what quadrant will the image be in? ____

9. If you rotate figure *A* 360° clockwise, what quadrant will the image be in? ____

10. If the measures of two angles in figure *A* are 60° and 120°, what will the measure of those two angles be in the rotated figure?

_____

Use the grid at the right for Exercises 11–12.

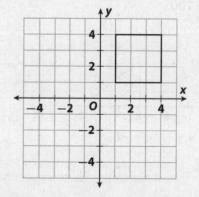

11. Draw a square to show a rotation of 90° clockwise about the origin of the given square in quadrant I.

12. What other transformation would result in the same image as you drew in Exercise 11?

_____

LESSON 9-3

Properties of Rotations

Practice and Problem Solving: C

Tell whether each triangle shows a rotation of triangle A about the origin. If a rotation is shown, give the number of degrees and the direction of the rotation. If a rotation is not shown, explain why it is not a rotation.

1. Triangle *B*_____

   _____

2. Triangle *C*_____

   _____

3. Triangle *D*_____

   _____

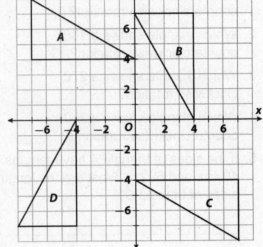

Solve.

4. You rotate an equilateral triangle clockwise 60° as shown at the right. If you continue to make 60° rotations, what larger figure will be formed?

   _____

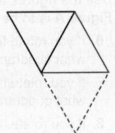

5. You draw square *S* with one vertex at the origin and one side along the *x*-axis. You rotate square *S* clockwise about the origin. You rotate square *S* through 90°, 180°, and 270°. Describe the large figure that is formed by the four squares. Include the size of the sides in relation to square *S*.

   _____

   _____

Draw the image of the figure after the given rotation about the origin.

6. 180°

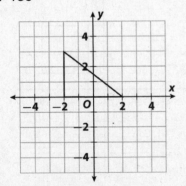

7. 90° counterclockwise

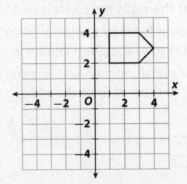

LESSON 9-3

Properties of Rotations
Practice and Problem Solving: D

Use the figures at the right for Exercises 1–5.
Rectangle A has been rotated about the origin.
The first one has been done for you.

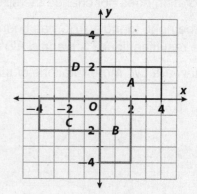

1. Which rectangle shows a 270°
   counterclockwise rotation? __**B**__

2. Which rectangle shows a 180°
   clockwise rotation? ____

3. Which rectangle shows a 90°
   clockwise rotation? ____

4. Which rectangle shows a 90°
   counterclockwise rotation? ____

5. If two sides of rectangle A have lengths of
   2 cm and 4 cm, what are the lengths of the
   two corresponding sides of rectangle C?

   _____

Use the figure at the right for Exercises 6–9.
Figure A is to be rotated about the origin. The
first one has been done for you.

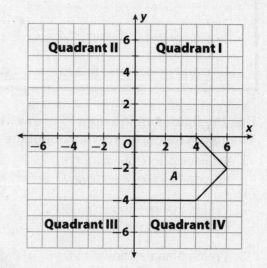

6. If you rotate figure A 270° clockwise,
   what quadrant will the image be in? __**I**__

7. If you rotate figure A 90° counterclockwise,
   what quadrant will the image be in? ____

8. If you rotate figure A 90° clockwise,
   what quadrant will the image be in? ____

9. If you rotate figure A 180° clockwise,
   what quadrant will the image be in? ____

Use the grid at the right for Exercises 10–11.

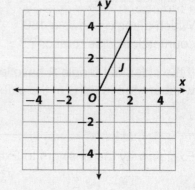

10. Draw a triangle to show a rotation of 180° clockwise
    about the origin of triangle J. Label the image
    triangle as K.

11. Suppose you rotate triangle J 180° counterclockwise
    about the origin. Compare the image of that rotation
    with triangle K.

    _____

    _____

Name _____ Date _____ Class _____

LESSON 9-3 Properties of Rotations
Reteach

A **rotation** is a change in position of a figure.

A rotation will *turn* the figure around a point called the **center of rotation**.

A rotation does not change the size of the figure.

At the right, triangle *ABC* has been rotated 90° clockwise. The resulting figure is triangle *A'B'C'*.

Below are two more rotations of triangle *ABC*.

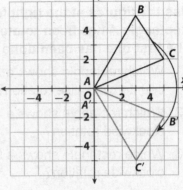

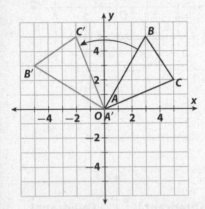

90° counterclockwise rotation

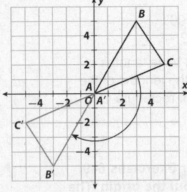

180° clockwise rotation

Use the figures at the right to answer each question.
Triangle *A* has been rotated about the origin.

1. Which triangle shows a 90° counterclockwise rotation? ____

2. Which triangle shows a 180° clockwise rotation? ____

3. Which triangle shows a 90° clockwise rotation? ____

4. Which triangle shows a 180° counterclockwise rotation? ____

5. If the sides of triangle *A* have lengths of 3 cm, 4 cm, and 5 cm, what are the lengths of the sides of triangle *B*?

_____

6. Explain why the answers to Exercises 2 and 4 are the same.

_____

_____

LESSON 9-3 **Properties of Rotations**

Reading Strategies: Using Visual Clues

Rotate the arrow 90° counterclockwise about the origin.

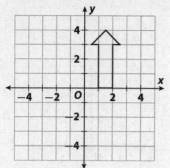

In which quadrant will the image be located?
Think:

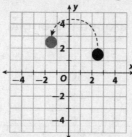

Counterclockwise goes from 12 to 9. The image will be in quadrant II.

How will the shape turn? What will it look like?

↑ Think: Go from 12 to 9 on a clock.

Where will the image be on the grid?

Think: Any vertices at the origin? No
           Any vertices on an axis? If so, which axis will the image be on and where? One side is from 1 to 2 on the x-axis. The image will be from 1 to 2 on the y-axis.

What else can help me?

Think: The point of the arrow is at (1.5, 4). The image will be in quadrant II, 1.5 units up from the x-axis and 4 units from the y-axis.

Use your clues to draw the image.

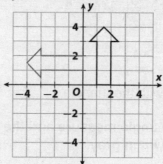

Rotate the figure on the grid 90° clockwise.

1. Write the clues you can use.

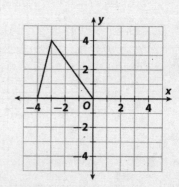

   _____

   _____

   _____

   _____

2. Draw the image of the figure after a 90° clockwise rotation.

Properties of Rotations

LESSON 9-3

Success for English Learners

A **rotation** turns a figure around a point called the **center of rotation**.

Problem 1

Rotate the triangle 90° clockwise around the origin.

Clockwise moves like clock hands.

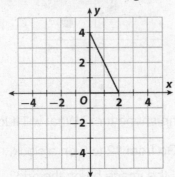

Start with the triangle.

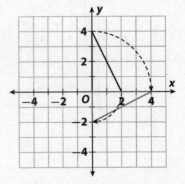

Each vertex turns 90°.

Problem 2

Rotate the triangle 180° counterclockwise around the origin.

Counterclockwise moves opposite of clock hands.

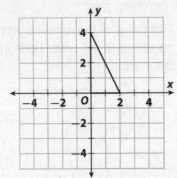

Start with the triangle.

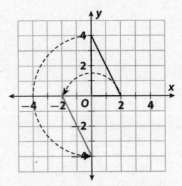

Each vertex turns 180°.

Describe each rotation by giving the angle measure and the direction of rotation. The rotated image is shown in gray.

1. _____

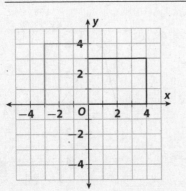

2. _____

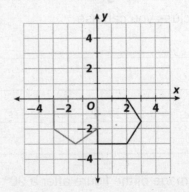

LESSON 9-4

Algebraic Representations of Transformations

Practice and Problem Solving: A/B

Write an algebraic rule to describe each transformation of figure A to figure A'. Then describe the transformation.

1.

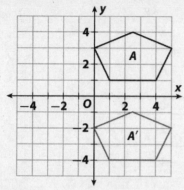

_____

_____

2.

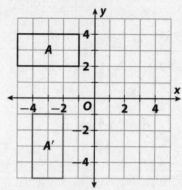

_____

_____

Use the given rule to graph the image of each figure. Then describe the transformation.

3. $(x, y) \rightarrow (-x, y)$

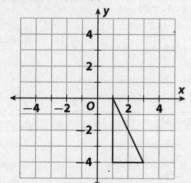

_____

4. $(x, y) \rightarrow (-x, -y)$

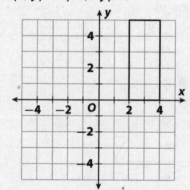

_____

Solve.

5. Triangle *ABC* has vertices *A*(2, –1), *B*(–3, 0), and *C*(–1, 4). Find the vertices of the image of triangle *ABC* after a translation of 2 units up.

_____

6. Triangle *LMN* has *L* at (1, –1) and *M* at (2, 3). Triangle *L'M'N'* has *L'* at (–1, –1) and *M'* is at (3, –2). Describe the transformation.

_____

LESSON
9-4
Algebraic Representations of Transformations
Practice and Problem Solving: C

**Write an algebraic rule to describe each transformation of figure
A to figure *A'*. Then describe the transformation.**

1.
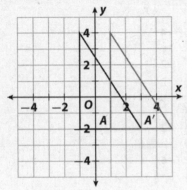

_____

_____

2.
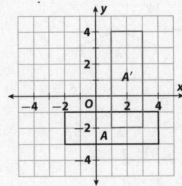

_____

_____

**Use the given rule to graph the image of each figure. Then describe
the transformation.**

3. $(x, y) \rightarrow (x, -y)$

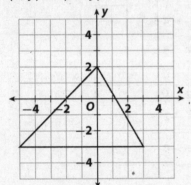

_____

4. $(x, y) \rightarrow (-x, -y)$

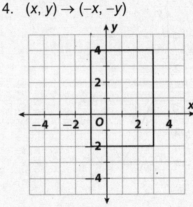

_____

Solve.

5. Triangle *ABC* has vertices *A*(2, −1), *B*(0, 0), and *C*(−1, 4). State a rule
   for an algebraic transformation where vertex *B* will **not** be at the origin.

_____

6. Triangle *LMN* has *L* at (1, −1) and *M* at (2, 3). Triangle *L'M'N'* has *L'* at
   (−1, −1), *M'* is at (3, −2), and *N'* is at (−3, 0). What are the coordinates
   of vertex *N*? Describe the transformation.

_____

LESSON 9-4
Algebraic Representations of Transformations
Practice and Problem Solving: D

**Complete the algebraic rule to describe each transformation of figure
A to figure *A'*. Then complete the description of the transformation.
The first one is done for you.**

1.

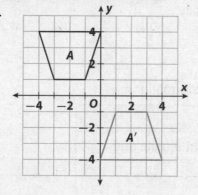

$(x, y) \rightarrow$ _____**(−x, −y)**_____

rotation of **180°** _____**clockwise**_____

2.

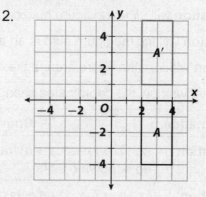

$(x, y) \rightarrow$ _____

translation _____ of ____ units

3.

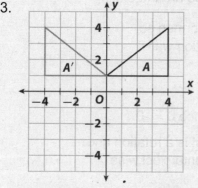

$(x, y) \rightarrow$ _____

reflection over the ___ -axis

4.

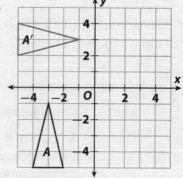

$(x, y) \rightarrow$ _____

rotation of ____ ° _____

**Figure *A* is shown on at the right. Use the rule
$(x, y) \rightarrow (x, -y)$ to give the coordinates of the image
of figure *A*. The first one is done for you.**

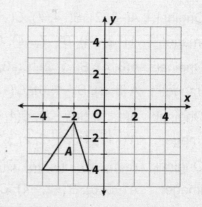

5. $(-4, -4) \rightarrow ($ __−4__, __4__ $)$

6. $(-1, -4) \rightarrow ($ ___, ___ $)$

7. $(-2, -1) \rightarrow ($ ___, ___ $)$

8. Graph the image of figure *A* for the rule
$(x, y) \rightarrow (x, -y)$.

LESSON 9-4

Algebraic Representations of Transformations
Reteach

A **transformation** is a change in size or position of a figure. The transformations below change only the position of the figure, not the size.

- A **translation** will *slide* the figure horizontally and/or vertically.

- A **reflection** will *flip* the figure across an axis.

- A **rotation** will *turn* the figure around the origin.

This table shows how the coordinates change with each transformation.

Transformation	Coordinate Mapping
Translation	$(x, y) \rightarrow (x + a, y + b)$ translates left or right a units and up or down b units
Reflection	$(x, y) \rightarrow (-x, y)$ reflects across the y-axis $(x, y) \rightarrow (x, -y)$ reflects across the x-axis
Rotation	$(x, y) \rightarrow (-x, -y)$ rotates 180° around origin $(x, y) \rightarrow (y, -x)$ rotates 90° clockwise around origin $(x, y) \rightarrow (-y, x)$ rotates 90° counterclockwise around origin

A triangle with coordinates of (0, 0), (1, 4), and (3, –2) is transformed so the coordinates are (0, 0), (–4, 1), and (2, 3). What transformation was performed?

Analyze each corresponding pairs of coordinates:

(0, 0) to (0, 0)	Think:	Could be reflection or rotation since 0 = –0.
(1, 4) to (–4, 1) (3, –2) to (2, 3)	Think:	Since x and y are interchanged, it is a rotation and y changes sign, so it is a 90° counterclockwise rotation around origin.

Identify the transformation from the original figure to the image.

1. Original: $A(-2, -4)$, $B(5, 1)$, $C(5, -4)$

   Image: $A'(2, -4)$, $B'(-5, 1)$, $C'(-5, -4)$ _____

2. Original: $A(-8, 2)$, $B(-4, 7)$, $C(-7, 2)$

   Image: $A'(-2, -8)$, $B'(-7, -4)$, $C'(-2, -7)$ _____

3. Original: $A(3, 4)$, $B(-1, 2)$, $C(-3, -5)$

   Image: $A'(3, 8)$, $B'(-1, 6)$, $C'(-3, -1)$ _____

4. Original: $A(1, 1)$, $B(2, -2)$, $C(4, 3)$

   Image: $A'(-1, -1)$, $B'(-2, 2)$, $C'(-4, -3)$ _____

5. Original: $A(-5, -6)$, $B(-2, 4)$, $C(3, 0)$

   Image: $A'(-5, 6)$, $B'(-2, -4)$, $C'(3, 0)$ _____

Name _____ Date _____ Class_____

LESSON
9-4

Algebraic Representations of Transformations
Reading Strategies: Use a Graphic Organizer

A **transformation** is a change in size or position of a figure. The transformations below change only the position of the figure, not the size.

- A **translation** will *slide* the figure horizontally and/or vertically.

- A **reflection** will *flip* the figure across an axis.

- A **rotation** will *turn* the figure around the origin.

$(x, y) \rightarrow (x + a, y + b)$ Analysis: Each value of *x* and/or *y* changes by a certain amount, *a* for *x* and *b* for *y*. Transformation: Translation over *a* units and/or up or down *b* units	$(x, y) \rightarrow (-x, -y)$ Analysis: The sign of both *x* and *y* change. Transformation: Rotation of 180° around origin

Analyzing changes in ordered pairs in transformations.

$(x, y) \rightarrow (-x, y)$ and $(x, y) \rightarrow (x, -y)$ Analysis: The sign of either *x* or *y* changes. Transformation: Reflection across the *y*-axis if the sign of *x* changes Reflection across the *x*-axis if the sign of *y* changes	$(x, y) \rightarrow (y, -x)$ and $(x, y) \rightarrow (-y, x)$ Analysis: The coordinates are switched and the sign of one changes. Transformation: Rotation of 90° clockwise if the sign of *x* changes Rotation of 90° counterclockwise if the sign of *y* changes

Identify the transformation from the original figure to the image.

1. Original: *A*(−1, −4), *B*(5, 1), *C*(5, −4)

   Image: *A'*(1, −4), *B'*(7, 1), *C'*(7, −4) _____

2. Original: *A*(6, 2), *B*(−4, 2), *C*(−1, −4)

   Image: *A'*(2, −6), *B'*(2, 4), *C'*(−4, 1) _____

3. Original: *A*(3, −4), *B*(−1, 2), *C*(3, −5)

   Image: *A'*(−3, 4), *B'*(1, −2), *C'*(−3, 5) _____

4. Original: *A*(1, 1), *B*(2, −2), *C*(4, 3)

   Image: *A'*(−1, 1), *B'*(−2, −2), *C'*(−4, 3) _____

Algebraic Representations of Transformations

LESSON 9-4

Success for English Learners

Some transformations change the position of a figure, but do not change the size of the figure.

Problem 1

How the positions change

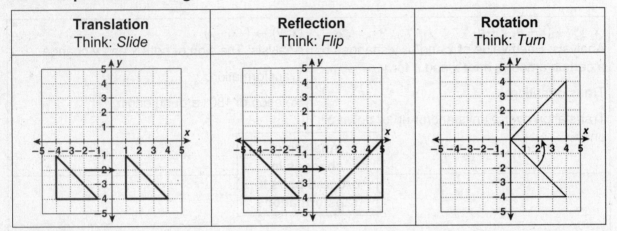

Translation Think: *Slide*	Reflection Think: *Flip*	Rotation Think: *Turn*

Problem 2

How the coordinates change

Translation Think: *Slide*	Reflection Think: *Flip*	Rotation Think: *Turn*
$(x, y) \rightarrow (x + a, y + b)$ translates left or right a units and up or down b units	$(x, y) \rightarrow (-x, y)$ reflects across the y-axis $(x, y) \rightarrow (x, -y)$ reflects across the x-axis	$(x, y) \rightarrow (-x, -y)$ rotates 180° around origin $(x, y) \rightarrow (y, -x)$ rotates 90° clockwise around origin $(x, y) \rightarrow (-y, x)$ rotates 90° counterclockwise around origin

Tell which transformation was used to change the position of the first arrow so it looks like the second arrow.

1. $\Rightarrow$ → $\Leftarrow$ 2. $\Leftarrow$ → $\Leftarrow$ 3. ⇑ → ⇓

_____   _____   _____

Tell which transformation is shown by the change in ordered pairs.

4. (3, 4), (2, −1), (0, 0) → (4, −3), (−1, −2), (0, 0)   _____

5. (−2, 0), (0, −2), (2, 2) → (0, 0), (2, −2), (4, 2)   _____

6. (1, 5), (1, −1), (−3, −2) → (1, −5), (1, 1), (−3, 2)   _____

LESSON 9-5

Congruent Figures

Practice and Problem Solving: A/B

Identify a sequence of transformations that will transform figure A into figure C.

1. What transformation is used to transform figure A to figure B?

   _____

2. What transformation is used to transform figure B to figure C?

   _____

3. What sequence of transformations is used to transform figure A to figure C? Express the transformations algebraically.

   _____

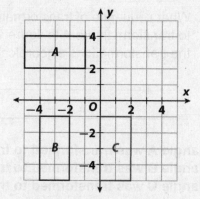

Complete each transformation.

4. Transform figure A by reflecting it over the y-axis. Label the new figure, B.

5. Transform figure B to figure C by applying $(x, y) \rightarrow (x, y + 5)$.

6. Transform figure C to figure D by rotating it 90° counterclockwise around the origin.

7. Compare figure A with figure D. Are the two figures congruent? _____

8. Do figures A and D have the same or different orientation? _____

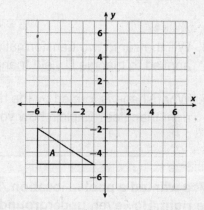

Alice wanted a pool in location A on the map at the right. However, underground wires forced her to move the pool to location B.

9. What transformations were applied to the pool at location A to move it to location B?

   _____

   _____

10. Did the relocation change the size or orientation of the pool?

   _____

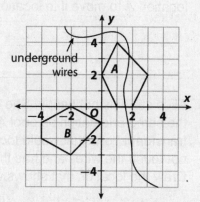

LESSON 9-5

Congruent Figures

Practice and Problem Solving: C

A transformation of figure *A* produces figure *B*. A second transformation produces figure *C*.

1. What sequence of transformations is used to transform figure *A* to figure *C*? Express the transformations algebraically.

   _____

   _____

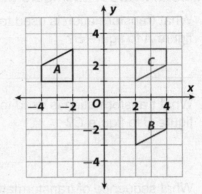

Triangle A was transformed to triangle B.
Triangle B was transformed to triangle C.
Triangle C was transformed to triangle D.

2. Each transformation included the same two transformations. Express those two transformations algebraically.

   _____

   _____

3. Will the same two transformations applied to triangle D yield triangle A? _____

4. What shape is formed by the hypotenuses of the right triangles? Explain how you know.

   _____

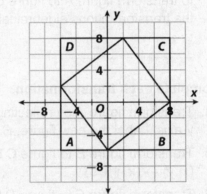

Alice wanted a pool in location *A* on the map at the right. However, underground wires forced her to move the pool to location *B*.

5. What transformations were applied to the pool at location *A* to move it to location *B*?

   _____

   _____

6. Alice still was not happy. She wants the pool to have the same orientation as pool *A*. Describe possible transformations that would locate the pool so that it does not touch the wires and has the same orientation as pool *A*. Draw the location that shows your suggested transformations.

   _____

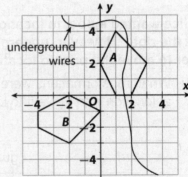

_____

LESSON 9-5

Congruent Figures

Practice and Problem Solving: D

Identify a sequence of transformations that will transform figure A into figure C. The first one is done for you.

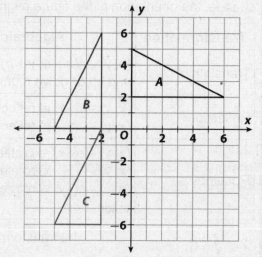

1. What transformation is used to transform figure A to figure B?

   rotation 90° counterclockwise

2. What transformation is used to transform figure B to figure C?

   _____

3. What sequence of transformations is used to transform figure A to figure C? Express the transformations algebraically.

   _____

   _____

Complete each transformation. The first one is done for you.

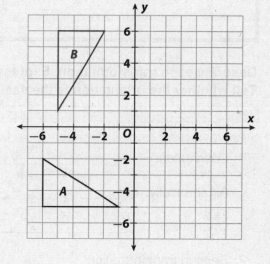

4. Transform figure A to figure B by rotating it 90° clockwise around the origin, so $(x, y) \rightarrow (y, -x)$.

5. Compare figure A with figure B. Are the two figures congruent? _____

6. Do figures A and B have the same or different orientation? _____

7. Transform figure B to figure C by translating it 8 units right, so $(x, y) \rightarrow (x + 8, y)$.

8. Compare figure B with figure C. Are the two figures congruent? _____

9. Do figures B and C have the same or different orientation? _____

10. Transform figure C to figure D by reflecting it over the x-axis so $(x, y) \rightarrow (x, -y)$.

11. Compare figure C with figure D. Are the two figures congruent? _____

12. Do figures C and D have the same or different orientation? _____

13. Compare figure A with figure D. Are the two figures congruent? _____

14. Do figures A and D have the same or different orientation? _____

LESSON 9-5

Congruent Figures
Reteach

When combining the transformations below, the original figure and transformed figure are **congruent**. Even though the size does not change, the orientation of the figure might change.

Transformation	Algebraic Coordinate Mapping	Orientation
Translation	$(x, y) \rightarrow (x + a, y + b)$ translates left or right a units and up or down b units	same
Reflection	$(x, y) \rightarrow (-x, y)$ reflects across the y-axis $(x, y) \rightarrow (x, -y)$ reflects across the x-axis	different
Rotation	$(x, y) \rightarrow (-x, -y)$ rotates 180° around origin $(x, y) \rightarrow (y, -x)$ rotates 90° clockwise around origin $(x, y) \rightarrow (-y, x)$ rotates 90° counterclockwise around origin	different

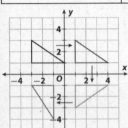

1st transformation: translation right 4 units
$(x, y) \rightarrow (x + 4, y)$,   orientation: same

2nd transformation: reflection over the x-axis
$(x, y) \rightarrow (x, -y)$,   orientation: different

3rd transformation: rotation 90° clockwise
$(x, y) \rightarrow (y, -x)$ orientation: different

**Describe each transformation. Express each algebraically.
Tell whether the orientation is the same or different.**

1. First transformation

   Description: _____

   Algebraically: _____

   Orientation: _____

2. Second transformation

   Description: _____

   Algebraically: _____

   Orientation: _____

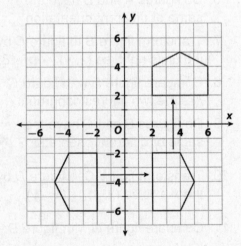

LESSON 9-5

Congruent Figures

Reading Strategies: Compare and Contrast

Some **transformations** create **congruent** figures.
These transformations are translations, rotations, and reflections.

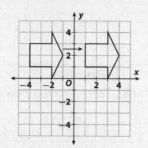

Identify the transformation:
Translation 5 units right

Compare and contrast:
Each value of x changes by 5.

Algebraic notation:

$$(x, y) \rightarrow (x + 5, y)$$

The figures are congruent.

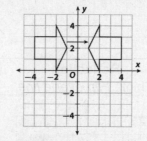

Identify the transformation:
Reflection over the y-axis

Compare and contrast:
The value of x changes signs.

Algebraic notation:

$$(x, y) \rightarrow (-x, y)$$

The figures are congruent.

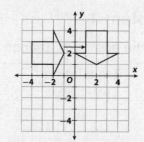

Identify the transformation:
90° rotation clockwise

Compare and contrast:
The x and y are switched, and x changes signs.

Algebraic notation:

$$(x, y) \rightarrow (y, -x)$$

The figures are congruent.

Use the figure for Exercises 1–4.

1. Identify the transformation.

   _____

2. Compare and contrast changes.

   _____

3. Algebraic notation: $(x, y) \rightarrow$ _____

4. Are the figures congruent? _____

Use the figure for Exercises 5–8.

5. Identify the transformation. _____

6. Compare and contrast changes.

   _____

7. Algebraic notation: $(x, y) \rightarrow$ _____

8. Are the figures congruent? _____

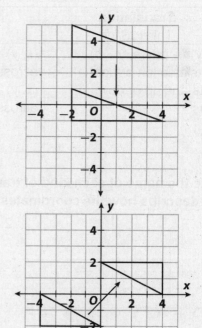

Congruent Figures
Success for English Learners

Some transformations change the position of a shape but do not change its size. Translations, reflections, and rotations all produce congruent figures.

Problem 1

How the positions change

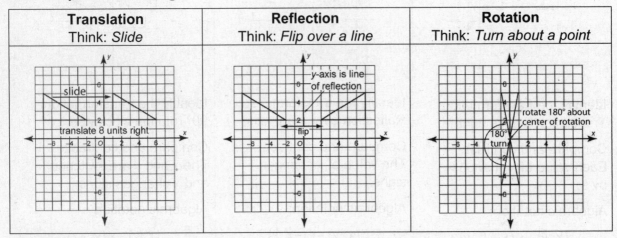

Translation	Reflection	Rotation
Think: *Slide*	Think: *Flip over a line*	Think: *Turn about a point*

Problem 2

How the coordinates change

Translation	Reflection	Rotation
Think: *Slide*	Think: *Flip*	Think: *Turn*
$(x, y) \rightarrow (x + a, y + b)$ translates left or right a units and up or down b units	$(x, y) \rightarrow (-x, y)$ reflects across the y-axis $(x, y) \rightarrow (x, -y)$ reflects across the x-axis	$(x, y) \rightarrow (-x, -y)$ rotates $180°$ around origin $(x, y) \rightarrow (y, -x)$ rotates $90°$ clockwise around origin $(x, y) \rightarrow (-y, x)$ rotates $90°$ counterclockwise around origin

Write the name of each kind of transformation. Use *x* and *y* to describe how the coordinates change.

1.

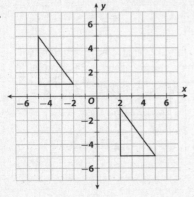

_____

2.

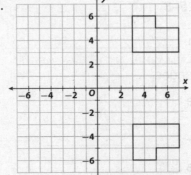

_____

3.

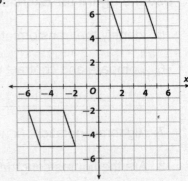

_____

MODULE 9 — Transformations and Congruence

Challenge

In this module the transformations you dealt with are called isometric transformations. Isometric means "has the same measures" so these transformations produce congruent images. There are two types of isometric transformations:

Direct—the original figure and the image have the same size, shape, and orientation. If the figure is named by letters they are not reversed.

Opposite—the original figure and the image have the same size and shape, but the orientation is not preserved. The image may point in a different direction and lettered points may be reversed.

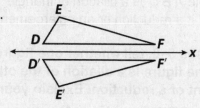

For each of Exercises 1–4 write an algebraic rule for the coordinates of the image. Then identify the type of transformation and state whether it is direct or opposite.

1.

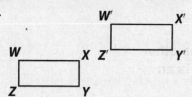

_____

_____

2.

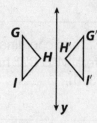

_____

_____

3.

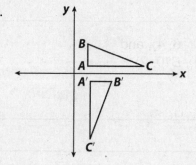

_____

_____

4.

_____

_____

Look at the coordinate pairs for each type of isometric transformation.

5. Which transformations are direct?

_____

6. Which transformations are opposite?

_____

LESSON 10-1

Properties of Dilations

Practice and Problem Solving: A/B

Use triangles *ABC* and *A'B'C'* for Exercises 1–4.

1. Use the coordinates to find the lengths of the sides.

   Triangle *ABC*: *AB* = ____ ; *BC* = ____

   Triangle *A'B'C'*: *A'B'* = ____ ; *B'C'* = ____

2. Find the ratios of the corresponding sides.

   $\dfrac{A'B'}{AB} = $ ——— = ——— $\dfrac{B'C'}{BC} = $ ——— = ———

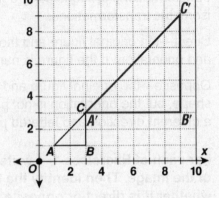

3. Is triangle *A'B'C'* a dilation of triangle *ABC*? _____

4. If triangle *A'B'C'* is a dilation of triangle
   ABC, is it a reduction or an enlargement? _____

For Exercises 5–8, tell whether one figure is a dilation of the other or not. If one figure is a dilation of the other, tell whether it is an enlargement or a reduction. Explain your reasoning.

5. Triangle *R'S'T'* has sides of 3 cm, 4 cm, and 5 cm. Triangle *RST* has sides of 12 cm, 16 cm, and 25 cm.

   _____

   _____

6. Quadrilateral *WBCD* has coordinates of *W*(0, 0), *B*(0, 4), *C*(–6, 4), and *D*(–6, 0). Quadrilateral *W'B'C'D'* has coordinates of *W'*(0, 0), *B'*(0, 2), *C'*(–3, 2), and *D'*(–3, 0).

   _____

   _____

7. Triangle *MLQ* has sides of 4 cm, 4 cm, and 7 cm. Triangle *M'L'Q'* has sides of 12 cm, 12 cm, and 21 cm.

   _____

   _____

8. Do the figures at the right show a dilation? Explain.

   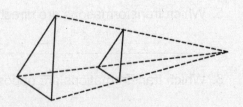

   _____

   _____

   _____

LESSON 10-1

Properties of Dilations

Practice and Problem Solving: C

Identify the scale factor used in each dilation.

1.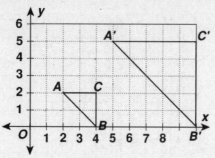

   scale factor: ____

2.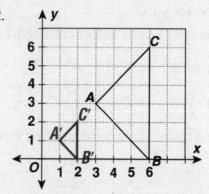

   scale factor: ____

Find the center of dilation for each pair of figures.

3.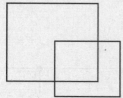

4.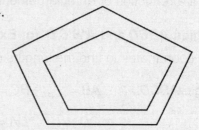

Solve.

5. A rectangle on the coordinate plane has vertices at (0, 0), (3, 0), (3, 2), and (0, 2). A dilation of the rectangle has vertices at (0, 0), (9, 0), (9, 6), and (0, 6). Find the scale factor and area of each rectangle.

   scale factor: ____ ; area of original rectangle: ____ ; area of dilation: ____

6. A rectangle on the coordinate plane has vertices at (0, 0), (4, 0), (4, 2), and (0, 2). A dilation of the rectangle has vertices at (0, 0), (2, 0), (2, 1), and (0, 1). Find the scale factor and area of each rectangle.

   scale factor: ____ ; area of original rectangle: ____ ; area of dilation: ____

7. Use the answers to Exercises 5 and 6. Make a conjecture about the relationship of the scale factor to the area of an original rectangle and its dilation.

   _____

   _____

LESSON
10-1

Properties of Dilations

Practice and Problem Solving: D

Use triangles *ABC* and *A'B'C'* for Exercises 1–4. The first one is done for you.

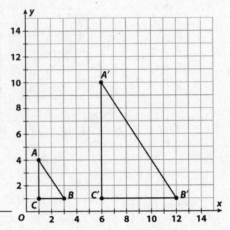

1. Use the coordinates to find the lengths of the sides.

   Triangle *ABC*: *AC* = __3__ ; *BC* = __2__

   Triangle *A'B'C'*: *A'C'* = __9__ ; *B'C'* = __6__

2. Find the ratios of the corresponding sides.

   $\dfrac{A'C'}{AC}$ = ——— = _____ $\dfrac{B'C'}{BC}$ = ——— = _____

3. Is triangle *A'B'C'* a dilation of triangle *ABC*? _____

4. If triangle *A'B'C'* is a dilation of triangle *ABC*, is it a reduction or an enlargement? _____

Use rectangles *ABCD* and *A'B'C'D'* for Exercises 5–8.

5. Use the coordinates to find the lengths of the sides.

   Rectangle *ABCD*:   *AB* = ___ ; *BC* = ___ ;

                          CD = ___ ; *DA* = ___

   Rectangle *A'B'C'D'*:   *A'B'* = ___ ; *B'C'* = ___ ;

                          C'D' = ___ ; *D'A'* = ___

6. Find the ratios of the corresponding sides.

   $\dfrac{A'B'}{AB}$ = ——— = _____ $\dfrac{B'C'}{BC}$ = ——— = _____

   $\dfrac{C'D'}{CD}$ = ——— = _____ $\dfrac{D'A'}{DA}$ = ——— = _____

7. Is rectangle *A'B'C'D'* a dilation of rectangle *ABCD*?   YES   NO

8. If rectangle *A'B'C'D'* is a dilation of rectangle *ABCD*, is it a reduction or an enlargement? _____

Solve.

9. If the scale factor is greater than one, is the new figure an enlargement or a reduction of the original figure? _____

LESSON
10-1

Properties of Dilations

Reteach

A **dilation** can change the size of a figure without changing its shape.

Lines drawn through the corresponding vertices meet at a point called the **center of dilation**.

To determine whether a transformation is a dilation, compare the ratios of the lengths of the corresponding sides.

$$\frac{A'B'}{AB} = \frac{2}{1} = 2$$

$$\frac{B'C'}{BC} = \frac{6}{3} = 2$$

The ratios are equal, so the triangles are similar, and the transformation is a dilation.

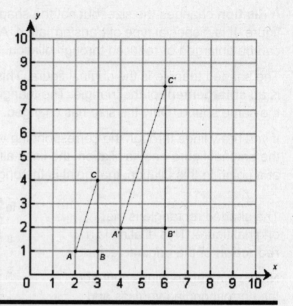

Determine whether each transformation is a dilation.

1.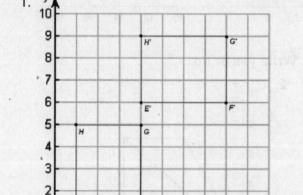

$$\frac{E'F'}{EF} = \frac{\rule{1cm}{0.4pt}}{\rule{1cm}{0.4pt}} = \rule{1cm}{0.4pt}$$

$$\frac{F'G'}{FG} = \frac{\rule{1cm}{0.4pt}}{\rule{1cm}{0.4pt}} = \rule{1cm}{0.4pt}$$

Are the ratios equal?_____

Is this a dilation?_____

2.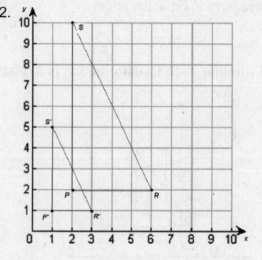

$$\frac{P'R'}{PR} = \frac{\rule{1cm}{0.4pt}}{\rule{1cm}{0.4pt}} = \rule{1cm}{0.4pt}$$

$$\frac{P'S'}{PS} = \frac{\rule{1cm}{0.4pt}}{\rule{1cm}{0.4pt}} = \rule{1cm}{0.4pt}$$

Are the ratios equal?_____

Is this a dilation?_____

Properties of Dilations

Reading Strategies: Use a Visual Aid

A **dilation** changes the size, but not the shape, of a figure. It is a special type of transformation. A figure can be enlarged or reduced through dilation.

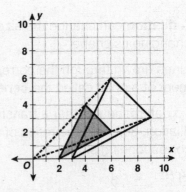

The shaded triangle is the original figure. This dilation is an **enlargement** of the triangle. The triangles have the same shape. Only the size has changed.

If you draw lines through the corresponding vertices of the original figure and its dilation, the lines all intersect at a point. In this dilation, that point is the origin.

The shaded rectangle is the original figure. This dilation is a **reduction** of the original rectangle.

Notice the dashed lines connect the corresponding vertices and intersect at a single point. The point of intersection does not always have to be at the origin.

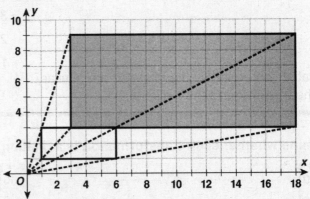

Tell whether each transformation is a dilation. Write *yes* or *no*.

1.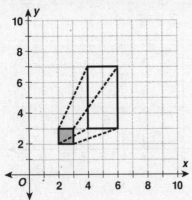

_____

2.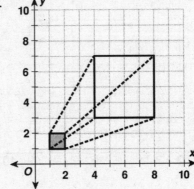

_____

LESSON 10-1 Properties of Dilations
Success for English Learners

A **dilation** changes the size of a figure without changing its shape.
Some dilations are **enlargements**. Some dilations are **reductions**.
In a dilation, the **ratios** of the lengths of corresponding sides are equal.

Problem 1

Do the figures at the right show a dilation? If so, is it an enlargement or a reduction?

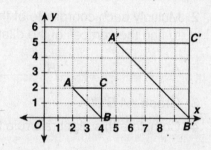

$\left.\begin{array}{l} \dfrac{A'C'}{AC} = \dfrac{5}{2} = 2.5 \\[3mm] \dfrac{B'C'}{BC} = \dfrac{5}{2} = 2.5 \end{array}\right\}$ These are equal. This is a dilation.

A'B'C' is an **enlargement** of *ABC* because:

• the ratio of corresponding lengths is greater than 1, and

• *A'B'C'* is the same shape as *ABC*, but larger.

Problem 2

Do the figures at the right show a dilation? If so, is it an enlargement or a reduction?

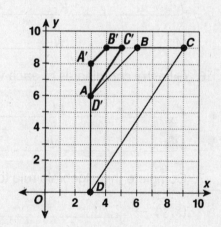

$\left.\begin{array}{l} \dfrac{A'D'}{AD} = \dfrac{2}{6} = \dfrac{1}{3} \\[3mm] \dfrac{B'C'}{BC} = \dfrac{1}{3} \end{array}\right\}$ These are equal. This is a dilation.

A'B'C'D' is a **reduction** of *ABCD* because:

• the ratio of corresponding lengths is less than 1, and

• *A'B'C'D'* is the same shape as *ABCD*, but smaller.

Tell whether each dilation is an enlargement or a reduction.

1.

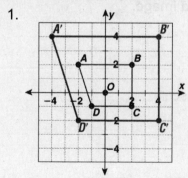

2.

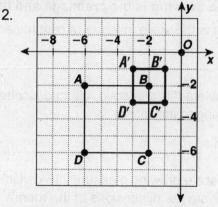

_____   _____

**LESSON
10-2**

Algebraic Representations of Dilations

Practice and Problem Solving: A/B

Use triangle *ABC* for Exercises 1–4.

1. Give the coordinates of each vertex of △*ABC*.

   *A*_____ *B*_____ *C*_____

2. Multiply each coordinate of the vertices of △*ABC* by 2
   to find the vertices of the dilated image △*A'B'C'*.

   *A'*_____ *B'*_____ *C'*_____

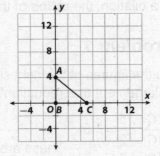

3. Graph △*A'B'C'*.

4. Complete this algebraic rule to describe the dilation.

   $(x, y) \rightarrow$ _____

Use the figures at the right for Exercises 5–7.

5. Give the coordinates of each vertex of figure *JKLM*.

   *J*_____ *K*_____ *L*_____

   *M*_____ *N*_____

6. Give the coordinates of each vertex of figure *J'K'L'M'*.

   *J'*_____ *K'*_____ *L'*_____

   *M'*_____ *N'*_____

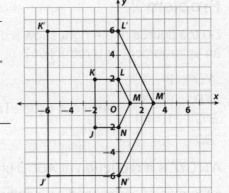

7. Complete this algebraic rule to describe the dilation.

   $(x, y) \rightarrow$ _____

**Li made a scale drawing of a room. The scale used was 5 cm = 1 m.
The scale drawing is the preimage and the room is the dilated image.**

8. What is the scale in terms of centimeters to centimeters?

   _____

9. Complete this algebraic rule to describe the dilation from the scale
   drawing to the room.

   $(x, y) \rightarrow$ _____

10. The scale drawing measures 15 centimeters by 20 centimeters.
    What are the dimensions of the room?

   _____

LESSON
10-2

Algebraic Representations of Dilations
Practice and Problem Solving: C

**Judy drew the gray square shown at the right.
Then she drew an enlargement of that square
and a reduction of that square.**

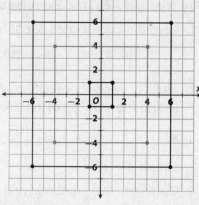

1. Complete this algebraic rule to describe the enlargement.

   $(x, y) \rightarrow$ _____

2. Complete this algebraic rule to describe the reduction.

   $(x, y) \rightarrow$ _____

**Roland made a scale drawing of a rectangular flower garden.
The scale used was 1 in. $= \dfrac{3}{4}$ ft. The scale drawing is the preimage
and the flower garden is the dilated image.**

3. The coordinates of three of the vertices of the scale drawing are (–3, 3),
   (2, 3), and (2, –1). What are the coordinates of the fourth vertex?

   _____

4. Complete this algebraic rule to describe the dilation from the scale
   drawing to the garden.

   $(x, y) \rightarrow$ _____

5. The scale drawing measures 5 in. by 4 in. What are the dimensions
   of the garden?

   _____

6. Roland decides to make the dimensions of his garden 50% larger.
   What are the coordinates of the new scale drawing?

   _____

7. What are the dimensions of the new scale drawing?

   _____

8. What are the dimensions of the new garden?

   _____

9. If Roland makes the dimensions of the original garden 50% smaller,
   what would the dimensions of the garden be?

   _____

LESSON 10-2

Algebraic Representations of Dilations

Practice and Problem Solving: D

Use triangle ABC for Exercises 1–4. The first one is done for you.

1. Give the coordinates of each vertex of △ABC.

   A_____(0, 6)_____ B_____(0, 0)_____ C_____(4, 0)_____

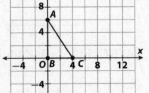

2. Multiply each coordinate of the vertices of △ABC by 2 to find the vertices of the dilated image △A'B'C'.

   A'_____ B'_____ C'_____

3. Graph △A'B'C'.

4. Complete this algebraic rule to describe the dilation.

   $(x, y) \rightarrow$ _____

Use the figures at the right for Exercises 5–7. The first one is done for you.

5. Give the coordinates of each vertex of figure JKLM.

   J_____(−2, −2)_____ K_____(−2, 2)_____

   L_____(2, 2)_____ M_____(2, −2)_____

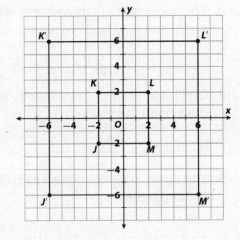

6. Give the coordinates of each vertex of figure J'K'L'M'.

   J'_____ K'_____

   L'_____ M'_____

7. Complete this algebraic rule to describe the dilation.

   $(x, y) \rightarrow$ _____

Li made a scale drawing of a room. The scale used was 1 in. = 1 ft. The scale drawing is the pre-image and the room is the dilated image. The first one is done for you.

8. What is the scale in terms of inches to inches?

   1 inch = 12 inches

9. Complete this algebraic rule to describe the dilation from the scale drawing to the room.

   $(x, y) \rightarrow$ _____

10. The scale drawing measures 10 inches by 12 inches. What are the dimensions of the room?

   _____

LESSON
10-2

Algebraic Representations of Dilations
Reteach

You dilate a figure using the origin as the center of dilation. Multiply each coordinate by the scale factor. The scale factor is the number that describes the change in size in a dilation.

Using the origin O as the center of dilation, dilate $\triangle ABC$ by a scale factor of 2.5.

$A(2, 2) \rightarrow A'(2.5 \bullet 2, 2.5 \bullet 2)$ or $A'(5, 5)$

$B(4, 0) \rightarrow B'(2.5 \bullet 4, 2.5 \bullet 0)$ or $B'(10, 0)$

$C(4, 2) \rightarrow C'(2.5 \bullet 4, 2.5 \bullet 2)$ or $C'(10, 5)$

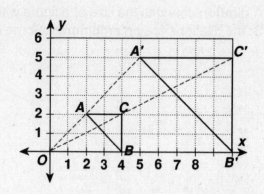

Using the origin as the center of dilation, dilate $\triangle ABC$ by a scale factor of 2. Graph the dilation.

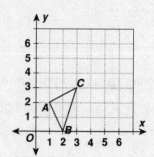

1. $A(1, 2) \rightarrow A'(2 \bullet 1, 2 \bullet 2)$ or $A'(\_\_\_\_ , \_\_\_\_)$

$B(2, 0) \rightarrow B'(\_\_\_\_ \bullet 2, \_\_\_\_ \bullet 0)$ or $B'(\_\_\_\_ , \_\_\_\_)$

$C(3, 3) \rightarrow C'(\_\_\_\_ \bullet 3, \_\_\_\_ \bullet 3)$ or $C'(\_\_\_\_ , \_\_\_\_)$

When the scale factor is a fraction between 0 and 1, the image is smaller than the original figure.
Using the origin O as the center of dilation, dilate $\triangle ABC$ by a scale factor of $\frac{1}{3}$.

$A(3, 3) \rightarrow A'\left(\frac{1}{3} \bullet 3, \frac{1}{3} \bullet 3\right)$ or $A'(1, 1)$

$B(6, 0) \rightarrow B'\left(\frac{1}{3} \bullet 6, \frac{1}{3} \bullet 0\right)$ or $B'(2, 0)$

$C(6, 6) \rightarrow C'\left(\frac{1}{3} \bullet 6, \frac{1}{3} \bullet 6\right)$ or $C'(2, 2)$

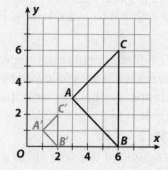

Using the origin as the center of dilation, dilate $\triangle ABC$ by a scale factor of $\frac{1}{2}$. Graph the dilation.

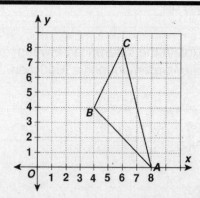

2. $A(8, 0) \rightarrow A'\left(\frac{1}{2} \bullet 8, \frac{1}{2} \bullet 0\right)$ or $A'(\_\_\_\_ , \_\_\_\_)$

$B(4, 4) \rightarrow B'(\_\_\_\_ \bullet 4, \_\_\_\_ \bullet 4)$ or $B'(\_\_\_\_ , \_\_\_\_)$

$C(6, 8) \rightarrow C'(\_\_\_\_ \bullet 6, \_\_\_\_ \bullet 8)$ or $C'(\_\_\_\_ , \_\_\_\_)$

LESSON 10-2
Algebraic Representations of Dilations
Reading Strategies: Build Vocabulary

A **dilation** changes the size of a figure without changing its shape.
Some dilations are **enlargements**. Some dilations are **reductions**.

dilations

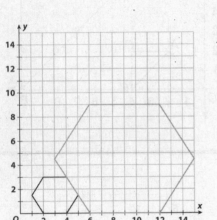

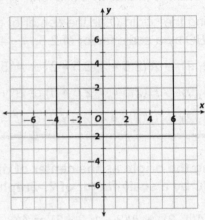

The gray figure is an **enlargement**.

The gray figure is a **reduction**.

The gray figures are called **images** of the black figure.

The black figures are the original figures.

Sometimes the original figures are called **preimages**.

Vertices of original figures or preimages are indicated with italic capital letters. For example, *ABC*.

Vertices of dilated figures or images are indicated with italic capital letters followed by a small mark called a prime symbol. For example, *A'B'C'*.

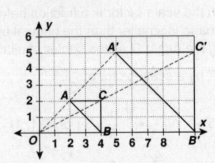

Complete.

1. The figures at the right show a reduction. Label the vertices of the original figure *MNP*. Label the vertices of the dilation *M'N'P'*.

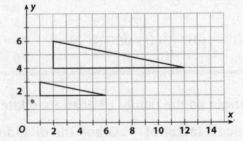

2. Explain the difference between an enlargement and a reduction.

_____

_____

Algebraic Representations of Dilations

LESSON 10-2

Success for English Learners

A **dilation** changes the size of a figure without changing its shape.
Some dilations are **enlargements**. Some dilations are **reductions**.

Problem 1

What are the characteristics of an enlargement?

Look at the coordinates of corresponding vertices.

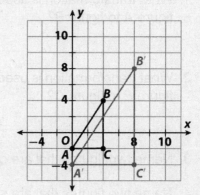

$A(0, -2) \rightarrow A'(0, -4)$

$B(4, 4) \rightarrow B'(8, 8)$

$C(4, -2) \rightarrow C'(8, -4)$

The absolute values of the coordinates of A', B', and C' are greater than the absolute values of the coordinates of A, B, and C.

$\dfrac{A'C'}{AC} = \dfrac{8}{4} = 2$

$\dfrac{B'C'}{BC} = \dfrac{12}{6} = 2$

Find the ratios of corresponding lengths. The ratios are equal and are greater than 1.

$A'B'C'$ is an **enlargement** of ABC because:

- The absolute values of the coordinates of the image are greater than the absolute values of the coordinates of the original figure.

- the ratio of corresponding lengths is greater than 1, and

- $A'B'C'$ is the same shape as ABC, but larger.

Problem 2

What are the characteristics of a reduction?

$A'B'C'D'$ is a **reduction** of $ABCD$ because:

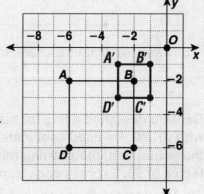

- The absolute values of the coordinates of the image are less than the absolute values of the coordinates of the original figure.

- the ratio of corresponding lengths is less than 1, and

- $A'B'C'D'$ is the same shape as $ABCD$, but smaller.

Tell whether each dilation is an enlargement or a reduction.

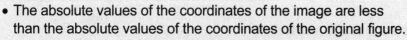

1. _____

2. _____

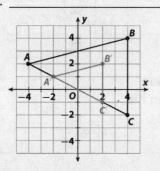

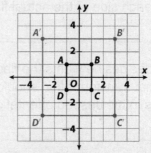

LESSON 10-3

Similar Figures

Practice and Problem Solving: A/B

Identify a sequence of transformations that will transform figure *A* into figure *C*. Express each transformation algebraically.

1. What transformation is used to transform figure *A* to figure *B*?

   _____

2. What transformation is used to transform figure *B* to figure *C*?

   _____

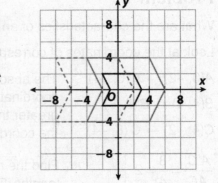

— Figure *A*
— Figure *B*
‐ ‐ Figure *C*

3. Name two figures that are congruent. _____

4. Name two figures that are similar, but not congruent. _____

Complete each transformation.

5. Transform figure *A* to figure *B* by applying $(x, y) \rightarrow (2x, 2y)$.

6. Transform figure *B* to figure *C* by rotating it 90° clockwise around the origin.

7. Name two figures that are congruent.

   _____

8. Name two figures that are similar, but not congruent.

   _____

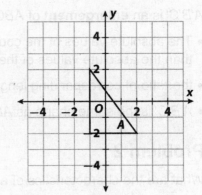

Geraldo designed a flag for his school. He started with △*ABC*. He used centimeter grid paper. To create the actual flag, the drawing must be dilated using a scale factor of 50. Express each transformation algebraically.

9. What transformation was used to create △*CBD* from △*ABC*?

   _____

10. How long will each side of the actual flag *ABD* be?

    _____

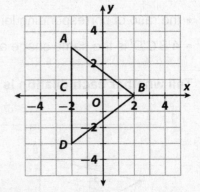

11. The principal decides he wants the flag to hang vertically with side *AD* on top. What transformation should Geraldo use on △*ABD* on his drawing so it is in the desired orientation?

    _____

LESSON 10-3

Similar Figures

Practice and Problem Solving: C

Identify a sequence of transformations that will transform figure A into figure C. Express each transformation algebraically.

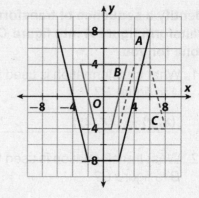

1. What transformation is used to transform figure *A* to figure *B*?

   _____

2. What two transformations are used to transform figure *B* to figure *C*?

   _____

3. Name two figures that are similar but not congruent.

   _____

Complete each transformation.

4. Transform figure *A* to figure *B* by applying

   $(x, y) \rightarrow \left(\dfrac{1}{3}x, \dfrac{1}{3}y\right)$.

5. Transform figure *B* to figure *C* with these two transformations:

   $(x, y) \rightarrow (-y, x)$
   $(x, y) \rightarrow (x + 6, y)$

6. If you performed the transformations of figure *B* to figure *C* in the opposite order, what would the coordinates of the right angle in figure *C* be?

   _____

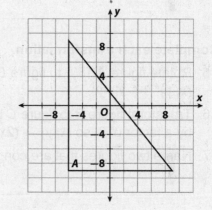

Use the grid at the right for 7–9.

7. Draw any rectangle *A* of your choosing.

8. Dilate rectangle *A*. Label it *B*. Describe the transformation algebraically.

   _____

9. Rotate rectangle *B* about the origin. Label it *C*. Describe the transformation algebraically.

   _____

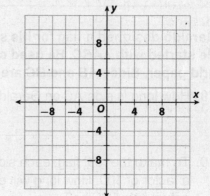

**LESSON
10-3**

Similar Figures

Practice and Problem Solving: D

Identify a sequence of transformations that will transform figure *A* into figure *C*. The first one is done for you.

1. What transformation is used to transform figure *A* to figure *B*?

   <u>$(x, y) \rightarrow (2x, 2y)$</u>

2. What transformation is used to transform figure *B* to figure *C*?

   _____

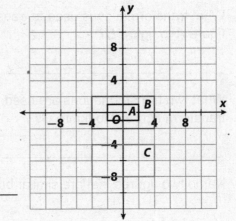

3. Name two figures that are congruent. _____

4. Name two figures that are similar but not congruent.

   _____

Complete each transformation.

5. Rotate figure *A* 180° to figure *B* by applying $(x, y) \rightarrow (-x, -y)$.

6. Transform figure B to figure C by dilating it by a factor of 2, so $(x, y) \rightarrow (2x, 2y)$.

7. Name two figures that are congruent.

   _____

8. Name two figures that are similar but not congruent.

   _____

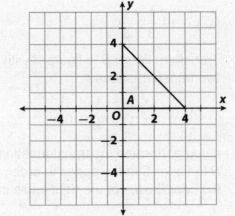

Geraldo designed a flag for his school. He started with △*ABC*. He used centimeter grid paper. Sides *AB* and *BC* are each 5 cm long.

9. How long is side *AC* on Geraldo's drawing?

   _____

10. To make the real flag, each side will be dilated by a factor of 100. How long will each side of the actual flag *ABC* be?

    _____

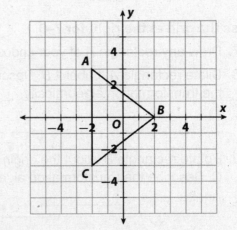

LESSON 10-3
Similar Figures
Reteach

Multiple dilations can be applied to a figure. If one of the transformations is a **dilation**, the figure and its image are **similar**. The size of the figure is changed but the shape is not.

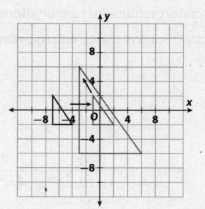

In a dilation, when the scale is a greater than 1, the image is an **enlargement**. When the scale is a fraction between 0 and 1, the image is a **reduction**.

1st transformation: translation right 6 units
$(x, y) \rightarrow (x + 6, y)$,
relative size: congruent

2nd transformation: dilation by a scale of 3
$(x, y) \rightarrow (3x, 3y)$
relative size: similar

The dilation at the right has a scale of $\frac{1}{4}$.

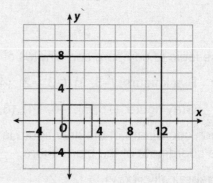

Algebraically it is $(x, y) \rightarrow \left(\frac{1}{4}x, \frac{1}{4}y \right)$

Describe each transformation. Express each one algebraically. Tell whether the figure and its image are congruent or are similar.

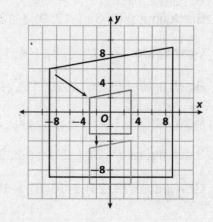

1. First transformation:

   Description: _____

   Algebraically: _____

   Relative size: _____

2. Second transformation:

   Description: _____

   Algebraically: _____

   Relative size: _____

LESSON
10-3

Similar Figures

Reading Strategies: Use Logical Reasoning

Transformations that are **dilations** create **similar** figures.

Some dilations create **enlargements**.

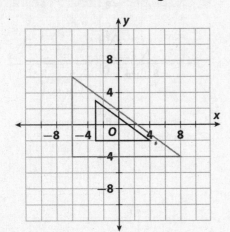

Some dilations create **reductions**.

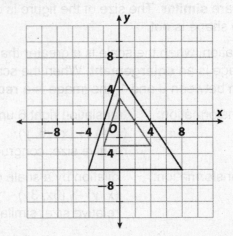

Use logic to compare coordinates of vertices.

    Black figure: (–3, 3), (–3, –2), (4, –2)

    Gray figure: (–6, 6), (–6, –4), (8, –4)

Each coordinate of the gray figure is twice the coordinate of the black figure.

Algebraically: $(x, y) \rightarrow (2x, 2y)$

This is an enlargement.

Use logic to compare coordinates of vertices.

    Black figure: (–4, –6), (0, 6), (8, –6)

    Gray figure: (–2, –3), (0, 3), (4, –3)

Each coordinate of the gray figure is one half the coordinate of the black figure.

Algebraically: $(x, y) \rightarrow \left(\dfrac{1}{2}x, \dfrac{1}{2}y\right)$

This is a reduction.

Use logic to compare coordinates. Describe the dilation algebraically.
Tell whether the dilation is an enlargement or a reduction.

1. Black figure: (6, 3), (–12, 9), (–12, 3)   Algebraically: $(x, y) \rightarrow$ _____

   Gray figure: (2, 1), (–4, 3), (–4, 1)   Enlargement or reduction? _____

2. Black figure: (5, 15), (–20, 15), (–10, 5)   Algebraically: $(x, y) \rightarrow$ _____

   Gray figure: (1, 3), (–4, 3), (–2, 1)   Enlargement or reduction? _____

3. Black figure: (1, 3), (–2, 1), (–2, 3)   Algebraically: $(x, y) \rightarrow$ _____

   Gray figure: (8, 24), (–16, 8), (–16, 24)   Enlargement or reduction? _____

Similar Figures

LESSON 10-3

Success for English Learners

When including dilations in combining transformations, some transformations will produce an **enlargement**. Other combinations will produce a **reduction**. The original figure and its enlargement or reduction are **similar**, not congruent.

Problem 1

Perform the transformations in order.

$(x, y) \rightarrow (-x, y)$

$(x, y) \rightarrow \left(\dfrac{1}{2}x, \dfrac{1}{2}y \right)$

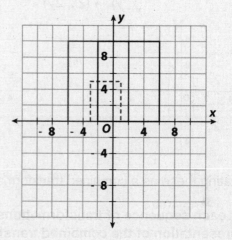

Original figure: $(-2, 10), (-2, 0), (6, 10), (6, 0)$

1st transformation: $(2, 10), (2, 0), (-6, 10), (-6, 0)$

2nd transformation: $(1, 5), (1, 0), (-3, 5), (-3, 0)$

The original figure is black.

The next figure is solid gray.

The final figure is dashed gray.

The final figure is smaller than the black figure.
The 2nd transformation produces a reduction.

Problem 2

Perform the transformations in order.

$(x, y) \rightarrow (-y, x)$

$(x, y) \rightarrow (3x, 3y)$

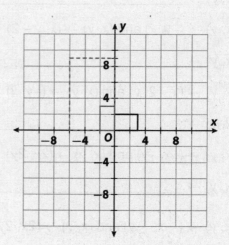

Original figure: $(0, 2), (0, 0), (3, 2), (3, 0)$

1st transformation: $(-2, 0), (0, 0), (-2, 3), (0, 3)$

2nd transformation: $(-6, 0), (0, 0), (-6, 9), (0, 9)$

The original figure is black.

The next figure is solid gray.

The final figure is dashed gray.

The final figure is larger than the black figure.
The 2nd transformation produces an enlargement.

Complete.

1. Write a combination of transformations that will produce an enlargement.

   _____

2. Write a combination of transformations that will produce a reduction.

   _____

MODULE 10

Transformations and Similarity
Challenge

You can combine transformations by performing a transformation on the original figure and then performing a second transformation on the image. The resulting image is called the final image. As with single transformations, the original figure and the final image are similar and may be congruent.

Treating each as a separate transformation, you would write:

$$(x, y) \rightarrow (2x, 2y) \quad \text{and} \quad (x, y) \rightarrow (-y, x).$$

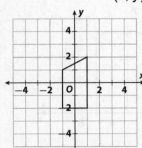 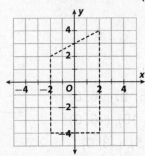 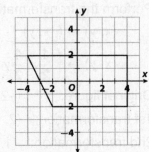

Treating these as a combined transformation, you would write: $(x, y) \rightarrow (-2y, 2x)$.

For each sequence of transformations, write the algebraic representation of the combined transformations. Then write the letter of the final image that shows the transformations.

Original Figure

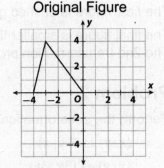

1. $(x, y) \rightarrow (-x, y)$ and $(x, y) \rightarrow (x + 2, y)$

   $(x, y) \rightarrow$ _____ ; figure ____

2. $(x, y) \rightarrow (-y, x)$ and $(x, y) \rightarrow (x, y - 2)$

   $(x, y) \rightarrow$ _____ ; figure ____

3. $(x, y) \rightarrow (x - 2, y)$ and $(x, y) \rightarrow (-y, x)$

   $(x, y) \rightarrow$ _____ ; figure ____

Final Images

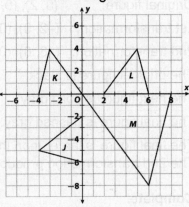

4. $(x, y) \rightarrow (-x, -y)$ and $(x, y) \rightarrow (2x, 2y)$

   $(x, y) \rightarrow$ _____ ; figure ____

5. $(x, y) \rightarrow (\frac{1}{2}x, \frac{1}{2}y)$ and $(x, y) \rightarrow (2x, 2y)$

   $(x, y) \rightarrow$ _____ ; figure ____

Use your answers to Exercises 1–5 to answer each question.

6. Does the order in which you perform combined transformations affect

   the final image?____

7. Which of the final images are congruent to the original figure? _____

LESSON 11-1 Parallel Lines Cut by a Transversal

Practice and Problem Solving: A/B

Use the figure at the right for Exercises 1–6.

1. Name both pairs of alternate interior angles.

   _____

2. Name the corresponding angle to ∠3. ____

3. Name the relationship between ∠1 and ∠5.

   _____

4. Name the relationship between ∠2 and ∠3.

   _____

5. Name an interior angle that is supplementary to ∠7. _____

6. Name an exterior angle that is supplementary to ∠5. _____

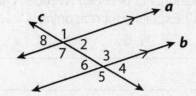

Use the figure at the right for problems 7–10. Line *MP* ∥ line *QS*. Find the angle measures.

7. m∠*KRQ* when m∠*KNM* = 146° ____

8. m∠*QRN* when m∠*MNR* = 52° ____

If m∠*RNP* = (8x + 63)° and m∠*NRS* = 5x°, find the following angle measures.

9. m∠*RNP* = _____

10. m∠*NRS* = _____

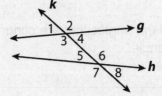

In the figure at the right, there are no parallel lines. Use the figure for problems 11–14.

11. Name both pairs of alternate exterior angles.

    _____

12. Name the corresponding angle to ∠4 ____

13. Name the relationship between ∠3 and ∠6.

    _____

14. Are there any supplementary angles? If so, name two pairs. If not, explain why not.

    _____

LESSON
11-1
Parallel Lines Cut by a Transversal
Practice and Problem Solving: C

At the right is a map of Littleton. North Street,
Center Street, and South Street are parallel.
Use the description to complete Exercises 1–2.

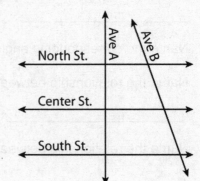

1. Avenue A is perpendicular to North Street. What is the relationship between Avenue A and South Street? Explain your reasoning.

   _____

   _____

2. Avenue B makes a 70° angle with Center Street. What are the measures of the angles that South Street makes with Avenue B?

   _____

In the figure at the right line *BD* || line *EG*.

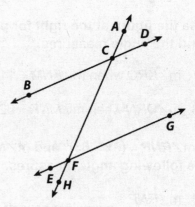

3. If m∠ACB = 5x°, what is m∠ACD in terms of x?

   _____

4. If m∠BCF = 4x° and m∠CFE = 11x°, what is m∠BCF and m∠CFE in degrees?

   _____

5. If m∠CFG = 3x° and m∠DCF = (7x + 40)°, what is m∠CFG and m∠DCF in degrees?

   _____

Use the figure at the right for Exercises 6–8.

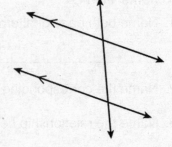

6. Label the parallel lines and the transversal with letters.

7. Name all the angles that are congruent to the smaller angle.

   _____

   _____

8. Write a problem about the figure.

   _____

   _____

LESSON 11-1

Parallel Lines Cut by a Transversal

Practice and Problem Solving: D

Use the figure at the right for Exercises 1–6. The first one is done for you.

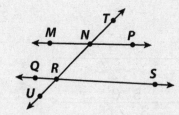

1. What do the arrows that are in the middle of lines *a* and *b* mean?

   The lines are parallel.

2. Name two parallel lines. _____

3. Name the transversal. _____

4. Name a pair of alternate exterior angles. _____

5. Name an angle that is congruent to ∠2. _____

6. Name an angle that is supplementary to ∠2. _____

Line *MP* ∥ line *QS*. Find the angle measure.
The first one is done for you.

7. m∠*TRS* when m∠*TNP* = 40° **40°**

8. m∠*QRU* when m∠*MNR* = 30° _____

9. m∠*MNR* when m∠*QRT* = 145° _____

10. m∠*PNU* when m∠*SRU* = 130° _____

11. In the space below, draw two lines that are NOT parallel. Label them line *g* and line *h*. Then draw a transversal and label it line *k*.

Name _____ Date _____ Class_____

LESSON 11-1

Parallel Lines Cut by a Transversal

Reteach

Parallel Lines	Parallel Lines Cut by a Transversal	
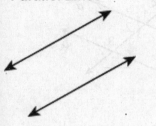 Parallel lines never meet.	A line that crosses parallel lines is a **transversal**. Eight angles are formed. If the transversal is not perpendicular to the parallel lines, then four angles are acute and four are obtuse. The acute angles are all congruent. The obtuse angles are all congruent. Any acute angle is supplementary to any obtuse angle.	$120°/60°$ $60°/120°$ $120°/60°$ $60°/120°$

In each diagram, parallel lines are cut by a transversal. Name the angles that are congruent to the indicated angle.

1.

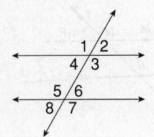

The angles congruent to

∠1 are: _____

2.

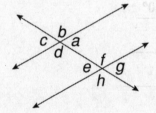

The angles congruent to

∠a are: _____

3.

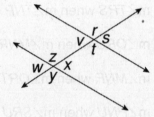

The angles congruent to

∠z are: _____

In each diagram, parallel lines are cut by a transversal and the measure of one angle is given. Write the measures of the remaining angles on the diagram.

4.

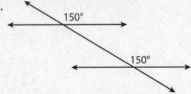

5.

6.

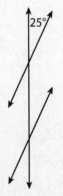

LESSON
11-1

Parallel Lines Cut by a Transversal

Reading Strategies: Build Vocabulary

When parallel lines are cut by a third line, called a **transversal**, some pairs of angles are **congruent**. Congruent angles have the same measure.

Alternate angles lie on opposite sides of the transversal.

Adjacent angles share a common side.

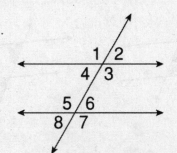

Alternate interior angles are not adjacent angles and are between the parallel lines.

∠3 and ∠5 are one pair of alternate interior angles.

∠4 and ∠6 are another pair of alternate interior angles.

Alternate exterior angles are not adjacent angles and are outside the parallel lines.

∠1 and ∠7 are one pair of alternate exterior angles.

∠2 and ∠8 are another pair of alternate exterior angles.

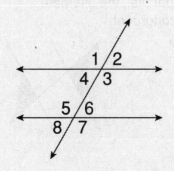

Corresponding angles are angles that lay on the same side of the transversal and on the same side of the two parallel lines.

∠1 and ∠5 are one pair of corresponding angles.

∠2 and ∠6 are a second pair of corresponding angles.

∠3 and ∠7 are a third pair of corresponding angles.

∠4 and ∠8 are a fourth pair of corresponding angles.

Label one pair of angles with 1 and 2 for each type of angle pairs.

1. Corresponding angles

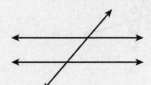

2. Alternate interior angles

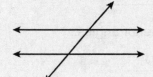

3. Alternate exterior angles

LESSON
11-1

Parallel Lines Cut by a Transversal
Success for English Learners

Problem 1

Below are pairs of **corresponding angles**. When two of the lines are parallel, the corresponding angles are **congruent**. Congruent angles have the same measure.

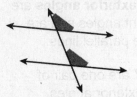 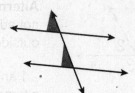 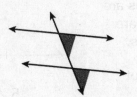 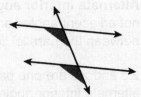

Problem 2

Below are pairs of **alternate interior angles**. When two lines are parallel, the alternate interior angles are congruent.	Below are pairs of **alternate exterior angles**. When two lines are parallel, the alternate exterior angles are congruent.

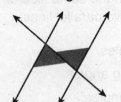  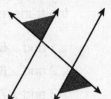 

Use the figure at the right to answer the questions below.

1. Identify all the pairs of corresponding angles.

   _____

   _____

2. Identify all the pairs of alternate interior angles.

   _____

3. Identify all the pairs of alternate exterior angles.

   _____

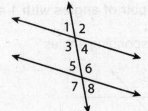

LESSON 11-2

Angle Theorems for Triangles

Practice and Problem Solving: A/B

Find the unknown angle measure in each triangle. Choose the letter for the best answer.

1.

   A 45°   C 90°

   B 55°   D 135°

2.

   A 40°   C 60°

   B 50°   D 70°

Find the unknown angle measure in each triangle.

3.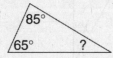

   _____

4.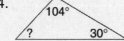

   _____

5.

   _____

Find the value of the variable in problems 6–8.

6.

   _____

7.

   _____

8.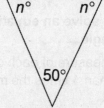

   _____

Use the diagram at the right to answer each question below.

9. What is the measure of ∠DEF?

   _____

10. What is the measure of ∠DEG?

    _____

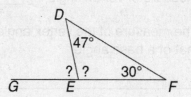

11. A triangular sign has three angles that all have the same measure. What is the measure of each angle?

    _____

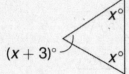

Name _____ Date _____ Class _____

LESSON 11-2

Angle Theorems for Triangles

Practice and Problem Solving: C

Find the value of each variable.

1.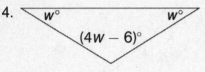

_____

2.

_____

3.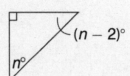

_____

4.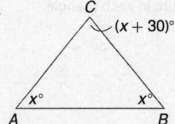

_____

5.

_____

6.

_____

Write and solve an equation to find the measures of the angles of each triangle.

7. The measure of each of the base angles of an isosceles triangle is 9°
   less than 4 times the measure of the vertex angle.

   _____

   measure of each base angle = _____

   measure of vertex angle = _____

8. The measure of the vertex angle of an isosceles triangle is one-fourth
   that of a base angle.

   _____

   measure of each base angle = _____

   measure of vertex angle = _____

9. The second angle in a triangle is twice as large as the first. The third
   angle is three times as large as the first. Find the angle measures.

   _____

LESSON 11-2

Angle Theorems for Triangles
Practice and Problem Solving: D

Find the measure of each unknown angle. The first one is done for you.

1.

$$85° + 40° = 125°$$
$$180° - 125° = 55°$$

2.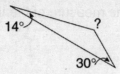

_____

3.

_____

4.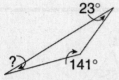

_____

5.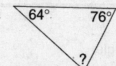

_____

6.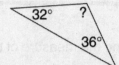

_____

7.

_____

8.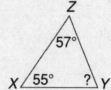

_____

9.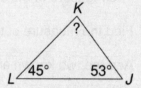

_____

Find the value of each variable. The first one is done for you.

10.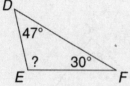

$$55° + 60° = 115°$$
$$180° - 115° = 65°$$

11.

_____

12.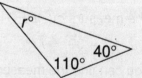

_____

LESSON 11-2

Angle Theorems for Triangles

Reteach

If you know the measure of two angles in a triangle, you can subtract their sum from 180°. The difference is the measure of the third angle.

The two known angles are 60° and 55°.

$60° + 55° = 115°$

$180° − 115° = 65°$

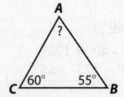

Solve.

1. Find the measure of the unknown angle.

   Add the two known angles: ____ + ____ = ____

   Subtract the sum from 180°: 180 − ____ = ____

   The measure of the unknown angle is: ____

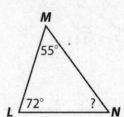

2. Find the measure of the unknown angle.

   Add the two known angles: ____ + ____ = ____

   Subtract the sum from 180°: 180 − ____ = ____

   The measure of the unknown angle is: ____

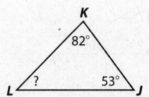

∠*DEG* is an **exterior angle**.

The measure of ∠*DEG* is equal to the sum of ∠D and ∠F.

$47° + 30° = 77°$

You can find the measure of ∠*DEF* by subtracting 77° from 180°.

$180° − 77° = 103°$

The measure of ∠*DEF* is 103°.

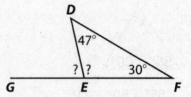

Solve.

3. Find the measure of angle *y*.

   $85° + 65° =$ _____

4. Find the measure of angle *x*.

   $180° −$ ____ = ____

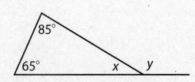

LESSON 11-2 Angle Theorems for Triangles
Reading Strategies: Identify Relationships

An **interior angle** of a triangle is an angle that is inside the triangle, and is formed by two sides of the triangle. Angles *A, B,* and *C* are the interior angles.

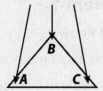

interior angles

The three **interior angles** of a triangle always have a sum of 180°.

Write an equation to find an unknown interior angle in a triangle.

$$m\angle A + m\angle B + m\angle C = 180°$$

Find the measure of each unknown angle.

1.

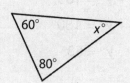

_____

2.

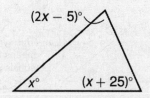

_____

_____

_____

An **exterior angle** is an angle on the outside of a triangle, formed by two of the sides of a triangle. ∠*D* is formed by *BC* and *AC*.

The **remote interior angles** are the two interior angles that are not next to the exterior angle.

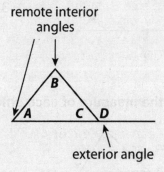

remote interior angles

In this triangle, ∠*A* and ∠*B* are the remote interior angles to ∠*D*.

The sum of the measures of the two remote interior angles is equal to the measure of the exterior angle.

You can find an unknown exterior angle in a triangle by adding the measures of the remote interior angles.

exterior angle

$$m\angle A + m\angle B = m\angle D$$

Solve.

3. Find the measure of the exterior angle.

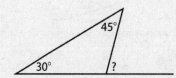

_____

**LESSON
11-2**

Angle Theorems for Triangles
Success for English Learners

Problem 1

What I know:

- One angle measures 37°.
- The sum of the angle measures has to equal 180°.

What I need:

- Another angle measure

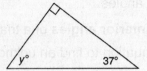

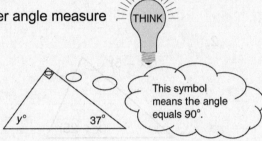

This symbol means the angle equals 90°.

Now I can find $y°$.

$$37° + 90° + y° = 180°$$
$$127° + y° = 180°$$
$$y° = 53°$$

Problem 2

What is m?

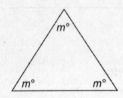

$$m° + m° + m° = 180°$$
$$3m° = 180°$$
$$\frac{3m°}{3} = \frac{180°}{3}$$
$$m = 60°$$

Remember:

All equilateral triangles have angle measures of 60°.

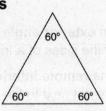

Find the measure of each unknown angle in the triangles shown below.

1.

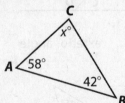

2.

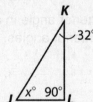

**LESSON
11-3**

Angle-Angle Similarity

Practice and Problem Solving: A/B

Explain whether the triangles are similar.

1.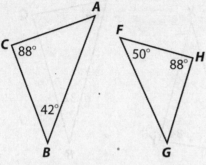

2.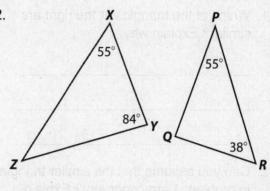

_____

_____

_____

_____

_____

_____

The diagram below shows a Howe roof truss, which is used to frame the roof of a building. Use it to answer problems 3–5.

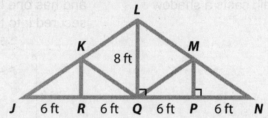

3. Explain why △*LQN* is similar to △*MPN*.

_____

4. What is the length of support *MP*?_____

5. Using the information in the diagram, can you determine whether
   △*LQJ* is similar to △*KRJ*? Explain.

_____

6. In the diagram at the right, sides *SV* and
   RW are parallel.
   Explain why △*RTW* is similar to △*STV*.

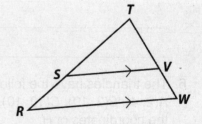

_____

_____

_____

LESSON 11-3

Angle-Angle Similarity

Practice and Problem Solving: C

Solve.

1. Which of the triangles at the right are similar? Explain why.

   _____

   _____

   _____

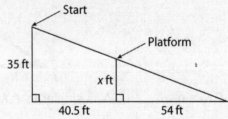

2. Can you assume that the similar triangles in problem 1 are congruent? Explain.

   _____

   _____

Find the unknown measure.

3. A tree casts a shadow 21 feet long, while Enzo, who is 5 feet tall, casts a shadow 6 feet long.

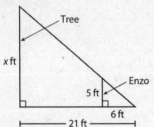

   Height of tree = _____

4. A zip line starts 35 feet above the ground and has one landing platform. The line is secured into the ground.

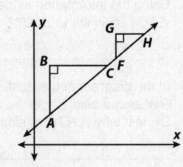

   Height of platform = _____

In the diagram, segments BC and GH are parallel. Use the diagram for Exercises 5–6.

5. Explain why △ABC is similar to △FGH.

   _____

   _____

   _____

6. The triangles have the following coordinates: A(2, 4), B(2, 10), C(10, 10), F(14, 13), G(14, 16). Find the coordinates of H.

   _____

Angle-Angle Similarity
Practice and Problem Solving: D

Find the missing angle measure in each triangle. The first one is done for you.

1.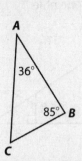

m∠C = **59°**

2.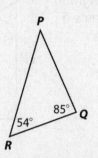

_____

3.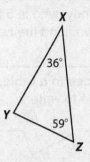

_____

4.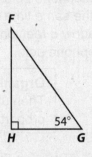

_____

5. Which two triangles in problems 1–4 are similar? Explain.

_____

A cactus casts a shadow 33 feet long. At the same time of day, Liam, who is 6 feet tall, casts a shadow 9 feet long, as shown.

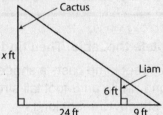

6. The triangles are redrawn below. Write the given information on the two new triangles.

7. Explain how you know that the two triangles are similar.

_____

_____

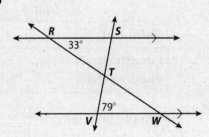

8. Complete and solve the proportion below to find the height of the cactus.

$$\frac{6}{\Box} = \frac{x}{\Box} \qquad x = \_\_\_ \text{ ft}$$

Answer the questions about the diagram, which shows two parallel lines cut by a transversal.

9. What are the measures of ∠RST and ∠VWT? Explain how you found the angle measures.

_____

_____

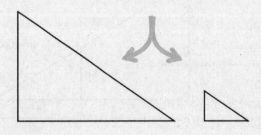

10. Explain whether △RST and △WVT are similar.

_____

LESSON 11-3

Angle-Angle Similarity
Reteach

When solving triangle similarity problems involving proportions, you can use a table to organize given information and set up a proportion.

A telephone pole casts the shadow shown on the diagram. At the same time of day, Sandy, who is 5 feet tall, casts a shadow 8 feet long, as shown. Find the height of the telephone pole.

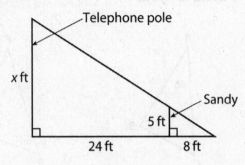

Organize distances in a table. Then use the table to write a proportion.

	Pole	**Sandy**
Height (ft)	x	5
Length of shadow (ft)	24 + 8, or 32	8

$$\frac{x}{32} = \frac{5}{8}$$

Solve the proportion. The height of the telephone pole is 20 feet.

Complete the table. Then find the unknown distance.

1. A street lamp casts a shadow 31.5 feet long, while an 8-foot tall street sign casts a shadow 14 feet long.

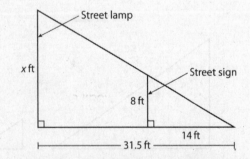

	Lamp	**Sign**
Height (ft)		
Length of shadow (ft)		

Height of street lamp = _____

2. A 5.5-foot woman casts a shadow that is 3 feet longer than her son's shadow. The son casts a shadow 13.5 feet long.

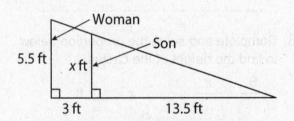

	Woman	**Son**
Height (ft)		
Length of shadow (ft)		

Height of son = _____

LESSON 11-3 Angle-Angle Similarity

Reading Strategies: Analyze Diagrams

For complicated diagrams that involve overlapping triangles, you can redraw the triangles so that they do not overlap. Transfer the information given in the original diagram to the new triangles.

The diagram shows the shadows cast by a tree and by Zachary at the same time of day.

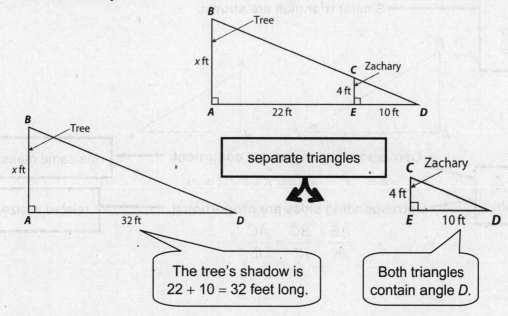

separate triangles

The tree's shadow is 22 + 10 = 32 feet long.

Both triangles contain angle *D*.

Solve.

1. What does *ED* represent? _____

2. What does *AB* represent? _____

3. Segment *AE* is not shown when the triangles are redrawn. What does *AE* represent?

   _____

4. Explain why △*ABC* is similar to △*ECD*.

   _____

5. Compete the statements about the similar triangles.

   a. Side *AD* corresponds to side _____

   b. Side *CE* corresponds to side _____

6. Write and solve a proportion to find the height of the tree.

   _____   _____

LESSON
11-3

Angle-Angle Similarity
Success for English Learners

Problem 1

What are similar triangles?

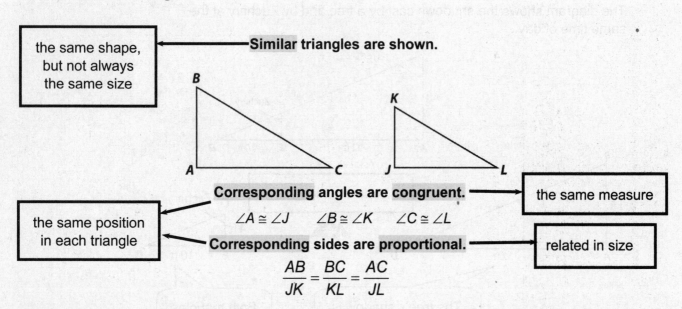

| the same shape, but not always the same size | ← **Similar** triangles are shown. |

Corresponding angles are congruent. → the same measure

$\angle A \cong \angle J \qquad \angle B \cong \angle K \qquad \angle C \cong \angle L$

the same position in each triangle ← **Corresponding sides are proportional.** → related in size

$$\frac{AB}{JK} = \frac{BC}{KL} = \frac{AC}{JL}$$

Problem 2

Explain whether the triangles are similar.

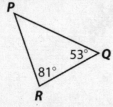

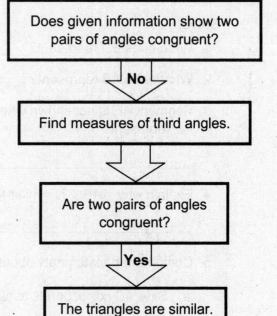

Does given information show two pairs of angles congruent?

No

Find measures of third angles.

$81° + 53° + m\angle P = 180° \qquad 81° + 46° + m\angle Z = 180°$

$134° + m\angle P = 180° \qquad\quad 127° + m\angle Z = 180°$

$m\angle P = 46° \qquad\qquad\quad m\angle Z = 53°$

Are two pairs of angles congruent?

1. Describe the relationship between the angles of similar triangles and the sides of similar triangles.

Yes

_____

The triangles are similar.

2. Explain how the measures of the angles of two triangles are used to show that the triangles are similar.

_____

MODULE 11

Angle Relationships in Parallel Lines and Triangles
Challenge

1. Use what you know about exterior angles and remote interior angles to find the measure of ∠x. Show your work.

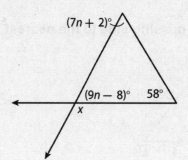

_____

_____

_____

_____

Use your observation about the alternate interior angles of parallel lines to find the measure of ∠x in each of these diagrams. Explain your reasoning.

2. _____

_____

_____

_____

_____

_____

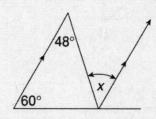

3. _____

_____

_____

_____

_____

_____

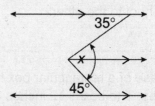

4. _____

_____

_____

_____

_____

_____

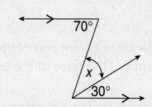

LESSON 12-1

The Pythagorean Theorem

Practice and Problem Solving: A/B

Find the missing side to the nearest tenth.

1.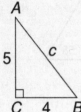

2.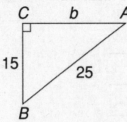

3.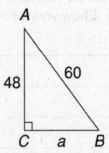

_____

4.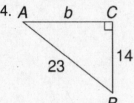

5.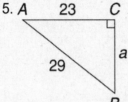

6.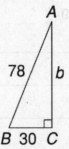

_____   _____   _____

Solve.

7. Jane and Miguel are siblings. They go to different schools. Jane walks 6 blocks east from home. Miguel walks 8 blocks north. How many blocks apart would the two schools be if you could walk straight from one school to the other?

_____

8. The base of a rectangular box has a width of 3 inches and a length of 4 inches. The box is 12 inches tall.

   a. Draw a picture of the box below.

   b. How far is it from one of the box's top corners to the opposite corner of the base of the box?

_____

LESSON
12-1

The Pythagorean Theorem
Practice and Problem Solving: C

In an isosceles right triangle the lengths of the sides $\overline{AC}$ and $\overline{BC}$ are equal.

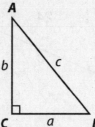

Find the length of the hypotenuse to the nearest tenth of a unit in these isosceles right triangles with the given leg lengths.

1. $AC = BC = 1$ inch

2. $AC = BC = 2.5$ kilometers

3. $AC = BC = \sqrt{3}$ feet

_____   _____   _____

In the isosceles triangle, find the length of $\overline{AB}$ when the lengths of $\overline{AC}$ and $\overline{CD}$ are given.

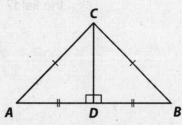

4. $AC = 4, CD = 2$

5. $AC = 10, CD = 6$

6. $AC = \sqrt{3}, CD = 1$

_____   _____   _____

7. A diagonal of a cube goes from one of the cube's top corners to the opposite corner of the base of the cube. Find the length of a diagonal *d* in a cube that has an edge of length 10 meters.

_____

_____

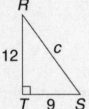

LESSON 12-1

The Pythagorean Theorem

Practice and Problem Solving: D

Find the length of the hypotenuse in each triangle using the Pythagorean Theorem, $a^2 + b^2 = c^2$. The first one is done for you.

1.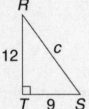

2.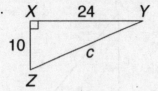

3.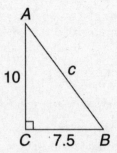

_____

$12^2 + 9^2 = c^2$

_____

$c = 15$

_____

Write the correct answer. Round your answers to the nearest tenth. The first one is done for you.

4. A right triangle has legs that are 10 meters and 3 meters in length. How long is its hypotenuse?

   Solution:

   $c^2 = 10^2 + 3^2$

   $c^2 = 100 + 9$

   $c^2 = 109$

   $c \approx 10.4$ meters

5. A soccer field is 120 yards long and 60 yards wide. How long is the diagonal of the field?

_____

Solve.

6. Find the length of diagonal $\overline{AB}$ shown by filling in the steps. The first one is done for you.

   Step 1: $3^2 + 6^2 = 9 + 36 = 45$

   Step 2: diagonal of base = $\sqrt{45} \approx$ _____

   Step 3: $4^2 + (\sqrt{45})^2 = (AB)^2$

   Step 4: $(AB)^2 =$ _____

   Step 5: $AB \approx$ _____ meters

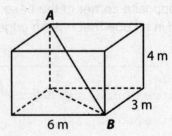

LESSON 12-1
The Pythagorean Theorem
Reteach

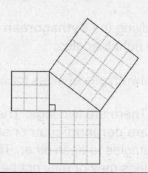

In a **right triangle,**

the sum of the areas of the squares on the legs
<u>is equal to</u>
the area of the square on the hypotenuse.

$3^2 + 4^2 = 5^2$
$9 + 16 = 25$

Given the squares that are on the legs of a right triangle, draw the square for the hypotenuse below or on another sheet of paper.

1. leg   leg   hypotenuse

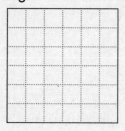

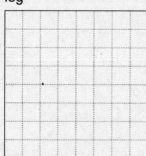

Without drawing the squares, you can find a missing leg or the hypotenuse when given the other sides.

Model   **Example 1**   **Example 2**

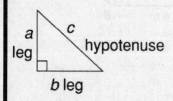

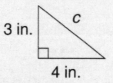

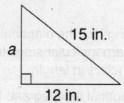

Solution 1   **Solution 2**
$a^2 + b^2 = c^2$ $a^2 + b^2 = c^2$
$3^2 + 4^2 = c^2$ $a^2 + 12^2 = 15^2$
$9 + 16 = c^2$ $a^2 = 225 - 144$
$25 = c^2$, so $c = 5$ in. $a^2 = 81$, so $a = 9$ in.

Find the missing side.

2.
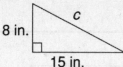

3.
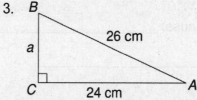

LESSON
12-1
The Pythagorean Theorem
Reading Strategies: Build Vocabulary

When studying the **Pythagorean Theorem**, you have to use terms that are specific to right triangles.

There are two types of sides for a right triangle:

→ There are two **legs**. The legs are **perpendicular** or at right angles to each other. The two legs may or may not be equal.

→ There is the **hypotenuse** which connects the ends of the two legs. Neither leg is as long as the hypotenuse.

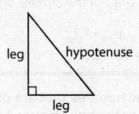

In real-world problems, the **hypotenuse** is often called a **diagonal**.

• The diagonal often connects the opposite ends of two perpendicular line segments.

• In three-dimensional problems in which a **diagonal** is calculated, the Pythagorean Theorem often has to be used twice.

Example
To find the length of diagonal $\overline{AB}$, two calculations have to be made.

• First, calculate the length of the diagonal connecting the two perpendicular sides that are 3 meters and 6 meters in length.

• Then use the first diagonal as a leg and the 4-meter side as the second leg to find the length of diagonal $\overline{AB}$.

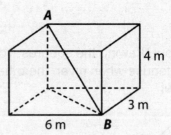

Identify the parts of the triangle by describing or listing the sides.

1.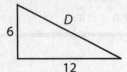

Hypotenuse: _____

Legs: _____

2.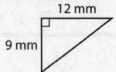

Hypotenuse: _____

Legs: _____

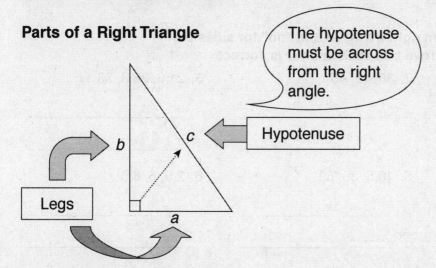

LESSON 12-1

The Pythagorean Theorem
Success for English Learners

Parts of a Right Triangle

The hypotenuse must be across from the right angle.

Hypotenuse

b *c*

Legs

a

The Pythagorean Theorem

Substitute values for *a*, *b*, or *c* in the Pythagorean Theorem to find the lengths of other sides.

$$a^2 + b^2 = c^2$$

If $a = 2$ yards and $b = 3$ yards $\longrightarrow$ $2^2 + 3^2 = 4 + 9 = 13 = c^2$

To find *c*, take the square root ($\sqrt{}$) of c^2. $\longrightarrow$ $c = \sqrt{13}$

Round your answer to the nearest tenth. $\longrightarrow$ $c = \sqrt{13} \approx 3.6$

Problem 1

1. Name the parts of the right triangle:

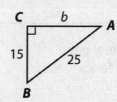

Leg: _____

Leg: _____

Hypotenuse: _____

2. Fill in the blanks to find the length of the missing leg.

Step 1 $\quad a^2 + b^2 = c^2$

Step 2 $\quad (\underline{\hspace{3cm}})^2 + b^2 = (\underline{\hspace{3cm}})^2$

Step 3 $\quad \underline{\hspace{3cm}} + b^2 = \underline{\hspace{3cm}}$

Step 4 $\quad b^2 = \underline{\hspace{3cm}} - \underline{\hspace{3cm}} = \underline{\hspace{3cm}}$

Step 5 $\quad b = \sqrt{\underline{\hspace{3cm}}} = \underline{\hspace{3cm}}$

LESSON 12-2

Converse of the Pythagorean Theorem
Practice and Problem Solving: A/B

Write "yes" for sides that form right triangles and "no" for sides that do not form right triangles. Prove that each answer is correct.

1. 7, 24, 25

2. 30, 40, 45

3. 21.6, 28.8, 36

_____

_____

4. 10, 15, 18

5. 10.5, 36, 50

6. 2.5, 6, 6.5

_____

_____

Solve.

7. A commuter airline files a new route between two cities that are 400 kilometers apart. One of the two cities is 200 kilometers from a third city. The other one of the two cities is 300 kilometers from the third city. Do the paths between the three cities form a right triangle? Prove that your answer is correct.

_____

_____

8. A school wants to build a rectangular playground that will have a diagonal length of 75 yards. How wide can the playground be if the length has to be 30 yards?

_____

9. A 250-foot length of fence is placed around a three-sided animal pen. Two of the sides of the pen are 100 feet long each. Does the fence form a right triangle? Prove that your answer is correct.

_____

_____

Converse of the Pythagorean Theorem
LESSON 12-2
Practice and Problem Solving: C

Problems 1–3 give the dimensions of isosceles triangles. Which triangles are right triangles? Prove your answer is correct.

1. Sides: 10

   Hypotenuse: 15

2. Sides: 2

   Hypotenuse: $2\sqrt{2}$

3. Sides: 300

   Hypotenuse: 700

_____

_____

Solve.

4. Can an equilateral triangle be a right triangle? Explain your answer.

   _____

   _____

5. A quadrilateral has two pair of opposite parallel sides. Each of one pair of parallel sides is 4 yards long. Each of the second pair of sides is 8 yards long. A diagonal connecting the opposite corners of the quadrilateral is 9 yards long. Is the quadrilateral a rectangle? Prove that your answer is correct.

   _____

   _____

6. A clear plastic prism has six faces, each of which is a parallelogram of side length 1 meter. A diagonal made of nylon filament line connecting two opposite vertices of the solid has a length of 4 meters. Is the solid a cube? Prove that your answer is correct.

   _____

A prism has a diagonal, _d_, connecting its opposite vertices. Give the lengths of the sides of the prism in each problem that will make it the solid described.

7. $d = 6$ meters; a cube

   _____

8. $d = \sqrt{6}$ feet; a rectangular solid with a pair of opposite square faces and two pair of rectangular faces in which the length is twice the width.

   _____

   _____

LESSON 12-2 Converse of the Pythagorean Theorem
Practice and Problem Solving: D

Problems 1–3 give the sides of a right triangle. In each case, which of the three sides is the hypotenuse? The first one is done for you.

1. 3, 4, 5

_____**5**_____

2. 5, 12, 13

_____

3. 1, 1, $\sqrt{2}$

_____

4. 2, 3, $\sqrt{13}$

_____

Do the sides given in 5–8 form a right triangle? Prove your answer is correct using the Pythagorean Theorem, $a^2 + b^2 = c^2$. The first one is done for you.

5. 8, 9, 10

_____ no; $8^2 + 9^2 \neq 10^2$ _____

6. 12, 14, 15

_____

7. 10, 24, 26

_____

8. 14, 15, 21

_____

A parking lot has four sides. One pair of opposite sides are 100 yards long. The other two sides are 60 yards long. The distance from one end of the longer side to the opposite end of the shorter side is 120 yards. Is the parking lot a rectangle? Answer the questions below to find out.

9. If the distances given form a right triangle, which number is the hypotenuse, and why?

_____

10. Which numbers are the two sides?

_____

11. Fill in the numbers in the Pythagorean Theorem for this problem.

Does $a^2 + b^2 = c^2$?

(_____)^2 + (_____)^2 $\overset{?}{=}$ (_____)^2

12. Simplify the numbers from problem 11.

Does _____ + _____ = _____?

Does _____ = _____?

13. Are the two sides of the equation equal? _____

14. Is the parking lot a rectangle? Explain.

_____

_____

LESSON 12-2
Converse of the Pythagorean Theorem
Reteach

Step 1 The first step in verifying that a triangle is a right triangle is to name the three sides. One side is the hypotenuse and the other two sides are legs.

- In a right triangle, the hypotenuse is opposite the right angle.

  ⟶ The hypotenuse is 5 cm.

- The hypotenuse is greater than either leg.

  ⟶ 5 cm > 4 cm and 5 cm > 3 cm

Step 2 Next, the lengths of the hypotenuse and legs must satisfy the Pythagorean Theorem.

$$(\text{hypotenuse})^2 = (\text{first leg})^2 + (\text{second leg})^2$$

In the example above, $5^2 = 3^2 + 4^2 = 25$, so the triangle is a right triangle.

Conclusion If the lengths of the hypotenuse and the two legs satisfy the conditions of the Pythagorean Theorem, then the triangle is a right triangle. If they do not satisfy the conditions of the Pythagorean Theorem, the triangle is not a right triangle.

Find the length of each hypotenuse.

1.

8 in. 6 in.

_____

2. 12 mm

9 mm

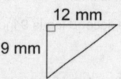

_____

First, fill in the length of the hypotenuse in each problem. Then, determine if the sides form a right triangle.

3. 1, 2, 3

Hypotenuse: _____

_____

4. 8, 7, 6

Hypotenuse: _____

_____

5. 15, 20, 25

Hypotenuse: _____

_____

Show that these sides form a right triangle.

6. 2, 3, $\sqrt{13}$

_____

7. 3, 6, $3\sqrt{5}$

_____

LESSON 12-2 **Converse of the Pythagorean Theorem**
Reading Strategies: Draw Conclusions

Earlier, you learned about the Pythagorean Theorem.
One way to state the Pythagorean Theorem is:

→ "If a triangle is a right triangle with legs a and b and a hypotenuse c, then $a^2 + b^2 = c^2$."

In this lesson, you studied the **converse** of the Pythagorean Theorem.
One way to state it is like this.

→ "If a triangle has sides of lengths a, b, and c and the lengths of the sides are related by the formula $a^2 + b^2 = c^2$, then the triangle is a right triangle with a hypotenuse c and legs a and b."

In both cases, a condition is given that allows you to **draw a conclusion**. These are called **"if-then" statements**. Look at the examples below.

Example 1

A right triangle has a hypotenuse of 15 inches. One of its legs is 12 inches. How long is the other leg?

Solution Using the Pythagorean Theorem, *if* a triangle is a right triangle, *then* its side lengths are related by the equation $a^2 + b^2 = c^2$.

Substitute what you know: $12^2 + b^2 = 15^2$

Solve for what you want to find: $b^2 = 15^2 - 12^2 = 225 - 144 = 81$

Find b: $b = \sqrt{81} = 9$; the second leg is 9 inches.

Example 2

A triangle has sides of 3 meters, 5 meters, and 7 meters. Is it a right triangle?

Solution Using the **converse** of the Pythagorean Theorem, *if* the sides of a triangle satisfy the formula $a^2 + b^2 = c^2$, *then* the triangle is a right triangle.

Substitute: $3^2 + 5^2 = 34$; $7^2 = 49$

Does $a^2 + b^2 = c^2$? No. You can draw the conclusion that a triangle with sides of lengths 3 meters, 5 meters, and 7 meters is *not* a right triangle.

Write an "if-then" statement for each problem using the Pythagorean Theorem and its converse as shown above. Then use your statement to answer the question.

1. A right triangle has sides of 5 and 12. What is its third side?

   "If _____,

   then _____."

   _____

2. A triangle has sides of lengths 4, 4, and 6. Is it a right triangle?

   "If _____,

   then _____."

   _____

LESSON 12-2 Converse of the Pythagorean Theorem
Success for English Learners

Problem 1

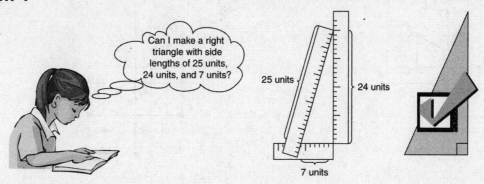

Problem 2

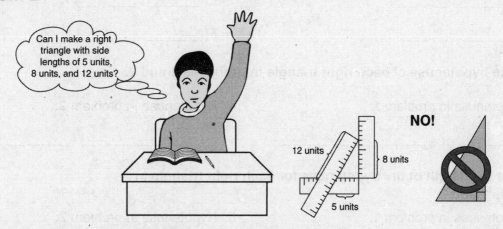

1. The **converse** of the Pythagorean Theorem is the "opposite" of the Pythagorean Theorem. It states that *if* the square of the hypotenuse equals the sum of the squares of the other two sides of a triangle, *then* the triangle is a right triangle.
   Explain how Problem 1 is an example of the converse of the Pythagorean Theorem.

   _____

   _____

   _____

2. In Problem 2, does the hypotenuse need to be longer or shorter to form a right triangle?

   _____

   _____

LESSON **12-3**

Distance Between Two Points

Practice and Problem Solving: A/B

Name the coordinates of the points.

1.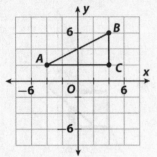

2.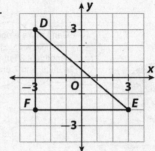

A(_____ , _____)

B(_____ , _____)

C(_____ , _____)

D(_____ , _____)

E(_____ , _____)

F(_____ , _____)

Name the hypotenuse of each right triangle in problems 1 and 2.

3. Hypotenuse in problem 1:

_____

4. Hypotenuse in problem 2:

_____

Estimate the length of the hypotenuse for each right triangle in problems 1 and 2.

5. Hypotenuse in problem 1:

_____

6. Hypotenuse in problem 2:

_____

Use the distance formula to calculate the length of the hypotenuse for each right triangle.

7. Hypotenuse in problem 1:

_____

_____

8. Hypotenuse in problem 2:

_____

_____

9. Use the distance formula to find the distance between the points (−4, −4) and (4, 4).

_____

LESSON 12-3

Distance Between Two Points
Practice and Problem Solving: C

1. Use the distance formula to determine if the three points, $A(1, 3)$, $B(-2, 4)$, and $C(1, 4)$, form a right triangle.

_____

_____

_____

2. A triangular-shaped forest preserve is formed by roads AB, BC, and CA as shown on the map. Find its perimeter using the distance formula. The distances are in kilometers.

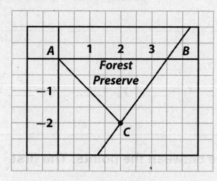

_____

_____

_____

_____

The distance d between two points is 5. Find the missing coordinate of the second point that will give this distance. Show your work.

3. $A(-5, 7)$; $B(x, 3)$

_____

_____

_____

4. $C(3, -4)$; $D(6, y)$

_____

_____

_____

LESSON 12-3

Distance Between Two Points

Practice and Problem Solving: D

Find the distance between the points by filling in the steps. The first one is done for you.

1. $A(1, 2)$ and $B(3, 4)$

$d = \sqrt{(x_2 - x_1)^2 + (y_2 - y_1)^2}$; $x_2 = $ **3**; $x_1 = $ **1**; $y_2 = $ **4**; $y_1 = $ **2**

$= \sqrt{(3-1)^2 + (4-2)^2} = \sqrt{(2)^2 + (2)^2} = \sqrt{4+4} = \sqrt{8} = 2\sqrt{2}$

2. $C(-1, 3)$ and $D(-5, 7)$

$d = \sqrt{(x_2 - x_1)^2 + (y_2 - y_1)^2}$; $x_2 = $ ___ ; $x_1 = $ ___ ; $y_2 = $ ___; $y_1 = $ ___

3. $E(0, -5)$ and $F(10, -15)$

$d = \sqrt{(x_2 - x_1)^2 + (y_2 - y_1)^2}$; $x_2 = $ ___ ; $x_1 = $ ___ ; $y_2 = $ ___; $y_1 = $ ___

Use the graph to _estimate_ the distance between the points. The first one is done for you.

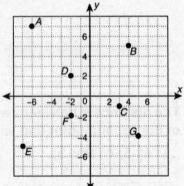

4. A and B

   x-distance between

   points = 10;

   $AB = $ more than 10

5. C and D

6. E and F

7. F and G

If the x-coordinates of two points are equal, the distance between the points can be found by taking the absolute value of the difference of the y-coordinates of the two points. Find the distance between the points. The first one is done for you.

8. $A(-2, 5)$ and $B(-2, 1)$

   The difference of the

   y-coordinates is $|5 - 1|$

   or 4.

9. $C(1, -4)$ and $D(1, -1)$

10. $E(0, -6)$ and $F(0, 9)$

LESSON 12-3

Distance Between Two Points
Reteach

There are three cases of distance between two points on a coordinate plane. The first two have fewer steps than the third, but you have to be able to identify when to use them.

Case 1

The *x*-coordinates of the two points are the same.

If the *x*-coordinates are the same, the distance between the two points is the **absolute value** of the *difference* of the *y*-coordinates.

The line connecting the two points is a *vertical* line.

Example 1

Find the distance between the two points $A(-3, 5)$ and $B(-3, -4)$.

⟶ The *x*-coordinates are the same.

⟶ Difference of the *y*-coordinates:
$$5 - (-4) = 9$$

⟶ The absolute value of 9 is 9.

Case 2

The *y*-coordinates of the two points are the same.

If the *y*-coordinates are the same, the distance between the two points is the **absolute value** of the *difference* of the *x*-coordinates.

The line connecting the two points is a *horizontal* line.

Example 2

Find the distance between the two points $C(1, 3)$ and $D(6, 3)$.

⟶ The *y*-coordinates are the same.

⟶ Difference of the *x*-coordinates:
$$1 - 6 = -5$$

⟶ The absolute value of −5 is 5.

Case 3

If the *x* and *y*-coordinates of the two points are different, use the distance formula:

$$d = \sqrt{(x_2 - x_1)^2 + (y_2 - y_1)^2}$$

The *x* and *y*-coordinates are different if $x_1 \neq x_2$ and $y_1 \neq y_2$.

The line connecting the two points can be thought of as the *hypotenuse* of a right triangle.

Example 3

Find the distance between the two points $E(-9, 5)$ and $F(-4, 0)$.

⟶ Use the distance formula.

⟶ $d = \sqrt{(-4 + 9)^2 + (0 - 5)^2}$

$= \sqrt{5^2 + (-5)^2} = 5\sqrt{2}$

Tell whether the points given are endpoints of a vertical line, a horizontal line, or neither.

1. (−8, 1), (−5, 1)　　　2. (4, 3), (2, 1)　　　3. (0, 0), (0, 100)　　　4. (3, 3), (3, 3)

_____　　_____　　_____　　_____

Use the distance formula to find the distance between the two points.

5. (0.5, 1.3), (−0.4, −1.2)　　　　　6. (6, −3), (2, −4)

_____　　_____

_____　　_____

LESSON 12-3

Distance Between Two Points
Reading Strategies: Identify Relationships

Look at the triangles shown below.

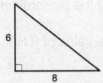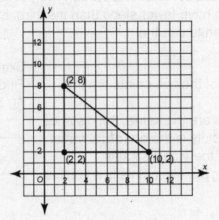

1. Are the triangles the same size? _____

2. What formula should you use to find the length of the hypotenuse

   for the triangle on the left? _____

3. What formula should you use to find the length of the hypotenuse

   for the triangle on the right? _____

4. Using the Pythagorean Theorem:

$$a^2 + b^2 = c^2$$

$$\underline{\hphantom{xx}}^2 + \underline{\hphantom{xx}}^2 = c^2$$

$$\underline{\hphantom{xx}} + \underline{\hphantom{xx}} = c^2$$

$$\underline{\hphantom{xx}} = c^2$$

$$\sqrt{\underline{\hphantom{xx}}} = c$$

$$\underline{\hphantom{xx}} = c$$

5. Using the Distance Formula:

$$d = \sqrt{(x_1 - x_2)^2 + (y_1 - y_2)^2}$$

$$d = \sqrt{(\underline{\hphantom{x}} - \underline{\hphantom{x}})^2 + (\underline{\hphantom{x}} - \underline{\hphantom{x}})^2}$$

$$d = \sqrt{(\underline{\hphantom{x}})^2 + (\underline{\hphantom{x}})^2}$$

$$d = \sqrt{\underline{\hphantom{x}} + \underline{\hphantom{x}}}$$

$$d = \sqrt{\underline{\hphantom{xx}}}$$

$$d = \underline{\hphantom{x}}$$

6. What do you notice about the last two steps of the formulas above?

_____

_____

LESSON 12-3 Distance Between Two Points

Success for English Learners

Problem 1

How do you know which coordinate is which in the distance formula?

Here are two points: $A(1, 2)$ and $B(4, 7)$.

Step 1 The Distance Formula: $d = \sqrt{(x_2 - x_1)^2 + (y_2 - y_1)^2}$

Step 2 What is "x_1"? ⟶ "x_1" is the x-coordinate of point A, the first point.

Step 3 What is "x_2"? ⟶ "x_2" is the x-coordinate of point B.

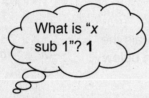

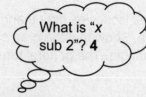

Point A: (**1**, 2)   Point B: (**4**, 7)

Step 4 What is y_1 in (1, **2**)? ⟶ y_1 = "y sub one" = **2**

Step 5 What is y_2 in (4, **7**)? ⟶ y_2 = "y sub two" = **7**

Problem 2

Find the distance between the two points using the Distance Formula.

Here's the formula: $d = \sqrt{(x_2 - x_1)^2 + (y_2 - y_1)^2}$

Substitute the numbers from Problem 1: $d = \sqrt{(4 - 1)^2 + (7 - 2)^2}$

Simplify: $d = \sqrt{(4 - 1)^2 + (7 - 2)^2} = \sqrt{3^2 + 5^2} = \sqrt{9 + 25} = \sqrt{34}$.

You can leave the answer as a square root, or you can use a calculator to find that the square root of 34 is about 5.8.

Name x_1, x_2, y_1, and y_2. Then, find the distance between the points.

1. $C(6, 4)$ and $D(9, 5)$

   x_1: ____ ; x_2: ____ ; y_1: ____ ; y_2: ____

   $d = \sqrt{(x_2 - x_1)^2 + (y_2 - y_1)^2}$

   _____

   _____

2. $X(0, 6)$ and $Y(1, 8)$

   x_1: ____ ; x_2: ____ ; y_1: ____ ; y_2: ____

   $d = \sqrt{(x_2 - x_1)^2 + (y_2 - y_1)^2}$

   _____

   _____

MODULE 12

The Pythagorean Theorem
Challenge

Pythagoras Without Squares

The Pythagorean Theorem describes squares constructed on the sides of a right triangle. But, the constructed figures do not necessarily need to be square. See what happens for similar figures of different shapes.

Figure 1

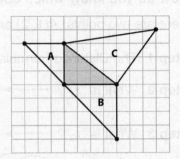

1. Show that the Pythagorean Theorem is true for a 3-4-5 right triangle. Then write the general formula using *a*, *b*, and *c* for the side lengths, where *c* is the hypotenuse.

   _____

2. In Figure 1, the three isosceles right triangles are each one-half of a square. Show that the area sum A + B equals the area of C for this triangle. The general formula is shown below Figure 1.

   _____

$$\frac{1}{2}a^2 + \frac{1}{2}b^2 = \frac{1}{2}c^2$$

For each figure, the area sum A + B equals the area C on the hypotenuse. Show this is true for the specific figure. Then write a general formula using *a*, *b*, and *c* for the side lengths.

3. **Figure 2**

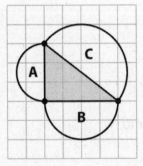

_____

_____

4. **Figure 3**

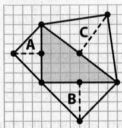

_____

_____

5. Create your own variation on the Pythagorean Theorem by constructing similar figures on the sides of a right triangle.

LESSON 13-1
Volume of Cylinders
Practice and Problem Solving: A/B

Find the volume of each cylinder. Round your answer to the nearest tenth if necessary. Use 3.14 for π.

1.

_____

2.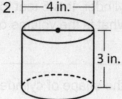

_____

3. A cylindrical oil drum has a diameter of 2 feet and a height of 3 feet. What is the volume of the oil drum?

_____

4. New Oats cereal is packaged in a cardboard cylinder. The packaging is 10 inches tall with a diameter of 3 inches. What is the volume of the New Oats cereal package?

_____

5. A small plastic storage container is in the shape of a cylinder. It has a diameter of 7.6 centimeters and a height of 3 centimeters. What is the volume of the storage cylinder?

_____

6. A can of juice has a diameter of 6.6 centimeters and a height of 12.1 centimeters. What is the total volume of a six-pack of juice cans?

_____

7. Mr. Macady has an old cylindrical grain silo on his farm that stands 25 feet high with a diameter of 10 feet. Mr. Macady is planning to tear down the old silo and replace it with a new and bigger one. The new cylindrical silo will stand 30 feet high and have a diameter of 15 feet.

  a. What is the volume of the old silo? _____

  b. What is the volume of the new silo? _____

  c. How much greater is the volume of the new silo than the old silo?

_____

Name _____ Date _____ Class _____

Volume of Cylinders

Practice and Problem Solving: C

Solve. Use 3.14 for π. Round your answer to the nearest tenth, if necessary. Show your work.

1. A feeding trough was made by hollowing out half of a log. The trough is shaped like half a cylinder. It is 5 feet long and has an interior diameter of 1.5 feet. What is the volume of oats that will fill the trough?

   _____

2. You buy 3 candles in the shape of cylinders as shown below.

   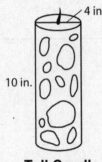
   Tall Candle

   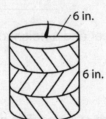
   Medium Candle

   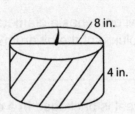
   Short Candle

   a. Use the dimensions shown above to find the volume of each candle to the nearest hundredth. Complete the table.

Candle Size	Radius	Height	Volume
Tall Candle			
Medium Candle			
Short Candle			

   b. Which candle has the most wax?

   _____

   c. How much more wax does this candle have than the candle with the least wax?

   _____

   d. Write an inequality that shows the amount of wax in the three candles ordered from least to greatest.

   _____

3. A cylinder has a height of 8 feet and a volume of 628 cubic feet. Find the radius of the cylinder. Use 3.14 for π. Show your work.

   _____

   _____

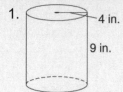

Volume of Cylinders

Practice and Problem Solving: D

Find the volume of each cylinder. Round your answer to the nearest tenth if necessary. Use 3.14 for π. Show your work by filling in the blanks with values from the diagrams. The first one is done for you.

1.

4 in.

9 in.

$V = \pi r^2 h$

$V = \underline{\ 3.14\ } \cdot \underline{\ 4^2\ } \times \underline{\ 9\ }$

$V = \underline{\ 3.14\ } \cdot \underline{\ 16\ } \times \underline{\ 9\ }$

$V \approx \underline{452.2}$ in³

2.

3.4 ft

12 ft

$V = \pi r^2 h$

$V = \underline{\hspace{1.2cm}} \cdot \underline{\hspace{1.2cm}} * \underline{\hspace{1.2cm}}$

$V = \underline{\hspace{1.2cm}} \cdot \underline{\hspace{1.2cm}} * \underline{\hspace{1.2cm}}$

$V \approx \underline{\hspace{1.5cm}}$

Find the volume of each cylinder. Round your answer to the nearest tenth if necessary. Use 3.14 for π. The first one is done for you.

3. 4 cm

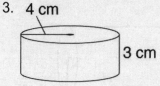

3 cm

_____ **150.7 cm³** _____

4. 5 cm

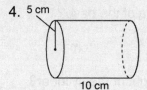

10 cm

_____

Solve. The first one is done for you.

5. A can of beans is 4.5 inches high and has a diameter of 3 inches Find the volume of the can to the nearest tenth of a unit. Use 3.14 for π.

____ **31.8 in³** _____

6. A telephone pole is 30 feet tall with a diameter of 12 inches. Jacob is making a replica of a telephone pole and wants to fill it with sand to help it stand freely. Find the volume of his model, which has a height of 30 inches and a diameter of 1 inch, to the nearest tenth of a unit. Use 3.14 for π.

_____

_____

LESSON
13-1
Volume of Cylinders
Reteach

You can use your knowledge of how to find the area of a circle to find the volume of a cylinder.

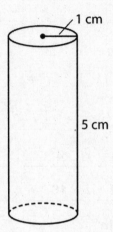

1 cm

5 cm

1. What is the shape of the base of the cylinder?

   circle

2. The area of the base is $B = \pi r^2$.

   $B = 3.14 \cdot \underline{\ 1\ }^2 = \underline{\textbf{3.14}}$ cm²

3. The height of the cylinder is __**5**__ cm.

4. The volume of the cylinder is

   $V = B \cdot h = \underline{\textbf{3.14}} \cdot \underline{\ \textbf{5}\ } = \underline{\textbf{15.7}}$ cm³

The volume of the cylinder is 15.7 cm³.

---

1. a. What is the area of the base?

   $B = 3.14 \cdot \underline{\quad}^2 = \underline{\quad}$ cm²

   b. What is the height of the cylinder? _____ cm

   c. What is the volume of the cylinder?

   $V = B \cdot h = \underline{\quad} \cdot \underline{\quad} = \underline{\quad}$ cm³

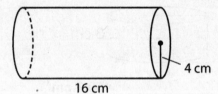

4 cm

16 cm

2. a. What is the area of the base?

   $B = 3.14 \cdot \underline{\quad}^2 = \underline{\quad}$ cm²

   b. What is the height of the cylinder? _____ cm

   c. What is the volume of the cylinder?

   $V = B \cdot h = \underline{\quad} \cdot \underline{\quad} = \underline{\quad}$ cm³

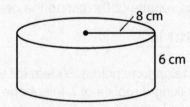

8 cm

6 cm

Name _____ Date _____ Class_____

LESSON 13-1

Volume of Cylinders

Reading Strategies: Use Diagrams

You can use diagrams to help solve problems. Use the information from the diagram below to find the area of the base and volume of a cylinder.

Example 1

What is the **area of the base** of the cylinder?

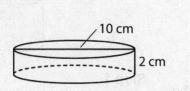

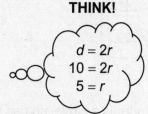

THINK!

$d = 2r$
$10 = 2r$
$5 = r$

Step 1: Write the formula for the area of the base of a cylinder.

$B = \pi r^2$

Step 2: Substitute the values you know. Evaluate.

$B = 3.14 \cdot (5)^2$

$B = 3.14 \cdot 25$

$B = 78.5 \text{ cm}^2$

Example 2

What is the **volume** of the cylinder?

Step 1: Write the formula for the volume of a cylinder.

$V = Bh$ or $V = \pi r^2 h$

Step 2: Substitute the values you know. Evaluate.

$V = \underline{\textbf{78.5}} \cdot \underline{\textbf{2}}$

$V = \underline{\textbf{157 cm}^3}$

Solve.

1. What is the area of the base of the cylinder?

_____

2. What is the volume of the cylinder?

_____

_____

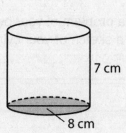

7 cm

8 cm

LESSON 13-1 Volume of Cylinders

Success for English Learners

Problem 1

Find the area of the base of the cylinder.

4 in.

Step 1

The base of a cylinder is a circle, so use the formula for the area of a circle.

$B = \pi r^2$

Step 2

Substitute the values. Use 3.14 for π. Then evaluate.

$B \approx 3.14 \cdot 4^2$

$B \approx 3.14 \cdot 16$

$B \approx 50.24 \text{ in}^2$

Problem 2

Find the volume of the cylinder. Round to the nearest tenth, if necessary.

4 in.
7 in.

Step 1

Multiply the area of the base (*B*) by the height (*h*) of the cylinder to find its volume. Use the formula for the volume of a cylinder.

$V = Bh$

Step 2

Substitute the values. Then evaluate.

$V = (50.24 \text{ in}^2) \cdot (7 \text{ in.})$

$V = 351.68 \text{ in}^3$

1. What formula is the same as $B = \pi r^2$?

_____

_____

2. Why is the volume of the cylinder expressed in cubic inches?

_____

_____

3. Write a problem of your own about finding the volume of a cylinder.
   Make a sketch of your cylinder at the right. Then solve the problem.

_____

_____

_____

LESSON
13-2

Volume of Cones

Practice and Problem Solving: A/B

Find the volume of each cone. Round your answer to the nearest tenth if necessary. Use 3.14 for π.

1.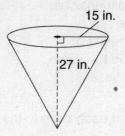
15 in.
27 in.

2.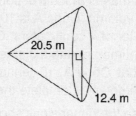
20.5 m
12.4 m

_____   _____

3. The mold for a cone has a diameter of 4 inches and is 6 inches tall. What is the volume of the cone mold to the nearest tenth?

_____

4. A medium-sized paper cone has a diameter of 8 centimeters and a height of 10 centimeters. What is the volume of the cone?

_____

5. A funnel has a diameter of 9 in. and is 16 in. tall. A plug is put at the open end of the funnel. What is the volume of the cone to the nearest tenth?

_____

6. A party hat has a diameter of 10 cm and is 15 cm tall. What is the volume of the hat?

_____

7. Find the volume of the composite figure to the nearest tenth. Use 3.14 for π.

    a. Volume of cone:

    _____

    b. Volume of cylinder:

    _____

    c. Volume of composite figure:

    _____

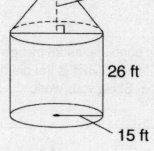
21 ft
26 ft
15 ft

LESSON 13-2

Volume of Cones

Practice and Problem Solving: C

Find the volume of each cone. Use 3.14 for π. Round your answer to the nearest tenth, if necessary. Show your work.

1. Lucas makes models of cones to explore how changing dimensions affect volume. Cone A is 10 centimeters high and its base has a diameter of 4 centimeters. Cone B is twice as tall with a height of 20 centimeters and a diameter of 4 centimeters. Cone C is the same height as Cone A, 10 centimeters, but the diameter of its base is 8 centimeters. Complete the table below.

   a. Use the dimensions shown above to find the volume of each cone to the nearest hundredth. Complete the table.

Cone Size	Radius	Height	Volume
Cone A			
Cone B			
Cone C			

   b. Which cone has the greatest volume?

   _____

   c. How much greater is the volume of Cone B than that of Cone A?

   _____

   d. Write an inequality that shows the volume of all three cones ordered from greatest to least.

   _____

   e. Does the volume of a cone increase more when you double the height of the original or when you double its radius? Explain why.

   _____

   _____

Solve.

2. A large traffic cone stands 28 inches in height and has a volume of 732.7 cubic inches. What is the diameter of the base of the cone? Use 3.14 for π. Show your work.

   _____

   _____

   _____

LESSON
13-2

Volume of Cones

Practice and Problem Solving: D

Find the volume of each cone. Round your answer to the nearest tenth if necessary. Use 3.14 for π. Show your work by filling in the blanks with values from the diagrams. The first one is done for you.

1.

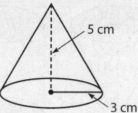

5 cm

3 cm

$V = \frac{1}{3}\pi r^2 h$

$V = \frac{1}{3} \cdot \underline{3.14} \cdot \underline{3^2} \times \underline{5}$

$V = \frac{1}{3} \cdot \underline{3.14} \cdot \underline{9} \times \underline{5}$

$V = \underline{47.1 \text{ cm}^3}$

2.

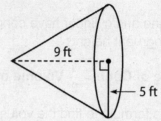

9 ft

5 ft

$V = \frac{1}{3}\pi r^2 h$

$V = \frac{1}{3} \cdot \underline{\hspace{1cm}} \cdot \underline{\hspace{1cm}} \times \underline{\hspace{1cm}}$

$V = \frac{1}{3} \cdot \underline{\hspace{1cm}} \cdot \underline{\hspace{1cm}} \times \underline{\hspace{1cm}}$

$V = \underline{\hspace{2cm}}$

Find the volume of each cone. Round your answer to the nearest tenth if necessary. Use 3.14 for π. The first one is done for you.

3.

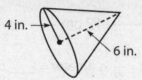

4 in.

6 in.

100.5 in³

4.

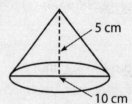

5 cm

10 cm

_____

Solve. The first one is done for you.

5. A cone has a diameter of 4 cm and a height of 11 cm. What is the volume of the cone to the nearest tenth? Use 3.14 for π.

46.1 cm³

6. A cloth pastry bag is shaped like a cone. It has a radius of 1.5 inches and a height of 8.5 inches. What is the volume of the pastry bag to the nearest tenth? Use 3.14 for π.

_____

_____

**LESSON
13-2**

Volume of Cones

Reteach

You can use your knowledge of how to find the volume of a
cylinder to help find the volume of a cone.

This cone and cylinder have congruent bases
and congruent heights.

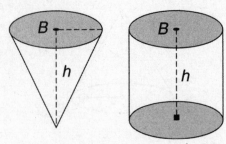

Volume of Cone = $\frac{1}{3}$ **Volume of Cylinder**

Use this formula to find the volume of a cone.

$$V = \frac{1}{3}Bh$$

Complete to find the volume of each cone.

1.

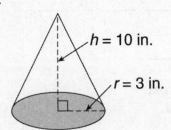

$h = 10$ in.

$r = 3$ in.

radius r of base = ____ in.

$V = \frac{1}{3}Bh$

$V = \frac{1}{3}(\pi r^2)h$

$V = \frac{1}{3}(\pi \times \underline{\ \ \ }) \times \underline{\ \ \ }$

$V = \frac{1}{3}(\underline{\ \ \ }) \times \underline{\ \ \ }$

$V = \underline{\ \ \ } \times \underline{\ \ \ }$

$V = \underline{\ \ \ \ \ \ }$

$V \approx \underline{\ \ \ }$ in³

2.

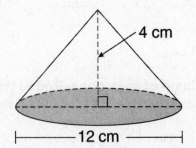

4 cm

12 cm

radius $r = \frac{1}{2}$ diameter = ____ cm

$V = \frac{1}{3}Bh$

$V = \frac{1}{3}(\pi r^2)h$

$V = \frac{1}{3}(\pi \times \underline{\ \ \ }) \times \underline{\ \ \ }$

$V = \frac{1}{3}(\underline{\ \ \ }) \times \underline{\ \ \ }$

$V = \underline{\ \ \ } \times \underline{\ \ \ }$

$V = \underline{\ \ \ \ \ \ }$

$V \approx \underline{\ \ \ }$ cm³

**LESSON
13-2**

Volume of Cones

Reading Strategies: Use Diagrams

Reading a diagram accurately is important when solving problems.

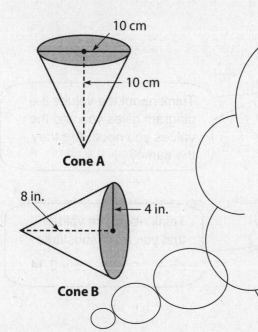

Cone A

Cone B

THINK!

- The base is shaded to show its area.

- The diameter and the radius of the base are shown by a solid line.

- The height of the cone is shown by a dashed line.

- Find the area of the base by using the formula $B = \pi r^2$.

- Check the diagram to see if it shows the diameter or the radius of the base of the cone.

- The formula asks for the radius. Remember that the diameter is twice the radius. So,

$$d = 2r \text{ and } r = \frac{d}{2}$$

Use the diagrams to answer the questions. Use 3.14 for π. Round your answer to the nearest tenth, if necessary.

1. Does the diagram of Cone A show the radius or the diameter of the base?

   _____

2. What is the radius of the base of Cone A?

   _____

3. What is the area of the base of Cone A?

   _____

4. What is the height of Cone A?

   _____

5. What is the volume of Cone A?

   _____

6. What is the volume of Cone B?

   _____

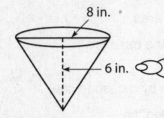

Volume of Cones

LESSON 13-2

Success for English Learners

Problem 1

What is the **area** of the base of this cone?

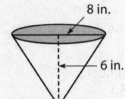

8 in.

6 in.

The **radius** is half the diameter.

So, 8 ÷ 2 = 4

Think about the values the diagram gives you and the values you need. Are they the same?

8 in.

6 in.

$B = \pi r^2$
$B = 3.14 \cdot 16$
$B = 50.24$ in^2

Think about the values that you must substitute.

$r = 4$ $r^2 = 16$ $\pi = 3.14$

Problem 2

What is the **volume** of this cone?

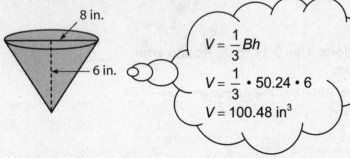

8 in.

6 in.

$V = \frac{1}{3} Bh$

$V = \frac{1}{3} \cdot 50.24 \cdot 6$

$V = 100.48$ in^3

Think about the values that you must substitute.

$B = 50.24$ $h = 6$

1. What must you do to find the radius of the base of a cone when a diagram gives you the measure of its diameter?

_____

2. Write a problem of your own about finding the volume of a paperweight in the shape of a cone. Then, solve.

_____

_____

_____

LESSON 13-3

Volume of Spheres

Practice and Problem Solving: A/B

Find the volume of each sphere. Round your answer to the nearest tenth if necessary. $V = \frac{4}{3}\pi r^3$. **Use 3.14 for** π. **Show your work.**

1.

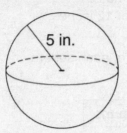

5 in.

_____

2.

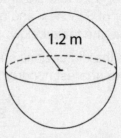

1.2 m

_____

3. $r = 3$ inches

_____

4. $d = 9$ feet

_____

5. $r = 1.5$ meters

_____

6. A globe is a map of Earth shaped as a sphere. What is the volume, to the nearest tenth, of a globe with a diameter of 16 inches?

_____

7. The maximum diameter of a bowling ball is 8.6 inches. What is the volume to the nearest tenth of a bowling ball with this diameter?

_____

8. According to the National Collegiate Athletic Association men's rules, a tennis ball must have a diameter of more than $2\frac{1}{2}$ inches and less than $2\frac{5}{8}$ inches.

   a. What is the volume of a sphere with a diameter of $2\frac{1}{2}$ inches?

   _____

   b. What is the volume of a sphere with a diameter of $2\frac{5}{8}$ inches?

   _____

   c. Write an inequality that expresses the range in the volume of acceptable tennis balls.

   _____

LESSON 13-3

Volume of Spheres

Practice and Problem Solving: C

Find the volume of each sphere. Use 3.14 for π. $V = \dfrac{4}{3}\pi r^3$. Show your work.

1. A basic sphere has a diameter of 6 inches, a mini sphere has a diameter of 3 inches, and a maxi sphere has a diameter of 12 inches. Complete the table below.

   a. Use the dimensions shown above to find the volume of each sphere to the nearest hundredth. Complete the table.

Sphere Size	Radius	Volume
Basic Sphere		
Mini Sphere		
Maxi Sphere		

   b. How does the volume of the mini sphere compare to the volume of the basic sphere?

   _____

   c. How does the volume of the maxi sphere compare to the volume of the basic sphere?

   _____

   d. Write an inequality that shows the volume of all 3 spheres ordered from least to greatest.

   _____

2. What is the radius of a sphere with a volume of 4186 in^3 to the nearest tenth of an inch?

   _____

   _____

3. If the radius of a sphere is equal to the length of the sides of a cube, are their volumes equal? Why or why not?

   _____

   _____

   _____

   _____

LESSON 13-3

Volume of Spheres

Practice and Problem Solving: D

Find the volume of each sphere. Round your answer to the nearest tenth if necessary. Use 3.14 for π. Show your work by filling in the blanks with values from the diagrams. The first one is done for you.

1.

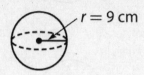

$r = 9$ cm

$V = \dfrac{4}{3}\pi r^3$

$V = \dfrac{4}{3} \cdot \underline{\ 3.14\ } \cdot \underline{\ 9^3\ }$

$V = \dfrac{4}{3} \cdot \underline{\ 3.14\ } \cdot \underline{\ 729\ }$

$V \approx \underline{\ 3{,}052.1\ } $ cm^3

2.

2 m

$V = \dfrac{4}{3}\pi r^3$

$V = \dfrac{4}{3} \cdot \underline{\ \ \ \ } \cdot \underline{\ \ \ \ } * \underline{\ \ \ \ }$

$V = \dfrac{4}{3} \cdot \underline{\ \ \ \ } \cdot \underline{\ \ \ \ } * \underline{\ \ \ \ }$

$V = \underline{\ \ \ \ \ \ \ \ }$

Find the volume of each sphere. Round your answer to the nearest tenth if necessary. Use 3.14 for π. The first one is done for you.

3.

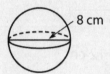

8 cm

_____ 267.9 cm^3

4.

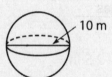

10 m

_____

Solve. The first one is done for you.

5. What is the volume to the nearest tenth of a spherical scoop of frozen yogurt with a diameter of 5.6 cm? Use 3.14 for π.

_____ 91.9 cm^3

6. Mike makes homemade apple lollipops. Each lollipop has a diameter of 2 in. What is the volume of the lollipop to the nearest tenth? Use 3.14 for π.

_____

LESSON
13-3

Volume of Spheres
Reteach

- All points on a sphere are the same distance from its center.

- Any line drawn from the center of a sphere to its surface is a radius of the sphere.

- The radius is half the measure of the diameter.

- Use this formula to find the volume of a sphere.

$$V = \frac{4}{3}\pi r^3$$

Complete to find the volume of each sphere to the nearest tenth.
Use 3.14 for π. The first one is done for you.

1. A regular tennis ball has a diameter of 2.5 inches.

   diameter = __**2.5 inches**__

   radius = __**1.25 inches**__

   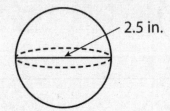

   $V = \frac{4}{3}\pi r^3$

   $V = \frac{4}{3} \cdot$ __**3.14**__ $\cdot$ __**1.25³**__

   $V = \frac{4}{3} \cdot$ __**3.14**__ $\cdot$ __**1.95**__

   $V =$ __**8.164**__

   $V \approx$ __**8.2 in³**__

2. A large grapefruit has a diameter of 12 centimeters.

   diameter = _____

   radius = _____

   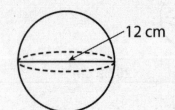

   $V = \frac{4}{3}\pi r^3$

   $V = \frac{4}{3} \cdot$ _____ $\cdot$ _____

   $V = \frac{4}{3} \cdot$ _____ $\cdot$ _____

   $V =$ _____

   $V \approx$ _____

Volume of Spheres
Reading Strategies: Build Vocabulary

Sphere: A 3-D figure shaped like a ball.

Diameter: Passes through the center and connects two points on the surface.

Radius: Connects the center with one point on the surface.

Center
Radius | Radius
Diameter

Think!
Diameter d = twice radius r

Use the diagram and vocabulary to answer the questions.

1. What is one example of a real-world object shaped like a sphere?

   _____

2. What passes through the center of a sphere and touches the surface at two points?

   _____

3. What connects the center of a sphere to one point on the surface?

   _____

4. If you are given the diameter of a sphere, how can you find its radius?

   _____

5. If you are given the radius of a sphere, how can you find its diameter?

   _____

**LESSON
13-3**

Volume of Spheres

Success for English Learners

Problem 1

What is the volume of a sphere with a diameter of 20 cm?

Use the formula $V = \dfrac{4}{3}\pi r^3$. Use 3.14 for π.

Round your answer to the nearest tenth.

The radius is half
the diameter.

$20 \div 2 = 10$

$r = 10$ cm

What is r^3?

$r^3 = r \cdot r \cdot r$

$10 \cdot 10 \cdot 10 = 1,000$

$r^3 = 1,000$ cm^3

What does the formula for the volume of a sphere look like when you plug
in numbers from the problem?

$V = \dfrac{4}{3}\pi r^3$

$V = \dfrac{4 \cdot 3.14 \cdot 1,000}{3}$

What operations must you perform next to find the volume of the sphere?

First, multiply. ⟹   **Next, divide.** ⟹   **Finally, round**

$V = \dfrac{12,560}{3}$

$V = 4186.66...$

$V \approx 4186.7$ cm^3

1. What does cm^3 in the answer mean?

_____

2. Write a problem of your own about finding the volume of a sphere.
   Then, solve.

_____

_____

_____

MODULE 13

Volume
Challenge

Use 3.14 for π.

1. Design a cylinder that has a volume of between 430 and 450 cubic inches. Sketch the cylinder and label the radius or diameter and the height. Prove your cylinder meets these conditions by showing your calculations.

   _____

   _____

   _____

   _____

   _____

2. Design a cone that has a volume of between 90 and 100 cubic inches. Sketch the cone and label the radius or diameter and the height. Prove your cone meets these conditions by showing your calculations.

   _____

   _____

   _____

   _____

   _____

3. Design a sphere that has a volume of between 980 and 1,005 cubic centimeters. Sketch the sphere and label the radius or diameter. Prove your sphere meets these conditions by showing your calculations.

   _____

   _____

   _____

   _____

   _____

LESSON 14-1

Scatter Plots and Association

Practice and Problem Solving: A/B

1. Use the given data to make a scatter plot.

Calories and Fat Per Portion of Meat and Fish

Food (Meat or Fish)	Fat (grams)	Calories
Fish Sticks (breaded)	3	50
Shrimp (fried)	9	190
Tuna (canned in oil)	7	170
Ground beef (broiled)	10	185
Roast beef (relatively lean)	7	165
Ham (light cure, lean and fat)	19	245

Calories and Fat Per Portion of Meat and Fish

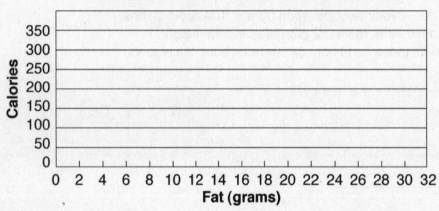

Do the data sets have a positive, a negative, or no correlation?

2. The size of the bag of popcorn and the price of popcorn

_____

3. The temperature and number of snowboards sold

_____

4. Use the data to predict how much money Tyler would be paid for babysitting $7\frac{1}{2}$ hours.

Amount Tyler Earns Babysitting

Hours	1	2	3	4	5	6	7	8
Amount	$8	$16	$24	$32	$40	$48	$56	$64

5. According to the data, Tyler would be paid _____ for babysitting $7\frac{1}{2}$ hours.

Scatter Plots and Association

LESSON 14-1

Practice and Problem Solving: C

An office supply store reported the following sales of ink cartridges for each month of a year:

January:	211	February:	358	March:	262
April:	265	May:	280	June:	305
July:	315	August:	345	September:	352
October:	382	November:	385	December:	355

1. Express the data as ordered pairs. Let *x* represent the month, using 1 for January, 2 for February, and so on. Let *y* represent the number of cartridges sold that month.

x												
y												

2. Make a scatter plot for the data.
   Use the horizontal axis for the months.

3. Answer these questions to describe trends in the data.

   a. Is the association positive, negative, or zero? Explain your answer.

   _____

   b. Do the data exhibit a linear relationship? Explain.

   _____

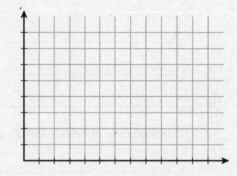

4. Are there clusters or outliers in the data? If so, where are the clusters and outliers and what real-world occasion might account for each?

   _____

5. a. Using 1 for the month with the most sales and 12 for the month with the least sales, rank the months from 1 to 12 for sales.

   _____

   b. Based on sales records for prior years, the manager of the supply store knows that if the store lowers the price of a print cartridge by 25% then the number of cartridges purchased increases by 35%. Suppose the store had lowered the price of print cartridges by 25% in May. What would be the ranking for May? Explain.

   _____

LESSON 14-1

Scatter Plots and Association

Practice and Problem Solving: D

The data below represent times and distances for car trips. Use the data to answer parts a, b, and c. Part a is done for you.

Time (hours)	5	10	3	6	8	4
Distance (miles)	250	200	140	320	425	210

1. a. Make a scatter plot of the data.

   Label the axes. Use the first variable, time, for the horizontal axis and use the second variable, distance, for the vertical axis. Then plot the ordered pairs.

   b. Describe the association between time and distance.

   _____

   _____

   _____

   _____

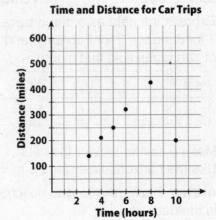

   c. Describe any outlier(s) in the scatter plot.

   _____

   _____

2. The data below represent the number of registers at grocery stores and the number of minutes shoppers wait until scanning the groceries.

Number of registers	10	5	12	8	4	6
Wait in minutes	3	7	2	4	1	6

   a. Make a scatter plot of the data.

   b. Describe the association between number of registers and wait time

   _____

   _____

   c. Describe any outlier(s) in the scatter plot.

   _____

Registers and Wait Times

LESSON 14-1

Scatter Plots and Association

Reteach

Many problems involving scatter plots have two parts.

Part I. Make a scatter plot from the following data values.

x	5	7	8	10	12	15	17	20	21	23
y	9	11	10	13	15	17	18	19	19	20

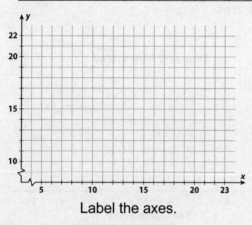

Label the axes.

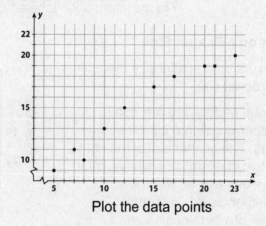

Plot the data points

Part 2. Interpret the scatter plot.

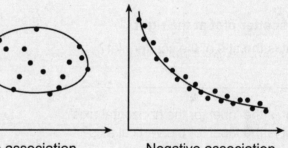

Positive association

linear

Zero association

Negative association

nonlinear

To interpret a scatter plot, data have a *positive association* if the points get higher from left to right. Data have a *negative association* if the points get lower from left to right. Also, the association is *linear* if the points lie along a line. The association is *nonlinear* if the points do not lie along a line.

1. Make a scatter plot for the given data.
   Then interpret the scatter plot.

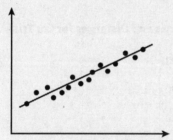

x	3	5	6	8	9
y	5	5	6	6	8

x	10	12	13	16	17
y	12	15	16	16	15

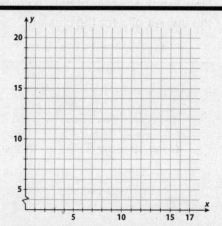

LESSON 14-1

Scatter Plots and Association

Reading Strategies: Read a Scatter Plot

The Organization of a Scatter Plot

horizontal axis   The horizontal and vertical axes have labels.

vertical axis   Each axis is numbered, usually starting with zero.

title   Usually a scatter plot has a title. The title usually refers to the information labeled on the axes.

Dots on a Scatter Plot

Each dot on a scatter plot represents an ordered pair.

A group of dots that are close together is called a *cluster* of data points. The scatter plot at the right has two clusters. One cluster is for the values of *x* between 1 and 4. The other cluster is for the values of *x* between 13 and 17.

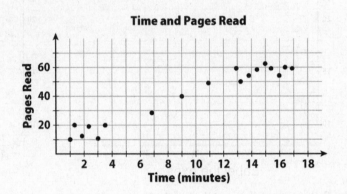

Use the scatter plot at the right.

1. What is the title of the scatter plot?

   _____

2. What is the label for the horizontal axis?
   What is the label for the vertical axis?

   _____

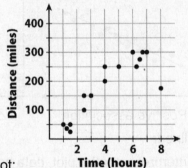

3. Complete the following ordered pairs for the scatter plot:

   (1, ____), (3, ____), (____ , 275), (____ , 175)

4. How many clusters of data values are in the scatter plot? What are the values of *x* for the clusters?

   _____

**LESSON
14-1**

Scatter Plots and Association
Success for English Learners

Important terms for scatter plots.

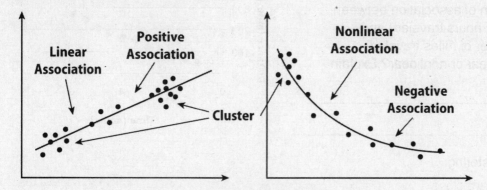

Cluster: Data points grouped closely together
Positive Association: Data points go up from left to right
Negative Association: Data points go down from left to right
Linear Association: Data points lie along a line
Nonlinear Association: Data points do not lie along a line

Use the letters in these scatter plots to answer the questions.

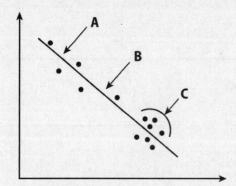
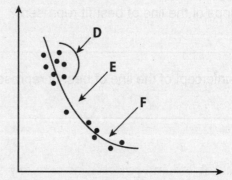

1. Which letter(s) point to a cluster? _____

2. Which letter(s) point to a positive association? _____

3. Which letter(s) point to a negative association? _____

4. Which letter(s) point to a linear association? _____

5. Which letter(s) point to a nonlinear association? _____

LESSON 14-2
Trend Lines and Predictions
Practice and Problem Solving: A/B

Use the scatter plot for Exercises 1–6.

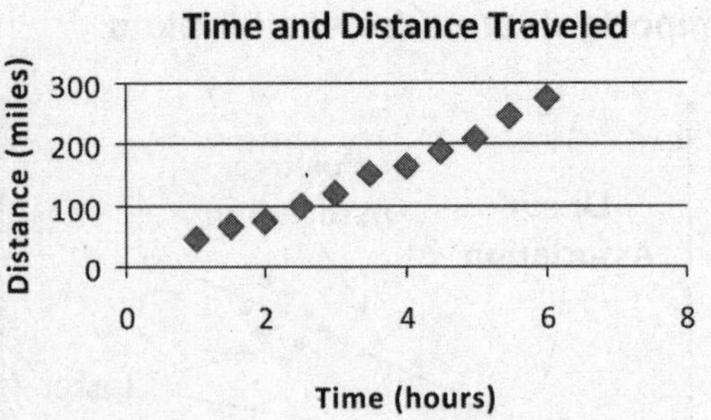

1. Does the pattern of association between time (number of hours traveled) and distance (number of miles traveled) appear to be linear or nonlinear? Explain.

   _____

   _____

Time and Distance Traveled

2. Explain any clustering.

   _____

3. Identify any possible outliers.

   _____

4. Write an equation for the line of best fit.

   _____

5. What does the slope of the line of best fit represent?

   _____

6. What does the *y*-intercept of the line of best fit represent?

   _____

LESSON 14-2

Trend Lines and Predictions

Practice and Problem Solving: C

Use the diagram and the description to complete Exercises 1–5.

Two students found equations for trend lines for this scatter plot.

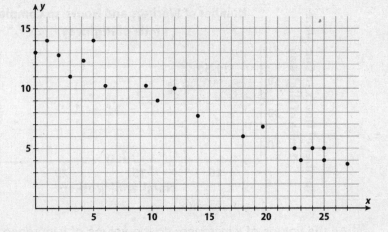

1. Clarisse used the ordered pairs (0, 13) and (24, 5) for her trend line. What equation did she get?

   _____

2. Anthony used the ordered pairs (12, 10) and (24, 5) for his trend line. What equation did he get?

   _____

3. Clarisse and Anthony used their equations to predict the value of y when x is 36. What values did they get?

   _____

4. When Clarisse and Anthony use their equations to predict a value for y, when will Clarisse's prediction be greater than Anthony's prediction? When will Anthony's prediction be greater?

   _____

5. There is a value of x so for which Clarisse's equation and Anthony's equation will predict the same y value. What is that x value? How is that ordered pair (x, y) related to the two trend lines?

   _____

   _____

LESSON 14-2 Trend Lines and Predictions

Practice and Problem Solving: D

Use the scatter plot for Exercises 1–5.

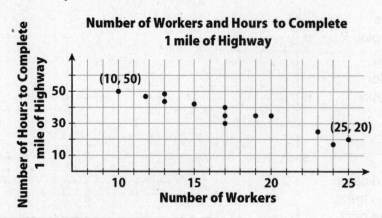

**Number of Workers and Hours to Complete
1 mile of Highway**

1. As the values of *x* increase, do the values of *y* increase, decrease, or remain the same?

   _____

2. Two ordered pairs in the scatter plot are (10, 50) and (25, 20). What is the slope of the line through those two points?

   _____

3. Use the slope from Exercise 2 and use the ordered pair (25, 20). What is the equation of the line for that slope and point? Use the slope-intercept form $y = mx + b$.

   _____

4. Is the relationship between the two variables a positive association, a negative association, or a zero association? Explain.

   _____

   _____

5. How is your answer to Exercise 4 related to the value of the slope from Exercise 2?

   _____

   _____

LESSON 14-2 Trend Lines and Predictions
Reteach

Here is another way to find the equation of a trend line.

Find the equation of a trend line that passes through the points (6, 9) and (12, 13).

Step 1.　Find the slope: $m = \dfrac{y_2 - y_1}{x_2 - x_1} = \dfrac{13 - 9}{12 - 6} = \dfrac{4}{6} = \dfrac{2}{3}$

Step 2.　Substitute $(x_1, y_1) = (6, 9)$ and $m = \dfrac{2}{3}$ into the

equation $y - y_1 = m(x - x_1)$.

$$y - y_1 = m(x - x_1) \rightarrow y - 9 = \frac{2}{3}(x - 6)$$

$$y - 9 = \frac{2}{3}x - 4$$

$$y = \frac{2}{3}x + 5$$

Note: The equation $y - y_1 = m(x - x_1)$ is called the point-slope form of an equation.

Find the equation of the line through each pair of points. Use the equation $y - y_1 = m(x - x_1)$ to find the equation.

1. (4, −10) and (10, −28)

2. (3, −14) and (20, 3)

3. (2, −6) and (20, −15)

4. (1, 6) and (8, 48)

Find the equation of the trend line for the given pair of points. Then use your equation to predict the y value for the given x value.

5. (3, 1) and (24, 15); predict y if $x = 15$.

6. (3, −8) and (8, −33); predict y if $x = 11$.

Trend Lines and Predictions
Reading Strategies: Analyze Information

The scatter plot and trend line shown
at the right provide many kinds of
information.

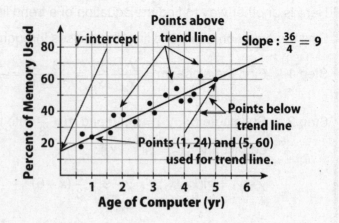

- General: The age of a computer
  and percent of memory used
  increase together.

- The same number of data points
  appear above the trend line and
  below the trend line.

- The trend line goes through
  (1, 24) and (5, 60).

- Slope = 9; that means about 9% of memory is used each year.

- y-intercept = 15; that means the computers had 15% of memory used when brand new.

Use the scatter plot below to answers the questions.

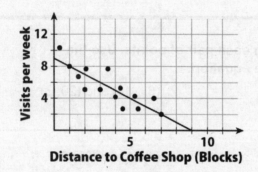

1. Write a general description about the scatter plot.

   _____

2. How many points are above the
   trend line? How many are below it?

   _____

3. What are the coordinates of the
   two points on the trend line?

   _____

4. What is an interpretation of the slope and y-intercept of the trend line?

   _____

LESSON
14-2

Trend Lines and Predictions

Success for English Learners

To write an equation for a trend line:

- Select two ordered pairs.

- Find the slope for those points.

- Write the equation.

Here are two ways to write an equation for the trend line in the scatter plot at the right.

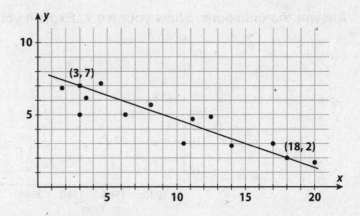

Problem 1

Method:

1. Select two ordered pairs.
   (3, 7) and (18, 2)

2. Calculate the slope.
   $$\frac{7-2}{3-18} = \frac{5}{-15} = -\frac{1}{3}$$

3. Find the y-intercept.
   $y = mx + b$
   $$7 = -\frac{1}{3}(3) + b$$
   $$7 = -1 + b; \ b = 8$$

4. Write the equation.
   $$y = -\frac{1}{3}x + 8$$

Problem 2

Method:

1. Select two ordered pairs.
   (3, 7) and (18, 2)

2. Calculate the slope.
   $$\frac{7-2}{3-18} = \frac{5}{-15} = -\frac{1}{3}$$

3. Find the equation.
   $$y - y_1 = m(x - x_1)$$
   $$y - 7 = -\frac{1}{3}(x - 3)$$
   $$y - 7 = -\frac{1}{3}x + 1$$
   $$y = -\frac{1}{3}x + 8$$

Use the two ordered pairs to write an equation. Use either method.

1. (8, −17) and (11, −23)

_____

2. (2, −30) and (5, −75)

_____

3. (4, 7) and (20, 11)

_____

4. (10, −3) and (20, −7)

_____

MODULE
14

Scatter Plots
Challenge

Answer the questions. Show your work. Explain your answers.

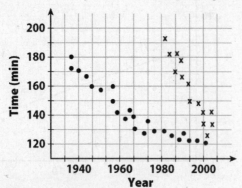

The scatter plot shows the winning time, in minutes, of a men's marathon foot race that has been held since the 1940s. Around 1980, women started running in the marathon, too. The men's winning times are shown as dots. The women's winning times are marked with "x's."

1. Describe the scatter plot for the men's and women's winning times from the 1940s to the twenty-first century.

   _____

2. Draw a line of best fit on the scatter plot for the points representing the men's scores.

   _____

3. Write an equation for the line of best fit for the men's scatter plot. Use points on the line.

   _____

4. Draw a line of best fit for the points representing the women's scores.

   _____

5. Write an equation for the line of best fit for the women's scatter plot. Use points on the line.

   _____

6. What do the *slopes* of these lines of best fit mean about the *trend* of the winning times of men and women for the marathon?

   _____

7. Will these lines continue to predict the winning times by 2020? Explain using specific examples.

   _____

LESSON 15-1

Two-Way Frequency Tables

Practice and Problem Solving: A/B

Complete the table. Then answer the questions that follow.

	Siblings	No Siblings	TOTAL
Boys	12	1. _____	25
Girls	10	14	2. _____
TOTAL	3. _____	4. _____	5. _____

6. What is the relative frequency of selecting a boy?

_____

7. What is the relative frequency of selecting a boy out of the children who have siblings?

_____

8. Compare the relative frequencies. Is there an association between being a boy and having siblings? Explain.

_____

_____

Complete the table. Then answer the questions that follow.

	Blooms	Does Not Bloom	TOTAL
Grows in Shade	75	9. _____	125
Grows in Sunlight	10. _____	85	110
TOTAL	100	11. _____	12. _____

13. What is the relative frequency of selecting a plant that blooms?

_____

14. Out of plants that grow in the shade, what is the relative frequency of

selecting one that blooms? _____

15. Compare the relative frequencies. Is there an association between a plant that blooms and a plant that grows in the shade? Explain.

_____

LESSON 15-1

Two-Way Frequency Tables

Practice and Problem Solving: C

Complete the table. Then answer the questions that follow.

Middle School Students' Favorite Subjects

	6th Grade	7th Grade	8th Grade	TOTAL
Math	75	60	65	1. _____
Reading	80	70	60	2. _____
Science	65	80	70	3. _____
Other	100	95	85	4. _____
TOTAL	5. _____	6. _____	7. _____	8. _____

9. Among 6th graders, name two subjects that, taken together, got more favorite votes than Other.

_____

10. For which grade was math the **least** favorite class?

_____

11. Among 7th graders, what percentage of the favorite-subject votes went to math **or** reading?

_____

12. What does the answer to Exercise 1 mean relative to the total number of students who participated in the survey?

_____

13. Compare the percentage of students in the whole school who chose science as their favorite subject to the percentage of 8th graders who chose science as their favorite subject.

_____

14. Among students in which grade did Other receive the least percentage of votes for favorite class?

_____

LESSON 15-1

Two-Way Frequency Tables
Practice and Problem Solving: D

Study the table. Then answer questions 1–5. The first one is done for you. Finally, use the answers you have found to complete the table.

Fruit Consumption and Weight Gain

	Weight Gain	No Weight Gain	TOTAL
Fruit as a Dessert	5	24	1. ___**29**___
No Fruit as a Dessert	15	4. _____	25
TOTAL	3. _____	5. _____	2. _____

1. How many people had fruit as a dessert? ___**29**___

2. How many people were surveyed? _____

3. How many people gained weight? _____

4. How many people did **not** eat fruit and did **not** gain weight? _____

5. How many people did **not** gain weight? _____

Use the information in the table above that you completed to answer the questions below.

6. Of the people who ate fruit, what percentage of them gained weight?
   Think: 5 out of 29.

   _____

7. What percentage of the people surveyed gained weight?

   _____

8. What kind of association can be made between eating or not eating fruit and weight gain?

   _____

   _____

   _____

LESSON 15-1

Two-Way Frequency Tables
Reteach

A two-way frequency table allows you to see the relationships among two or more pairs of variables in a real-world situation.

Automobile Gas Mileage and Commuting Distance

	Mileage < 20 mi/gal	Mileage ≥ 20 mi/gal	TOTAL
3-Mile Commute	18	3	21
30-Mile Commute	5	24	29
TOTAL	23	27	50

Notice that a total value is shown for each column or row, and that the total for the far right column and the bottom row are the same, 50. This is the total number of commuters surveyed.

Looking for an Association The table can show whether there is a relationship between commuting distance and gas mileage.

3-Mile Commute and Mileage

What fraction of commuters drove 3 miles and got 20 miles per gallon or more?

Number who drove 3 miles: **21**

Number of those with mileage ≥ 20 mi/gal: **3**

The fraction is $\frac{3}{21}$, or about 14%.

30-Mile Commute and Mileage

What fraction of commuters drove 30 miles and got 20 miles per gallon or more?

Number who drove 30 miles: **29**

Number of those with mileage ≥ 20 mi/gal: **24**

The fraction is $\frac{24}{29}$, or about 83%.

Use the table above to answer the questions.

1. What association exists between commuters who drove 3 miles and commuters who got **less than** 20 miles per gallon? Use the data in your answer.

_____

_____

2. What association exists between commuters who drove 30 miles and commuters who got **less than** 20 miles per gallon? Use the data in your answer.

_____

_____

3. What other factors besides gas mileage should be considered when making an analysis of the costs of commuting 3 miles and 30 miles?

_____

_____

LESSON 15-1

Two-Way Frequency Tables

Reading Strategies: Read a Table

To make an association between the factors in a two-way frequency table, first you need to be able to understand the data presented.

The table below shows data about a number of athletes, the time they spent training, and their maximum bench press at the end of training.

Maximum Bench Press and Training Time

	< 150 lb	≥ 150 lb	TOTAL
3 Months Training	11	12	23
6 Months Training	13	15	28
TOTAL	24	27	51

Tell what the data in each shaded row or column represents.

1.

	< 150 lb	≥ 150 lb	TOTAL
3 Months Training	11	12	23
6 Months Training	13	15	28
TOTAL	24	27	51

_____

2.

	< 150 lb	≥ 150 lb	TOTAL
3 Months Training	11	12	23
6 Months Training	13	15	28
TOTAL	24	27	51

_____

3.

	< 150 lb	≥ 150 lb	TOTAL
3 Months Training	11	12	23
6 Months Training	13	15	28
TOTAL	24	27	51

_____

4.

	< 150 lb	≥ 150 lb	TOTAL
3 Months Training	11	12	23
6 Months Training	13	15	28
TOTAL	24	27	51

_____

5. What association can you make between the two factors in the table?

_____

LESSON 15-1

Two-Way Frequency Tables
Success for English Learners

Problem

**Number of 8ᵗʰ Graders Who Have a Bike
and Number of 8ᵗʰ Graders Who Have a Job**

	Bike	No Bike	TOTAL
Job	24	10	34
No Job	15	32	47
TOTAL	39	42	81

How many 8ᵗʰ graders have a bike? **39**

Write this number as a fraction of all the 8ᵗʰ graders.

$$\frac{\text{8th graders with bike}}{\text{all 8th graders}} = \frac{39}{81}$$

Rewrite this fraction as a percent of all the 8ᵗʰ graders.

$$\frac{39}{81} = 0.\overline{481} \approx 48\%$$

How many 8ᵗʰ graders have a job? **34**

Write this number as a fraction and as a percent of all the 8ᵗʰ graders.

$$\frac{\text{8th graders with job}}{\text{all 8th graders}} = \frac{34}{81} \approx 0.41975 \approx 42\%$$

> **Think:**
> **34** 8ᵗʰ graders have a job.
> **47** 8ᵗʰ graders have no job.
>
> So, the total number of
> 8ᵗʰ graders is
> **34 + 47 = 81.**

Answer the questions.

1. How many 8th graders who have a job also have a bike? Write your
   answer as a fraction and a percent.

   _____

2. How many 8ᵗʰ graders who do have a job do **not** have a bike? Write
   your answer as a fraction and a percent.

   _____

3. What association is there between having a job and having a bike?

   _____

4. What association is there between having a job and not having a bike?

   _____

Two-Way Relative Frequency Tables

LESSON 15-2

Practice and Problem Solving: A/B

Rewrite each frequency in the table as a relative frequency. Write each one as a percent to the nearest whole percent. Show your work.

Home Heating Energy Sources Sample

	Electric	Gas	TOTAL
Inside City Limits	35 1. _____	55 2. _____	90 3. _____
Outside City Limits	60 4. _____	15 5. _____	75 6. _____
TOTAL	95 7. _____	70 8. _____	165 9. _____

Complete.

10. Name the four joint relative frequencies (JRFs) shown in the table by using the names of the columns *and* rows. Give the percent for each. Show your work.

   JRF name: _____, _____   percent: _____

   JRF name: _____, _____   percent: _____

   JRF name: _____, _____   percent: _____

   JRF name: _____, _____   percent: _____

11. Name the four marginal relative frequencies (MRFs) in the table by using the name of the column *or* row. Give the percent for each. Show your work.

   MRF name: _____   percent: _____

   MRF name: _____   percent: _____

   MRF name: _____   percent: _____

   MRF name: _____   percent: _____

Calculate the conditional relative frequency.

12. Electric, Inside City Limits: 13. Gas, Outside City Limits:

   _____ ÷ _____ = _____   _____ ÷ _____ ≈ _____

LESSON 15-2 Two-Way Relative Frequency Tables

Practice and Problem Solving: C

The table below shows electric and gas usage for heating in a sample of homes inside the city limits and outside the city limits.

Home Heating Energy Sources Sample

	Electric	Gas	TOTAL
Inside City Limits	35	55	90
Outside City Limits	60	15	75
TOTAL	95	70	165

Use the table to answer the questions.

1. Without doing the calculations, how would you expect the joint relative frequency (JRF) for electric energy use inside the city limits to compare to the conditional relative frequency (CRF) for electric energy use inside the city limits?

   _____

   _____

2. Calculate the JRF and the CRF for electric use inside the city limits. Show your work.

   JRF: _____   CRF: _____

3. Do these calculations support your answer to Exercise 1? Explain.

   _____

   _____

4. Describe the associations you observe in electric usage for heat inside and outside the city limits. Use the terms *joint*, *marginal*, and *conditional relative frequency* in your description.

   _____

   _____

   _____

LESSON 15-2

Two-Way Relative Frequency Tables

Practice and Problem Solving: D

Bowling Averages and Bowling Ball Ownership

	Average > 150	Average ≤ 150	TOTAL
Owns a Bowling Ball	21	17	38
Does Not Own a Bowling Ball	16	23	39
TOTAL	37	40	77

Find the relative frequencies for the data shown in the table above. The first one of each type has been done for you.

1. the joint relative frequency of averaging more than 150 and owning a bowling ball

   ___21___ ÷ ___77___ ≈ ___0.27___ = ___27___ %

2. the joint relative frequency of averaging 150 or less and owning a bowling ball

   _____ ÷ _____ ≈ _____ = _____ %

3. the marginal relative frequency of owning a bowling ball

   (___21___ + ___17___) ÷ ___77___ = ___38___ ÷ ___77___ ≈ ___0.49___ = ___49___ %

4. the marginal relative frequency of not owning a bowling ball

   (_____ + _____) ÷ _____ = _____ ÷ _____ ≈ _____ = _____ %

5. the conditional relative frequency of averaging more than 150 and owning a bowling ball

   ___21___ ÷ ___38___ ≈ ___0.55___ = ___55___ %

6. the conditional relative frequency of averaging 150 or less and owning a bowling ball

   _____ ÷ _____ ≈ _____ = _____ %

LESSON
15-2
Two-Way Relative Frequency Tables
Reteach

Comparison of the different relative frequencies in data can reveal associations or trends that the frequencies themselves might not show.

The table below compares the weights of corn chips found in two different sizes of bags of three brands.

Amount of chips in 24-Ounce Bags

	Bags with less than 24 ounces of chips	Bags with more than 24 ounces of chips	Bags with exactly 24 ounces of chips	TOTAL
Brand A	12	10	40	62
Brand B	9	15	55	79
Brand C	7	6	25	38
TOTAL	28	31	120	179

Marginal Relative Frequency (MRF)

The MRF is a fraction that compares the sum of all frequencies in one row or column to the total of all frequencies of all columns and rows.

Example

Find the MRF of all of Brand A's samples.

$$62 \div 179 = 0.35, \text{ or about } 35\%.$$

Conditional Relative Frequency (CRF)

The CRF is a fraction that compares one frequency in a row or column to the total of all factors in that row or column.

Example

Find the CRF of Brand A samples with less than 24 ounces of chips.

$$12 \div 62 = 0.19, \text{ or about } 19\%.$$

Solve. Show your work.

1. Which brand may have quality-control problems when it comes to selling the advertised amount of chips in its 24-ounce bag? Use MRF and/or CRF values to support your answer.

   _____

   _____

   _____

2. Which brand has the greatest CRF for **less than** the advertised weight of chips? What does this indicate about the accuracy of its label?

   _____

   _____

LESSON 15-2

Two-Way Relative Frequency Tables
Reading Strategies: Understand Vocabulary

The four terms that are introduced in this lesson have specific meanings in two-way frequency tables. However, each term is made up of words that you may have encountered in other situations.

Refer to the table below as you review the four terms and answer the questions.

Automobile Gas Mileage and Commuting Distance

	Mileage < 30 mi/gal	Mileage ≥ 30 mi/gal	TOTAL
3-Mile Commute	36%	6%	42%
30-Mile Commute	10%	48%	58%
TOTAL	46%	54%	100%

Relative Frequency (RF) The frequency is "relative" to another frequency, namely the grand total of all the frequencies.

Relative frequency is found by dividing a frequency by the grand total of all frequencies in a two-way frequency table.

1. Name the 8 relative frequencies shown in the table. _____

2. Which frequency is **not** a relative frequency? Why? _____

_____

Joint Relative Frequency (JRF) The *joint* relative frequency "joins" or "combines" two factors in the table. Joint relative frequency is found by dividing a frequency that is **not** in the total column or row by the grand total of all frequencies.

3. Name the 4 joint relative frequencies shown in the table. _____

Marginal Relative Frequency (MRF) The *marginal* relative frequency is "in the margin" of the table. It is a total for a column or a row but not the grand total. Marginal relative frequency is found by dividing a column or row total by the grand total.

4. Name the 4 marginal relative frequencies shown in the table. _____

Conditional Relative Frequency (CRF) The *conditional* relative frequency is a frequency that "depends on" the column or row in which a relative frequency is found. It is not shown in the example. It is a joint relative frequency in a row or column divided by the marginal relative frequency of the column or row.

5. Calculate the 8 conditional relative frequencies. _____

LESSON 15-2 Two-Way Relative Frequency Tables

Success for English Learners

Problem 1

Use the table to find the **relative frequencies**.

8th Graders with Bike and Jobs

	Bike	No Bike	TOTAL
Job	30%	10%	40%
No Job	15%	45%	60%
TOTAL	45%	55%	100%

Joint Relative Frequency
Example:
Bike and a Job: **30%**

Name the **joint relative frequencies**.

Bike and a Job: 30%   Bike and No Job: 15%

No Bike and Job: 10%   No Bike and No Job: 45%

Problem 2

a. Find the **marginal relative frequencies**.

Example:
Bike, Job, and No Job:
30% + 15% = 45%

b. Find the **conditional relative frequencies**.

Examples:
Bike only, and a Job:
$$\frac{\text{Bike and Job}}{\text{Bike Total}} = \frac{30}{45} \approx 67\%$$

Bike only, and No Job:
$$\frac{\text{Bike and No Job}}{\text{Bike Total}} = \frac{15}{45} \approx 33\%$$

Answer the questions.

1. In the top row of the table, where does the value 40% come from?

_____

2. How is the conditional relative frequency in Problem 2 different from the joint relative frequency in Problem 1?

_____

_____

_____

MODULE 15 Two-Way Tables
Challenge

The table shows the frequencies *a – f*, *x*, *y*, and *z* of part failures of three vehicle models. Complete the table.

New Part Failures in Three Vehicle Models

Model	More than 30 part failures	More than 75 part failures	More than 120 part failures	TOTAL
Compact	*a*	*b*	*c*	1. _____
Mid-Size	*d*	*e*	*f*	2. _____
SUV	*x*	*y*	*z*	3. _____
TOTAL	4. _____	5. _____	6. _____	7. _____ _____

8. Compare the sums for Exercises 1–3 and for Exercises 4–6. Do they

   agree? Write the sum. _____

Write an expression for each sum of *relative* frequency rates.

9. *a* + *c*: _____ 10. *b* + *d*: _____

11. *e* + *x*: _____ 12. *f* + *y*: _____

Write two fractional expressions for each of these *conditional relative frequency* variables.

13. *a*   14. *e*   15. *z*

   _____   _____   _____

   _____   _____   _____

16. How do these conditional relative frequencies compare with their joint
    failure rates? Use specific data from the table and your answers to
    Exercises 8–10 to prove your answer.

    _____

    _____

    _____

UNIT 1: Real Numbers, Exponents, and Scientific Notation

MODULE 1 Real Numbers

LESSON 1-1

Practice and Problem Solving: A/B

1. 0.125
2. 0.5625
3. 0.5$\overline{5}$
4. 5.32
5. 0.9$\overline{3}$
6. 2.58$\overline{3}$
7. 0.03
8. 3.2
9. 5, −5
10. 1, −1
11. $\frac{5}{2}$, $-\frac{5}{2}$
12. $\frac{11}{7}$, $-\frac{11}{7}$
13. 2
14. 6
15. 1
16. 13
17. 5.66
18. 10.86
19. 4.24
20. 17.86
21. 2.83

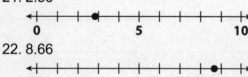

22. 8.66

23. $1\frac{23}{100}$ lb
24. 288 in²

Practice and Problem Solving: C

1. 1.17 in.
2. 7.64 in.
3. Since $\frac{41}{50} = 0.82, \frac{9}{11} = 0.\overline{81}$, and
$\frac{10}{11} = 0.\overline{90}$, $\frac{41}{50}$ is closer to $\frac{9}{11}$.
4. $\pm\frac{1}{2}$
5. $\pm\frac{1}{4}$
6. $\approx \pm\frac{2}{3}$
7. ≈ 1.73
8. ≈ 4.24

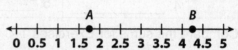

9. When you find a square root, you find two factors that are the same. They can be positive or negative. When you find a cube root, you find three factors that are the same. They are positive.
10. The length of one photo album page is 25 cm. The width of the page is 32 cm.

Practice and Problem Solving: D

1. 0.$\overline{1}$
2. 0.55
3. 0.5625
4. $\frac{129}{500}$
5. $4\frac{4}{5}$
6. $\frac{333}{1000}$
7. 4, −4
8. 7, −7

9. $\dfrac{5}{2}$, $-\dfrac{5}{2}$

10. 7

11. 1

12. $\dfrac{2}{3}$

13. 5.66

14. 7.68

15. 10.86

16. 0.17 mi^2

17. 5 ft

Reteach

1. 3.75

2. $0.8\overline{3}$

3. $3.\overline{6}$

4. 9, −9

5. 7, −7

6. $\dfrac{5}{6}$, $-\dfrac{5}{6}$

7. 3

8. 5

9. 9

Reading Strategies

1. Yes, because it can be written as a fraction: $0.62 = \dfrac{62}{100} = \dfrac{31}{50}$.

2. No, because it cannot be written as a decimal that terminates or repeats.

3. Yes, as long as the decimal is infinite and nonrepeating, such as 0.31311311131111....

4. Yes, for example, $\dfrac{2}{3} = 0.\overline{6}$.

5. A decimal that is an irrational number is infinite and nonrepeating, such as the value for π.

6. Both are real numbers and both can be written as decimals.

Success for English Learners

1. $\dfrac{1}{4} = 0.25$

2. Possible answer: If you have a square with a side length of 5, then 5^2 is how you find the area of that square.

3. Because the answer is an approximation.

LESSON 1-2

Practice and Problem Solving: A/B

1. real, rational

2. real, irrational

3. real, rational, integer

4. real, rational, integer

5. real, rational

6. real, rational, integer, whole

7. false; irrational real numbers include nonterminating decimals

8. true; whole numbers are nonnegative integers.

9. rational; all money amounts can be written as fractions

10. real numbers; the temperature can be any number between 0 and 100 degrees Celsius

11. rational, real

12. integers, rational, real

13. irrational, real

14. whole numbers, integers, rational, real

Practice and Problem Solving: C

1. real, irrational

2. integers, rational, real

3. irrational, real

4. whole numbers, integers, rational, real

5. real, rational

6. real, rational, integer, whole

7. integers; possible points are positive and negative numbers

8. real; elevation can be any number above or below zero

9. no; there are an infinite number of rational numbers between any two integers

10. 10 will be whole numbers (square roots of 1, 4, 9, 16, 25, 36, 49, 64, 81, and 100); 90 will be irrational numbers

11. all of the negative numbers that are not fractions or decimals

12. all fractions, irrational numbers, or decimals less than 0

Practice and Problem Solving: D

1. real, rational

2. real, irrational

3. real, rational

4. real, rational, integer

5. real, rational

6. real, rational, integer, whole

7. true; all fractions are rational numbers, and all rational numbers are real numbers

8. false; Negative fractions and decimals are not integers.

9. whole numbers; There are 0 or more people in a movie theater.

10. real numbers; The square root of 1, 4, or 9 would be whole numbers, but the square root of 2, 3, 5, 6, 7, 8, 10, 11, or 12 would be irrational numbers. (Each cube can show 1 through 6, so the sum can be 2 through 12. Of these numbers, 4 and 9 are perfect squares, so their square roots are whole numbers. The other possible sums have square roots that are irrational. The set of numbers that contains whole numbers and irrational numbers is the real numbers.)

11. rational

12. integers

13. rational

14. whole numbers

Reteach

1. Yes

2. Yes; $\sqrt{16} = 4$, which can be written as $\frac{4}{1}$.

3. Yes

4. Is it a whole number? Yes.

5. real, rational, integer, whole

Reading Strategies

1. rational; irrational

2. fraction; decimal

3. terminating; repeating

4. opposites

5. counting

6. a. integers

   b. rational numbers

   c. whole numbers

   d. irrational numbers

Success for English Learners

1. real

2. not real

3. real, rational

4. real, rational, integer

LESSON 1-3

Practice and Problem Solving: A/B

1. <

2. <

3. <

4. >

5. >

6. >

7. Great white, White–angled sulphur, Large orange sulphur, Apricot sulphur

8. Between Large orange sulphur and Apricot sulphur

9. $\frac{\sqrt{7}}{2}$, 2, $\sqrt{8}$

10. π, $\sqrt{12}$, 3.5

11. –20, $\sqrt{26}$, $\sqrt{35}$, 13.5

12. –5.25, $\frac{3}{2}$, $\sqrt{6}$, 5

13. $1 + \frac{\pi}{2}$, $\frac{5}{2}$, $\sqrt{12} - 1$, 2.25

Practice and Problem Solving: C

1. a. $2\pi - 1.68$; $\sqrt{13} + 1$; $4.\overline{6}$

b. Yes, if you used
$\pi \approx \dfrac{22}{7}$, then $2\pi - 1.68 \approx 4.6057142$,
which would be greater than
$\sqrt{13} + 1 \approx 4.6055512$, so from least to
greatest the order would be $\sqrt{13} + 1$,
$2\pi - 1.68$, and $4.\overline{6}$.

2. a. $\dfrac{\sqrt{23}}{2} - 1 \approx 1.40$; $1 + \dfrac{\pi}{9} \approx 1.35$;
$\sqrt{12} - 2.2 \approx 1.26$; 1.18

b.

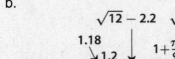
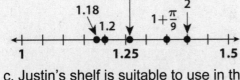

c. Justin's shelf is suitable to use in the closet. The other shelves are too long. Justin's shelf is shorter than the closet width, but it can be held up using the 3.5–centimeter brackets.

Practice and Problem Solving: D

1. <
2. >
3. <
4. >
5. >
6. =
7.

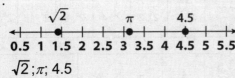

$\sqrt{2}$; π; 4.5

8. -10, $\dfrac{\sqrt{2}}{2}$, 2

9. $\sqrt{3}$, π, 7

10. -4, 1.5, $\sqrt{8}$

11. -5.5, $\dfrac{3}{2}$, $\sqrt{6}$

12. $\dfrac{5}{2}$, 2.6, $1 + \sqrt{3}$, $\sqrt{8}$

Reteach

1. $\sqrt{8}$, π, 4
2. 5, $\pi + 2$, $\dfrac{17}{3}$
3. -2, $\sqrt{2}$, 1.7
4. $\dfrac{3}{2}$, $\sqrt{5}$, 2.5
5. $\sqrt{13}$, 3.7, $\pi + 1$
6. $\dfrac{\sqrt{5}}{2}$, $\pi - 2$, $\dfrac{5}{4}$

Reading Strategies

1. The square root of thirteen is less than four.
2. Five-hundred-and-one thousandths is approximately one half.
3. The square root of 25 equals 5.
4. Pi plus one is greater than two thirds. OR The sum of pi and one is greater than two thirds.
5. $\dfrac{18}{2} = 9$
6. $5.17 > \sqrt{23}$
7. $\dfrac{2}{3} < \pi$

Success for English Learners

1. <
2. $\pi + 1$, $\sqrt{19}$, 4.4
3. Answers may vary. Sample answer: when comparing runners' marathon times

MODULE 1 Challenge

1. No square numbers are prime. No S is P.
2. Some prime numbers are odd. Some P is O.
3. All even numbers are integers. All E is I.
4.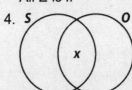

5.

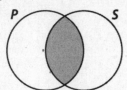

6.

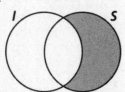

7.

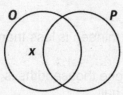

MODULE 2 Exponents and Scientific Notation

LESSON 2-1

Practice and Problem Solving: A/B

1. 125
2. $\frac{1}{49}$
3. 51
4. $\frac{1}{81}$
5. 1
6. 1
7. $\frac{1}{64}$
8. 64
9. 100,000
10. 6
11. 6
12. 3
13. 35
14. 5
15. $\frac{1}{16}$

16. 4,096
17. 2^3 in^3; 10^3 in^3
18. 125
19. Sample answer: The box will hold the same number of balls as small boxes. With the balls, there is empty space.
20. 125; Sample answer: Find the volume of the box and of the cube. Divide the box volume by the cube volume.

Practice and Problem Solving: C

1. 1,024
2. $\frac{1}{4}$
3. $\frac{2}{5}$
4. 10,000
5. $\frac{1}{144}$
6. 2,048
7. 1; Explanations will vary. Sample answer: If you add all the exponents, you get $n - 21$ and when $n = 3$, $7n - 21 = 0$; $2^0 = 1$.
8. Predictions will vary.
9.

Number of Folds	0	1	2	3	4	5
Number of Rectangles	2^0, 1	2^1, 2	2^2, 4	2^3, 8	2^4, 16	2^5, 32

Number of Folds	6	7	8	9	10
Number of Rectangles	2^6, 64	2^7, 128	2^8, 256	2^9, 512	2^{10}, 1,024

10. Answers will vary.
11. Predictions will vary.
12. Answers will vary. Sample answer: Raise 2 to the power of the cut to see how many pieces. On the 5th cut, $2^5 = 32$ pieces.

Practice and Problem Solving: D

1. $\dfrac{1}{4\times4\times4\times4}=\dfrac{1}{256}$

2. $6\times6=36$

3. $3\times3\times3\times3\times3=243$

4. 1

5. $\dfrac{1}{7\times7}=\dfrac{1}{49}$

6. $10\times10\times10\times10\times10=100,000$

7. $\dfrac{(3\bullet2)^6}{(7-1)^4}=\dfrac{6^6}{6^4}=6^{6-4}=6^2=36$

8. $(3)^2\bullet(3^1)=3^{2+1}=3^3=27$

9. $4^2\bullet4^3=4^{2+3}=4^5=1,024$

10. $(4^2)^3=4^{2\bullet3}=4^6=4,096$

11. $(4-3)^2\bullet(5\bullet4)^0=1^2\bullet20^0=1\bullet1=1$

12. $(2+3)^5\div(5^2)^2=5^5\div5^4=5^{5-4}=5^1=5$

13. $(2^2)^3=2^6=64;(2^3)^2=2^6=64$; Both are equal. Explanations will vary.

Reteach

1. subtract; 27

2. add; $\dfrac{1}{8}$

3. multiply; 729

4. add; 625

5. subtract; $\dfrac{1}{16}$

6. multiply; 1,296

Reading Strategies

1. The exponent decreases by 1 as you move down the column.

2. 3

3. 3

4. 4

5. 4

6.

Column 1	Column 2	Column 3
$5^3=125$	$6^3=216$	$10^3=1,000$
$5^2=25$	$6^2=36$	$10^2=100$
$5^1=5$	$6^1=6$	$10^1=10$
$5^0=1$	$6^0=1$	$10^0=1$
$5^{-1}=\dfrac{1}{5}$	$6^{-1}=\dfrac{1}{6}$	$10^{-1}=\dfrac{1}{10}$
$5^{-5}=\dfrac{1}{25}$	$6^{-2}=\dfrac{1}{36}$	$10^{-2}=\dfrac{1}{100}$

Success for English Learners

1. Answers will vary. Sample answer: A negative exponent tells you how many times you use the base as a divisor.

2. 9

3. 64

4. x^{20}

5. 4,096

6. 12

7. z^{12}

LESSON 2-2

Practice and Problem Solving: A/B

1. 10^2

2. 10^4

3. 10^5

4. 10^7

5. 10^6

6. 10^3

7. 10^9

8. 10^0

9. 1,000

10. 100,000

11. 10

12. 1,000,000

13. 100

14. 1

15. 10,000

16. 10,000,000

17. 2.5×10^3

18. 3×10^2

19. 4.73×10^4

20. 2.4×10^1

21. 1.4565×10^4

22. 7.001×10^3

23. 1.905×10^7

24. 3.3×10^1

25. 6,000

26. 450

27. 70,000,000

28. 10,500

29. 3,052

30. 5

31. 98.7

32. 54.3

33. 3.844×10^5 km

34. 6,380 km

Practice and Problem Solving: C

1. $2,500 < 2,500,000$

2. $5,000,000 > 2,500,000$

3. $3 < 10$

4. $4,025 < 10,250$

5. 4.50×10^2; 1.2×10^3

6. 2.3×10^5; 3.2×10^4

7. 2.35×10^5; 3.25×10^5; 5.32×10^5; 2.35×10^6; 3.25×10^6; 5.32×10^6

8. 0×10^0; 1×10^0; 5×10^0; 1×10^1; 5×10^1

9. False; 1×10^3 m = $1 \times 10^3 \times 10^1$ cm = 1×10^4 cm, which is less than 1×10^6 cm

10. False; 9×10^1 m = $9 \times 10^1 \times 10^3$ mm = 9×10^4 mm, which is not equal to 9×10^1 mm

11. $15,000 - 9,000 = 6,000$; 6,000 tickets are available

12. $1.5 \times 10^4 = 15,000$, and $15,000 > 2,500$, so the athletic team is more popular

Practice and Problem Solving: D

1. 100

2. 100,000

3. 10,000

4. 1,000

5. $10 \times 10 \times 10 \times 10 \times 10$

6. $10 \times 10 \times 10 \times 10 \times 10 \times 10 \times 10$

7. $10 \times 10 \times 10 \times 10$

8. $10 \times 10 \times 10 \times 10 \times 10 \times 10 \times 10 \times 10 \times 10 \times 10 \times 10$

9. 10^3

10. 10^1

11. 10^5

12. 10

13. 1,000

14. 10,000

15. 1,000,000,000

16. 100,000

17. 1

18. 3

19. 2

20. 6

21. 0

22. 3,560

23. 9,000

24. 68,750

25. 4,005,000

26. 1,000 ft^3

Reteach

1. 3.46; 4; 3.46×10^4

2. 1.0502; 6; 1.0502×10^6

3. 1,057

4. 300,000,000

5. 524,000

Reading Strategies

1. 2; 2.95; 2; 2.95×10^2

2. 1; 1.05; 4; 1.05×10^4

3. 4; 4.505; 6; 4.505×10^6

4. between 2 and 9; 4; 25,000

5. after the 7; 5; 700,000

6. between 1 and 2; 3; 1,234

Success for English Learners

1. $3.28 \times 10^5 > 3.28 \times 10^3$ because
   $3.28 \times 10^5 = 328,000$ and
   $3.28 \times 10^3 = 3,280$.

2. A car; $3 \times 10^6 = 3,000,000$ g, or 3,000 kg, and a car would weigh many kilograms but a hair would not.

3. 1.86×10^5

4. 4,567.89

LESSON 2-3

Practice and Problem Solving: A/B

1. 10^{-2}
2. 10^{-4}
3. 10^{-5}
4. 10^{-7}
5. 10^{-6}
6. 10^{-3}
7. 10^{-9}
8. 10^{-1}
9. 0.001
10. 0.00001
11. 0.1
12. 0.000001
13. 0.01
14. 0.000000001
15. 0.0001
16. 0.0000001
17. 2.5×10^{-2}
18. 3×10^{-1}
19. 4.73×10^{-4}
20. 2.4×10^{-3}
21. 1.4565×10^{-5}
22. 7.001×10^{-1}
23. 1.905×10^{-2}
24. 3.3×10^{-3}
25. 0.006
26. 0.045
27. 0.0000007
28. 0.00000105
29. 0.00000003052

30. 0.5
31. 0.000987
32. 0.0000543
33. 0.0000005 m
34. 1.7×10^{-5} m

Practice and Problem Solving: C

1. 0.0052; 0.0000052; >
2. 0.000005; 0.000025; <
3. 3; 0.1; >
4. 0.00502; 0.000205; >
5. 1.2×10^{-3}; 4.5×10^{-1}
6. 3.2×10^{-4}; 2.3×10^{-6}
7. 2.35×10^{-6}, 3.25×10^{-6}, 5.32×10^{-6}, 2.35×10^{-5}, 3.25×10^{-5}, 5.32×10^{-5}
8. 0×10^0, 1×10^{-1}, 5×10^{-1}, 1×10^0, 5×10^0
9. 1×10^{-3} m = 1 mm; 1×10^{-1} cm = 1 mm; equal, so false
10. 7×10^{-1} cm = 7 mm; 7×10^{-3} m = 7 mm; equal, so false
11. 3.5×10^{-1} cm = 3.5 mm; 3.5×10^{-3} m = 3.5 mm; equal, so true
12. 9×10^{-1} mm; 9×10^{-4} m = 9×10^{-1} mm; equal, so true
13. 9×10^{-3} liters = 0.009 liters; 3×10^{-5} liters = 0.00003; 0.009 ÷ 0.00003 = 300 drops
14. 0.00025 meters = 2.5×10^{-4}; 0.000125 meters = 1.25×10^{-4}; area = length × width = $(2.5 \times 10^{-4}) \times (1.25 \times 10^{-4}) = 3.125 \times 10^{-8}$ square meters

Practice and Problem Solving: D

1. $\frac{1}{100}$
2. $\frac{1}{100,000}$
3. $\frac{1}{10,000}$
4. $\frac{1}{1,000}$
5. $\frac{1}{10 \times 10 \times 10 \times 10 \times 10}$

6. $\dfrac{1}{10 \times 10 \times 10 \times 10 \times 10 \times 10 \times 10}$

7. $\dfrac{1}{10 \times 10 \times 10 \times 10}$

8. $\dfrac{1}{10 \times 10 \times 10 \times 10 \times 10 \times 10 \times 10 \times 10 \times 10 \times 10 \times 10}$

9. $\dfrac{1}{10^3} = 10^{-3}$

10. $\dfrac{1}{10^1} = 10^{-1}$

11. $\dfrac{1}{10^2} = 10^{-2}$

12. $\dfrac{1}{10^4} = 10^{-4}$

13. $\dfrac{1}{10}$

14. $\dfrac{1}{1,000}$

15. $\dfrac{1}{10,000}$

16. $\dfrac{1}{1,000,000,000}$

17. $\dfrac{1}{100,000}$

18. $\dfrac{1}{1,000,000,000,000}$

19. -4

20. -1

21. -8

22. -3

23. 0.00356

24. 0.00009

25. 0.0006875

26. 0.000004005

27. 0.15 ft^2; 1.5×10^{-1}

Reteach

1. 2.79×10^{-2}

2. 7.1×10^{-5}

3. 5.06×10^{-7}

4. 0.000235

---

5. 0.0065

6. 0.0000707

Reading Strategies

1. 1; 3; right; -3; 1.23×10^{-3}

2. 5; 6; right; -6; 5.67×10^{-6}

3. -8; left; 8; 0.000000067

4. -4; left; 4; 0.000321

Success for English Learners

1. $5.75 \times 10^{-3} > 5.75 \times 10^{-4}$ because $5.75 \times 10^{-3} = 0.00575$ and $5.75 \times 10^{-4} = 0.000575$.

2. A hair; $3 \times 10^{-7} = 0.0000003$ g, and a hair would have a mass that is less than a gram, but a bicycle would not.

3. 4.93×10^{-4}

4. 0.0000321

LESSON 2-4

Practice and Problem Solving: A/B

1. 2.79×10^4

2. 3.83×10^6

3. 6.67×10^9

4. 4.48×10^4

5. 4.16×10^{17}

6. 2.0×10^3

7. 8.85×10^{10}

8. 6.0×10^7

9. $4.1E + 4$

10. $9.4E - 6$

11. 5.2×10^{-6}

12. 8.3×10^2

13. 7.0×10^4

14. 1.4×10^4

15. 1.6×10^4

16. about 3.0×10^4, or about 30,000 strides

Practice and Problem Solving: C

1. 3.574×10^4

2. 5.416×10^4

3. 1.6897×10^7

4. 7.08×10^3

5. 2.496×10^{13}

6. 7.0×10^{12}

7. 2.89×10^{-2}

8. 2.3×10^{-4}

9. 6.0×10^{-2}

10. 3.65×10^2

11. 3.15×10^8

12. 6.8985×10^9 kilowatt hours; 6,898,500,000 kilowatt hours

13. 459,900 households

Practice and Problem Solving: D

1. 4.044×10^4

2. 1.028×10^4

3. 2.8×10^6

4. 5.65×10^4

5. 2.048×10^{13}

6. 1.92×10^1

7. 1.025×10^9

8. 2.0×10^8

9. 3.3×10^{-3}, 6.9×10^5

10. $7.1E + 5$, $4.4E - 3$

11. 1.0×10^6

12. $\dfrac{1.0 \times 10^6}{8.64 \times 10^4} \approx$ 0.116×10^2 or $1.16 \times 10^1 \approx 11.6$ days

Reteach

1. 6.5×10^2

2. 1.5×10^6

3. 2.1×10^8

Reading Strategies

1. 2.82×10^4

2. 1.92×10^{10}

3. 2.0×10^3

4. 2.0×10^{-1}

5. 3.07×10^8

6. 3.29×10^{10}

Success for English Learners

1. Sample answer: When dealing with very large or very small numbers

2. 5.5×10^2

3. 1.5×10^6

4. 1.45×10^{10}

5. 3.74×10^5

6. 6.12×10^{11}

7. 5.6×10^4

MODULE 2 Challenge

1. 9,460,528,400,000,000 m; rounded, this is 9 trillion km

2. 9,460,528,400,000 km; 9.4605284×10^{12} km; almost 10 trillion

3. $(9.4605284 \times 10^{12}$ km$)(3.26)$; 3.08×10^{13} km

4. 0.000000001 m; 1×10^{-9} m

5. $(1 \times 10^{-9}$ m$)(0.1) = 1 \times 10^{-10}$ m

6. $(1 \times 10^{-9}$ m$)(1,000) = 1 \times 10^{-6}$ m

7. $\dfrac{3.08 \times 10^{16}}{1.0 \times 10^{-9}} = 3.08 \times 10^{25}$; 1 parsec is about 3×10^{25} nanometers

UNIT 2: Proportional and Nonproportional Relationships and Functions

MODULE 3 Proportional Relationships

LESSON 3-1

Practice and Problem Solving: A/B

1.

Feet	1	2	3	4	5	6
Inches	12	24	36	48	60	72

2. 12; 2; 36; 48; 5; 72; $\frac{12}{1}$ or 12

3. $y = 12x$, or $x = \frac{12}{y}$ or, $x = \frac{1}{12}y$

4. yes; let x = lemons and y = sugar; $y = 1.5x$ or let x = sugar and y = lemons; $y = \frac{x}{1.5}$

5. yes; let x = sugar and y = water; $y = 4\frac{2}{3}x$ or $y \approx 4.7x$, or let x = water and y = sugar; $y = \frac{3}{14}x$ or $y \approx \frac{x}{4.7}$

6. not a proportional relationship

Practice and Problem Solving: C

1. a. yes

   b. $y = 1.9x$

2. about 6.6 ft

3 a. yes

   b. $y = 50x$

   c. 456.25 mi

   d. 11

Practice and Problem Solving: D

1.

Yards	1	2	3	4	5	6
Feet	3	6	9	12	15	18

2. 2, 9, 4, $\frac{15}{5}$, 3

3. $y = 3x$

4. $y = 50x$

5. yes
6. yes
7. yes

Reteach

1.

Distance Driven (mi)	100	200	300	400	500	600
Gas Used (gal)	5	10	15	20	25	30

2. a. 10; 300; 20; $\frac{500}{25}$

   b. 20

3 a. number of miles driven

   b. $y = 20x$

Reading Strategies

1. $y = 0.25x$

2. $87.50

3.

Planet	Mercury	Venus	Earth	Mars	Jupiter
Diameter (mi)	3,032	7,521	7,926	4,222	88,846
Distance from Sun (millions of mi)	36.0	67.2	93.0	141.6	483.6
Ratio	84.2	111.9	85.2	29.8	183.7

4. No; The ratio between each pair of numbers is not the same.

Success for English Learners

1. 31 mi

2. Real-world distance is greater: 1 mile is greater than 1 inch.

LESSON 3-2

Practice and Problem Solving: A/B

1. −2

2. $\frac{4}{3}$

3. $6.49

4. 65 mi/h

5. 30 gal/min

6. No; the size of the tank does not matter. The rate of water flow will stay the same.

7. $n = -4$

Practice and Problem Solving: C

1.

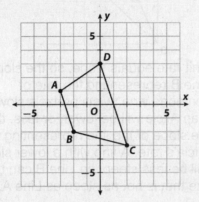

2. −3

3. $-\dfrac{1}{4}$

4. −3

5. $\dfrac{2}{3}$

6. One pair of opposite sides ($\overline{AB}$ and $\overline{CD}$) has the same slope so those sides are parallel. The other pair has different slopes so those sides are not parallel.

7. trapezoid

8. slope $= \dfrac{1}{46}$

9. 1,840 peanuts

10. A right triangle; The side with a slope of 0 is horizontal and the side with an undefined slope is vertical. Those two sides are perpendicular to each other, so the triangle is a right triangle.

Practice and Problem Solving: D

1. constant

2. variable

3. −3

4. 1

5. $\dfrac{1}{2}$

6. $-\dfrac{2}{5}$

7. 218 gal/h

8. 50 mi/h

Reteach

1. increase

2. down

3. When the slope is positive, as the value of y increases, the value of x increases.

4. When the slope is positive, as you move from left to right, the line goes up.

5. slope $= 1$

Reading Strategies

1. (5, 4), (10, 8), (15, 12)

2.

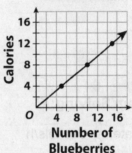

Calories in Blueberries

3. $\dfrac{4}{5}$

4. No; Since the points lie in a line, the slope between any two points is the same.

Success for English Learners

1. If both the rise and the run are positive, the slope of the line is positive. The line slants upward from left to right.

2. If either the rise or the run is negative, the slope of the line is negative. The line slants downward from left to right.

3. When the points form a line, the ratio of rise to run for any two points will be the same.

LESSON 3-3

Practice and Problem Solving: A/B

1. $\dfrac{4}{5}$; $\dfrac{4}{5}$ mi/h

2. $\dfrac{6}{5}$; $\dfrac{6}{5}$ mi/h

3. Piyush walks faster. Laura's rate is equal to the slope 3.5, or 3.5 mph. Piyush's rate is equal to the slope of the line $\frac{9}{2}$ or 4.5 mph. 4.5 > 3.5, so Piyush walks faster.

4. a.

Time (h)	3	6	9	12
Rainfall (in.)	2	4	6	8

b.

Rainfall

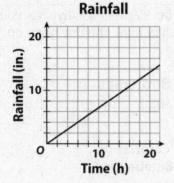

c. $\frac{2}{3}$

d. $\frac{2}{3}$ in./h

Practice and Problem Solving: C

1. a. slope = $\frac{9}{2}$; unit rate: $\frac{9}{2}$ bushels/h

b.

Time (h)	3	6	9	12
Fruit (bushels)	10	20	30	40

c. Shawn's rate is $\frac{9}{2}$ bushels/h. Carla's rate is $\frac{10}{3}$ bushels/h. $\frac{9}{2} = \frac{27}{6}$, and $\frac{10}{3} = \frac{20}{6}$. $\frac{27}{6} > \frac{20}{6}$, so Shawn picked fruit at a faster rate.

2. No, the slope and unit rate for both Bridge A and Bridge B would be the same. Bridge A's slope and unit rate is 20 vehicles per hour. Bridge B's slope and unit rate is $\frac{40}{2}$, or 20 vehicles per hour, which is the same as Bridge A.

3. a. Answers may vary. Sample answer:

Pretzel Twisting

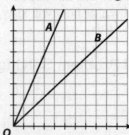

b. Unit rate equals slope, so the slope of Line B representing the rate of someone who twists pretzels slower than Alicia will be lower, or less, than the slope of the line representing Alicia's rate. A line with a lower slope will be less steep, so Line B can be any line that is not as steep as Line A.

Practice and Problem Solving: D

1. $\frac{2}{3}$; $\frac{2}{3}$ mi/h

2. $\frac{1}{2}$; $\frac{1}{2}$ mi/h

3. a. $\frac{4}{1}$ or 4

b. 4 mi/h

c. 3

d. 3 mi/h

e. Poonam walks faster. Latrice's speed is 3 mi/h. Poonam's speed is 4 mi/h. 4 > 3, so Poonam walks faster.

Reteach

1. $\frac{3}{5}$; $\frac{3}{5}$

2. $\frac{9}{4}$; $\frac{9}{4}$

Reading Strategies

1. 8 in.

2. 0.8 in.

3. 0.8; 0.8 in./h

4. 12 in.

5. 3 in.

6. 3 in./h

7. The slope would be 3, because the slope of the graph is equal to the unit rate.

Success for English Learners

1. 4 mi
2. about 2.7 mi

MODULE 3 Challenge

1. $200 = k \cdot 6^3$

   $k = \dfrac{200}{6^3}$

   $k \approx 0.93$

   $y = 0.93x^3$

2. $200 = k \cdot 6^2$

   $k = \dfrac{200}{6^2}$

   $k \approx 5.56$

   $y = 5.56x^2$

3. 7440 lb

4. 2224 lb

5. Its legs would not be strong enough to support its weight.

6.

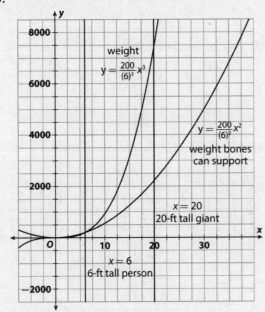

7. The weight of the creature increases much more quickly than the weight its bones can support at values of $x > 6$.

MODULE 4 Nonproportional Relationships

LESSON 4-1

Practice and Problem Solving: A/B

1.

x	−2	−1	0	1	2
y	−5	−1	3	7	11

2.

x	−8	−4	0	4	8
y	−4	−3	−2	−1	0

3.

x	−4	−2	0	2	4
y	3	2	1	0	−1

4.

x	−2	−1	0	1	2
y	−1	2	5	8	11

5.

x	−2	−1	0	1	2
y	−3	−1	1	3	5

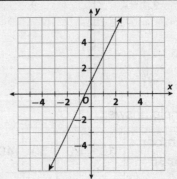

6.

x	−4	−2	0	2	4
y	−1	−2	−3	−4	−5

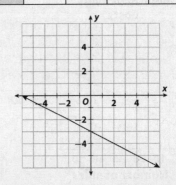

7. Solid line; Sample answer: The height of the tree can be measured at any moment in time.

8. Set of unconnected points; You cannot buy a fractional part of a DVD.

Practice and Problem Solving: C

1.

x	−6	−3	0	3	6
y	−1	0	1	2	3

2. Sample answer:

x	−2	−1	0	1	2
y	−4.4	−4.2	−4	−3.8	−3.6

3. Sample answer:

x	−4	−2	0	2	4
y	1	1.5	2	2.5	3

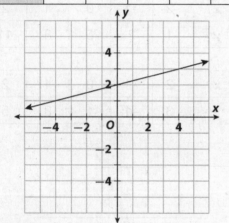

4. a. Sample answer:

x (Number of Miles)	10	20	30	40	50
y (Cost of Delivery)	15	20	25	30	35

b.

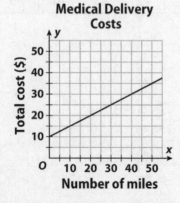

Medical Delivery Costs

c. Sample answer: The graph does not include the origin.

d. Yes, the number of miles can be in fractional increments.

Practice and Problem Solving: D

1.

x	−2	−1	0	1	2
y	−4	−1	2	5	8

2.

x	−2	−1	0	1	2
y	1	0	−1	2	−3

3.

x	−2	−1	0	1	2
y	−7	−2	3	8	13

4.

x	−4	−2	0	2	4
y	1	2	3	4	5

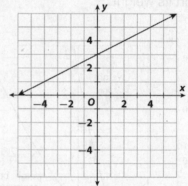

5.

x	−2	−1	0	1	2
y	−4	−3	−2	−1	0

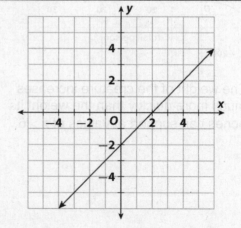

6.

x	−2	−1	0	1	2
y	5	3	1	−1	−3

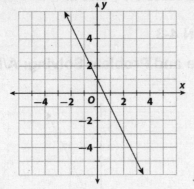

Reteach

1.

x	−2	−1	0	1	2
y	−5	−2	1	4	7

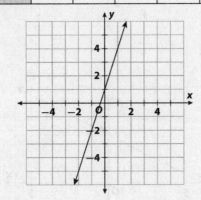

2.

x	−2	−1	0	1	2
y	0	−1	−2	−3	−4

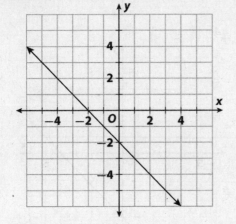

Reading Strategies

1. nonproportional; the relationship is nonproportional because each $\frac{y}{x}$ ratio is not constant.

2. proportional; the relationship is proportional because each $\frac{y}{x}$ ratio is constant.

Success for English Learners

1. Every ratio $\frac{y}{x}$ will be equal.

2. The graph will be a straight line that passes through the origin.

LESSON 4-2

Practice and Problem Solving: A/B

1. 1; 3

2. $-\frac{4}{5}$; 4

3. 3; 1

4. 0.5; 1

5. The y-intercept represents the cost of a pizza with no toppings. The slope represents the rate of change ($2 per topping).

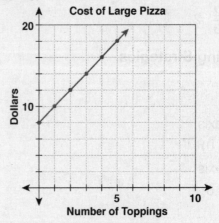

Practice and Problem Solving: C

1. a. $120 to rent the truck; $0.50 per mile

   b. $47.50; (45 miles × $0.50 per mile + $120) ÷ 3 = $47.50

2. The rate of change is $2.50 per ride. The initial value is $12, which is a flat fee no matter how many rides are ridden.

3. a. The rate of change is $29.50 per session. The initial value is $10.

  b. The rate of change is $19.50 per session. The initial value is $10.

  c. Both rates of change are constant, but the group sessions compensate more. There is a flat fee of $10 no matter which type of session the tutor teaches.

4. After mowing 6 lawns; Miguel earns a fixed weekly salary of $150 plus $30 for each lawn he mows. He earns the same in fees as his fixed salary for mowing $150 \div 30 = 5$ lawns.

Practice and Problem Solving: D

1. $-\frac{1}{2}$; 5

2. 3; 6

3. $\frac{5}{6}$; −5

4. $-\frac{3}{4}$; 1

5. 2; 3

6. $\frac{1}{2}$; 5

Reteach

1. 2; 3

2. $-\frac{2}{3}$; 2

Reading Strategies

1. 0

2. 0

3. x-axis

4. (9, 0)

5. y-axis

6. (0, 6)

7. 6

8. 9

9. $-\frac{6}{9}$ or $-\frac{2}{3}$

Success for English Learners

1. They both have a zero as one of their coordinates. The x-intercept has a zero y-coordinate and the y-intercept has a zero x-coordinate.

2. $-\frac{3}{4}$

3. The line slopes downward from left to right and crosses the y-axis at $\frac{9}{7}$.

LESSON 4-3

Practice and Problem Solving: A/B

1. 2; −1

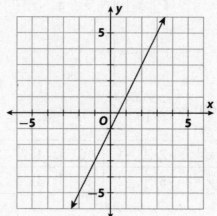

2. $\frac{1}{2}$; 3

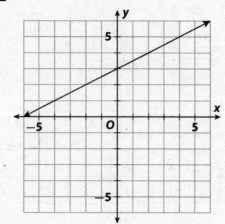

3. 1, −4

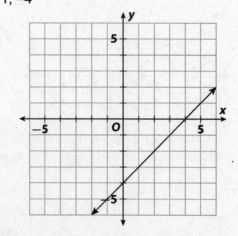

4. −1; −2

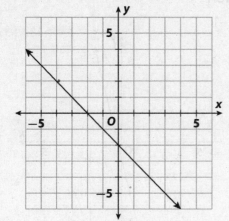

5. a.

Math Quiz Scoring

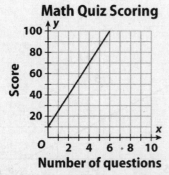

b. The slope, 15, means that each question is worth 15 points. The *y*-intercept, 10, is the number of points given for taking the test; it is the minimum score.

c. 85

Practice and Problem Solving: C

1. a.

Gallons of Gas

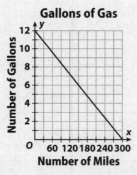

b. The slope, −0.04, means that each mile driven uses 0.04 gallons of gas. The *y*-intercept, 12, is the number of gallons of gas in the car.

c. 4

2. a.

Savings Account

b. The slope, 100, means that each month you deposit $100. The *y*-intercept, 250, is the amount of money you initially deposited in your account.

c. $950

3. a.

Cell Phone

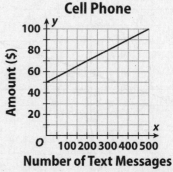

b. The slope, 0.1, means that each text message sent or received costs $0.10. The *y*-intercept, 50, is the cost of your cell phone plan before adding the cost of each text message sent or received.

c. $81.50

Practice and Problem Solving: D

1. −2; 1

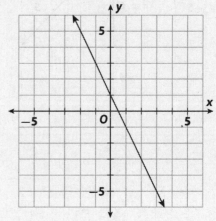

2. 3; −2

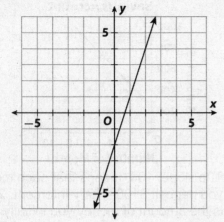

3. $\frac{1}{3}$; 1

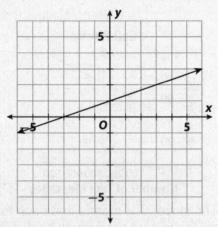

4. −1; 3

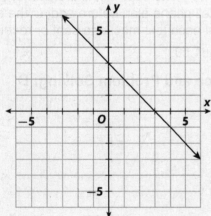

1. 4; −1

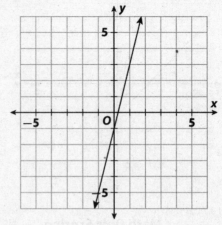

2. $-\frac{1}{2}$; 2

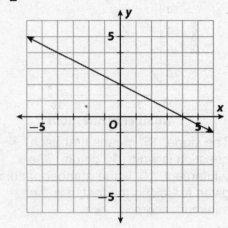

3. −1; 1

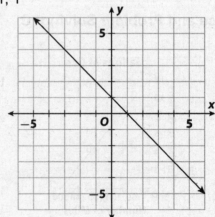

4. 2; −3

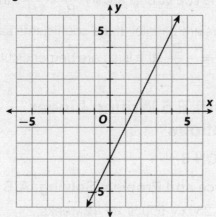

Reading Strategies

1. slope: 2; y-intercept −8

2.

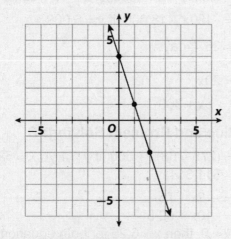

Success for English Learners

1. Plot the point that contains the y-intercept. Use the slope to find a second point. Draw a line through the points.

2. The slope tells the rate of change for the situation. The y-intercept tells an initial starting point for the situation.

LESSON 4-4

Practice and Problem Solving: A/B

1. nonproportional; the line does not include the origin

2. proportional; the line includes the origin

3. proportional; when the equation is written in the form $y = mx + b$, the value of b is 0.

4. nonproportional; when the equation is written in the form $y = mx + b$, the value of b is not 0.

5. nonproportional; the equation is not linear.

6. nonproportional; the equation is not linear.

7. nonproportional; the relationship is not linear.

8. proportional; the quotient of y and x is constant, 9, for every number pair.

Practice and Problem Solving: C

1. The number of cats is nonproportional to the number of dogs, because the quotient when you divide the number of cats by the number of dogs is not constant.

2. a. proportional; the graph passes through the origin, so $b = 0$ and it is proportional.

   b. $m = 8.5$, $b = 0$; each mile takes Brittany 8.5 minutes to jog. It takes 0 minutes for Brittany to jog 0 miles.

3. a. Yes; using Equation B you see that the y-intercept is 0, so the graph includes the origin. Using Table C you see that the quotient of C to I is 0.39, which is constant.

   b. Yes; Equation A is in the form $y = mx + b$, with F being used instead of y and I being used instead of x. The value of b is 0. Since b is 0, the relationship is proportional.

Practice and Problem Solving: D

1. nonproportional; when the equation is written in the form $y = mx + b$, the value of b is not 0.

2. proportional; when the equation is written in the form $y = mx + b$, the value of b is 0.

3. proportional; the quotient of y and x is constant, 8, for every number pair.

4. nonproportional; when the equation is written in the form $y = mx + b$, the value of b is not 0.

5. proportional; the line includes the origin

6. nonproportional; the line does not include the origin

Reteach

1. nonproportional; the line does not include the origin

2. proportional; the quotient of y and x is constant, 12, for every number pair.

3. nonproportional; the equation is not linear.

4. proportional; when the equation is written in the form $y = mx + b$, the value of b is 0.

Reading Strategies

1. nonproportional; the line does not go through the origin

2. proportional; the quotient of y and x is constant, 3, for every number pair

3. proportional; the equation linear with a y-intercept equal to 0

4. nonproportional; when the equation is written in the form $y = mx + b$, the value of b is not 0.

Success for English Learners

1. The graph will be a straight line that passes through the origin.

2. The equation will be linear and when the equation is written in the form $y = mx + b$ the value of b is 0.

MODULE 4 Challenge

1. pencil through (0, 6)

2. pencil through (2, 0)

3. parallel lines with slope 3

4. parallel lines with slope –0.5

5. pencil through (4, 6)

6. pencil through (–4, –6)

7. pencil through (4, –6)

8. parallel lines with slope 2

9. The system is a pencil of lines through (h, k).

10. Sample answers: $\frac{3}{5} = \frac{6}{10}$, $3x + 5y = 10$, $6x + 10y = -2$

11. Sample answers: $\frac{3}{5} = \frac{6}{10}$, $3x + 5y = 10$, $10x - 6y = -2$

12. If the coefficients satisfy $\frac{A_1}{B_1} = \frac{A_2}{B_2}$, the lines are parallel. If the coefficients satisfy $\frac{A_1}{B_1} = -\frac{B_2}{A_2}$, the lines are perpendicular.

MODULE 5 Writing Linear Equations

LESSON 5-1

Practice and Problem Solving: A/B

1. $y = 250x + 500$; if $x = 12$ weeks, $y = \$3,500$.

2. $y = -12x + 75$; if $y = 0$, $x = 6.25$ days.

3. $y = 3x$; if $y = 54$ houses, $x = 18$ weeks.

4. $y = -450x + 18,000$; if $y = 6,000$, $x = 26 \frac{2}{3}$ days.

5. $y = 20x$

6. $y = -6x + 360$

Practice and Problem Solving: C

1. $y = (275 - 68)x + 550$; if $y = 1$ yr, $x = 52$, $y = \$11,314$.

2. $y = -12x + 75$
   $y = -10x + 62.5$
   If $y = 0$, then $x = 6.25$ for both equations. The fields will be harvested after 6.25 days.

3. $y = 4.5x$, if $y = 55$, $x = 12.2$ weeks
   $12.2 \div 4.5 = 2.7$ months

4. $y = -650x + 24,000$; if $y = 16,000$, $x = 12.3$ days or 295.2 h

5. $y = 20x$

6. $y = -6x + 360$

Practice and Problem Solving: D

1. 35

2. Answers may vary, e.g. –5, –10 etc., depending on the two points.

3. Answers may vary, e.g. +1, +2 etc., depending on the two points.

4. –5

5. –5

6. $y = -5x + 30$

7. 0

8. $\frac{1}{2}$ or 0.5

9. $y = 0.5x$

10. Move the line up so that it begins at (0, 4) and includes (17, 12).

Reteach

1. 1.5; 0; $d = 1.5t$

2. 75; 50; $n = 75t + 50$

Reading Strategies

1. horizontal axis

2. vertical axis

3. *CD* and *DE*

4. The "rise" is 0 to 8 mph, or 8 mph, and the "run" from 2:15 P.M. to 2:18 P.M. is 3 minutes or 3. Therefore, the slope is $\frac{8}{3}$.

5. She increases her speed from 0 mph to 8 mph from point *C* to point *D* and she runs at a constant speed of 8 miles per hour from point *D* to point *E*.

6. These lines are not linear or straight, so the slope is not constant.

Success for English Learners

1. 3; 0; $y = 3x$

2. 6; 4; $y = 6x + 4$

LESSON 5-2

Practice and Problem Solving: A/B

1.

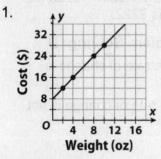

slope: 2

y-intercept: 8

equation: $y = 2x + 8$

2.

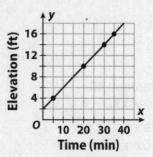

slope: 0.4; *y*-intercept: 2;
equation: $y = 0.4x + 2$

3. $y = 5x + 100$

4. $y = -10x + 375$

5. $y = 3x + 8$

6. 26 in.

Practice and Problem Solving: C

1.

Servings, *x*	0	1	2	3
Total Cost ($), *y*	70.00	70.20	70.40	70.60

$y = 0.2x + 70$

2.

Games bowled, *x*	1	2	3	4
Total Cost ($), *y*	4.50	6.00	7.50	9.00

$y = 1.5x + 3$

3. negative; as the time increases, the height decreases.

4. a. Gym A: $y = 20x + 50$, Gym B: $y = 25x + 30$; the slope represents the monthly cost, and the *y*-intercept represents the membership fee.

   b. Gym A; For 10 months of membership, Gym A costs $250 and Gym B costs $280. So Gym A is less expensive.

Practice and Problem Solving: D

1. B

2. C

3. C

4. 8

5. $\frac{1}{4}$ or 0.25

6. 1

7. 4

8. 6

9. 15

10. $y = 6x + 15$

11. $87

Reteach

1. slope: 0.2, y-intercept: 40,
   equation: $y = 0.2x + 40$

2. slope: 2.5, y-intercept: 2.5,
   equation: $y = 2.5x + 2.5$

Reading Strategies

1. The variable y represents the height
   (in inches) of the plant x days after it was
   planted.

2. The description states that the relationship
   is a linear relationship. A linear
   relationship can be represented by a
   linear equation.

3. Yes; as the x-values increase, the
   y-values increase as well. So, the slope
   is positive.

4. The growth rate of the plant in inches per
   day

5. The slope (using (0, 15) and (2, 20)) is:
   $$m = \frac{y_2 - y_1}{x_2 - x_1} = \frac{20 - 15}{2 - 0} = \frac{5}{2} = 2.5.$$

6. On the y-axis; the y-intercept is 15.

7. $y = 2.5x + 15$

Success for English Learners

1. slope: 250

2. y-intercept: 800

3. $y = 250x + 800$

4. Graph the ordered pairs from the table,
   draw a line through the points, and find
   the point where the line cross the y-axis;
   Sample answer: It may be difficult to
   determine the exact value for the
   y-intercept when reading it from a graph.

LESSON 5-3

Practice and Problem Solving: A/B

1. Yes; the rate of change is constant.

2. No; the rate of change is not constant.

3. $y = 4x$

4. $y = 2x + 8$

5. yes; $y = 0.5x + 4$

6. 11 min

7.

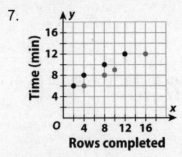

Rows completed

No; the points do not lie on a straight line,
so the rate of change is not constant.

Practice and Problem Solving: C

1. Linear; the rate of change is constant; the
   gallons y of water in the tank is $y = 6x + 7$
   after x minutes.

2. Not linear; the rate of change is not
   constant.

3. $120

4. 6 weeks

5. Lara; Adrian's account balance will be
   $100, and Lara's account balance will be
   $120. Lara's account has the greater
   balance.

6.

Tickets	Total Cost ($)
2	72
4	132
8	252

The relationship is linear; an equation for
the relationship is $y = 30x + 12$, so the
cost of 7 tickets is $222.

Practice and Problem Solving: D

1. Yes, because the rate of change is
   constant.

2. No, because the rate of change is not
   constant.

3. A

4. B

5. C

6. B

7. Linear; the rate of change is the
   babysitter's pay per hour, which is
   constant.

8. Not linear; the rate of change in the height increases and then decreases as the horizontal distance traveled increases.

9. Linear; the rate of change in the perimeter is 4, which is constant.

Reteach

1.

Time (h)	Snow Accumulation (in.)
1	5
2	7
3	9
4	11
5	13

9 inches

2.

Prints	Total Cost ($)
2	3.00
3	4.50
4	6.00
5	7.50
6	9.00
7	10.50

$9.00

Reading Strategies

1. If the graph is a line, then the relationship is linear. If the graph is not a line, then the relationship is nonlinear.

2. A linear relationship has a constant rate of change, and a nonlinear relationship does not have a constant rate of change.

3. Find the rate of change of the data values. A linear relationship has a constant rate of change, and a nonlinear relationship does not have a constant rate of change.

4. Yes; use two points on the line to find the slope, and use the slope and one point on the line to find the y-intercept. Write an equation using the slope and y-intercept.

Success for English Learners

1. The slope represents the hourly rate of the plumber. The y-intercept represents the cost of the materials.

2. Answers will vary. Sample answer: The table can represent the speed y (in miles per hour) that a train travels after x hours.

MODULE 5 Challenge

1. The slope of $\overline{MN}$ is found by using $M(0, 3)$ and $N(4, 0)$: $m = \dfrac{3-0}{0-4} = -\dfrac{3}{4}$.
The y-intercept comes from point M: $b = 3$. Use the slope-intercept form : $y = mx + b = -\dfrac{3}{4}x + 3$. Rearrange into the standard form: $y = -\dfrac{3}{4}x + 3$; $4y = -3x + 12$ or $3x + 4y = 12$.

2. Find the slope of $\overline{JL}$ using the points $J(4, -2)$ and $L(6, 6)$: $m = \dfrac{-2-6}{4-6} = \dfrac{-8}{-2} = 4$.
Use one of the two points and the point-slope form. Using point $J(4, -2)$, $y - (-2) = 4(x - 4)$ or $y + 2 = 4x - 16$. Rearrange into standard form: $-4x + y = -18$.

MODULE 6 Functions

LESSON 6-1

Practice and Problem Solving: A/B

1. not a function
2. function
3. function
4. not a function
5. not a function
6. function
7. function
8. not a function
9. function
10. not a function
11. Yes. Each input value (the hours studied) is paired with only one output value (the grade).

12. If she got a grade of anything but a 95, it would no longer be a function because the input value, 2 hours, would be paired with two different output values.

Practice and Problem Solving: C

1. not a function; input value 2 is paired with more than one output value, 8 and 9

2. function; each input value is paired with only one output value

3. No; There are at least four Mondays, each likely to have a different output value (different amounts of mulch applied). Also, there are at least four of each other day, with different outputs likely.

4. Yes. For each weight of beads she buys (input), there can only be one dollar amount representing the amount of money she pays (output).

5. There is only one number of animals for each day, so each input is paired with only one output.

6. No; Each day (input) would then most likely have two number of animals (outputs) paired with it.

Practice and Problem Solving: D

1. function
2. not a function
3. not a function
4. function
5. not a function
6. function
7. not a function
8. function
9. C
10. It is a function because there is only one year number (input) paired with each number of elephants (output).

Reteach

1. { ((1) 1), ((2) 3), ((3) 5) }
2. { ((6) 2), ((5) 3), ((4) 8) }
3. Yes; Each input value is paired with only one output value.
4. No; The input value 1 is paired with both 2 and 8.

5. Yes; Each input value is paired with only one output value.

6. No; The input value 1 is paired with both 1 and 2.

Reading Strategies

1. Sample answer:

Input	1	2	3	4
Output	1	2	3	4

2. Answers will vary. Sample answer:

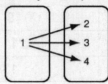

3. Answers will vary. Sample answer: because the input value 1 is paired with more than one output value

4. no
5. no
6. yes

Success for English Learners

1. If any input (x-value) has more than one output (y-value), the relation is not a function.

2. Yes. Since the input values 3 and 5 are each only paired with one output value, it is a function.

LESSON 6-2

Practice and Problem Solving: A/B

1.

Input, x	−1	0	1	2	4
Output, y	−3	0	3	6	12

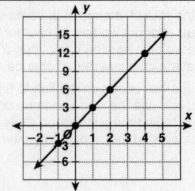

Linear

2.

Input, x	-2	-1	0	1	2
Output, y	5	2	1	2	5

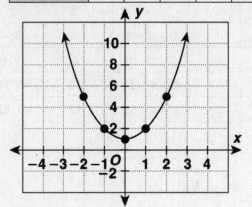

nonlinear

3. No.

4. Yes; $y = x + 4$

5. Yes; $y = -2x + 3$

6.

Time (min), x	0	1	2	3	4
Water (gal), y	0	20	40	60	80

7.

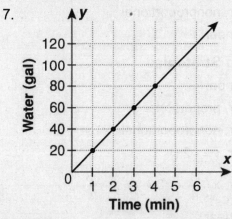

8. 120 gal

9. It is linear; the solutions lie on a line.

Practice and Problem Solving: C

1. nonproportional

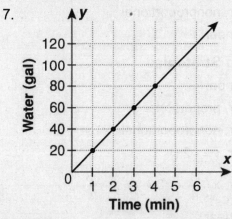

2. $y - 5 = -2(3x - 1)$

$y - 5 = -6x + 2$

$y = -6x + 7$

Since the equation can be written in $y = mx + b$ form it is linear. The equation is not true for (0, 0), $0 \neq 7$, therefore the relationship between x and y is not proportional.

3. Yes it is linear since the equation is of the form $y = mx + b$. No it is not proportional because the equation is not true for (0, 0), $0 \neq 3$. She would spend $63 on groceries since $y = 2(30) + 3 = 63$.

4. $y = 12x + 5$; $60 = 12x + 5$, so $x = \frac{55}{12}$ h or 275 min.

5. It is not linear. The graph is a V-shape. Therefore, it is nonproportional.

Practice and Problem Solving: D

1.

Input, x	$x - 1$	Output, y	(x, y)
-1	$-1 - 1$	-2	$(-1, -2)$
0	$0 - 1$	-1	$(0, -1)$
1	$1 - 1$	0	$(1, 0)$
2	$2 - 1$	1	$(2, 1)$
3	$3 - 1$	2	$(3, 2)$

2.

Input, x	$2x + 6$	Output, y	(x, y)
-2	$2(-2) + 6$	2	$(-2, 2)$
-1	$2(-1) + 6$	4	$(-1, 4)$
0	$2(0) + 6$	6	$(0, 6)$
1	$2(1) + 6$	8	$(1, 8)$

3.

Input, x	−2x + 2	Output, y	(x, y)
−2	−2(−2) + 2	6	(−2, 6)
−1	−2(−1) + 2	4	(−1, 4)
0	−2(0) + 2	2	(0, 2)
1	−2(1) + 2	0	(1, 0)
2	−2(2) + 2	−2	(2, −2)

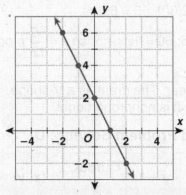

4.

Input, x	20x	Output, y	(x, y)
0	20(0) = 0	0	(0, 0)
1	20(1) = 20	20	(1, 20)
2	20(2) = 40	40	(2, 40)
3	20(3) = 60	60	(3, 60)

5.

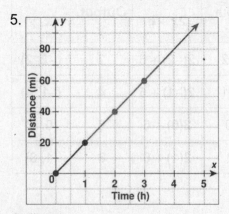

6. linear

7. The graph is linear and goes through (0, 0).

1.

Input, x	x + 4	Output, y	(x, y)
−2	−2 + 4 = 2	2	(−2, 2)
0	0 + 4 = 4	4	(0, 4)
2	2 + 4 = 6	6	(2, 6)
6	6 + 4 = 10	10	(6, 10)
8	8 + 4 = 12	12	(8, 12)

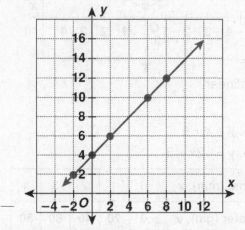

2. linear, proportional

3. linear, nonproportional

4. nonlinear

Reading Strategies

1. not linear

2. linear, proportional

3. linear, nonproportional

4. linear, $y = -2x + 1$

5. linear, $x = \frac{3}{4}$ or $0 \cdot y = x - \frac{3}{4}$

6. not linear

7. linear, $y = 8x - 1$

Success for English Learners

1. He should have moved 5 units right then 6 units up.

2. (1, −2)

3. Sample answer: Make a table of ordered pairs. Then graph them on a coordinate grid. If the graph is a line, the equation is a linear equation.

LESSON 6-3

Practice and Problem Solving: A/B

1. 5; 2; The slope of $f(x)$ is greater than the slope of $g(x)$.

2. –3, –1; The y-intercept of $f(x)$ is 2 less than the y-intercept of $g(x)$.

3. Connor: 200 ft; –10 ft/min; Pilar: 242 ft; –8 ft/min; Sample answer: Pilar started higher than Connor and climbed down more slowly than Connor did. It will take Pilar longer to get down the canyon wall.

Practice and Problem Solving: C

1. f slope: –3, f y-intercept: 5; g slope: –3, g y-intercept: 1; The graphs of the two functions are parallel lines with $f(x)$ 4 units above $g(x)$.

2. The slope of $f(x)$ is $\frac{1}{3}$, and the slope of $g(x)$ is –3. Both y-intercepts are –2. The graphs are perpendicular and intersect at $(0, -2)$.

3. Jing: $12.50, $0.50/year; Max: $10, $1/year; Sample answer: Jing starts at a higher wage, but gets a smaller raise each year. They both must work 6 years for Max to make more than Jing.

Practice and Problem Solving: D

1. f slope = 1; g slope = 2; f y-intercept = –1; g y-intercept = 4; The slope of $f(x)$ is less steep than the slope of $g(x)$. Both slopes are positive. There are 5 units between the y-intercepts.

2. f slope = –2; g slope = –2; f y-intercept = 2; g y-intercept = 0; The slope of both functions is the same and is negative. The lines are parallel. There are 2 units unit between the y-intercepts.

3. f slope = –1; g slope = 3; f y-intercept = 4; g y-intercept = 0; The slope of $f(x)$ is less than the slope of $g(x)$. One slope is negative and one slope is positive, so the lines intersect. There are 4 units between the y-intercepts.

Reteach

1. f slope $= -\frac{1}{2}$; g slope $= -\frac{3}{2}$; f y-intercept $= -2$; g y-intercept $= 1$; The slope of $f(x)$ is less steep than the slope of $g(x)$. Both slopes are negative. There are 3 units between the y-intercepts.

2. f slope = 6; g slope = –3; f y-intercept = –1; g y-intercept = 0; The slope of $f(x)$ is greater than the slope of $g(x)$. There is 1 unit between the y-intercepts.

Reading Strategies

1.

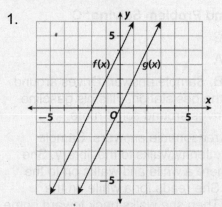

2. The slopes of $f(x)$ and $g(x)$ are the same. Both slopes are positive.

3. There are 4 units difference in the y-intercepts.

Success for English Learners

1. Choose two ordered pairs. Substitute the values into the slope formula:

$$m = \frac{y_2 - y_1}{x_2 - x_1}.$$

2. Answers will vary. Discuss with students that their choice of which representation to use may depend on what information they are asked to find.

LESSON 6-4

Practice and Problem Solving: A/B

1. The oven would be at room temperature, not zero.

2. The oven has reached the desired temperature and is maintaining that temperature.

3. Graph 1

4. Graph 3

5. Graph 2. Sample answer: The car eases into traffic and has to stop. After a while, it starts up fast and then stops.

6.

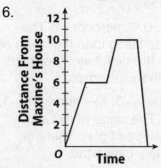

7. 20 mi

Practice and Problem Solving: C

1. Graph C

2. Graph A

3. Graph B; Sample answer: Drives around and to the gas station. Fills his gasoline tank. Drives around some more.

4. Accept reasonable answers. Sample answer: Jenny walks to the library. She stays there a while and walks on to the beach. She reads for a while on the beach. Then she walks back toward home and stops at the snack shop. Finally, she walks home.

5.

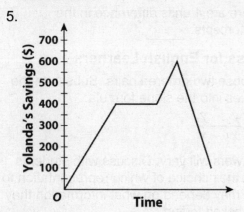

6. $100

Practice and Problem Solving: D

1. The water temperature went down after the ice was put in.

2. The water has been cooled and reached a steady temperature.

3. Graph B

4. Graph C

5. Graph A. Sample answer: Alexia jogs to the park. Then she turns around and jogs home.

6.

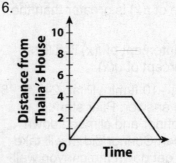

7. 8 miles

Reteach

1. Sample answer: I saved some money. I left it in the bank for a while. Then I took it all out of the bank to buy a bike.

2. Sample answer: I saved money until I had enough to buy a gym membership. Then I stopped saving and started paying for the gym membership until I ran out of money.

3. Sample answer:

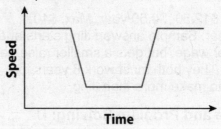

4. Sample answer:

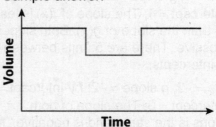

Reading Strategies

Accept reasonable answers. Sample answer: The gates opened and a lot of people came to the park. It started raining and about half the people went home. In the afternoon and evening the number of people slowly decreased as people went home.

Success for English Learners

1. A plane's altitude from take off to landing
2. 30 min
3. The plane descending and landing.

MODULE 6 Challenge

1. Table A missing values: −2, 4; equation: $y = 3x + 1$; This is a nonproportional linear function because the equation is in $y = mx + b$ form, but since (0, 0) is not a value of this function the graph does not go through the origin.

   Table B missing values: 2, 0; equation: $y = -2x$; This is a proportional linear function because the equation is in $y = mx + b$ form and the graph does go through the origin since (0, 0) is a value of this function.

   Table C missing values: 1, 2; equation: $y = |x|$; This is a nonlinear function because the equation cannot be put into $y = mx + b$ form.

   Table D missing values: 1, 4; equation: $y = x^2$; This is a nonlinear function because the equation cannot be put into $y = mx + b$ form.

2. Tree planter: $y = 15x - 18$; Cashier: $y = 9x + 30$;

   The intersection of the two lines is at (8, 102). This means that the tree planter job will pay the same as the cashier job for 8 hours of work. For 0 to less than 8 hours of work, the cashier job pays more. For more than 8 hours of work, the tree planter job pays more.

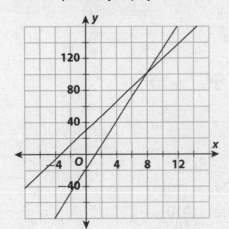

UNIT 3: Solving Equations and Systems of Equations

MODULE 7 Solving Linear Equations

LESSON 7-1

Practice and Problem Solving: A/B

1. $x = -4$

2. $x = 4$

3. $x = 1$

4. $4a - 3 = 2a + 7$

$$\frac{-2a \qquad -[2a]}{2a - 3 = 7}$$

$$\frac{+[3] + 3}{2a = [10]}$$

$$\frac{2a}{[\ 2\ ]} = \frac{10}{[2]}$$

$$a = [5]$$

5. $7x - 1 = 2x + 5$

$$\frac{-[\ 2x\ ] \qquad -2x}{5x - 1 = [5]}$$

$$\frac{+[1] \quad +1}{5x = [6]}$$

$$\frac{5x}{[5]} = \frac{6}{[5]}$$

$$x = \left[\frac{6}{5}\right]$$

6. $-3r + 9 = -4r + 5$

$$\frac{+[4r] \qquad +4r}{r + 9 = 5}$$

$$\frac{-[\ 9\ ] - 9}{r = [-4\ ]}$$

7. $y = 7$

8. $x = -\dfrac{1}{7}$

9. $y = 1$

10. $3n - 10 = n + 4; n = 7$

11. $6n + 4 = n - 11; n = -3$

12. $15 + 2h = 3h - 15; h = 30$

Practice and Problem Solving: C

1. $v = \dfrac{1}{2}$

2. $x = 3$

3. $r = -3$

4. $m = -4$

5. $x = -1$

6. $t = -5$

7. $12 - 2n = 8(n + 4); n = -2$

8. $3 + 8n = 3(2n - 1); n = -3$

9. $28,000 + 3,000n = 36,000 + 2,000n$; $n = 8$; Company C would need to give a raise of $4,250 per year to equal the salaries of Companies A and B, $52,000, after year 8.

10. Sample answer: Erin has already saved $60. She plans to save an additional $25 per week. Robin has already saved $20 and plans to save an additional $35 per week. After how many weeks will Robin and Erin have the same amount saved?
    $x = 4$ weeks

Practice and Problem Solving: D

1. $x = 3$

2. $x = -2$

3.
$$7y + 1 = 3y + 13$$
$$\underline{-[3y] \quad - 3y}$$
$$4y + 1 = 13$$
$$\underline{-1 \; - \; [1]}$$
$$4y = [12]$$
$$\frac{4y}{4} = \frac{12}{[4]}$$
$$y = [3]$$

4.
$$4w + 3 = 2w + 7$$
$$\underline{-[2w] \quad - 2w}$$
$$2w + 3 = 7$$
$$\underline{-3 - [3]}$$
$$2w = [4]$$
$$\frac{2w}{2} = \frac{4}{[2]}$$
$$w = [2]$$

5.
$$-2r + 4 = -3r + 9$$
$$\underline{+[3r] \qquad + 3r}$$
$$r + 4 = 9$$
$$\underline{-[4] \; -4}$$
$$r = [5]$$

6. $y = 6$

7. $x = -1$

8. $y = 1$

9. $4n - 5 = 2n + 3$; $n = 4$

10. $7 - 2n = n - 2$; $n = 3$

Reteach

1.
$$9m + 2 = 3m - 10$$
$$\underline{-[3m] \quad - [3m]}$$
$$6m + 2 = -10$$
$$\underline{-[2] \qquad -[2]}$$
$$6m = [-12]$$
$$\frac{6m}{[6]} = \frac{-12}{[6]}$$
$$m = [-2]$$

To collect on left side, subtract $\underline{3m}$ from both sides.

Subtract $\underline{2}$ from both sides.

Divide by $\underline{6}$.

Check: Substitute into the original equation.

$$9m + 2 = 3m - 10$$
$$9(\underline{-2}) + 2 \overset{?}{=} 3(\underline{-2}) - 10$$
$$\underline{-18} + 2 \overset{?}{=} \underline{-6} - 10$$
$$\underline{-16} = \underline{-16}$$

2.
$$-7d - 22 = 4d$$
$$\underline{+[7d] \qquad +[7d]}$$
$$-22 = 11d$$
$$\frac{-22}{[11]} = \frac{11d}{[11]}$$
$$[-2] = d$$

To collect on right side, add $\underline{7d}$ to both sides.

Divide by $\underline{11}$.

Check: Substitute into the original equation.

$$-7d - 22 = 4d$$
$$-7(\underline{-2}) - 22 \overset{?}{=} 4(\underline{-2})$$
$$\underline{14} - 22 \overset{?}{=} \underline{-8}$$
$$\underline{-8} = \underline{-8}$$

Reading Strategies

1. Get all the variables on one side of the equation.
2. $2x$ was subtracted from both sides.
3. $4x - 7 = 5$
4. Get all the constants on the other side of the equation.
5. 7 was added to both sides of the equation.
6. Both sides of the equation were divided by 4.

Success for English Learners

1. The length of the trail is the unknown value being solved for.
2. $2x$: distance of 2 laps around a trail in miles; $3x$: distance of 3 laps around a trail in miles
3. The variables must be all on one side and the constants must all be on the other side.
4. Sample answer: On Monday Julie ran 8 miles and two laps around a trail. On Tuesday she ran 6 laps around the trail. She ran the same distance both days. How many miles long is one lap around the trail? $x = 2$; One lap is 2 miles long.

LESSON 7-2

Practice and Problem Solving: A/B

1. 8
2. 12
3.

$$6\left(\frac{5}{6}x - 2\right) = 6\left(-\frac{2}{3}x + 1\right)$$

Multiply both sides by the LCM, 6.

$5x - 12 = -4x + 6$	Simplify.
$+4x \qquad -4x$	Add $4x$ to both sides.
$9x - 12 = \qquad 6$	Simplify.
$+12 \qquad +12$	Add 12 to both sides.
$9x = 18$	Simplify.
$\dfrac{9x}{9} = \dfrac{18}{9}$	Divide both sides by 9.

4. $x = 1$
5. $n = -4$
6. $h = -1$
7. $w = 50$
8. $y = 15\frac{1}{2}$
9. $a = -8$
10. Tina sold bags of popcorn at a bake sale. In the morning, Tina paid the booth fee of $18.50 and sold the bags for $0.75 each. In the afternoon she sold the bags for $0.65 each. Her profit in the morning was the same as her profit in the afternoon. How many bags of popcorn did Tina sell in the morning? $x = 185$; Tina sold 185 bags in the morning.

Practice and Problem Solving: C

1. $x = -2\frac{4}{5}$
2. $x = -1.5$
3. $r = \frac{4}{5}$
4. $x = -5\frac{1}{3}$
5. $x = -3\frac{17}{21}$
6. $t = \frac{12}{13}$
7. $2x = -\frac{23}{3}$ or $-7\frac{2}{3}$
8. $x - 0.8 = -2.8$
9. $0.75x - \$28.50 = \$36.75$; $x = 87$ muffins
10. Possible answer: Three more than two-thirds the number of hours Laura worked last week is the same as five-sixths times the hours she worked this week decreased by seven-eighths. $x = 23\frac{1}{4}$ hours

Practice and Problem Solving: D

1. 4
2. 6

3.

$$10\left(\frac{7}{10}x - 2\right) = 10\left(\frac{2}{5}x + 1\right)$$ Multiply

both sides by the LCM (10, 5), which is 10.

$7x - 20 = 4x + 10$	Simplify.
$\underline{-4x \qquad -4x}$	Subtract $4x$ from both sides.
$3x - 20 = \qquad 10$	Simplify.
$\underline{+20 \qquad +20}$	Add 20 to both sides.
$3x \quad = \qquad 30$	Simplify.
$\dfrac{3x}{3} = \dfrac{30}{3}$	Divide both sides by 3.

4. $n = \dfrac{1}{3}$

5. $r = -1$

6. $g = 8$

Reteach

1.

$$[\,20\,]\left(\frac{1}{4}x + 2\right) = [\,20\,]\left(\frac{2}{5}x - 1\right)$$

$$[20]\left(\frac{1}{4}x\right) + [20](2) = [20]\left(\frac{2}{5}x\right) - [20](1)$$

$$[5]x + [40] = [8]x - [20]$$

$$\underline{-5x \qquad\qquad -5x}$$

$$40 = 3x - 20$$

$$\underline{+20 \qquad\quad +20}$$

$$[60] = 3x$$

$$\frac{60}{\boxed{3}} = \frac{3x}{\boxed{3}}$$

$$[20] = x$$

Multiply both sides of the equation by <u>20</u> the LCM of 4 and 5.

Multiply each term by <u>20</u>.

Simplify.

Subtract <u>5x</u>.

Simplify.

Add <u>20</u>.

Simplify.

Divide both sides by <u>3</u>.

Simplify.

Check: Substitute into the original equation.

$$\frac{1}{4}x + 2 = \frac{2}{5}x - 1$$

$$\frac{1}{4}(20) + 2 \overset{?}{=} \frac{2}{5}(20) - 1$$

$$\underline{5} + 2 \overset{?}{=} \underline{8} - 1$$

$$\underline{7} = \underline{7}$$

Reading Strategies

1. Multiply every term by the LCM.

2. Multiply every term by a power of 10 to clear the decimals.

3. $x = -4$

4. $k = \dfrac{1}{2}$

5. $y = 24$

Success for English Learners

1. Subtract $15x$ from both sides. Then subtract 80 from both sides. $x = -120$

2. Sample answer: After adding 1 pound of peanuts to a bag that is 0.375 full the bag is now 0.4 full. How many pounds of peanuts does the bag hold when the bag is full? $x = 40$ pounds

3. LCM (2, 3, 4) = 12

4. 100

LESSON 7-3

Practice and Problem Solving: A/B

1. $x = 6$

2. $n = 9$

3. $y = -5$

4. $k = 3$

5. $m = -1$

6. $y = -5$

7. 20 mi

8. 28 mi

9. 1 error

10. 50 wpm

11. 365 words

Practice and Problem Solving: C

1. $x = 6$
2. $n = 2$
3. $y = 3$
4. $k = 9$
5. $m = \dfrac{1}{4}$
6. $x = -6$
7. 11 oz
8. 137 mi
9. Benjamin: 13; Kevan: 17
10. 11 mi
11. 19 quarters, 23 dimes

Practice and Problem Solving: D

1. $x = 10$
2. $n = 15$
3. $s = 2$
4. $p = \dfrac{1}{2}$
5. $y = -6$
6. $k = -1$
7. $m = 11$
8. $x = 6$
9. a. $k - 6$
   b. $2(k - 6)$
   c. $2(k - 6) = 18$
   d. Kevan is 9 and Katie is 15.

Reteach

1. $i = -3$
2. $n = 4$
3. $y = \dfrac{2}{3}$
4. $x = 14$

Reading Strategies

1. $-4(j + z) - 3j = 6$
   $-4j - 8 - 3j = 6$
   $-7j - 8 = 6$
   $-7j = 1$
   $j = -2$

2. $4n + 6 - 2n = 3(n + 3) - 11$
   $4n + 6 - 2n = 3n + 9 - 11$
   $2n + 6 = 3n - 2$
   $8 = n$

3. $5(r - 1) = 2(r - 4) - 6$
   $5r - 5 = 2r - 8 - 6$
   $5r - 5 = 2r - 14$
   $3r = -9$
   $r = -3$

4. $2\left(n + \dfrac{1}{3}\right) = \dfrac{3}{2}n + 1$
   $2n + \dfrac{2}{3} = \dfrac{3}{2}n + 1$
   $\dfrac{n}{2} = \dfrac{1}{3}$
   $n = \dfrac{2}{3}$

Success for English Learners

1. $x = 5$
2. 11 quarters; 20 pennies

LESSON 7-4

Practice and Problem Solving: A/B

1. zero solutions
2. infinitely many solutions
3. zero solutions
4. $n = -8$; one solution
5. zero solutions
6. infinitely many solutions
7. $y = 6$; one solution
8. zero solutions
9. infinitely many solutions
10. $x = 10$; one solution
11. Yes; 500 text messages will cost exactly the same from both companies.
12. No, the two tanks will never need the exact same amount of food.

Practice and Problem Solving: C

1. zero solutions
2. one solution; $m = 7$
3. infinitely many solutions
4. one solution; $n = -8$
5. one solution; $r = 14$

6. infinitely many solutions

7. one solution; $x = 0$

8. one solution; $q = -4$

9. No; $x + 2x + 200 = x + 85 + 2x$ results in no solutions.

10. a. Possible equation: $0.25x + 0.05(5 - x) = 0.50$

    b. $x = 1\frac{1}{4}$

    c. yes

    d. no; it is not possible to have $1\frac{1}{4}$ coins.

Practice and Problem Solving: D

1. zero solutions

2. infinitely many solutions

3. zero solutions

4. zero solutions

5. one solution; $r = 2$

6. infinitely many solutions

7. one solution; $x = -3$

8. one solution; $t = 10$

9. one solution; $d = -2$

10. infinitely many solutions

11. Any number may be added; Sample answer: $x + 2 = x + 2$

12. infinitely many solutions

13. Any number may be used to multiply; Sample answer: $4(x + 2) = 4(x + 2)$

14. infinitely many solutions

15. sample: $4x + 20 = 4(x + 5)$

16. infinitely many solutions

Reteach

1. $i = 6$; one solution

2. infinitely many solutions

3. Answers may vary; should have one solution

4. Answers may vary; should have no solution

5. Answers may vary; should have infinitely many solutions

Reading Strategies

1. infinitely many solutions

2. no solution

3. Answers may vary; should have one solution

4. Answers may vary; should have no solution

5. Answers may vary; should have infinitely many solutions

Success for English Learners

1. Answers will vary; should have no solution

2. Answers will vary; should have infinitely many solutions

Module 7 Challenge

1. HT: $25.00 + 8.50 (2.5) = 46.25$: RR: $20.75 + 9.75(2.5) = 45.13$; Rough Riders Ranch

2. $25.00 + 8.50x = 20.75 + 9.75x$; $4.25 = 1.25x$; $3.4 = x$; The two ranches would charge the same amount for 3.4 hours.

3. $5(5 + 1.7x) = 5(4.15 + 1.95x)$; $0.85 = 0.25x$; $3.4 = x$

4. infinitely many, the two sides of the equation are the same so any value of x will satisfy both

5. at 3:24 P.M.; $53.90

6. $53.90; For 3.4 hours, the two ranches charge the same amount.

7. Happy Trails; for any time over 3.4 hours Happy Trails is the better deal

MODULE 8 Solving Systems of Linear Equations

LESSON 8-1

Practice and Problem Solving: A/B

1.

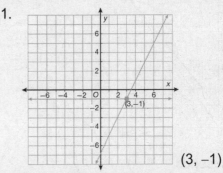

$(3, -1)$

2.

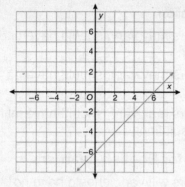

infinitely many solutions

3.

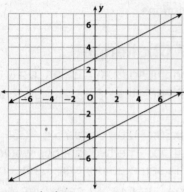

no solution

4.

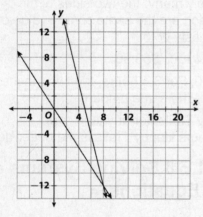

(2, 5)

5.

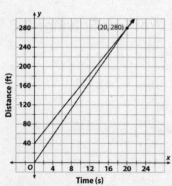

20 seconds

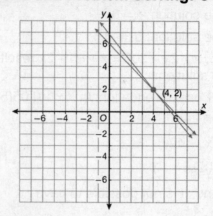

1. $x + y = 6$

2. $5x + 4y = 28$

3. x represents the number of chicken salads and y represents the number of egg salads

4. (4, 2); 4 chicken salads and 2 egg salads

5.

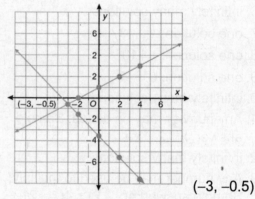

(−3, −0.5)

6.

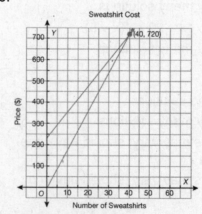

40 sweatshirts

Practice and Problem Solving: D

1.

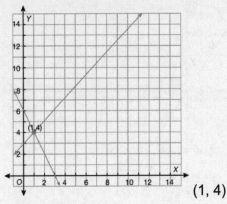

(1, 4)

2.

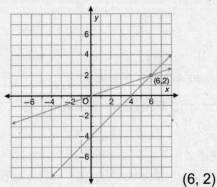

(2, 6)

3.

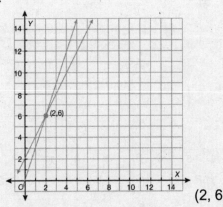

(6, 2)

4.

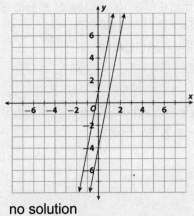

no solution

5.

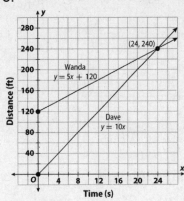

81 seconds

Reteach

1.

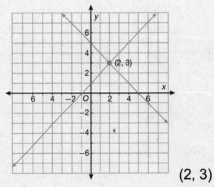

(2, 3)

2.

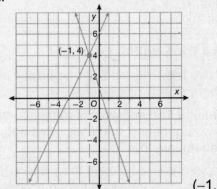

(−1, 4)

Reading Strategies

1. Drawings will vary. Sample drawing:

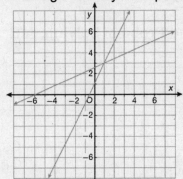

2. Drawings will vary. Sample drawing:

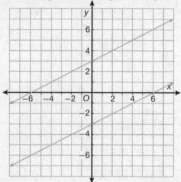

3. Drawings will vary. Sample drawing:

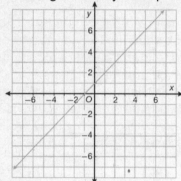

4. none

5. one

6. infinite

7. one

Success for English Learners

1. The two lines intersect at one point, so there is only one solution.

2. Substitute the ordered pair into each of the two equations, and check that both equations are true.

3. Sample answer: I plotted the *y*-intercept, and then used the slope to find another point. I then connected the two points with a straight line.

LESSON 8-2

Practice and Problem Solving: A/B

1. $(-1, -3)$

2. $(1, -4)$

3. $(1, -2)$

4.

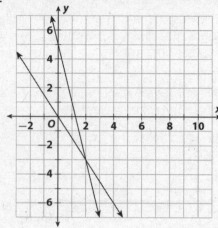

$(2, -3)$

5.

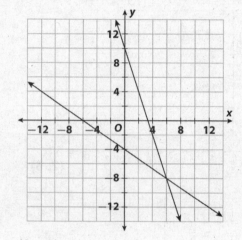

$(6, -8)$

6. $13/suit, $8/pair of shoes

Practice and Problem Solving: C

1. 1; 1

2. $0 \cdot x + y = 1$

3. No. The equations $4B + 6S = 150$ and $8B + 12S = 400$ have no solution, which means there are no values of *B* and *S* that satisfy both equations.

4. Round the coefficients.

$$4x - \frac{2}{3}y = 6 \text{ and } -2x = 10 + 6y$$

5. Multiply the coefficients by 1,000 and round: $y = 5$; $6x + 8y = 1$

6. Solve the inequalities $40 - 17n < 0$ and $35 - 15n < 0$ to find the smallest integers that make $x < 0$ and $y < 0$. n has to be 3 or greater.

7. Substitute $x = 20$ and $y = 30$ in the equations to see if an integer results; it does not in either case.

Practice and Problem Solving: D

1. $2x$; 2; 2; x; 2; 2; 2; 2; 6; 2; 6

2. $x - 3$; $x - 3$; $4x$; $4x$; 4; 4; x; 7; 7; 7; 7; 4; 7; 4

3. $(3, 12)$

4. $(2, 0)$

5. 50; 75; 60; 50; $y = 50x + 75$; $y = 60x + 50$; 2.5; 200

   For 2.5 hours both decorators charge the same amount, $200.

Reteach

1. $(2, 3)$

2. $(7, 9)$

3. $(-4, 1)$

4. $(17, 7)$

Reading Strategies

1. $(6, 4)$

2. $(-3, 5)$

Success for English Learners

1. Substitute the value of x into one of the equations to find y.

2. Option 1 charges $50 to set up the service and then $30 each month. Option 2 charges nothing to set up the service, but charges $40 each month.

LESSON 8-3

Practice and Problem Solving: A/B

1. $(10, 2)$

2. $(2, 0)$

3. $(6, 2)$

4. $\left(\dfrac{1}{2}, \dfrac{15}{2}\right)$

5. $\left(\dfrac{33}{10}, \dfrac{18}{50}\right)$

6. $\left(\dfrac{7}{2}, \dfrac{5}{2}\right)$

7. $b + 3m = 7.25$; $b + 2m = 6.00$; $3.50/bagel, $1.25/muffin

8. $2m + 3s = 25$; $3m + 4s = 35$; $9.00/ticket, $2.00/snack

9. Answers may vary, but students should realize that when the equations are subtracted, an untrue statement results $(0 = -12)$, which means that there is no common solution. A graph of this system will show two parallel lines.

10. Answers may vary, but students should realize that when the equations are subtracted, a true statement results $(0 = 0)$, which means that there are many combinations of x and y that make the equations true statements. A graph of this system will show only one line, since both equations have the same graph.

Practice and Problem Solving: C

1. a. 14

   b. $2x = 18$, or $x = 9$

   c. 9

   d. -3

   e. $x = 9$, $y = 5$, and $z = -3$; $(9, 5, -3)$

2. $\left(12, 20, \dfrac{15}{2}\right)$.

3. $\left(0, \dfrac{5}{3}, 2\right)$.

4. $(7, 4, 3)$

5. $(1.5, -2, 0)$

Practice and Problem Solving: D

1. 0, $3x$, 3, 3, 2, 2, 2, 2, 12, 4; 2, 4

2. $2y$; -7; $0y$; -3; -3; -1; -1; 3; 3; 3; 9; 9; 9; -2; 2; 2; -1; 3; -1

3. 2; 4; -16; 5; 10; 5; 10; 5; 5; 2; 2; 2; 2; 2; -10; -2; -2; 5; 2; 5

4. $(3, 4)$

5. $(6, -2)$

6. $(-8, -1)$

Reteach

1. Addition; $(4, -1)$
2. Subtraction; $(-6, 18)$

Reading Strategies

1. The hand towels are the variable to eliminate. Bath towels: $10; hand towels: $5
2. The adult movie ticket is the variable to eliminate. Adult tickets: $15; child tickets: $5

Success for English Learners

1. The y-variable is eliminated.
$-2y + 2y = 0$
2. The "$2D$" in both equations is eliminated, and you get $2L = 16$. The lunch combo is $8.

LESSON 8-4

Practice and Problem Solving: A/B

1. 4; 6
2. 42; 90
3. 24; 60
4. $\left(\dfrac{17}{5}, -\dfrac{29}{5} \right)$
5. $\left(-\dfrac{1}{2}, 3 \right)$
6. $(-4, -1)$
7. $2a + 3y = 134$; $3a + 2y = 146$; $22
8. $x + y = 19$; $0.25x + 0.3y = 5.1$; 7 Galas, 12 Granny Smith's

Practice and Problem Solving: C

1. $(-1, -2)$
2. $(-1, -2)$
3. $(-1, -2)$
4. The numbers are consecutive whole numbers.
5. $(-1, -2)$. They follow the pattern.
6. $y = \dfrac{2}{3}x - \dfrac{4}{3}$; $y = \dfrac{3}{4}x - \dfrac{5}{4}$; both slopes are close to but less than 1.
7. The slopes are getting larger and approaching positive one.

8. All of the lines would intersect at $(-1, -2)$ but would have different slopes less than $+1$ and different y-intercepts.
9. $(-1, 2)$

10–11.
Answers may vary, but the two systems should have equations of the form $nx + (n + 1)y = n + 2$ and $(n + 3)x + (n + 4)y = (n + 5)$, where n is an integer; $(-1, 2)$; $(-1, 2)$.

Practice and Problem Solving: D

1. 2; 4; –16; 5; 10; 5; 10; 5; 5; 2; 2; 2; 2; 2; –10; –2; –2; 5; 2; 5
2. 57; 9; 8; 25

Reteach

1. $\left(\dfrac{59}{7}, -\dfrac{22}{7} \right)$
2. $\left(69, \dfrac{111}{2} \right)$
3. $\left(\dfrac{135}{19}, -\dfrac{5}{19} \right)$
4. $\left(\dfrac{27}{10}, -\dfrac{119}{10} \right)$

Reading Strategies

1. Multiply the first equation by 3 and the second equation by 5 to get common coefficients of -15.
2. $\begin{cases} 4(9x - 10y = 7) \\ 5(5x + 8y = 31) \end{cases} \Rightarrow \begin{cases} 36x - 40y = 28 \\ 25x + 40y = 155 \end{cases}$
3. $(1, -3)$
4. $(10, -10)$

Success for English Learners

1. -3
2. Multiply the first equation by 3 and the second by -2, or the first by -3 and the second by 2.

LESSON 8-5

Practice and Problem Solving: A/B

1.

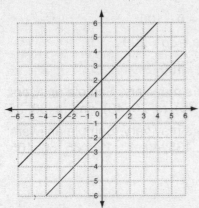

No solution; parallel lines with the same slopes.

2.

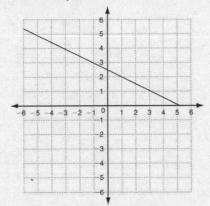

Many solutions; same lines

3. $\begin{cases} y = -2x + 1 \\ y = -2x - 3 \end{cases}$; same slope but different y-intercepts, so no solution.

4. $\begin{cases} y = -5x + 2 \\ y = 5x + 2 \end{cases}$; different slopes, so one solution.

5. $\begin{cases} y = 3x - 2 \\ y = 3x - 2 \end{cases}$; same slope and y-intercepts, so many solutions.

6. The rates of deposit are the same, since the 2nd sister's rate of $40 every 2 months is the same as the 1st sister's rate of $20 each month. They start with the same amount, too. The total amounts of their savings will only vary for the months in which sister 1 puts her $20 in before sister 2 puts in $40 every 2 months.

Practice and Problem Solving: C

1. $+3$; $-\dfrac{1}{3}$; $-\dfrac{1}{3}$

2. $y = 3x$; $x + 3y = 3$; $x + 3y = -9$

3. They are negative reciprocals.

4. They are the same.

5. $\left(\dfrac{3}{10}, \dfrac{9}{10} \right)$

6. Find the distances from the solution point to a point on line *A* and a point on line *B*. Then, find the distance between the points on lines *A* and *B*. Finally, check to see if the three distances satisfy the conditions for a right triangle, i.e. the square of the hypotenuse is equal to the sum of the squares of its two legs.

7. Yes, because the slopes, $+3$ and $-\dfrac{1}{3}$, are negative reciprocals.

8. No, because the slopes are positive reciprocals.

9. Yes, because the slopes, $\dfrac{3}{5}$ and $-\dfrac{5}{3}$, are negative reciprocals.

Practice and Problem Solving: D

1. $-2x$; $-2x$; $-2x$; 6; $-2x$; 6; 6; $-1x$; 3; $\dfrac{5}{2}$; $-\dfrac{1}{3}$; $\dfrac{5}{2}$

   $3x$; 3; 3; 3; -9; -9; -9; -1; 3; 9

2 $-\dfrac{1}{3}$; $-\dfrac{1}{3}$

3. $\dfrac{5}{2}$; $\dfrac{-5}{9}$

4. No solutions, because the lines have the same slope and different y-intercepts.

5. none

6. none

7. many

Reteach

1. many solutions
2. no solution
3. no solution

Reading Strategies

1. No solution. A false statement means that the lines are parallel.
2. One solution.

Success for English Learners

1. In one case, an untrue statement, $0 = 1$, results; in the other case, a true statement results, $0 = 0$:
2. An untrue outcome means that the system of equations has no solution. A true outcome means that the system has many solutions.

Module 8 Challenge

1. $c + e + p = 100$
2. $c + 2e + 3p = 200$
3. $\begin{cases} c + e + p = 100 \\ c + 2e + 3p = 200 \end{cases}$
4. $e + 2p = 100$
5. Answers may vary. Sample answers: $(c, 10, 45)$, $(c, 20, 40)$, and $(c, 30, 35)$
6. Answers may vary. Sample answers: 45, 20, 135; 40, 40, 120; 35, 60, 105

MODULE 9 Transformations and Congruence

LESSON 9-1

Practice and Problem Solving: A/B

1. 5 units right and 8 units down

2. 2 units left and 9 units up

3.

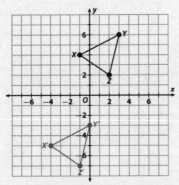

4.

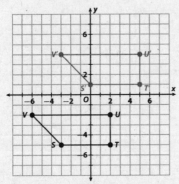

5. a.

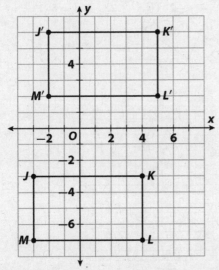

b. Area of *JKLM* = 28 square units, area of *J′K′L′M′* = 28 square units

c. No; the image and preimage are congruent, so they have the same size. This means that the areas are the same.

Practice and Problem Solving: C

1.

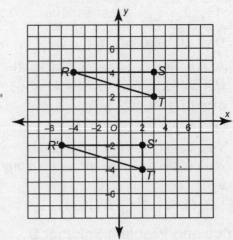

2.

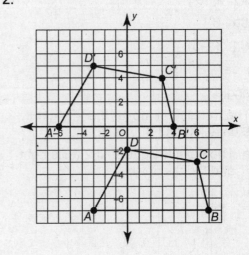

3.

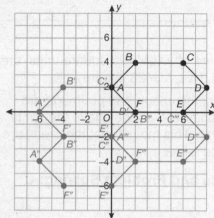

a. $A'(-6, 0)$, $B'(-4, 2)$, $C'(0, 2)$,
$D'(2, 0)$, $E'(0, -2)$, $F'(-4, -2)$

b. $A''(-6, -4)$, $B''(-4, -2)$, $C''(0, -2)$,
$D'(2, -4)$, $E''(0, -6)$, $F'(-4, -6)$

c. $A'''(0, -2)$, $B'''(2, 0)$, $C'''(6, 0)$,
$D'''(8, -2)$, $E'''(6, -4)$, $F'''(2, -4)$

d. Yes; the figures cover the plane
without overlapping and without any
gaps.

4. $P'(-8, 6)$, $Q'(-5, 6)$, $R'(-6, 4)$

Practice and Problem Solving: D

1. $A'(-7, -2)$

2. $B(6, 6)$

3. $C'(-3, -5)$

4. side $A'B'$

5. angle C'

6. The translation moves the triangle
9 units left and 6 units down.

7. a. The point is translated 2 units right
and 8 units down.

b.

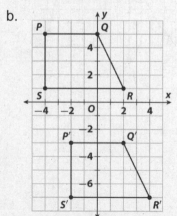

c. They are congruent.

8.

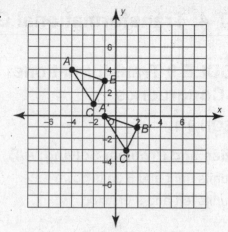

9.

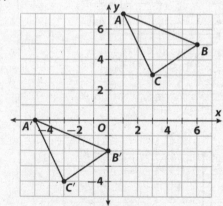

Reteach

1.

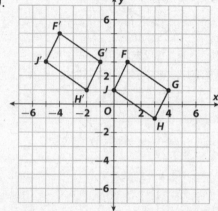

2.

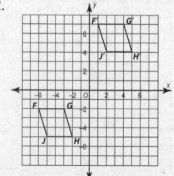

3. Yes; translations preserve the size and shape of a figure. Even after two translations, the resulting figure is congruent to the original figure.

Reading Strategies

1. Triangle *A'B'C'*

2. Triangle *ABC*

3. 3 vertices

4. Yes; a translation produces a figure (image) that is congruent to the original figure (preimage).

5. The translation moves the triangle 5 units left and 7 units up.

6. A transformation is an operation that changes the position, size, or shape of a figure. A translation is a type of transformation that changes only the position of a figure.

Success for English Learners

1. The translation moved the triangle 5 units to the right.

2. Yes; the new translation is the same as the one in Problem 2, except that the vertical movement is described first and the horizontal movement is second.

LESSON 9-2

Practice and Problem Solving: A/B

1. Quadrilateral *G*

2. Quadrilaterals *F* and *G*

3. One is a translation of the other.

4.

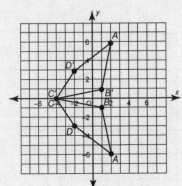

5.

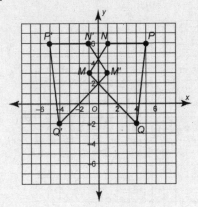

6. a.

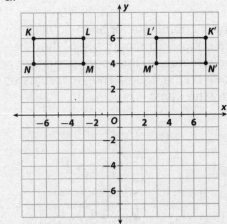

b. Perimeter of *KLMN* = 12 units, perimeter of *K'L'M'N'* = 12 units

c. No; the image and preimage are congruent, so they have the same size. This means that the perimeters are the same.

Practice and Problem Solving: C

1.

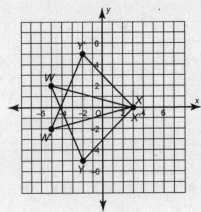

2.

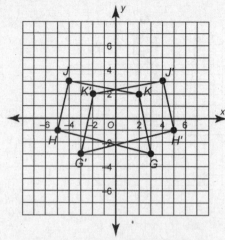

3. The *x*-coordinate for each point on the image is the opposite of the *x*-coordinate of the corresponding point on the figure. The *y*-coordinates stay the same.

4.

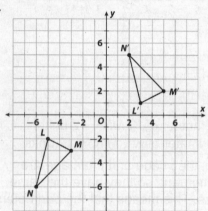

5.

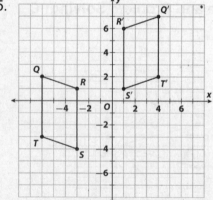

Practice and Problem Solving: D

1. *A*′(6, 2)

2. *B*(−5, 6)

3. *C*′(3, 7)

4. side *C*′*D*′

5. angle *D*′

6. a reflection across the *y*-axis

7.

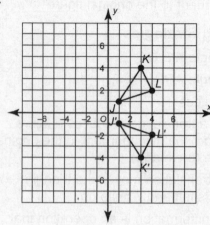

8.

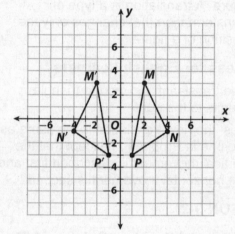

9. flips

10. always

11. *y*-coordinate

Reteach

1.

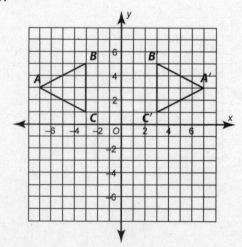

2.

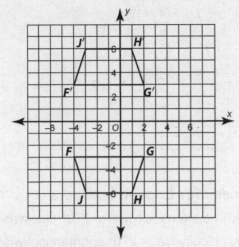

Reading Strategies

1. Triangle C'D'E'

2. Triangle CDE

3. Sample answer: C and C'

4. a reflection across the y-axis

5. a. quadrilateral PQRS

   b. reflection

6. The corresponding points are the same distance from the line of reflection.

Success for English Learners

1. Reflection across the y-axis

2. Connect the reflected vertices to form triangle A'B'C'.

LESSON 9-3

Practice and Problem Solving: A/B

1. B
2. C
3. B
4. D
5. 30 cm, 40 cm, and 50 cm
6. III
7. I
8. IV
9. II
10. 60° and 120°

11.

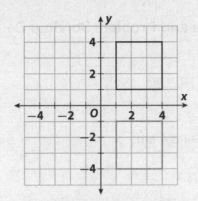

12. Accept: reflection over x-axis, translation of 5 units down, or rotation of 270° counterclockwise.

Practice and Problem Solving: C

1. Sample answer: Not a rotation because triangle B is flipped from where it would be after a rotation.

2. A rotation of 180°

3. A rotation of 90° counterclockwise OR 270° clockwise

4. a regular hexagon

5. A large square is formed with its center at the origin and each side is twice as long as the side of square S.

6.

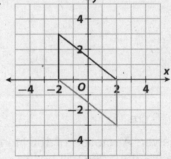

7.

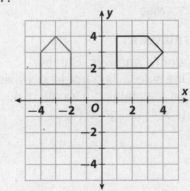

Practice and Problem Solving: D

1. *B*

2. *C*

3. *B*

4. *D*

5. 2 cm and 4 cm

6. I

7. I

8. III

9. II

10.

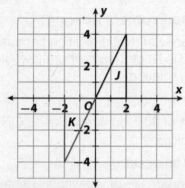

11. The image will be the same as triangle *K*.

Reteach

1. *D*

2. *B*

3. *C*

4. *B*

5. 3 cm, 4 cm, 5 cm

6. Sample answer: A rotation of 180° turns the figure a half-turn and will be the same whether turned clockwise or counterclockwise.

Reading Strategies

1. Check student's answers. Sample answer: One side will go from the *x*-axis to the *y*-axis maintaining a length of 4. Vertex at (−3, 4) will go to (4, 3)

2.

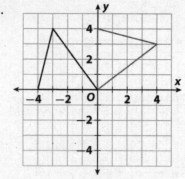

Success for English Learners

1. 90° counterclockwise or 270° clockwise

2. 90° clockwise or 270° counterclockwise

LESSON 9-4

Practice and Problem Solving: A/B

1. $(x, y) \rightarrow (x, y-5)$; translation down 5 units

2. $(x, y) \rightarrow (-y, x)$; rotation 90° counterclockwise

3. reflection over the *y*-axis

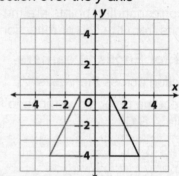

4. rotation of 180°

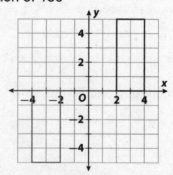

5. *A′* (2, 1), *B′* (−3, 2), *C′* (−1, 6)

6. a 90° clockwise rotation

Practice and Problem Solving: C

1. $(x, y) \rightarrow (x + 2, y)$; translation right 2 units

2. $(x, y) \rightarrow (-y, x)$; rotation 90° counterclockwise

3. reflection over the x-axis

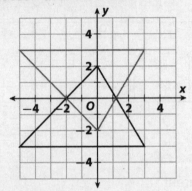

4. rotation of 180°

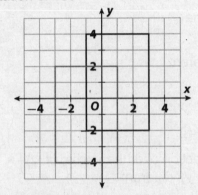

5. Possible answer: $(x, y) \rightarrow (x + 2, y)$

6. $(0, -3)$; rotation of 90° clockwise

Practice and Problem Solving: D

1. $(x, y) \rightarrow (-x, -y)$; rotation 180° clockwise OR counterclockwise

2. $(x, y) \rightarrow (x, y + 5)$; translation up 5 units

3. $(x, y) \rightarrow (-x, y)$; reflection over the y-axis

4. $(x, y) \rightarrow (y, -x)$; rotation 90° clockwise

5. $(-4, 4)$

6. $(-1, 4)$

7. $(-2, 1)$

8.

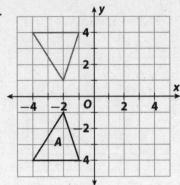

Reteach

1. reflection over the y-axis

2. 90° rotation counterclockwise

3. translation up 4 units

4. 180° rotation

5. reflection over the x-axis

Reading Strategies

1. translation up 2 units

2. 90° rotation clockwise

3. 180° rotation

4. reflection over the y-axis

Success for English Learners

1. reflection or rotation

2. translation

3. rotation

4. rotation 90° clockwise

5. translation right 2 units

6. reflection over x-axis

LESSON 9-5

Practice and Problem Solving: A/B

1. rotation 90° counterclockwise

2. translation right 4 units

3. $(x, y) \rightarrow (-y, x)$; $(x, y) \rightarrow (x + 4, y)$

4–6.

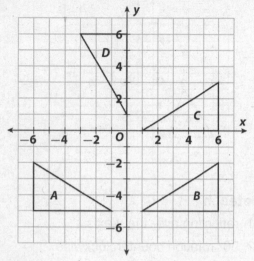

7. yes

8. different

9. Sample answer: rotation 90° clockwise, translation 4 units left

10. size: no; orientation: yes

Practice and Problem Solving: C

1. Sample answer: $(x, y) \rightarrow (-x, -y)$; $(x, y) \rightarrow (x, y + 4)$

2. Sample answer: $(x, y) \rightarrow (-y, x)$; $(x, y) \rightarrow (x + 2, y)$

3. yes

4. square; Sample explanation: Each side of the square is a hypotenuse of congruent triangles. Each angle is supplemental to two angles with a sum of 90°.

5. Sample answer: $(x, y) \rightarrow (y, -x)$; $(x, y) \rightarrow (x - 4, y)$

6. Accept answers that meet the criteria. Sample transformation of A: $(x, y) \rightarrow (x - 5, y)$

Practice and Problem Solving: D

1. rotation 90° counterclockwise

2. translation down 6 units

3. $(x, y) \rightarrow (-y, x)$; $(x, y) \rightarrow (x, y - 6)$

4. 7, and 10

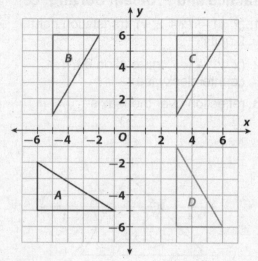

5. yes

6. different

8. yes

9. same

11. yes

12. different

13. yes

14. different

Reteach

1. reflection over the y-axis; $(x, y) \rightarrow (-x, y)$; different

2. 90° rotation counterclockwise; $(x, y) \rightarrow (-y, x)$; different

Reading Strategies

1. translation down 4 units

2. y decreases by 4

3. $(x, y - 4)$

4. yes

5. 180° rotation

6. x and y both change signs.

7. $(-x, -y)$

8. yes

Success for English Learners

1. translation; $(x, y) \rightarrow (x + 7, y - 6)$

2. reflection; $(x, y) \rightarrow (x, -y)$

3. rotation; $(x, y) \rightarrow (-x, -y)$

MODULE 9 Challenge

1. $(x, y) \rightarrow (x + h, y + k)$; translation, direct

2. $(x, y) \rightarrow (x - y)$; reflection across x-axis, opposite

3. $(x, y) \rightarrow (-y, x)$; rotation of 90°, opposite

4. $(x, y) \rightarrow (-x, y)$; reflection across y-axis, opposite

5. translation

6. rotation, reflection

MODULE 10 Transformations and Similarity

LESSON 10-1

Practice and Problem Solving: A/B

1. 2, 2; 6, 6

2. $\dfrac{6}{2} = 3; \dfrac{6}{2} = 3$

3. Yes

4. enlargement

5. No, the ratios are not all equal.
   $\dfrac{3}{12} = \dfrac{1}{4}; \dfrac{4}{16} = \dfrac{1}{4}; \dfrac{5}{25} = \dfrac{1}{5}$

6. Yes, this shows a reduction. The ratio of the lengths of corresponding sides is $\dfrac{1}{2}$.

7. Yes, this shows an enlargement. The ratio of the lengths of corresponding sides is $\dfrac{3}{1}$.

8. Yes; The lines drawn through corresponding vertices meet in a single point.

Practice and Problem Solving: C

1. 2.5

2. $\dfrac{1}{3}$

3.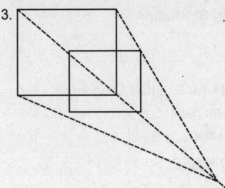

4.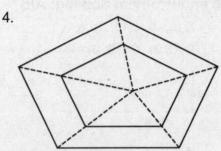

5. scale factor: 3; area of original rectangle: 6 square units; area of dilation: 54 square units

6. scale factor: $\dfrac{1}{2}$; area of original rectangle: 8 square units; area of dilation: 2 square units

7. Sample answer: The area of the image is the area of the original figure times the square of the scale factor.

Practice and Problem Solving: D

1. 3; 2; 9; 6

2. $\dfrac{9}{3} = 3; \dfrac{6}{2} = 3;$

3. Yes

4. Enlargement

5. 6, 6, 6, 6; 3, 3, 3, 3

6. $\dfrac{3}{6} = \dfrac{1}{2}; \dfrac{3}{6} = \dfrac{1}{2}; \dfrac{3}{6} = \dfrac{1}{2}; \dfrac{3}{6} = \dfrac{1}{2}$

7. Yes

8. Reduction

9. Enlargement

Reteach

1. $\dfrac{4}{3} = 1\dfrac{1}{3}; \dfrac{3}{4} = \dfrac{3}{4}$; no; no

2. $\dfrac{2}{4} = \dfrac{1}{2}; \dfrac{4}{8} = \dfrac{1}{2}$; yes; yes

Reading Strategies

1. no

2. yes

Success for English Learners

1. enlargement

2. reduction

LESSON 10-2

Practice and Problem Solving: A/B

1. A (0, 4), B (0, 0), C (5, 0)

2. A′(0, 8), B′(0, 0), C′(10, 0)

3.

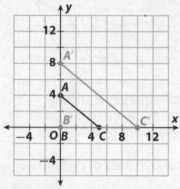

4. (2x, 2y)

5. J(–2, –2), K(–2, 2), L(0, 2), M(1, 0), N(0, –2)

6. J′(–6, –6), K′(–6, 6), L′(0, 6), M′(3, 0), N′(0, –6)

7. (3x, 3y)

8. 1 cm = 20 cm

9. (20x, 20y)

10. 300 cm by 400 cm or 3 m by 4 m

Practice and Problem Solving: C

1. $\left(1\frac{1}{2}x, 1\frac{1}{2}y\right)$

2. $\left(\frac{1}{4}x, \frac{1}{4}y\right)$

3. (–3, –1)

4. (9x, 9y)

5. 45 in. by 36 in.

6. $\left(-4\frac{1}{2}, 4\frac{1}{2}\right), \left(3, 4\frac{1}{2}\right), \left(3, -1\frac{1}{2}\right),$
   $\left(-4\frac{1}{2}, -1\frac{1}{2}\right)$

7. $7\frac{1}{2}$ in. by 6 in.

8. $67\frac{1}{2}$ in. by 54 in.

9. $22\frac{1}{2}$ in. by 18 in.

Practice and Problem Solving: D

1. A (0, 6), B (0, 0), C (4, 0)

2. A′(0, 12), B′(0, 0), C′(8, 0)

3.

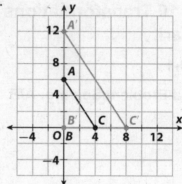

4. (2x, 2y)

5. J(–2, –2), K(–2, 2), L(2, 2), M(2, –2)

6. J′(–6, –6), K′(–6, 6), L′(6, 6), M′(6, –6)

7. (3x, 3y)

8. 1 in. = 12 in.

9. (12x, 12y)

10. 120 in. by 144 in. or 10 ft by 12 ft

Reteach

1. A(1, 2) → A′(2 • 1, 2 • 2) or A′(2, 4)
   B(2, 0) → B′(2 • 2, 2 • 0) or B′(4, 0)
   C(3, 3) → C′(2 • 3, 2 • 3) or C′(6, 6)

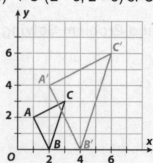

2. $A(8, 0) \rightarrow A'\left(\frac{1}{2} \cdot 8, \frac{1}{2} \cdot 0\right)$ or $A'(4, 0)$

$B(4, 4) \rightarrow B'\left(\frac{1}{2} \cdot 4, \frac{1}{2} \cdot 4\right)$ or $B'(2, 2)$

$C(6, 8) \rightarrow C'\left(\frac{1}{2} \cdot 6, \frac{1}{2} \cdot 8\right)$ or $C'(3, 4)$

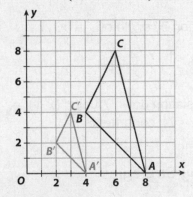

Reading Strategies

1. Sample answer:

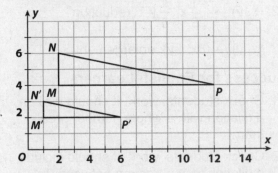

2. Sample answer: In an enlargement, the image is larger than the original figure. In a reduction, the image is smaller than the original figure.

Success for English Learners

1. reduction

2. enlargement

LESSON 10-3

Practice and Problem Solving: A/B

1. $(x, y) \rightarrow (2x, 2y)$
2. $(x, y) \rightarrow (x - 4, y)$
3. Figures B and C
4. Figures A and B or Figures A and C

5–6.

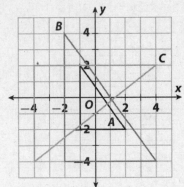

7. Figures B and C
8. Figures A and B or Figures A and C
9. $(x, y) \rightarrow (x, -y)$
10. $AB = 250$ cm; $BD = 250$ cm; $AD = 300$ cm
11. $(x, y) \rightarrow (y, -x)$

Practice and Problem Solving: C

1. $(x, y) \rightarrow \left(\frac{1}{2}x, \frac{1}{2}y\right)$

2. Sample answer: $(x, y) \rightarrow (x, -y)$; $(x, y) \rightarrow (x + 5, y)$

3. Figures A and B or Figures A and C

4–5.

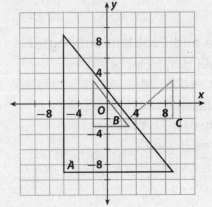

6. $(3, 4)$

7. Check students' work. Sample answer:

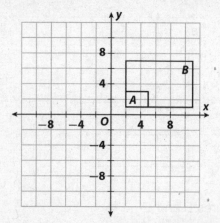

8. Sample answer: $(x, y) \rightarrow (3x, 3y)$

9. Sample answer: $(x, y) \rightarrow (-x, y)$

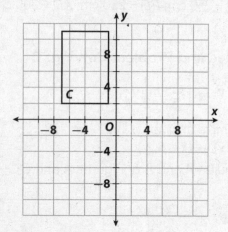

Practice and Problem Solving: D

1. dilating by a factor of 2 OR
   $(x, y) \rightarrow (2x, 2y)$

2. translating down 6 units OR
   $(x, y) \rightarrow (x, y - 6)$

3. Figures B and C

4. Figures A and B or Figures A and C

5–6.

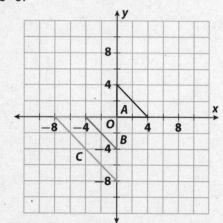

7. Figures A and B

8. Figures A and C or Figures B and C

9. 6 cm

10. $AB = 500$ cm; $BC = 500$ cm;
    $AC = 600$ cm

Reteach

1. dilation by scale of $\frac{1}{3}$; $(x, y) \rightarrow$
   $\left(\frac{1}{3}x, \frac{1}{3}y\right)$; similar

2. translation down 7 units; $(x, y) \rightarrow$
   $(x, y - 7)$; congruent

Reading Strategies

1. $(x, y) \rightarrow \left(\frac{1}{3}x, \frac{1}{3}y\right)$; reduction

2. $(x, y) \rightarrow \left(\frac{1}{5}x, \frac{1}{5}y\right)$; reduction

3. $(x, y) \rightarrow (8x, 8y)$; enlargement

Success for English Learners

1. Check students' work. It should include a dilation with a whole number greater than 1.

2. Check students' work. It should include a dilation with a fraction between 0 and 1.

MODULE 10 Challenge

1. $(-x + 2, y)$; L

2. $(-y, x - 2)$; J

3. $(-y, x - 2)$; J

4. $(-2x, -2y)$; M

5. (x, y); K

6. yes

7. J, K, L

UNIT 5: Measurement Geometry

MODULE 11 Angle Relationships in Parallel Lines and Triangles

LESSON 11-1

Practice and Problem Solving: A/B

1. ∠2 and ∠6, ∠3 and ∠7

2. ∠1

3. alternate exterior angles

4. Accept: same-side interior angles OR supplementary angles.

5. Accept ∠2 OR ∠6.

6. Accept: ∠4 OR ∠8.

7. 146°

8. 128°

9. 135°

10. 45°

11. ∠2 and ∠7, ∠1 and ∠8

12. ∠8

13. alternate interior angles

14. Yes; Accept any two pairs of supplementary angles.

Practice and Problem Solving: C

1. Avenue A and South Street are also perpendicular. Possible explanation: The measure of the angles formed by Avenue A and North Street is 90°. Then the measure of corresponding angles is also 90°, making Avenue A and South Street perpendicular.

2. 70° and 110°

3. (180 – 5x)°

4. m∠BCF = 48°; m∠CFE = 132°

5. m∠CFG = 42°; m∠DCF = 138°

6–8. Check students' work.

Practice and Problem Solving: D

1. The lines are parallel.
2. a and b
3. c

4. ∠1 and ∠5

5. ∠4

6. ∠1, ∠3, or ∠5

7. 40°

8. 30°

9. 35°

10. 130°

11. Check students' drawings. Sample answer:

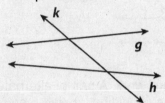

Reteach

1. ∠3, ∠5, ∠7

2. ∠c, ∠e, ∠g

3. ∠y, ∠t, ∠r

4.

30°   150°
150°   30°
30°   150°
150°   30°

5.

135°
45°   45°
135°
135°   45°
45°   135°

6.

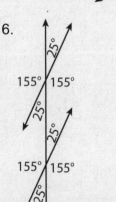

25°
155°   155°
25°
25°
155°   155°
25°

Reading Strategies

1. Check students' work. A pair of corresponding angles should be labeled 1 and 2.

Sample answer:

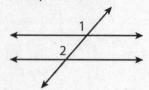

2. Check students' work. A pair of alternate interior angles should be labeled 1 and 2.

Sample answer:

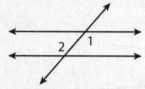

3. Check students' work. A pair of alternate exterior angles should be labeled 1 and 2.

Sample answer:

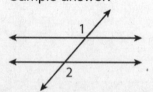

Success for English Learners

1. $\angle 1$ and $\angle 5$, $\angle 2$ and $\angle 6$, $\angle 3$ and $\angle 7$, $\angle 4$ and $\angle 8$

2. $\angle 3$ and $\angle 6$, $\angle 4$ and $\angle 5$

3. $\angle 1$ and $\angle 8$, $\angle 2$ and $\angle 7$

LESSON 11-2

Practice and Problem Solving: A/B

1. A
2. B
3. 30°
4. 46°
5. 55°
6. $x = 40°$
7. $y = 65°$
8. $n = 65°$
9. 103°
10. 77°
11. 60°

Practice and Problem Solving: C

1. $x = 59°$
2. $n = 46°$
3. $t = 60°$
4. $w = 31°$
5. $x = 50°$
6. $x = 30°$
7. $180 = (4x - 9) + (4x - 9) + x;$ base angles = 79°; vertex angle = 22°
8. $180 = 2x + \dfrac{x}{4}$; base angles = 80°; vertex angle = 20°
9. $180 = x + 2x + 3x$; 30°, 60°, 90°

Practice and Problem Solving: D

1. 55°
2. 136°
3. 74°
4. 16°
5. 40°
6. 112°
7. 103°
8. 68°
9. 82°
10. $x = 65°$
11. $y = 40°$
12. $r = 30°$

Reteach

1. $55s + 72° = 127°$; $180° - 127° = 53°$; 53°
2. $82° + 53° = 135°$; $180° - 135° = 45°$; 45°
3. $y = 150°$
4. 150°; 30°

Reading Strategies

1. 40°
2. 75°, 65°, 40°
3. 75°

Success for English Learners

1. $x = 80°$
2. $x = 58°$

LESSON 11-3

Practice and Problem Solving: A/B

1. △ABC has angle measures 42°, 50°, 88°, and △FGH has angle measures 42°, 50°, 88°. The triangles are similar because two angles in one triangle are congruent to two angles in the other triangle.

2. △XYZ has angle measures 41°, 55°, 84°, and △PRQ has angle measures 38°, 55°, 87°. The triangles are not similar because the triangles have only one congruent pair of angles.

3. Both triangles contain both ∠N and a right angle, so △LQN is similar to △MPN.

4. 4 ft

5. No; ∠J is in both △LQJ and △KRJ, but there is not enough information given to find any other congruent angles. ∠R looks like a right angle, but it is not given.

6. ∠TSV and ∠TRW are congruent because they are corresponding angles, and both triangles contain ∠T. By AA similarity, △RTW is similar to △STV.

Practice and Problem Solving: C

1. △XYZ and △RQP are similar. The triangles are similar because two angles in one triangle are congruent to two angles in the other triangle. Both triangles have angles measures 32°, 84°, 64°.

2. No, similar triangles have congruent corresponding angles. However, corresponding sides of similar triangles are proportional, not congruent.

3. 17.5 ft

4. 20 ft

5. ∠BCA and ∠GHF are congruent because they are corresponding angles, and both triangles contain right angles. By AA similarity, △ABC is similar to △FGH.

6. H(18, 16)

Practice and Problem Solving: D

1. m∠C = 59°

2. m∠P = 41°

3. m∠Y = 85°

4. m∠F = 36°

5. △ABC is similar to △XYZ by AA similarity.

6.

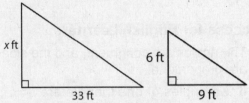

7. Both triangles contain the same angle at the far right, and a right angle, so the triangles are similar.

8. $\dfrac{6}{9} = \dfrac{x}{33}$; $x = 22$

9. m∠RST = 79°, m∠VWT = 33°; congruent alternate interior angles were used to find the angle measures.

10. △RST and △WVT are similar by AA similarity since the triangles contain two congruent angles.

Reteach

1.

	Lamp	Sign
Height (ft)	x	8
Length of shadow (ft)	31.5	14

18 ft

2.

	Woman	Son
Height (ft)	5.5	x
Length of shadow (ft)	3 + 13.5 = 16.5	13.5

4.5 ft

Reading Strategies

1. the length of Zachary's shadow

2. the height of the tree

3. the distance between the tree and Zachary

4. Both triangles contain angle *D* and a right angle. The triangles are similar by AA similarity.

5. a. *ED* b. *AB*

6. $\dfrac{x}{32} = \dfrac{4}{10}$; 12.8 ft

Success for English Learners

1. The angles are congruent, and the sides are proportional.

2. If two angles of one triangle are congruent to two angles of another triangle, the third angles are congruent and the triangles are similar.

MODULE 11 Challenge

1. $180 = 58 + 9n - 8 + 7n + 2$
$180 = 52 + 16n$
$128 = 16n$
$8 = n$
$9(8) - 8 = 72 - 8 = 64$
$\angle x = 180 - 64 = 116$
$m\angle x = 116°$

2. $m\angle x = 48°$ Angle *x* and the angle marked 48° are alternate interior angles, and therefore congruent.

3. $m\angle x = 35° + 45° = 80°$ Angle *x* is made up of two alternate interior angles. Part is an alternate interior angle to a 45° angle, and part is an alternate interior angle to a 35° angle. I can use those measures to add because the angles are congruent.

4. $m\angle x = 70° - 30° = 40°$ The angle marked 70° and the angles marked *x* and 30° are alternate interior angles and therefore congruent. I can subtract 30° from 70° to find the missing part, *x*, of the angle.

MODULE 12 The Pythagorean Theorem

LESSON 12-1

Practice and Problem Solving: A/B

1. $c = 6.4$

2. $b = 20$

3. $a = 36$

4. $b = 18.2$

5. $a = 17.7$

6. $b = 72$

7. 10 blocks

8. a. Drawings will vary, but should show a rectangular solid 12 units high with a base 3 units wide and 4 units long

   b. 13 in.

Practice and Problem Solving: C

1. 1.4 in.

2. 3.5 km

3. 2.4 ft

4. 6.9

5. 16

6. 2.8

7. 17.3 m

Practice and Problem Solving: D

1. $c = 15$

2. $c = 26$

3. $c = 12.5$

4. 10.4 m

5. 134.2 yd

6. 6.7; 61; 7.8

Reteach

1. Drawings may vary, but should be squares of side 10. Sample:

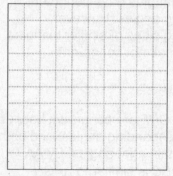

2. $c = 17$ in.

3. $a = 10$ cm

Reading Strategies

1. side *D*; sides of length 6 and 12

2. the side connecting the ends of the 9 mm and 12-mm legs; sides of length 9 mm and 12 mm.

Success for English Learners

1. Legs: $\overline{AC}$ and $\overline{BC}$; hypotenuse: $\overline{AB}$

2. Step 2: 15; 25

   Step 3: 225; 625

   Step 4: 625; 225; 400

   Step 5: 400; 20

LESSON 12-2

Practice and Problem Solving: A/B

1. Yes; $7^2 + 24^2 = 25^2 = 625$

2. No; $30^2 + 40^2 = 2,500$; $45^2 = 2,025$

3. Yes; $21.6^2 + 28.8^2 = 36^2 = 1,296$

4. No; $10^2 + 15^2 = 325$; $18^2 = 324$

5. No; $10.5^2 + 36^2 = 1,406.25$; $50^2 = 2,500$

6. Yes; $2.5^2 + 6^2 = 6.5^2 = 42.45$

7. No; $400^2 = 160,000$; $200^2 + 300^2 = 130,000$

8. Width = 68.7 yd (approx.)

9. No; the third side would have to be 50, which is less than each of the other sides. Also, there are two "longest" sides, so neither could be a hypotenuse.

Practice and Problem Solving: C

1. not a right triangle; $15^2 = 225$; $2(10)^2 = 200$

2. right triangle; $\left(2\sqrt{2}\right)^2 = 8$; $2(2)^2 = 8$

3. not a right triangle; $700^2 = 490,000$; $2(300)^2 = 180,000$

4. No, because the hypotenuse has to be longer than either of the two legs.

5. No; $9^2 = 81$; $4^2 + 8^2 = 80$

6. No; $\left(\sqrt{2}\right)^2 + 1^2 = 2 + 1 = 3$;

7.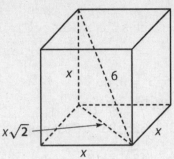

$6^2 = \left(x\sqrt{2}\right)^2 + x^2$

$36 = 2x^2 + x^2$

$36 = 3x^2$

$x^2 = 12$, $x = 2\sqrt{3}\,\text{m}$

8. Base: $\left(x\sqrt{2}\right)^2 + x^2 = 5x^2$, so diagonal of base is $x\sqrt{5}$;

   Solid diagonal: $\left(x\sqrt{5}\right)^2 + x^2 = \left(\sqrt{6}\right)^2$;

   $6x^2 = 6$; $x = 1$; dimensions of the rectangular solid are 1 foot by 1 foot by 2 feet.

Practice and Problem Solving: D

1. 5

2. 13

3. $\sqrt{2}$

4. $\sqrt{13}$

5. no; $8^2 + 9^2 \neq 10^2$;

6. no; $12^2 + 14^2 \neq 15^2$;

7. yes; $10^2 + 24^2 = 26^2$

8. no; $14^2 + 15^2 \neq 21^2$

9. 120 yd; it's the longest side.

10. 60 yd and 100 yd

11. 60; 100; 120

12. 3,600; 10,000; 14,400; 13,600; 14,400

13. No.

14. No; 120 yards would be the diagonal of the parking lot, and the two sides would be 60 yards and 100 yards, which would form a right triangle. The Pythagorean Theorem is not satisfied by the numbers 60, 100, and 120, so the triangle formed is not a right triangle.

Reteach

1. 10 in.

2. 15 mm

3. 3; $1^2 + 2^2 = 5$; $3^2 = 9$; no

4. 8; $6^2 + 7^2 = 85$; $8^2 = 64$; no

5. 25; $15^2 + 20^2 = 625$; $25^2 = 625$; yes

6. $2^2 + 3^2 = 13$; $\left(\sqrt{13}\right)^2 = 13$

7. $3^2 + 6^2 = 45$; $\left(3\sqrt{5}\right)^2 = 9(5) = 45$

Reading Strategies

1. Answers may vary. Sample answer: "If a right triangle has sides of 5 and 12, then its third side is the square root of 5 squared plus 12 squared, or 13."

2. Answers may vary. Sample answer: "If a triangle has sides 4, 4, and 8, then it is not a right triangle because the sum of 4 squared plus 4 squared is 32, which is not equal to 8 squared or 64."

Success for English Learners

1. The sides 7, 24, and 25 can be used to make a right triangle as shown, assuming that the 7 and 24 sides are perpendicular to each other and form a right angle. However, this is an informal proof by observation, not a formal proof using specific numbers from the problem.

2. Shorter, since a length longer than 12 would make the square of the hypotenuse ($12^2 = 144$) greater than the sum of the squares of the sides of the sides ($5^2 + 8^2 = 25 + 64 = 89$).

LESSON 12-3

Practice and Problem Solving: A/B

1. $A(-4, 2)$; $B(4, 6)$; $C(4, 2)$

2. $D(-3, 3)$; $E(3, -2)$; $F(-3, -2)$

3. $\overline{AB}$

4. $\overline{DE}$

5. Answers will vary. Sample answer: 9 units.

6. Answers will vary. Sample answer: 8 units.

7. $\overline{AB} = 4\sqrt{5}$

8. $\overline{DE} = \sqrt{61}$

9. $8\sqrt{2}$

Practice and Problem Solving: C

1. $d_{AB} = \sqrt{10}$; $d_{BC} = 3$; $d_{AC} = 1$; $\overline{AB}$ is the hypotenuse, so does $(\sqrt{10})^2 = 3^2 + 1^2$? Yes.

2. $AB = 3.5$ km; $BC = 2.5$ km; $CA = 2\sqrt{2}$, so the perimeter is $6 + 2\sqrt{2}$ or approx. 8.8 km

3. $d = \sqrt{(x+5)^2 + (3-7)^2} = \sqrt{(x+5)^2 + 16}$; for $d = 5$, $\sqrt{(x+5)^2 + 16}$; $= 5$ and $x + 5 = 3$. So $x = -2$.

4. $d = \sqrt{(6-3)^2 + (y+4)^2} = \sqrt{9 + (y+4)^2}$; for $d = 5$, $\sqrt{9 + (y+4)^2} = 5$ and $(y+4)^2 = 16$ and $(y+4) = -4$ and $y = -8$.

Practice and Problem Solving: D

1. $2\sqrt{2}$

2. $4\sqrt{2}$; $x_2 = -5$; $x_1 = -1$; $y_2 = 7$; $y_1 = 3$; $d = \sqrt{(-5+1)^2 + (7-3)^2}$

3. $10\sqrt{2}$; $x_2 = 10$; $x_1 = 0$; $y_2 = -15$; $y_1 = -5$; $d = \sqrt{(10-0)^2 + (-15+5)^2}$

4. Answers will vary.; Sample answer: x-distance between points = 10; AB = more than 10.

5. Answers will vary.; Sample answer: x-distance between points = 5; CD = more than 5.

6. Answers will vary.; Sample answer: x-distance between points = 5; EF = more than 5.

7. Answers will vary.; Sample answer: x-distance between points = 7; CD = more than 7.

8. The difference of the y-coordinates is $|5 - 1| = 4$.

9. The difference of the y-coordinates is $|-4 + 1| = 3$.

10. The difference of the y-coordinates is $|9 + 6| = 15$

Reteach
1. horizontal
2. neither
3. vertical
4. neither
5. $\sqrt{7.06}$
6. $\sqrt{17}$

Reading Strategies
1. Yes
2. the Pythagorean Theorem
3. the Distance Formula
4. $6^2 + 8^2 = c^2$
   $36 + 64 = c^2$
   $100 = c^2$
   $\sqrt{100} = c$
   $10 = c$
5. $d = \sqrt{(10-2)^2 + (2-8)^2}$
   $d = \sqrt{8^2 + 6^2}$
   $d = \sqrt{64 + 36}$
   $d = \sqrt{100}$
   $d = 10$
6. Answers may vary, but should mention, at a minimum, that both of the last two steps involve finding a square root.

Success for English Learners
1. 6, 9, 4, 5; $d = \sqrt{10}$ or about 3.2
2. 0, 1, 6, 8; $d = \sqrt{5}$ or about 2.2

MODULE 12 Challenge
1. $3^2 + 4^2 = 5^2$ because $9 + 16 = 25$;
   $a^2 + b^2 = c^2$
2. $\frac{1}{2}(3^2) + \frac{1}{2}(4^2) = \frac{1}{2}(5^2)$ because
   $4.5 + 8 = 12.5$

3. $\frac{\pi}{2}(3^2) + \frac{\pi}{2}(4^2) = \frac{\pi}{2}(5^2)$ because you can
   multiply both sides by $\frac{2}{\pi}$;
   $\frac{\pi}{2}(a^2) + \frac{\pi}{2}(b^2) = \frac{\pi}{2}(c^2)$
4. $\frac{1}{2}(6)(3) + \frac{1}{2}(8)(4) = \frac{1}{2}(10)(5)$ because
   $9 + 16 = 25$;
   $\frac{1}{2}(a)\left(\frac{a}{2}\right) + \frac{1}{2}(b)\left(\frac{b}{2}\right) = \frac{1}{2}(c)\left(\frac{c}{2}\right)$
5. Answers will vary. Sample answer: using equilateral triangles:

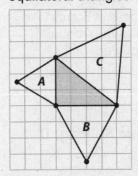

MODULE 13 Volume
LESSON 13-1
Practice and Problem Solving: A/B
1. 2,122.6 cm^3; $3.14 \cdot (6.5)^2 \cdot 16 = 3.14 \cdot 42.25 \cdot 16 = 2,122.64 \approx 2,122.6$
2. 37.7 cm^3; $3.14 \cdot (2)^2 \cdot 3 = 3.14 \cdot 4 \cdot 3 = 37.68 \approx 37.7$
3. 9.4 ft^3; $3.14 \cdot (1)^2 \cdot 3 = 3.14 \cdot 1 \cdot 3 = 9.42 \approx 9.4$
4. 70.7 in.^{3}; $3.14 \cdot (1.5)^2 \cdot 10 = 3.14 \cdot 2.25 \cdot 10 = 70.65 \approx 70.7$
5. 136 cm^3; $3.14 \cdot (3.8)^2 \cdot 3 = 3.14 \cdot 14.44 \cdot 3 = 136.0248 \approx 136$
6. 413.8 cm^3; $3.14 \cdot (3.3)^2 \cdot 12.1 = 3.14 \cdot 10.89 \cdot 12.1 = 413.75466 \approx 413.8$
7. a. 1,962.5 ft^3; $3.14 \cdot (5)^2 \cdot 25 = 3.14 \cdot 25 \cdot 25 = 1,962.5$
   b. 5,298.8 ft^3; $3.14 \cdot (7.5)^2 \cdot 30 = 3.14 \cdot 56.25 \cdot 30 = 5,298.8$
   c. 3,336.3 ft^3; $5,298.8 - 1,962.5 = 3,336.3$

Practice and Problem Solving: C

1. 8.8 ft^3; 3.14 • (0.75)^2 • 5 = 8.83125
2. a.

Candle Size	Radius	Height	Volume
Tall Candle	2 in.	10 in.	125.6 in.^{3}
Medium Candle	3 in.	6 in.	169.56 in.^{3}
Short Candle	2 in.	4 in.	200.96 in.^{3}

   b. The short candle has the most wax.

   c. 75.36 in^3; 200.96 − 125.6 = 75.36

   d. 125.6 < 169.56 < 200.96

3. 628 = (3.14)(r^2)(8)

   628 = 25.12r^2

    25 = r^2

     5 = r

Practice and Problem Solving: D

1. $V = \pi r^2 h$

   $V = 3.14 • 4^2 • 9$

   $V = 3.14 • 16 • 9$

   $V = 452.16 \approx 452.2$ in.^{3}

2. $V = \pi r^2 h$

   $V = 3.14 • 3.4^2 • 12$

   $V = 3.14 • 11.56 • 12$

   $V = 435.5808 \approx 435.6$ ft^3

3. 150.7 cm^3
4. 785 cm^3
5. 31.8 in^3
6. 23.6 in^3

Reteach

1. a. $B = \pi r^2$

   $B = 3.14 • 4^2 = 3.14 • 16 = 50.24$ cm^2

   b. 16 cm

   c. $V = Bh$

    $V = 50.24 • 16$

    $V = 803.84$ cm^3

2. a. $B = \pi r^2$

   $B = 3.14 • 8^2 = 200.96$ cm^2

   b. 6 cm

   c. $V = Bh$

    $V = 200.96 • 6$

    $V = 1,205.76$ cm^3

Reading Strategies

1. $B = \pi r^2$

   $B = 3.14 • 4^2$

   $B = 3.14 • 16$

   $B = 50.24$ cm^2

2. $V = Bh$

   $V = 50.24 • 7$

   $V = 351.68 \approx 351.7$ cm^3

Success for English Learners

1. the formula for the area of a circle ($A = \pi r^2$ and $B = \pi r^2$)

2. because you must multiply the area of the base (expressed in in^2), by the height (expressed in in.); so, in^2 multiplied by in. results in the volume being in in^3

3. Answers will vary. Sample answer: A cylinder has a radius of 5 inches and a height of 12 inches. What is the volume of the cylinder? Round the answer to the nearest tenth. (942 in^3)

LESSON 13-2

Practice and Problem Solving: A/B

1. 6,358.5 in.^{3}; $\frac{1}{3}$ • 3.14 • (15)^2 • 27 = $\frac{1}{3}$ •

   3.14 • 225 • 27 = $\frac{1}{3}$ • 19,075.5 = 6,358.5

2. 3,299.2 m^3; $\frac{1}{3}$ • 3.14 • (12.4)^2 • 20.5 = $\frac{1}{3}$ •

   3.14 • 153.76 • 20.5 = $\frac{1}{3}$ • 9,897.53 =

   3,299.18 ≈ 3,299.2

3. 25.1 in.^{3}; $\frac{1}{3} \bullet 3.14 \bullet (2)^2 \bullet 6 = \frac{1}{3} \bullet 3.14 \bullet$

$4 \bullet 6 = \frac{1}{3} \bullet 75.36 = 25.12 \approx 25.1$

4. 167.5 cm^3; $3.14 \bullet (4)^2 \bullet 10 = \frac{1}{3} \bullet 3.14 \bullet$

$16 \bullet 10 = 167.5$

5. 339.1 in.^{3}; $\frac{1}{3} \bullet 3.14 \bullet (4.5)^2 \bullet 16 = \frac{1}{3} \bullet$

$3.14 \bullet 20.25 \bullet 16 = \frac{1}{3} \bullet 1{,}017.36 = 339.12$

6. 392.5 cm^3; $\frac{1}{3} \bullet 3.14 \bullet (5)^2 \bullet 15 = \frac{1}{3} \bullet$

$3.14 \bullet 25 \bullet 15 = \frac{1}{3} \bullet 1{,}177.5 = 392.5$

7. a. $1{,}236.375$ ft^3; $\frac{1}{3} \bullet 3.14 \bullet (15)^2 \bullet 21 =$
   $4{,}945.5$ ft^3

   b. $4{,}592.25$ ft^3; $3.14 \bullet (15)^2 \bullet 26 =$
   $18{,}369$ ft^3

   c. $23{,}314.5$ ft^3

Practice and Problem Solving: C

1. a.

Cone Size	Radius	Height	Volume
Cone A	2 cm	10 cm	41.87 cm^3
Cone B	2 cm	20 cm	83.73 cm^3
Cone C	4 cm	10 cm	167.47 cm^3

   b. Cone C has the greatest volume.

   c. 41.9 cm^3; $83.73 - 41.86 = 41.87 \approx 41.9$

   d. $41.9 < 83.7 < 167.5$

   e. when you double the radius because
   the radius is squared

2. $732.7 = \frac{1}{3}(3.14)(r^2)(28)$

   $732.7 = 29.3 r^2$

   $25 = r^2$

   $5 = r$

   $d = 2r = 2(5) = 10$ in.

Practice and Problem Solving: D

1. $V = \frac{1}{3}\pi r^2 h$

   $V = \frac{1}{3} \bullet 3.14 \bullet 3^2 \bullet 5$

   $V = \frac{1}{3} \bullet 3.14 \bullet 9 \bullet 5$

   $V = 47.1$ cm^3

2. $V = \frac{1}{3}\pi r^2 h$

   $V = \frac{1}{3} \bullet 3.14 \bullet 5^2 \bullet 9$

   $V = \frac{1}{3} \bullet 3.14 \bullet 25 \bullet 9$

   $V = 235.5$ ft^3

3. 100.5 in.^{3}

4. 130.8 cm^3

5. 46.1 cm^3

6. 20 in.^{3}

Reteach

1. radius r of base = 3 in.

   $V = \frac{1}{3}Bh$

   $V = \frac{1}{3}(\pi r^2)h$

   $V = \frac{1}{3}(\pi \times 3^2) \times 10$

   $V = \frac{1}{3}(28.26) \times 10$

   $V = 9.42 \times 10$

   $V = 94.2$ in.^{3}

2. radius r of base = 6 cm

   $V = \frac{1}{3}Bh$

   $V = \frac{1}{3}(\pi r^2)h$

   $V = \frac{1}{3}(\pi \times 6^2) \times 4$

   $V = \frac{1}{3}(113.04) \times 4$

   $V = 37.68 \times 4$

   $V = 150.72$ cm^3

Reading Strategies

1. the diameter
2. 5 cm
3. 78.5 cm^2; $B = \pi r^2 = 3.14 \cdot 5^2 = 3.14 \cdot 25 = 78.5$ cm^3
4. 10 cm
5. $V = \dfrac{1}{3} Bh$

   $V = \dfrac{1}{3} \cdot 78.5 \cdot 10$

   $V = \dfrac{1}{3} \cdot 785$

   $V = 261.666 \approx 261.7$ cm^3
6. $V = \dfrac{1}{3} Bh$

   $V = \dfrac{1}{3} \cdot 50.24 \cdot 8$

   $V = \dfrac{1}{3} \cdot 401.92$

   $V = 133.97333 \approx 134$ cm^3

Success for English Learners

1. To find the radius, you must divide the diameter by 2.
2. Answers will vary. Sample answer: A paperweight is in the shape of a cone with a diameter of 3 in. and a height of 4 in.

   What is the volume of the cone? $V = \dfrac{1}{3}$

   $Bh = \dfrac{1}{3} \cdot 3.14 \cdot 1.5^2 \cdot 4 = \dfrac{1}{3} \cdot 3.14 \cdot$

   $2{,}25 \cdot 4 = \dfrac{1}{3} \cdot 28.26 = 9.42$ in.^{2}

LESSON 13-3

Practice and Problem Solving: A/B

1. $\dfrac{4}{3}(3.14)(5)^3 = \dfrac{4}{3}(3.14)(125) \approx 523.3333 \approx 523.3$ in.^{3}
2. $\dfrac{4}{3}(3.14)(1.2)^3 = \dfrac{4}{3}(3.14)(1.728) = 7.23456 \approx 7.2$ m^3

3. $\dfrac{4}{3}(3.14)(3)^3 = \dfrac{4}{3}(3.14)(27) = 113.04 \approx 113$ in.^{3}
4. $\dfrac{4}{3}(3.14)(4.5)^3 = \dfrac{4}{3}(3.14)(91.125) = 381.51 \approx 381.5$ m^3
5. $\dfrac{4}{3}(3.14)(1.5)^3 = \dfrac{4}{3}(3.14)(3.375) = 14.13 \approx 14.1$ m^3
6. $\dfrac{4}{3}(3.14)(8)^3 = \dfrac{4}{3}(3.14)(512) \approx 2{,}143.5733 \approx 2{,}143.6$ in^3
7. $\dfrac{4}{3}(3.14)(4.3)^3 \approx \dfrac{4}{3}(3.14)(79.507) = 332.8693 \approx 332.9$ in.^{3}
8. a. $\dfrac{4}{3}(3.14)(1.25)^3 \approx \dfrac{4}{3}(3.14)(1.953125) \approx 8.177 \approx 8.2$ in.^{3}

   b. $\dfrac{4}{3}(3.14)(1.3125)^3 = \dfrac{4}{3}(3.14)(2.261) \approx 9.4661 \approx 9.5$ in.^{3}

   c. 8.2 in.$^3 < x < 9.5$ in.^{3}

Practice and Problem Solving: C

Cone Size	Radius	Volume
Basic Sphere	3 in.	113 in.^{3}
Mini Sphere	1.5 in.	14.1 in.^{3}
Maxi Sphere	6 in.	904.3 in.^{3}

b. The mini sphere is $\dfrac{1}{8}$ the volume of the basic sphere.

c. The volume of the maxi sphere is 8 times greater than the volume of the basic sphere.

d. $14.1 < 113 < 904.3$

2. $V = \dfrac{4}{3}\pi r^3$.

   $4{,}186 = \dfrac{4(3.14)\, r^3}{3} = \dfrac{12.56\, r^3}{3}$

   $12{,}558 = 12.56\, r^3$

   $r^3 \approx 999.84$

   $r \approx 9.999 \approx 10$ in.

3. No. The volume of the sphere is always about 4.1866… times the volume of the cube when the radius of the sphere and the side of the cube are the same measure. The volume of the cube is the side raised to the power of 3, whereas the volume of the sphere is the same number raised to the power of 3 which is then multiplied by π and by 4 and finally divided by 3.

Practice and Problem Solving: D

1. $V = \frac{4}{3}\pi r^3$

   $V = \frac{4}{3} \bullet 3.14 \bullet 9^3$

   $V = \frac{4}{3} \bullet 3.14 \bullet 729$

   $V \approx 3{,}052.1 \text{ cm}^3$

2. $V = \frac{4}{3}\pi r^3$

   $V = \frac{4}{3} \bullet 3.14 \bullet 2^3$

   $V = \frac{4}{3} \bullet 3.14 \bullet 8$

   $V \approx 33.5 \text{ m}^3$

3. $V = \frac{4}{3}\pi r^3$

   $V = \frac{4}{3} \bullet 3.14 \bullet 2^3$

   $V = \frac{4}{3} \bullet 3.14 \bullet 8$

   $V \approx 33.5 \text{ cm}^3$

4. $V = \frac{4}{3}\pi r^3$

   $V = \frac{4}{3} \bullet 3.14 \bullet 5^3$

   $V = \frac{4}{3} \bullet 3.14 \bullet 125$

   $V \approx 523.3 \text{ m}^3$

5. $V = \frac{4}{3}\pi r^3$

   $V = \frac{4}{3} \bullet 3.14 \bullet 2.8^3$

   $V = \frac{4}{3} \bullet 3.14 \bullet 22$

   $V \approx 91.9 \text{ cm}^3$

6. $V = \frac{4}{3}\pi r^3$

   $V = \frac{4}{3} \bullet 3.14 \bullet 1^3$

   $V = \frac{4}{3} \bullet 3.14 \bullet 1$

   $V \approx 4.2 \text{ m}^3$

Reteach

1. diameter = 2.5 in.

   radius = 1.25 in.

   $V = \frac{4}{3} \bullet 3.14 \bullet 1.25^3$

   $V = \frac{4}{3} \bullet 3.14 \bullet 1.95$

   $V = 8.1771$

   $V \approx 8.2 \text{ in.}^3$

2. diameter = 12 cm

   radius = 6 cm

   $V = \frac{4}{3}(3.14 \times 6^3)$

   $V = \frac{4}{3}(3.14 \times 216)$

   $V = 904.32$

   $V \approx 904.3 \text{ cm}^3$

Reading Strategies

1. Answers will vary. Sample answers: baseball, basketball, marble, orange

2. diameter

3. radius

4. Divide the diameter by 2.

5. Multiply the radius by 2.

Success for English Learners

1. The expression cm^3 in the answer is the unit of measurement, and it stands for cubic centimeters.

2. Answers will vary. Sample answer: What is the volume of a sphere with a radius of 6 inches?

$$V = \frac{4}{3} \cdot 3.14 \cdot 6^3 = 904.32 \text{ in.}^3$$

MODULE 13 Challenge

1. Check students' drawings for correct labeling and proportionality to given measures.

   Sample answer. Other answers are possible.

   $$V = \pi r^2 h$$

   $$V \approx (3.14)(4.5^2)(7)$$

   $$V \approx (3.14)(20.25)(7)$$

   $$V \approx 445.095 \text{ in.}^3$$

   $$V \approx 445.1 \text{ in.}^3$$

2. Check students' drawings for correct labeling and proportionality to given measures.
   Sample answer. Other answers are possible.

   $$V = \frac{1}{3}\pi r^2 h$$

   $$V \approx \frac{1}{3}(3.14)(5^2)(3.5)$$

   $$V \approx \frac{1}{3}(3.14)(25)(3.5)$$

   $$V \approx 91.58 \text{ in.}^3$$

3. Check students' drawings for correct labeling and proportionality to given measures.
   Sample answer. Other answers are possible.

   $$V = \frac{4}{3}\pi r^3$$

   $$V \approx \frac{4}{3}(3.14)(6.2^3)$$

   $$V \approx \frac{4}{3}(3.14)(238.33)$$

   $$V \approx 997.81 \text{ cm}^3$$

UNIT 6: Statistics

MODULE 14 Scatter Plots

LESSON 14-1

Practice and Problem Solving: A/B

1.

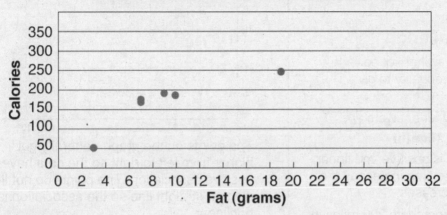

Calories and Fat Per Portion of Meat and Fish

2. positive

3. negative

4. $60

Practice and Problem Solving: C

1.

x	1	2	3	4	5	6	7	8	9	10	11	12
y	211	358	262	265	280	305	315	345	352	382	385	355

2.

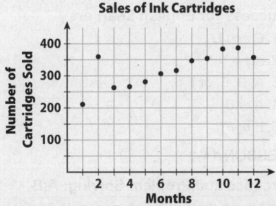

Sales of Ink Cartridges

3. a. The association is positive. In general, the sales of ink cartridges increase from month 1 through month 12.

b. The relationship does not seem linear. The sales generally increased during the year, but the trend changed for the last two months and actually decreased in December.

4. There are no clusters in the data. The data value for February is an outlier. Sample answer: There may have been a special sale in February on ink cartridges.

5. a. 1: November; 2: October; 3: February; 4: December; 5: September; 6: August; 7: July; 8: June; 9: May; 10: April; 11: March; 12: January

b. May would have sales of ink cartridges of about 1.35 × 280 or 378. That would rank May as the third highest month for sales, right below November (385) and October (382).

Practice and Problem Solving: D

a.

Time and Distance for Car Trips

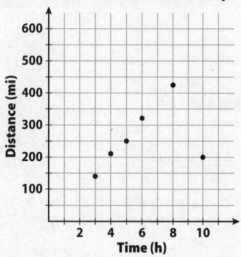

b. The association is positive and linear. In general, as the time increases the distance also increases.

c. The point that represents 200 miles in 10 hours seems to be an outlier because it does not fit the trend for the other data.

2. a.

Registers and Wait Times

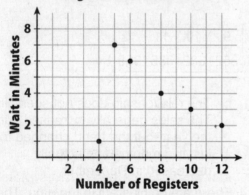

b. The association is negative and linear. In general, as the number of registers increases the wait in minutes decreases.

c. The point that represents 4 registers and a 1 minute wait seems to be an outlier because it does not fit the trend for the other data.

Reteach

1.

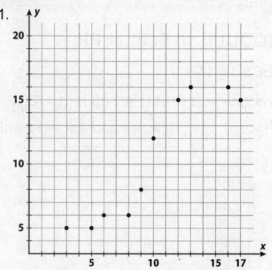

The points on the graph generally get higher from left to right so the data have a positive association. The points do not lie along a straight line so the association is nonlinear.

Reading Strategies

1. Times and Distances for Car Trips

2. Horizontal axis: Time (hours)
   Vertical axis: Distance (miles)

3. (1, 50), (3, 150), (6.5, 275), (8, 175)

4. Answers may vary. Sample answer: There are two clusters; one is for the values of x between 1 and 1.5 and the other is for the values of x between 6 and 7.

Success for English Learners

1. C and D

2. none

3. A, B, E, or F

4. A or B

5. E or F

LESSON 14-2

Practice and Problem Solving: A/B

1. Linear; the data points appear to lie along a line.

2. There is no clustering.

3. There are no outliers.

4. Sample answer: $y = 45x$

5. The slope represents the distance traveled per hour.

6. Sample answer: There is no y-intercept represented on this scatter plot, but if there were, it would have to be plotted at zero because you could not have traveled any distance in miles when you have not begun traveling (when time is zero).

Practice and Problem Solving: C

1. $y = -\dfrac{1}{3}x + 13$

2. $y = -\dfrac{5}{12}x + 15$

3. Clarisse: 1; Anthony: 0

4. Answers may vary. Sample answer: Clarisse will get greater y values for larger values of x; that is, when x is greater than 25 or so; Anthony will get greater y values for smaller values of x that is, when x is less than 20 or so.

5. When $x = 24$, Clarisse's equation gives

   $y = -\dfrac{1}{3}(24) + 13 = -8 + 13 = 5$ and

   Anthony's equation gives $y = -\dfrac{5}{12}(24) +$

   $15 = -10 + 15 = 5$, so both equations predict the same result. The ordered pair (24, 5) is the intersection of the two trend lines.

Practice and Problem Solving: D

1. decrease

2. -2

3. $y = -2x + 70$

4. It is a negative association. As the values increase on the horizontal axis, they decrease on the vertical axis.

5. Sample answer: If a scatter plot has a linear association that is negative, then the slope of the line of best fit for that scatter plot is negative.

Reteach

1. $y = -3x + 2$

2. $y = x - 17$

3. $y = -\dfrac{1}{2}x - 5$

4. $y = 6x$

5. $y = \dfrac{2}{3}x - 1$; $y = 9$

6. $y = -5x + 7$; $y = -48$

Reading Strategies

1. Sample answers: As the distance to the coffee shop increases, the number of visits per week decreases; there is a negative association between distance to the coffee shop and number of visits per week.

2. There are 6 data points above the trend line and 6 data points below the trend line.

3. (1, 8) and (7, 2)

4. An interpretation of the slope, -1, is that the number of visits decreases by 1 for each block of distance from the coffee shop. An interpretation of the y-intercept, 9, is that customers who live (or work) 0 blocks from the coffee shop will visit the coffee shop 9 times per week.

Success for English Learners

1. $y = -2x - 1$

2. $y = -15x$

3. $y = \dfrac{1}{4}x + 6$

4. $y = -\dfrac{2}{5}x + 1$

MODULE 14 Challenge

1. Answers will vary, but students should observe that there is a negative association between the winning times and the year, i.e. more recent winning times are less than earlier winning times.

2. Drawings will vary. Sample answer:

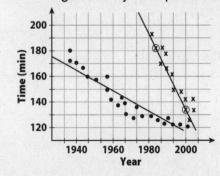

3. Answers will vary depending on the points chosen, but they should be similar to this:

Men: $T_M = -0.7Y + 175$

4 Drawings will vary. Sample answer: See above.

5. Answers will vary depending on the points chosen, but they should be similar to this: Women: $T_W = -3Y + 192$

6. Answers will vary, but students should observe that the absolute value of the *rate* at which the winning time is *decreasing* is *greater* for women than for men.

7. Answers will vary, but students should be able to see that the trend lines will not be accurate indefinitely. Sample answer: In 2020, the men's winning time will be a little less than two hours, whereas the women's winning time will be about 80 minutes. Both of these times may not be realistic in terms of human performance.

MODULE 15 Two-Way Tables

LESSON 15-1

Practice and Problem Solving: A/B

1. 13
2. 24
3. 22
4. 27
5. 49
6. 25 out of 49, or about 51%
7. 12 out of 22, or about 55%
8. There is an association that suggests that boys are as likely as girls to have siblings because slightly more than half (51%) of the total children (boys and girls) are boys, and because slightly more than half (55%) of the total children (boys and girls) with siblings are boys with siblings.
9. 50
10. 25
11. 135

12. 235
13. 100 out of 235, or about 43%
14. 75 out of 125, or 60%
15. There is an association which suggests that the plants bloom more in the shade, since 60% of the plants that bloom are plants that bloom in the shade, whereas about 43% of all of the plants bloom in the shade or in the sunlight.

Practice and Problem Solving: C

1. 200
2. 210
3. 215
4. 280
5. 320
6. 305
7. 280
8. 905
9. Answers will vary: math and reading; math and science; reading and science
10. 7th grade
11. $\frac{(60 + 70)}{305}$, or about 43%
12. 200 out of 905, or about 22% of students school-wide, listed math as their favorite class.
13. School-wide: $\frac{215}{905}$, or about 24%;

    8th grade: $\frac{70}{280}$, or 25%
14. 8th grade; About 30% of 8th graders chose Other, versus about 31% in 6th and 7th grades.

Practice and Problem Solving: D

1. 29
2. 54
3. 20
4. 10
5. 34
6. about 17%
7. about 37%

8. There seems to be a relationship between eating fruit and not gaining weight because, compared to the percent of all people surveyed who gained weight, the percent of people who ate fruit and gained weight was about half as great.

Reteach

1. 18 commuters out of 23, or about 78%, of commuters who got less than 20 miles per gallon, drove 3 miles, which suggests an association between short commuting distance and poor gas mileage.

2. 5 commuters out of 23, or about 22%, of commuters who got less than 20 miles per gallon, drove 30 miles, which suggests an association between longer commuting distances and better gas mileage.

3. Answers might vary, but students should suggest that the 30-mile commute might take more time and use more fuel than the 3-mile commute. Also, mileage will depend on the age and engine efficiency of the car used.

Reading Strategies

1. the number of athletes who trained for 3 months, and the portions of that number whose maximum bench press was either less than 150 lb or 150 lb or greater

2. the number of athletes who trained for 6 months, and the portions of that number whose maximum bench press was either less than 150 lb or 150 lb or greater

3. the total number of athletes, and the portions of that number whose maximum bench press is either less than 150 lb or is 150 lbs or greater

4. the total number of athletes whose maximum bench press was less than 150 lb, and the portions of that number who trained for either 3 months or 6 months

5. Answers may vary, but students should observe that there is a mild association between the number of athletes who trained for 6 months and those whose maximum bench press is 150 lb or greater. That is, slightly more athletes can lift 150 lb or more after 3 extra months of training.

Success for English Learners

1. 24 out of 81, or about 30%

2. 10 out of 81, or about 12%

3. Students who have a job are more likely to have a bike.

4. Students who do not have a job are less likely to have a bike.

LESSON 15-2

Practice and Problem Solving: A/B

Note: Due to rounding, percentages may not add up to the percentages shown in the "Total" columns in the table.

1. $\frac{35}{165} \approx 21\%$

2. $\frac{55}{165} \approx 33\%$

3. $\frac{90}{165} \approx 55\%$

4. $\frac{60}{165} \approx 36\%$

5. $\frac{15}{165} \approx 9\%$

6. $\frac{75}{165} \approx 45\%$

7. $\frac{95}{165} \approx 58\%$

8. $\frac{70}{165} \approx 42\%$

9. $\frac{165}{165} = 100\%$

10. Students may list the four JRFs in any order.

Electric, Inside City Limits; $\frac{35}{165} \approx 21\%$

Electric, Outside City Limits; $\frac{60}{165} \approx 36\%$

Gas, Inside City Limits; $\frac{55}{165} \approx 33\%$

Gas, Outside City Limits; $\frac{15}{165} \approx 9\%$

11. Students may list the four MRFs in any order.

Electric; $\frac{95}{165} \approx 58\%$

Gas; $\frac{70}{165} \approx 42\%$

Inside City Limits; $\frac{90}{165} \approx 55\%$

Outside City Limits; $\frac{75}{165} \approx 45\%$

12. 21; 58; about 36%

13. 9; 42; about 21%

Practice and Problem Solving: C

1. The JRF for electric use inside the city limits is $\frac{35}{165}$, whereas the CRF for electric use inside the city limits is $\frac{35}{95}$. The CRF should be greater than the JRF.

2. about 21%; about 37%

3. Yes, the CRF is greater because the frequency of electric use inside the city limits is divided by a smaller number, the combined use of electric energy inside and outside the city limits.

4. The marginal relative frequency (MRF) for electric use ($\frac{95}{165}$, or about 58%) is greater than the MRF for gas ($\frac{70}{165}$, or about 42%) both inside and outside the city limits. The joint relative frequency (JRF) for electric use is greater outside the city limits ($\frac{60}{165}$, or about 36%) than inside the city limits ($\frac{35}{165}$, or about 21%), whereas the JRF for gas use is greater inside the city limits than outside. The conditional relative frequencies (CRF) for electric and gas usage further supports the JRF associations, namely, that electric use is greater outside the city limits, and gas use is greater inside the city limits.

Practice and Problem Solving: D

1. 21; 77; 0.27; 27
2. 17; 77; 0.22; 22
3. 21; 17; 77; 38; 77; 0.49; 49
4. 16; 23; 77; 39; 77; 0.51; 51
5. 21; 38; 0.55; 55
6. 17; 38; 0.45; 45

Reteach

1. Brand A more than *or* less than 24 ounces: $\frac{10 + 12}{62} \approx 35\%$; Brand B more than *or* less than 24 ounces: $\frac{9 + 15}{79} \approx 30\%$; Brand C more than *or* less than 24 ounces: $\frac{7 + 6}{38} \approx 34\%$; So, Brand A has the greatest percentage of samples that deviate from exactly 24 ounces.

2. Brand A less than 24 ounces: $\frac{12}{62} \approx 19\%$; Brand B less than 24 ounces: $\frac{9}{79} \approx 11\%$; Brand C less than 24 ounces: $\frac{7}{38} \approx 18\%$; Brand A has the greatest percentage of samples that contain less than 24 ounces.

Reading Strategies

1. 36%, 6%, 42%, 10%, 48%, 58%, 46%, and 54%

2. 100%; It is the total of all the frequencies.

3. 36%, 6%, 10%, and 48%

4. 42%, 58%, 46%, and 54%

5. Note: Percents may not add to 100% due to rounding.

   3-mile commute with mileage < 30 mi/gal: 36% ÷ 42% = 85%;

   3-mile commute with mileage ≥ 30 mi/gal: 6% ÷ 42% = 14%;

   30-mile commute with mileage < 30 mi/gal: 10% ÷ 58% = 17%;

   30-mile commute with mileage ≥ 30 mi/gal: 48% ÷ 58% = 83%;

   mileage < 30 mi/g on a 3-mile commute: 36% ÷ 46% = 78%;

   mileage < 30 mi/gal on a 30-mile commute: 10% ÷ 46% = 22%;

   mileage ≥ 30 mi/gal on a 3-mile commute: 6% ÷ 54% = 12%;

   mileage ≥ 30 mi/gal on a 30-mile commute: 48% ÷ 54% = 89%

Success for English Learners

1. 40% is the row total, the sum of the 30% who have a Bike and a Job and the 10% who have a Job and No Bike.

2. With the conditional relative frequency, a joint relative frequency is divided by the column or row marginal relative frequency. With the joint relative frequency, a frequency is divided by the grand total in the last column and row.

MODULE 15 Challenge

1. $a + b + c$

2. $d + e + f$

3. $x + y + z$

4. $a + d + x$

5. $b + e + y$

6. $c + f + z$

7. $a + b + c + d + e + f + x + y + z$

8. yes; $a + b + c + d + e + f + x + y + z$

9. $\dfrac{a}{a+b+c+d+e+f+x+y+z} + \dfrac{c}{a+b+c+d+e+f+x+y+z}$ or $\dfrac{a+c}{a+b+c+d+e+f+x+y+z}$

10. $\dfrac{b}{a+b+c+d+e+f+x+y+z} + \dfrac{d}{a+b+c+d+e+f+x+y+z}$ or $\dfrac{b+d}{a+b+c+d+e+f+x+y+z}$

11. $\dfrac{e}{a+b+c+d+e+f+x+y+z} + \dfrac{x}{a+b+c+d+e+f+x+y+z}$ or $\dfrac{e+x}{a+b+c+d+e+f+x+y+z}$

12. $\dfrac{f}{a+b+c+d+e+f+x+y+z} + \dfrac{y}{a+b+c+d+e+f+x+y+z}$ or

$\dfrac{f+y}{a+b+c+d+e+f+x+y+z}$

13. $\dfrac{a}{a+d+x}$ or $\dfrac{a}{a+b+c}$

14. $\dfrac{e}{b+e+y}$ or $\dfrac{e}{d+e+f}$

15. $\dfrac{z}{c+f+z}$ or $\dfrac{z}{x+y+z}$

16. Sample answer: Compare $\dfrac{a}{a+b+c}$ and $\dfrac{a}{a+b+c+d+e+f+x+y+z}$; cross multiply and

simplify. $a+b+c < a+b+c+d+e+f+x+y+z$, so the fraction $\dfrac{a}{a+b+c}$ is greater

than the fraction $\dfrac{a}{a+b+c+d+e+f+x+y+z}$. The CRF will be greater than the JRF.